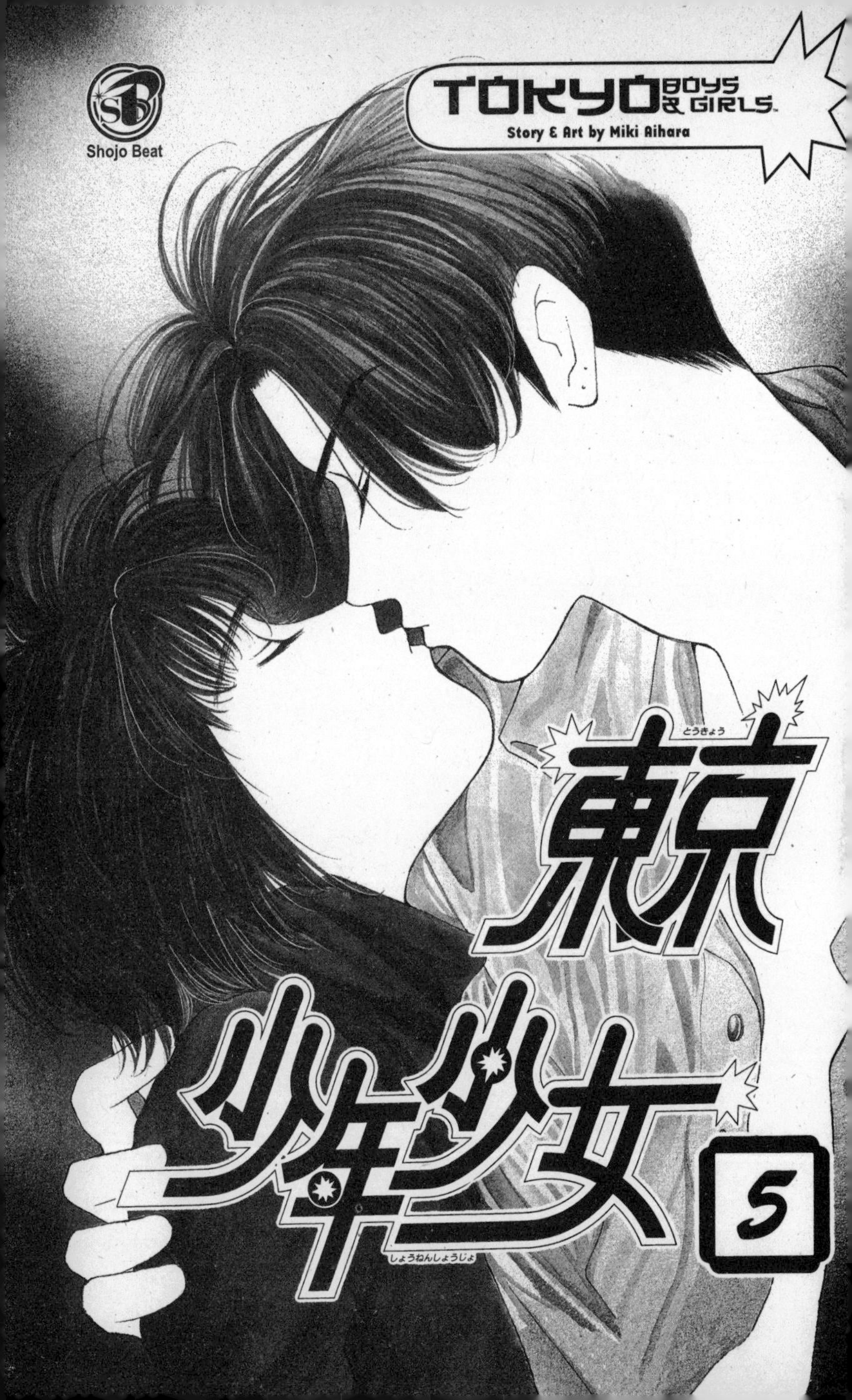
Shojo Beat
TOKYO BOYS & GIRLS
Story & Art by Miki Aihara
とうきょう
東京
少年少女
しょうねんしょうじょ
5

TOKYO BOYS & GIRLS

◆◆◆◆◆◆◆◆◆◆◆◆◆◆◆◆◆◆◆◆◆◆◆◆◆◆◆

The Story Thus Far

Mimori's dream has finally come true: she and Haruta are an item. But no sooner have they started dating than Haruta, still convinced that she's in love with Kuniyasu, pressures her to have sex. Confused, Mimori refuses, and she and Haruta break up. After realizing that she still loves Haruta, Mimori decides to patch things up with him. When her father suddenly moves to Kyushu alone, she goes to Kyushu to save her parents' marriage, and Haruta goes with her. During the trip, she begins to understand Haruta's feelings. But then she overhears Haruta explaining why, when they met on the first day of high school, he wanted revenge against her...

MAIN CHARACTERS

Mimori Kosaka

Member of Class 1-A, Girls' Division at Meidai Attached High School. A bright, outspoken girl. Possibly because of this, she's always screwing up...

Nana Takaichi

Mimori's classmate. Because she's so attractive, all the boys are obsessed with her. She's in love with Kuniyasu, but he brushes her off.

Atsushi Haruta

Member of Class 1-A, Boys' Division. Went to elementary school with Mimori. He's intimidating now, but he used to be bullied for looking like a girl.

Kazukita Kuniyasu

Member of Class 1-A, Boys' Division. Clear-headed, handsome, and cool toward girls.

Ran Shingyoji

Member of Class 1-A, Boys' Division. A hot-blooded type and Kuniyasu's closest friend. Fell in love with Nana at first sight. Is he upset with Mimori?

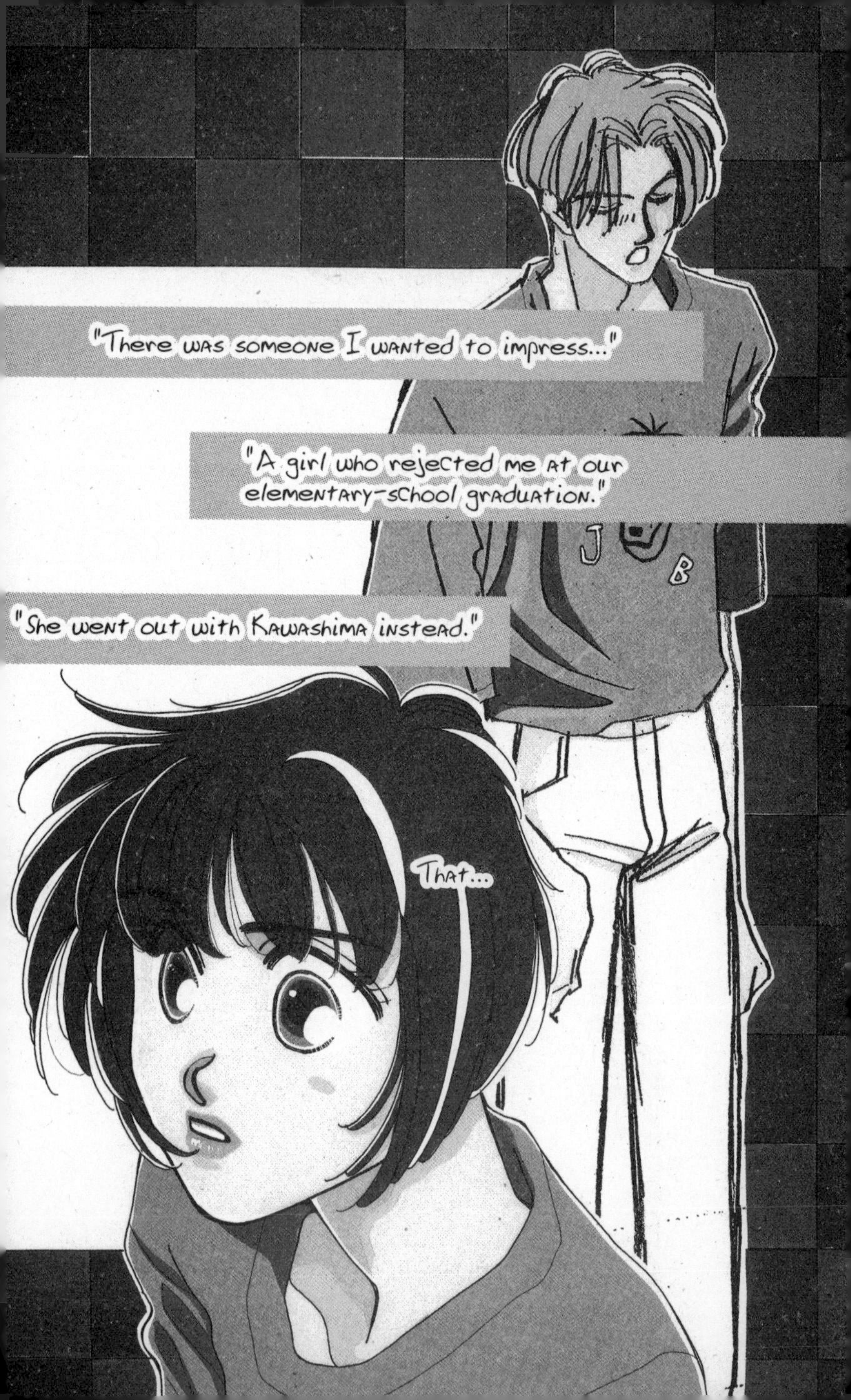
"There was someone I wanted to impress..."
"A girl who rejected me at our elementary-school graduation."
"She went out with Kawashima instead."
That...

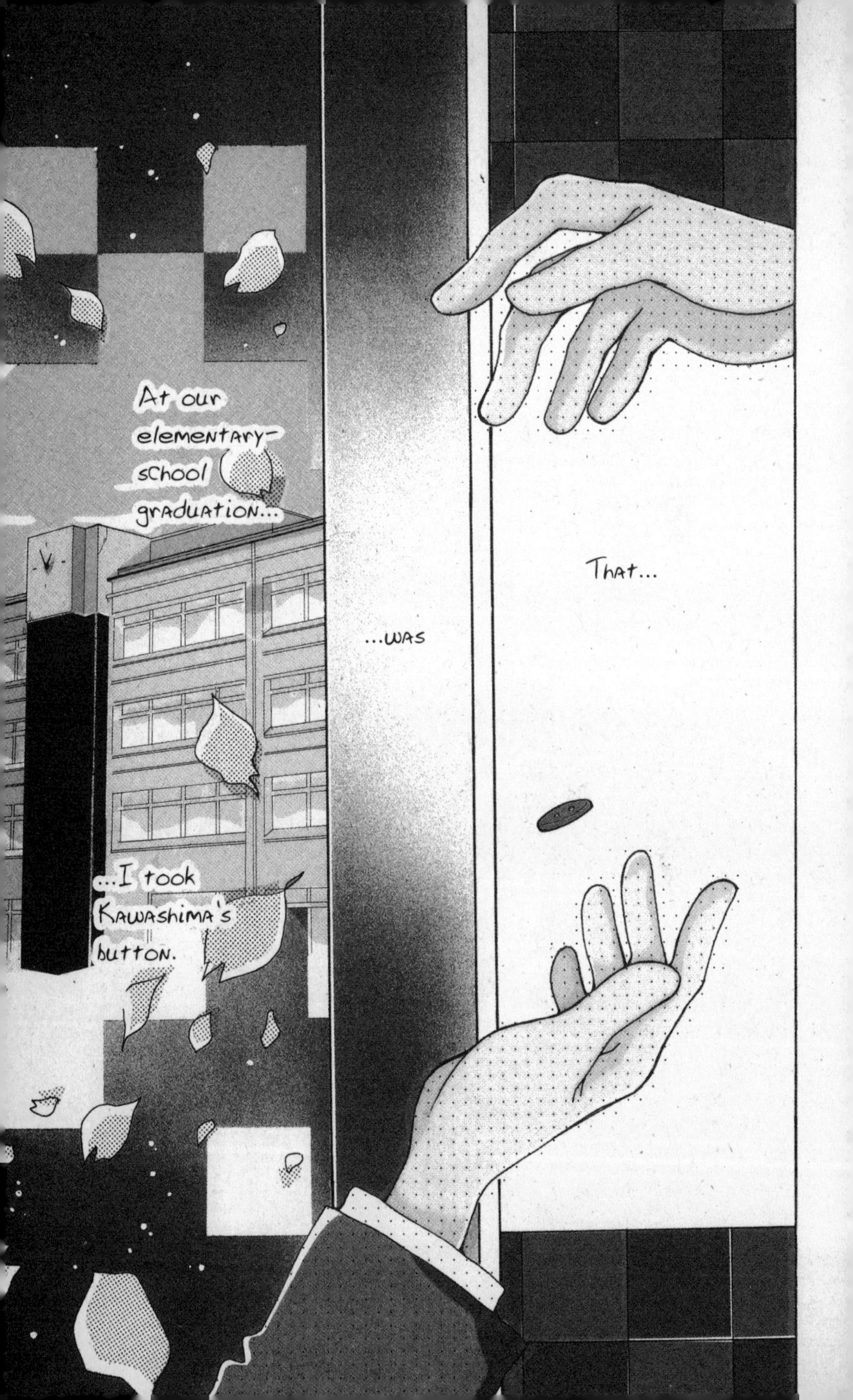
That...
...was
At our elementary-school graduation...
...I took Kawashima's button.

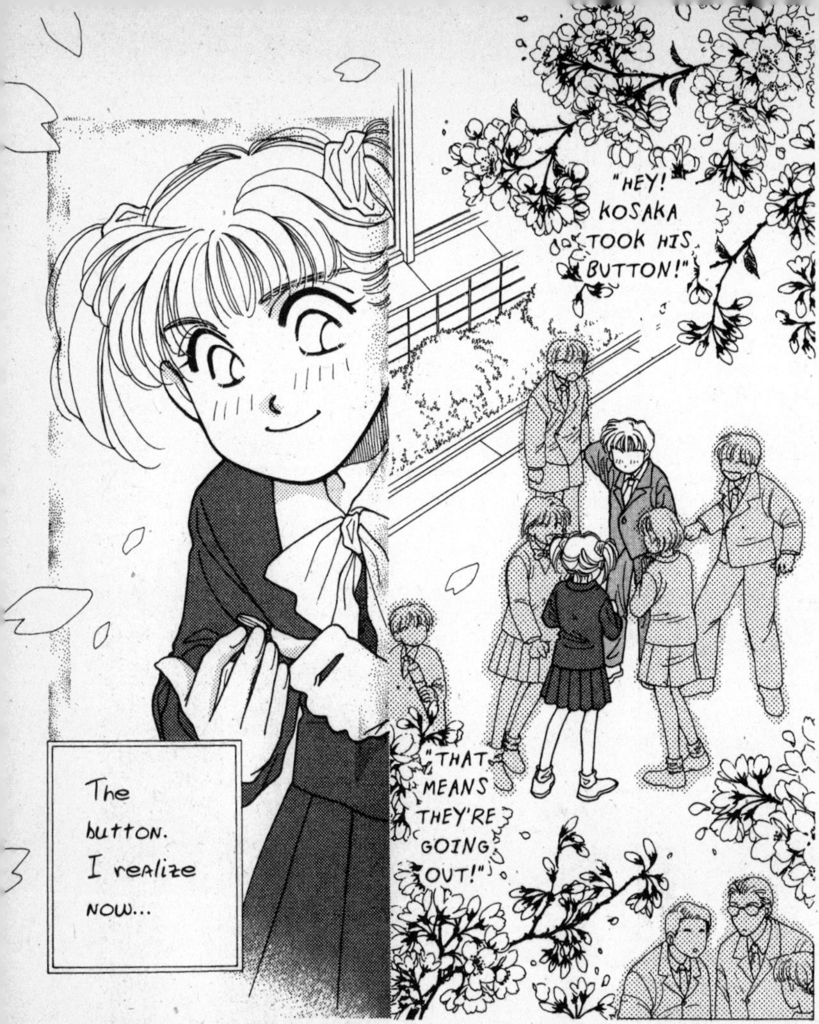
"HEY! KOSAKA TOOK HIS BUTTON!"
"THAT MEANS THEY'RE GOING OUT!"
The button. I realize now...

Hello!
This the final volume of Tokyo Boys and Girls. To the first-timers, thanks for joining us. To those of you who have followed from the beginning, thank you very much. I couldn't have continued or finished this manga without my assistants, my publisher, and you readers.
So...In this volume, starting on page 15, I'll show you the results of the popularity poll I ran in Volume 4.
Thank you for all your votes.

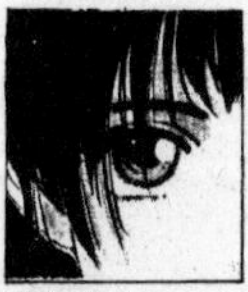

I'll do the serious stuff in the postscript.

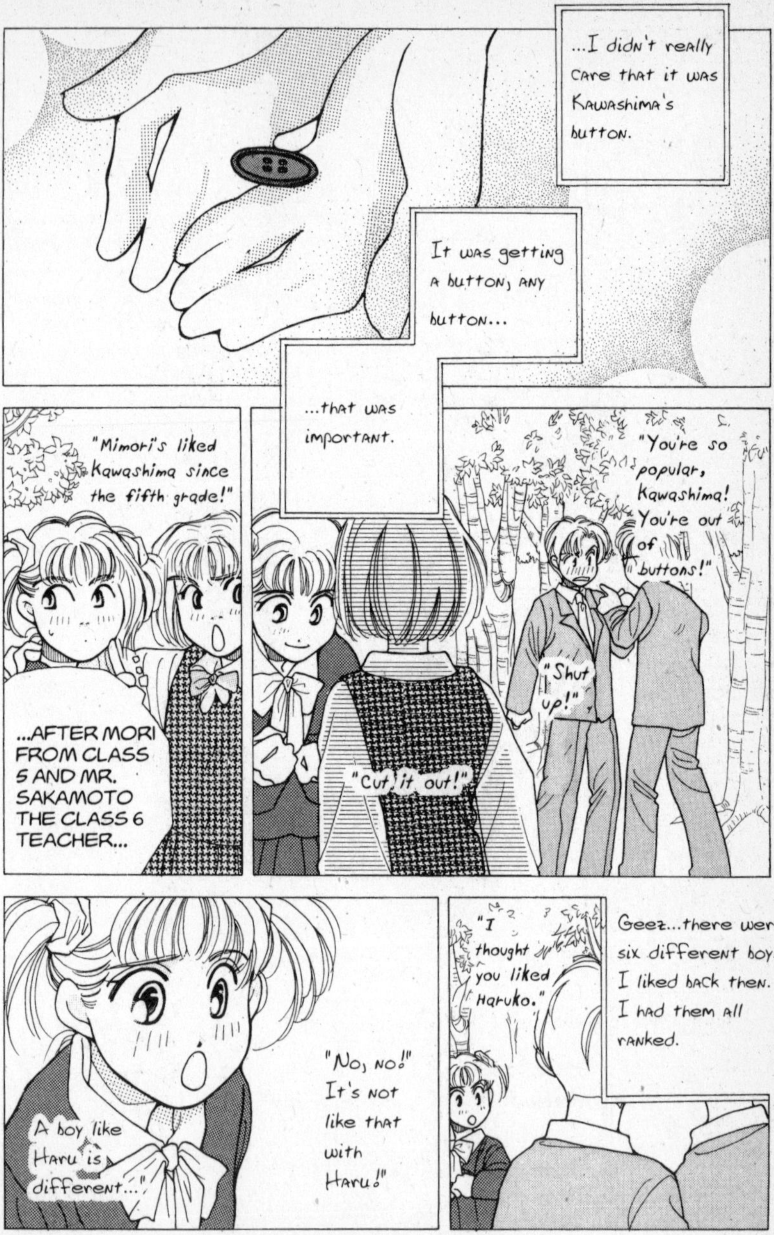
...I didn't really care that it was Kawashima's button.
It was getting a button, any button...
...that was important.
"You're so popular, Kawashima! You're out of buttons!"
"Shut up!"
"Cut it out!"
"Mimori's liked Kawashima since the fifth grade!"
...AFTER MORI FROM CLASS 5 AND MR. SAKAMOTO THE CLASS 6 TEACHER...
"I thought you liked Haruko."
Geez...there were six different boys I liked back then. I had them all ranked.
"No, no! It's not like that with Haru!"
A boy like Haru is different..."

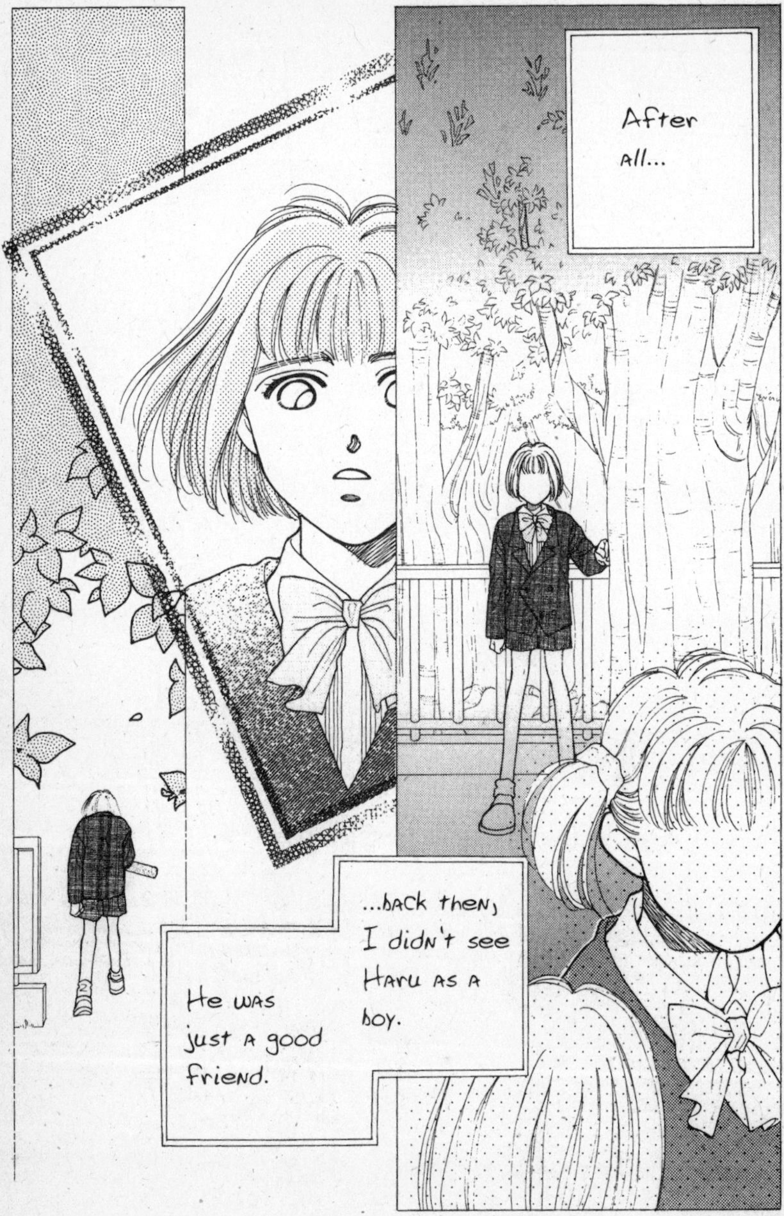
After all...
...back then, I didn't see Haru as a boy.
He was just a good friend.

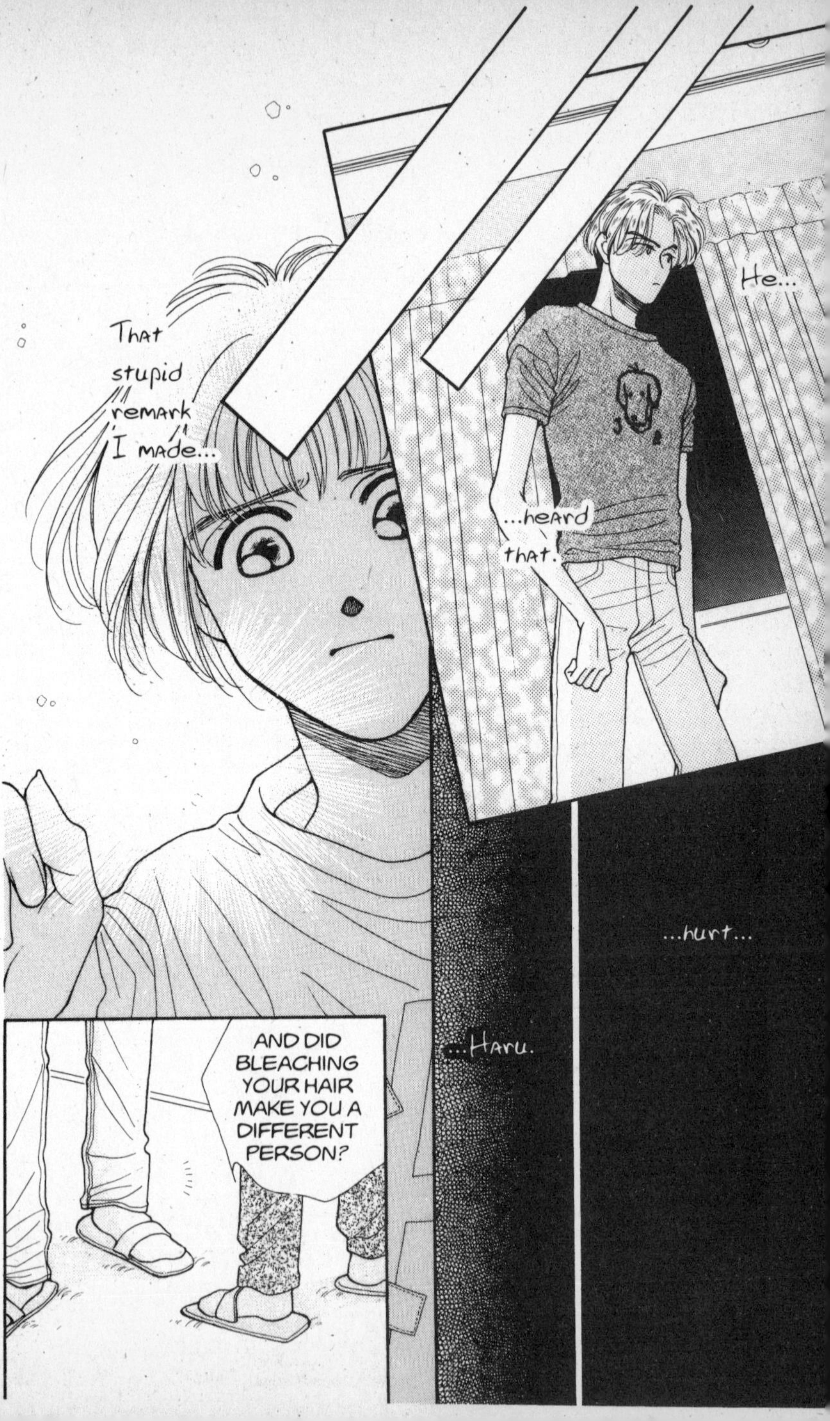
He...
...heard that.
That stupid remark I made...
...hurt...
...Haru.
AND DID BLEACHING YOUR HAIR MAKE YOU A DIFFERENT PERSON?

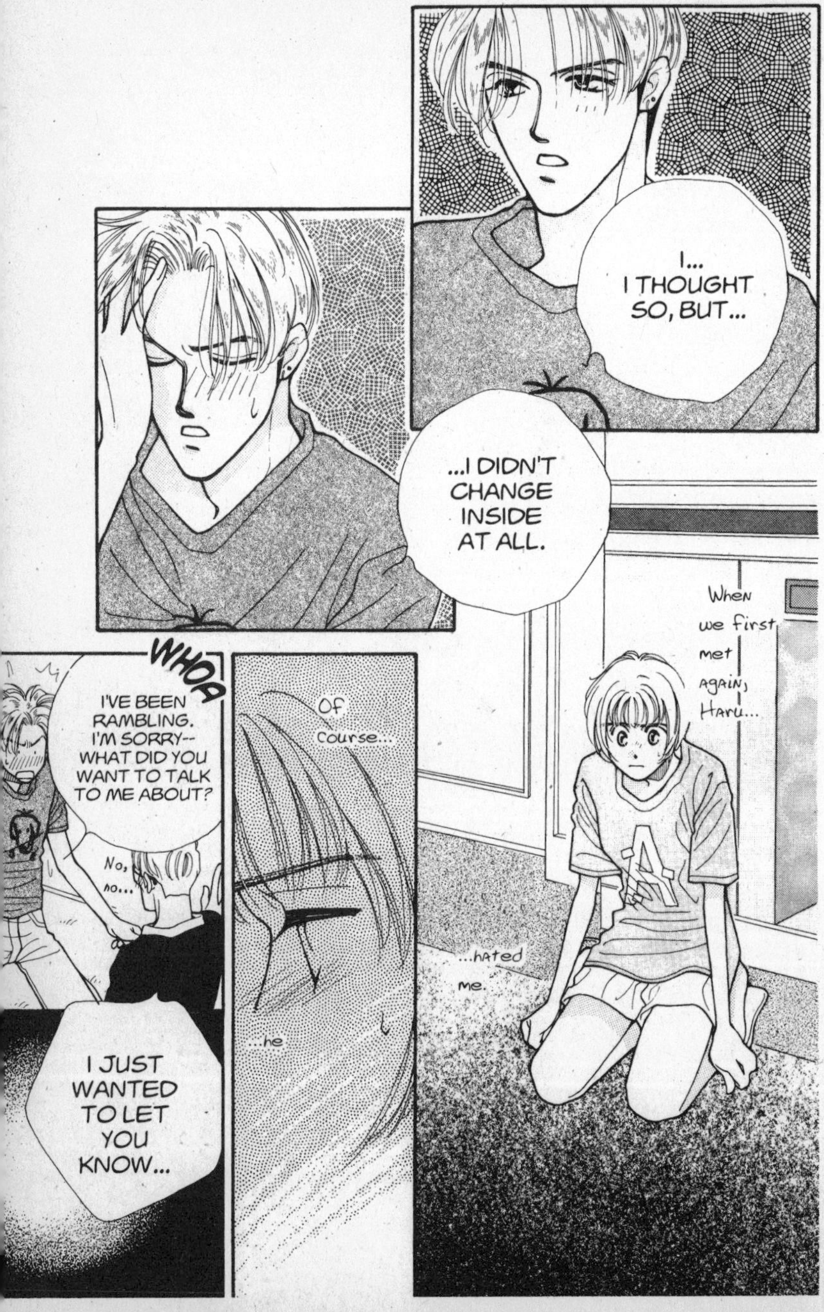
I...
I THOUGHT SO, BUT...
...I DIDN'T CHANGE INSIDE AT ALL.
When we first met again, Haru...
...hated me.
Of course...
...he
WHOA
I'VE BEEN RAMBLING. I'M SORRY-- WHAT DID YOU WANT TO TALK TO ME ABOUT?
No, no...
I JUST WANTED TO LET YOU KNOW...

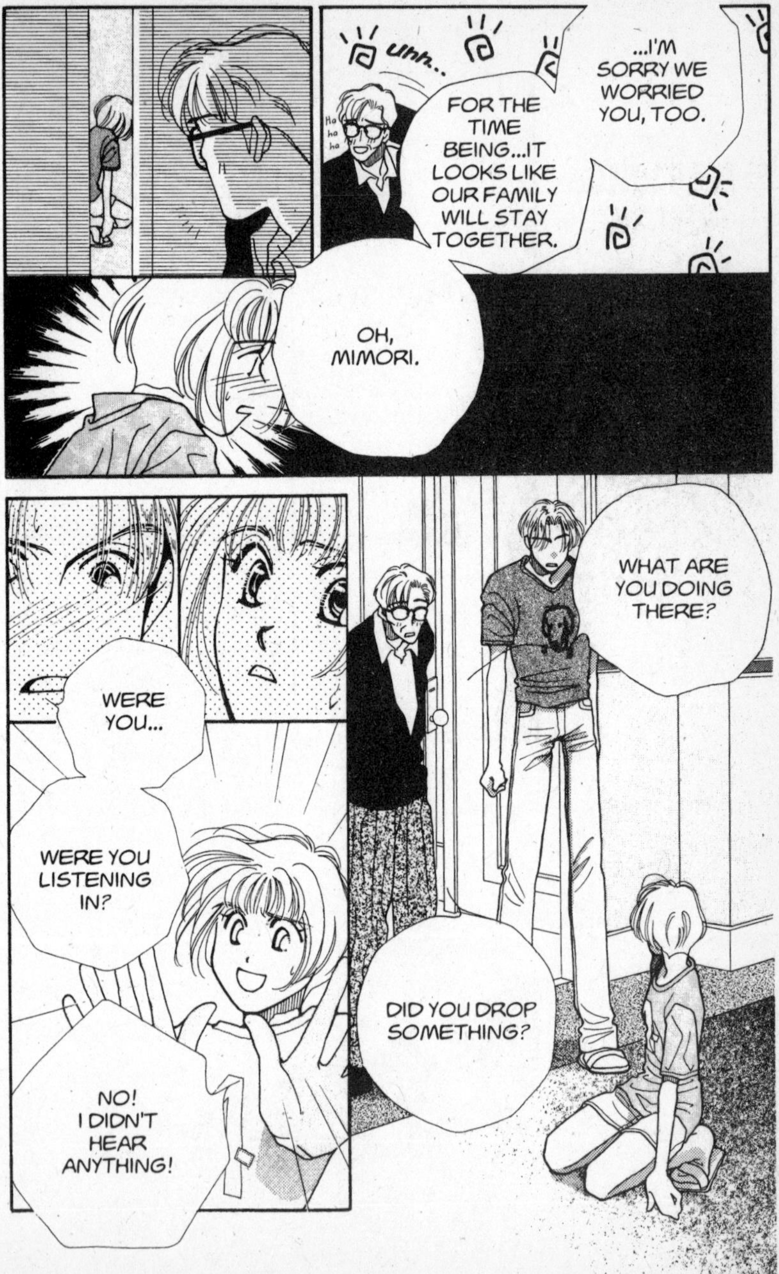
uhh..
Ha ha ha
FOR THE TIME BEING...IT LOOKS LIKE OUR FAMILY WILL STAY TOGETHER.
...I'M SORRY WE WORRIED YOU, TOO.
OH, MIMORI.
WHAT ARE YOU DOING THERE?
DID YOU DROP SOMETHING?
WERE YOU...
WERE YOU LISTENING IN?
NO! I DIDN'T HEAR ANYTHING!

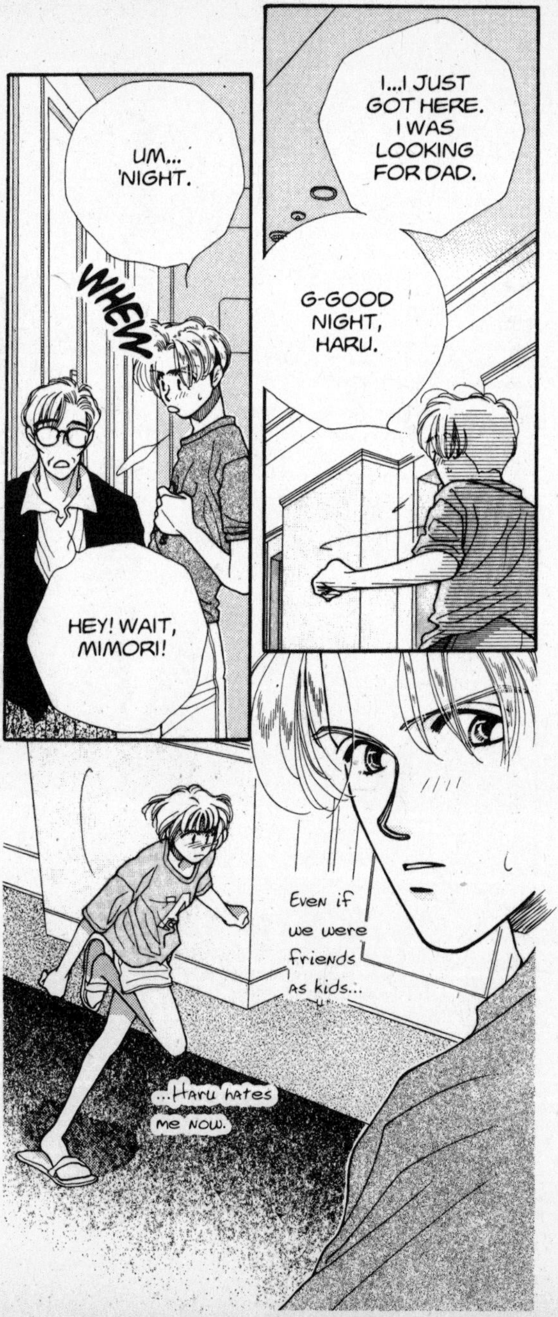
I...I JUST GOT HERE. I WAS LOOKING FOR DAD.
G-GOOD NIGHT, HARU.
UM... 'NIGHT.
WHEW
HEY! WAIT, MIMORI!
Even if we were friends as kids...
...Haru hates me now.

CHARACTER RANKING

NO.4 284 POINTS

• Ran Shingyoji •

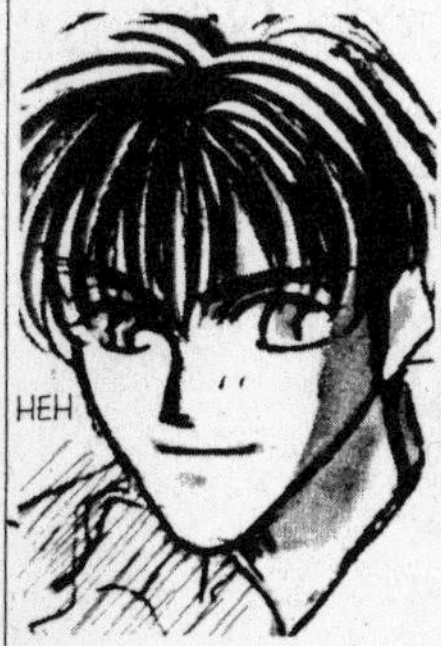
HEH

I drew him to look like an average guy on the street. Out of all the boys, he'd be the best boyfriend. I think he's very sweet.
Oh...but he's kind of conceited, and he's a sucker for hot girls.

He wouldn't look twice at me.

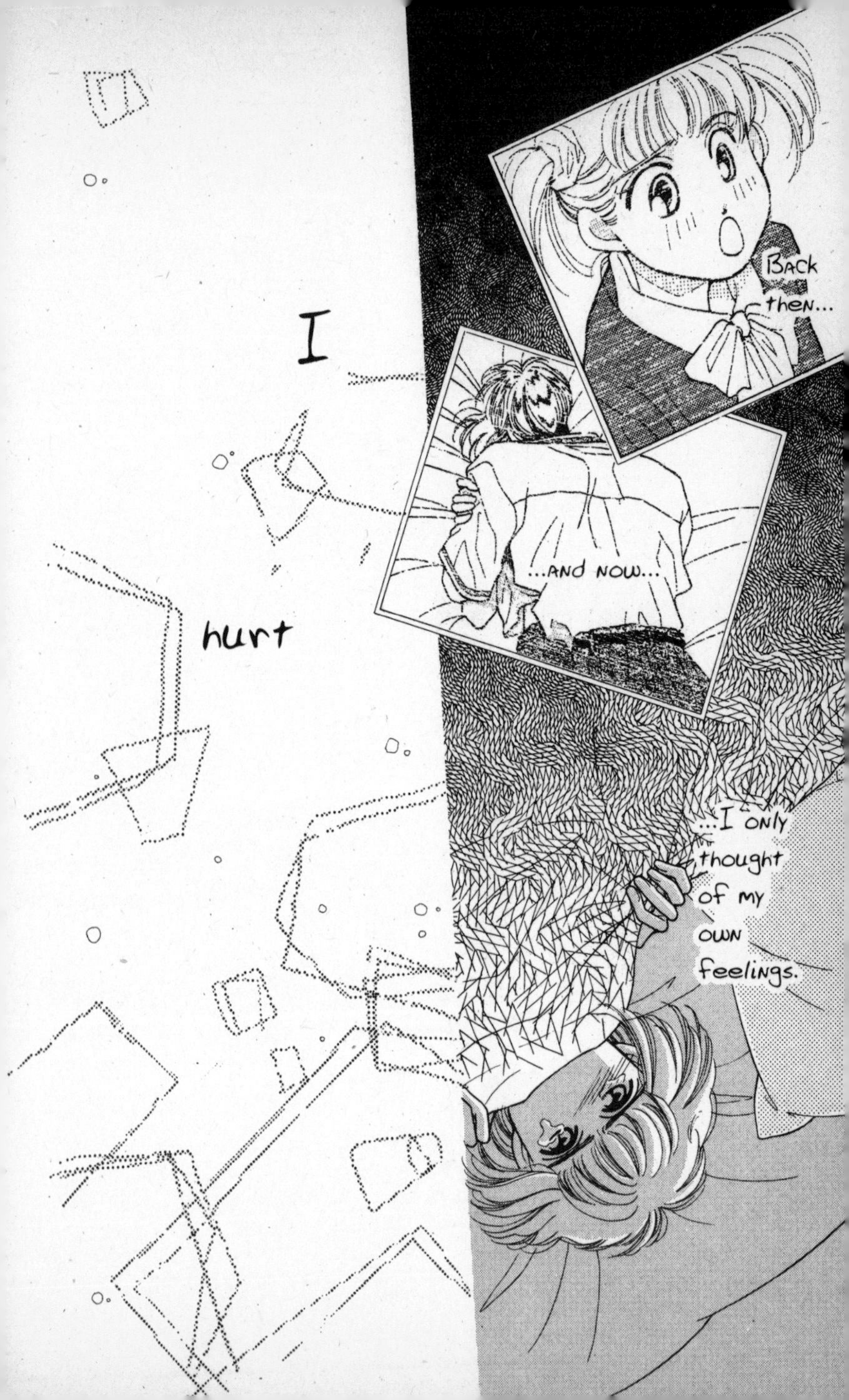
Back then...
...and now...
...I only thought of my own feelings.
I
hurt

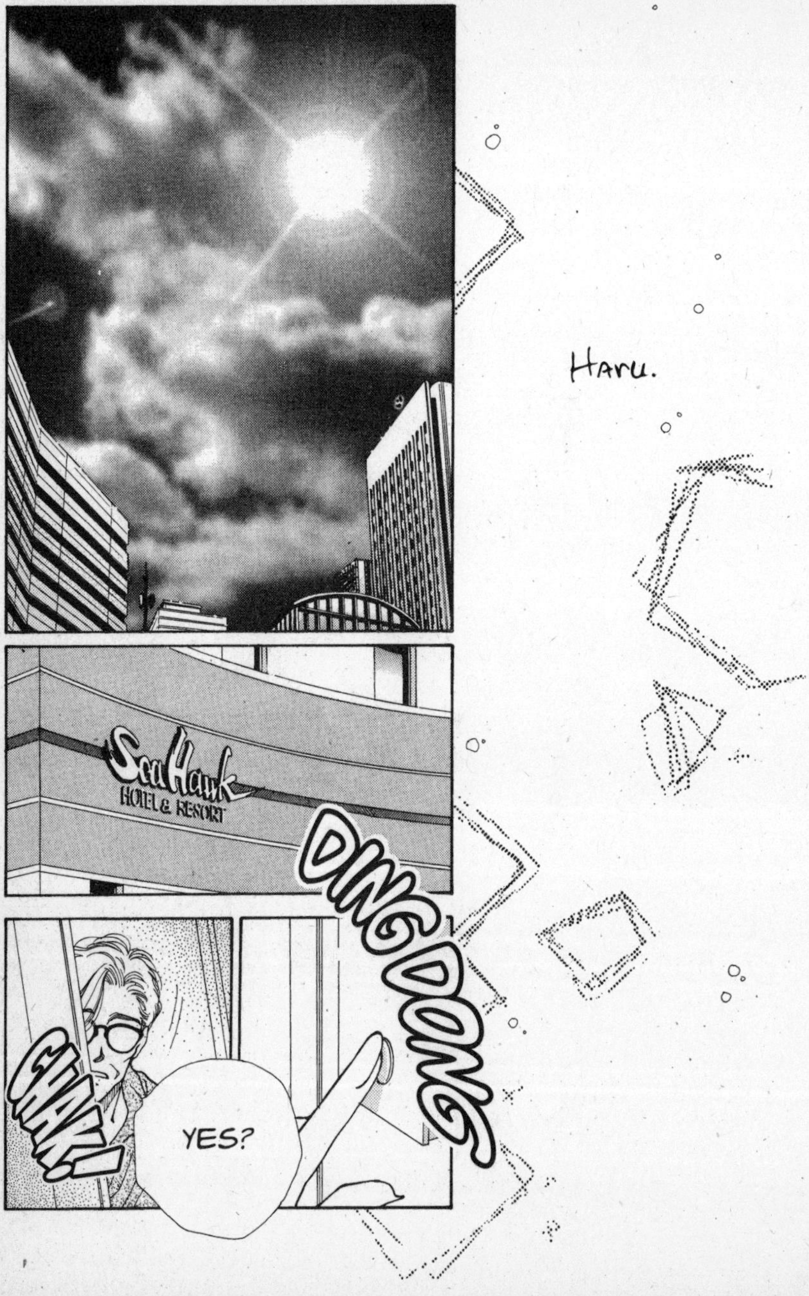
Haru.
Sea Hawk
HOTEL & RESORT
DING DONG
CHAK!!
YES?

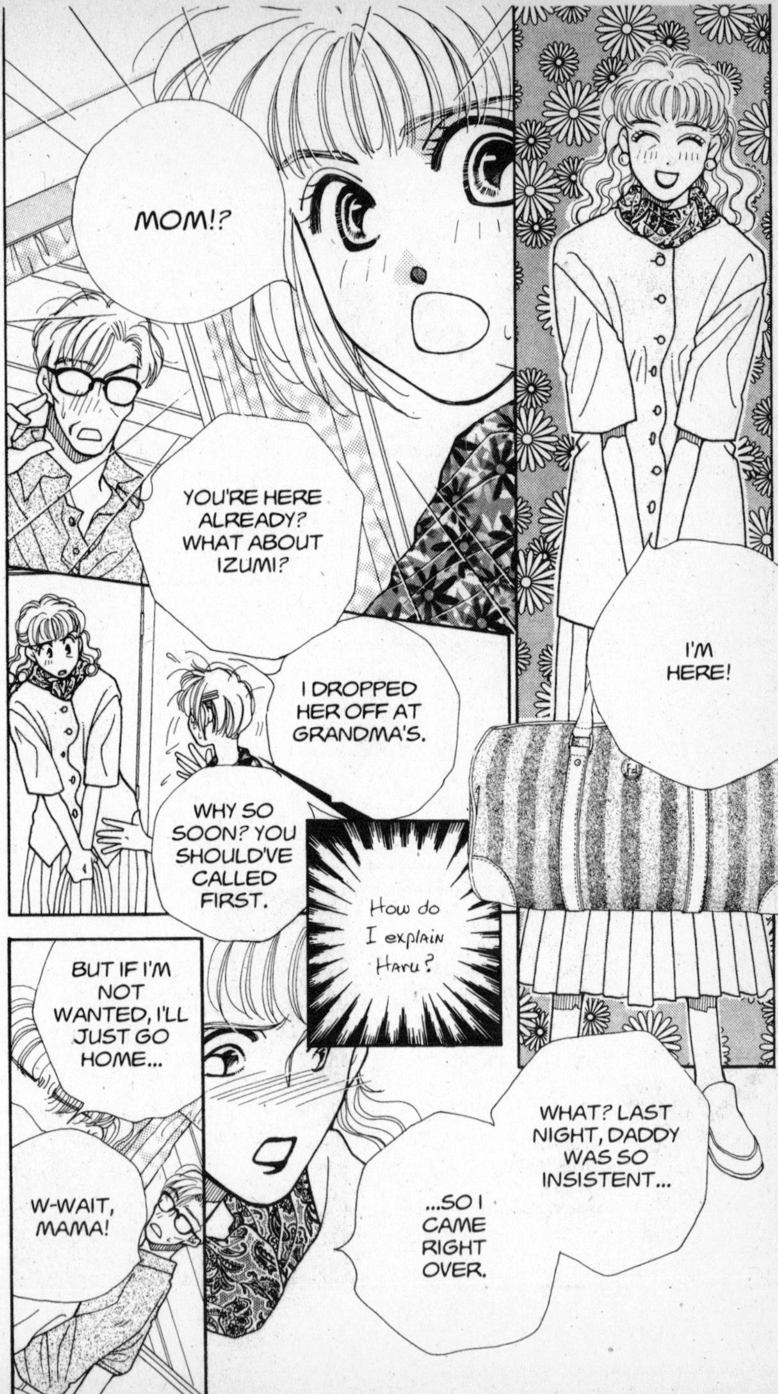
I'M HERE!
MOM!?
YOU'RE HERE ALREADY? WHAT ABOUT IZUMI?
I DROPPED HER OFF AT GRANDMA'S.
WHY SO SOON? YOU SHOULD'VE CALLED FIRST.
How do I explain Haru?
WHAT? LAST NIGHT, DADDY WAS SO INSISTENT...
...SO I CAME RIGHT OVER.
BUT IF I'M NOT WANTED, I'LL JUST GO HOME...
W-WAIT, MAMA!

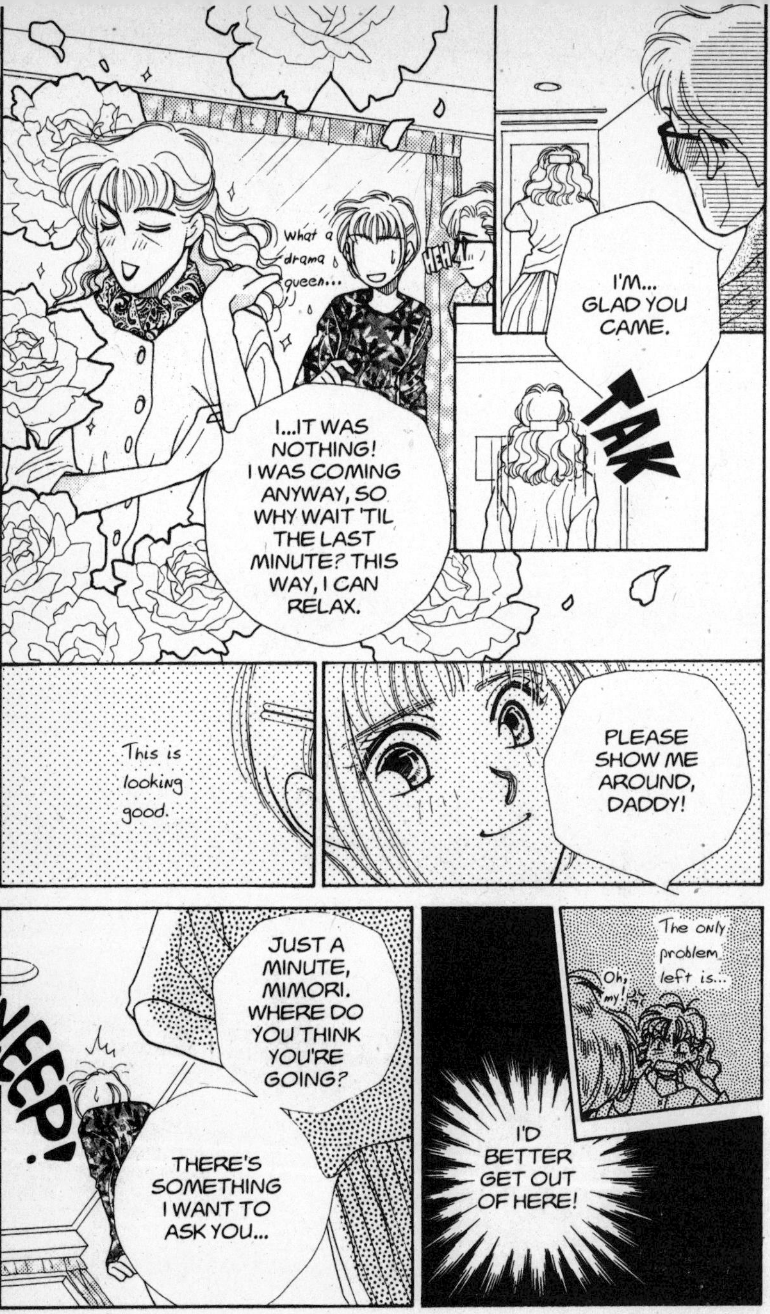
I'M... GLAD YOU CAME.
TAK
HEH
What a drama queen...
I...IT WAS NOTHING! I WAS COMING ANYWAY, SO WHY WAIT 'TIL THE LAST MINUTE? THIS WAY, I CAN RELAX.
PLEASE SHOW ME AROUND, DADDY!
This is looking good.
The only problem left is...
Oh, my!
I'D BETTER GET OUT OF HERE!
YEEP!
JUST A MINUTE, MIMORI. WHERE DO YOU THINK YOU'RE GOING?
THERE'S SOMETHING I WANT TO ASK YOU...

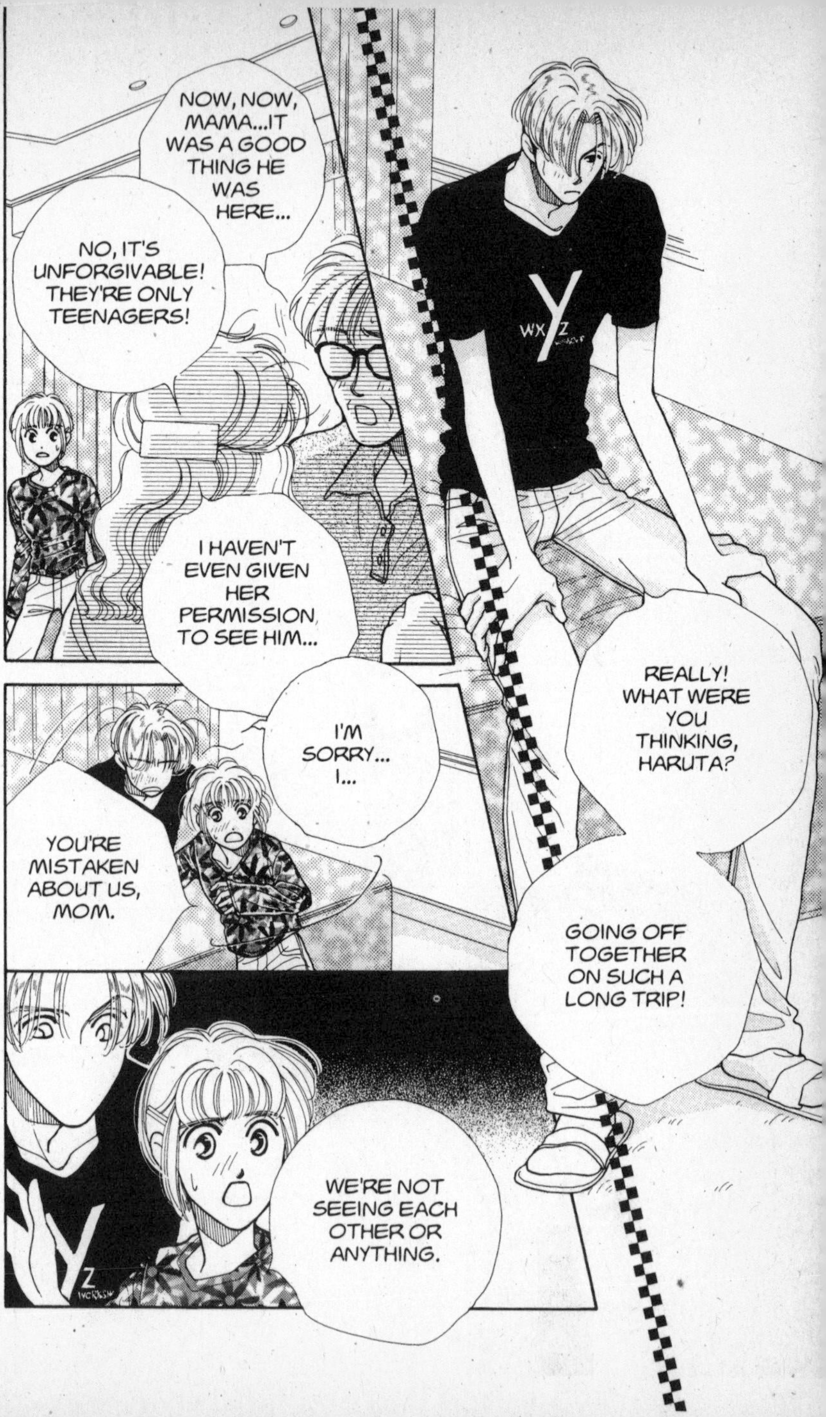
REALLY! WHAT WERE YOU THINKING, HARUTA?
GOING OFF TOGETHER ON SUCH A LONG TRIP!
NOW, NOW, MAMA...IT WAS A GOOD THING HE WAS HERE...
NO, IT'S UNFORGIVABLE! THEY'RE ONLY TEENAGERS!
I HAVEN'T EVEN GIVEN HER PERMISSION TO SEE HIM...
I'M SORRY... I...
YOU'RE MISTAKEN ABOUT US, MOM.
WE'RE NOT SEEING EACH OTHER OR ANYTHING.

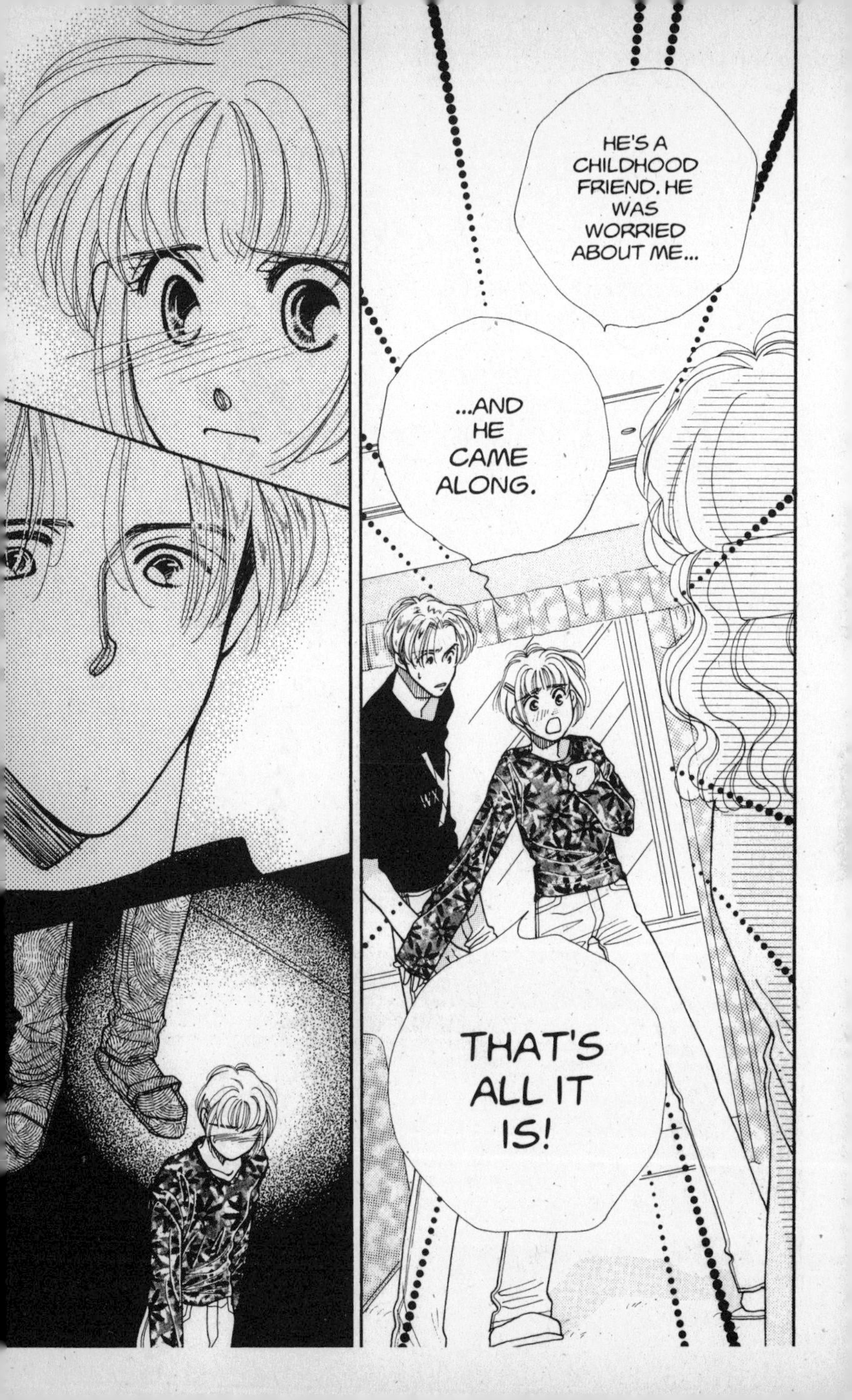
HE'S A CHILDHOOD FRIEND. HE WAS WORRIED ABOUT ME...
...AND HE CAME ALONG.
THAT'S ALL IT IS!

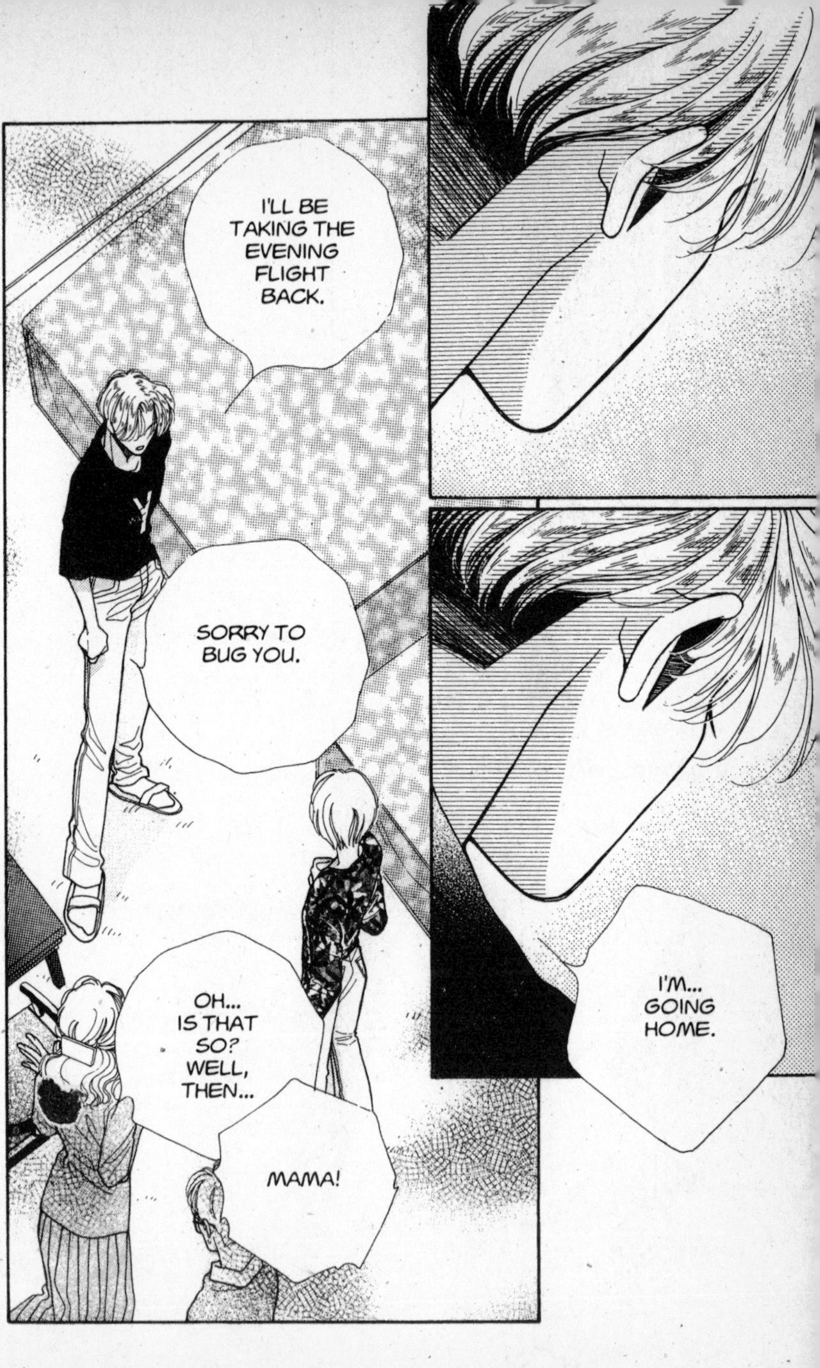
I'M... GOING HOME.
I'LL BE TAKING THE EVENING FLIGHT BACK.
SORRY TO BUG YOU.
OH... IS THAT SO? WELL, THEN...
MAMA!

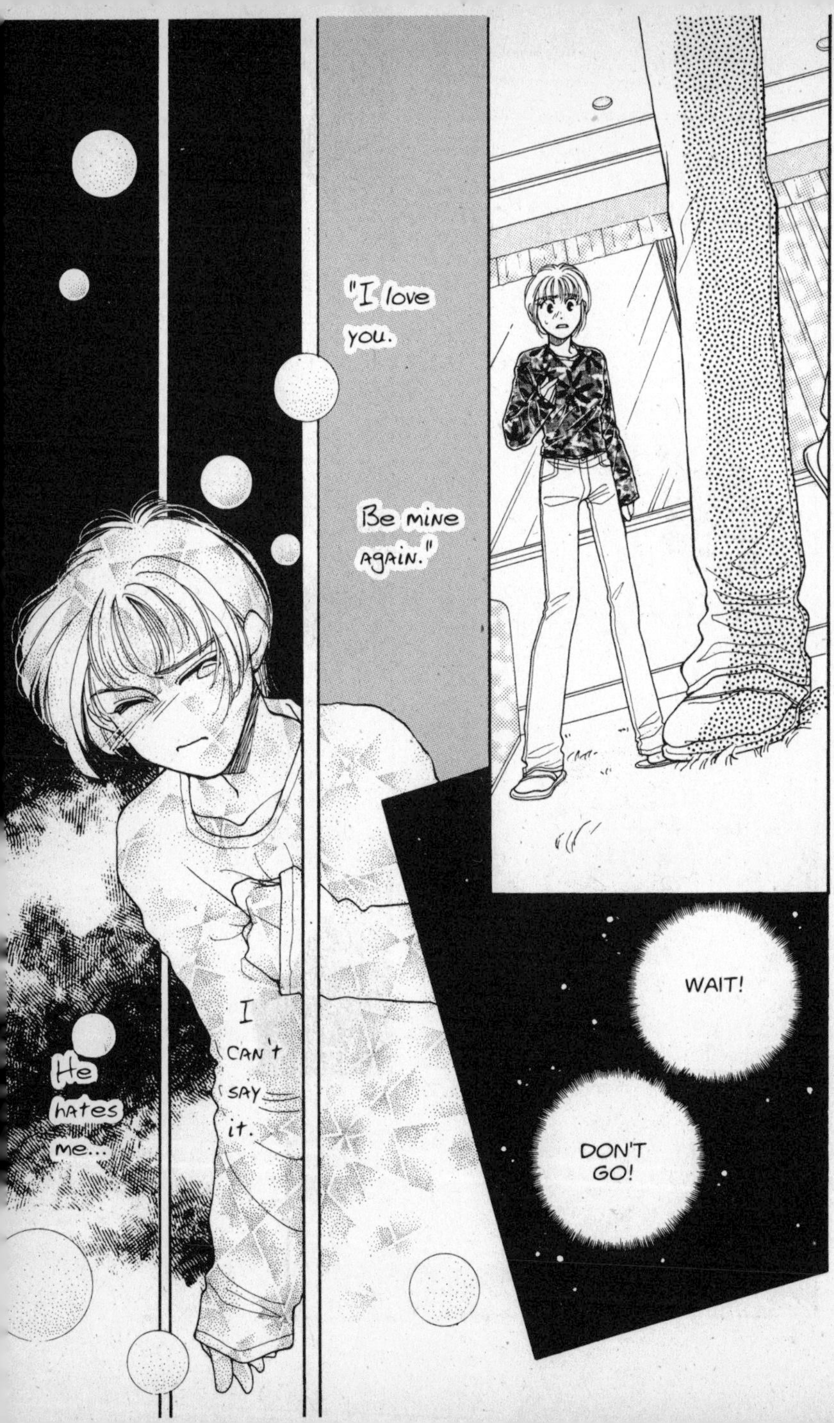
WAIT!
DON'T GO!
"I love you. Be mine again."
I can't say it.
He hates me...

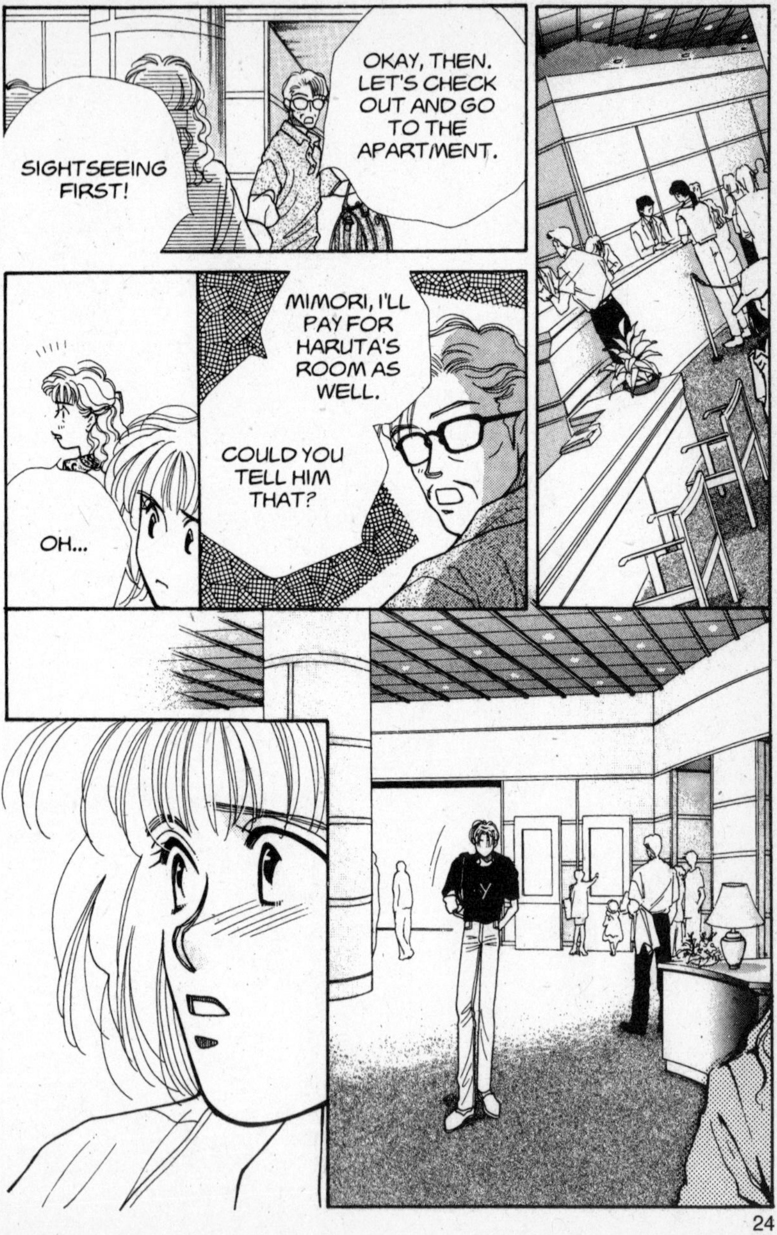
OKAY, THEN. LET'S CHECK OUT AND GO TO THE APARTMENT.
SIGHTSEEING FIRST!
MIMORI, I'LL PAY FOR HARUTA'S ROOM AS WELL.
COULD YOU TELL HIM THAT?
OH...

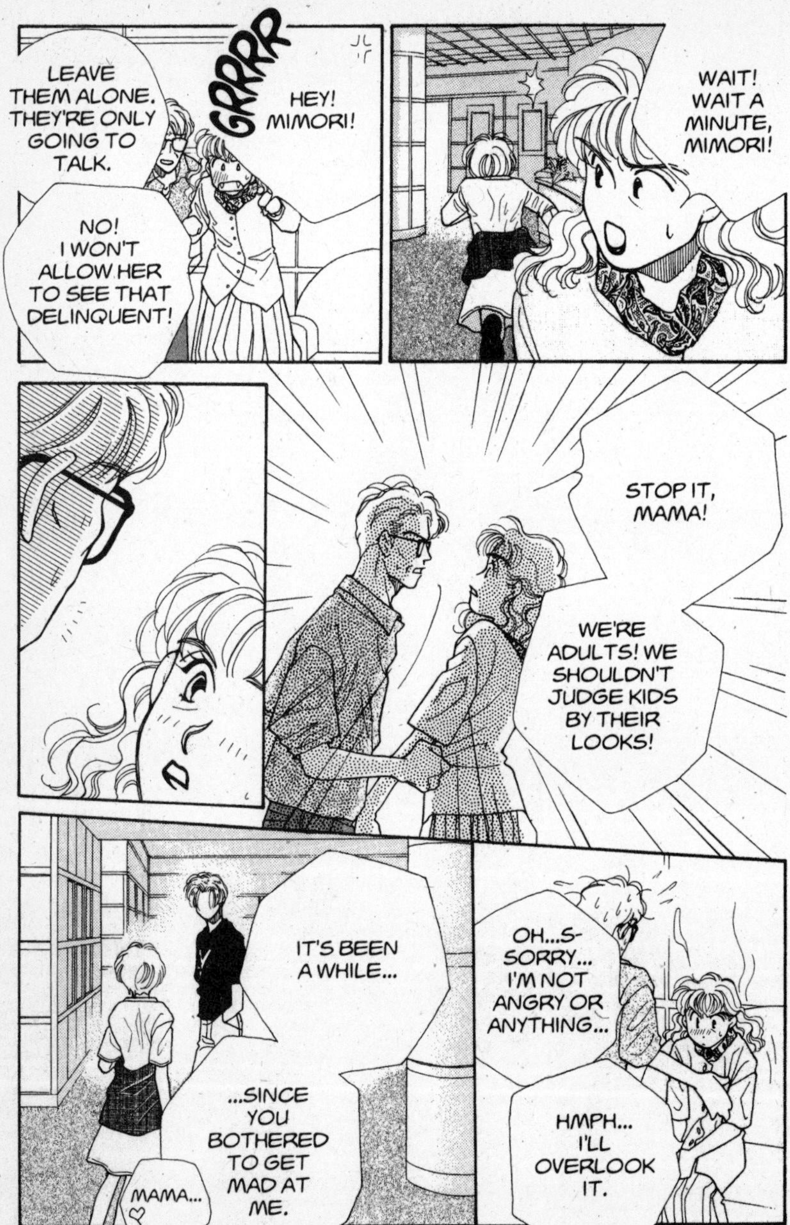
WAIT! WAIT A MINUTE, MIMORI!
HEY! MIMORI!
GRRRR
LEAVE THEM ALONE. THEY'RE ONLY GOING TO TALK.
NO! I WON'T ALLOW HER TO SEE THAT DELINQUENT!
STOP IT, MAMA!
WE'RE ADULTS! WE SHOULDN'T JUDGE KIDS BY THEIR LOOKS!
OH...S-SORRY... I'M NOT ANGRY OR ANYTHING...
HMPH... I'LL OVERLOOK IT.
IT'S BEEN A WHILE...
...SINCE YOU BOTHERED TO GET MAD AT ME.
MAMA...♡

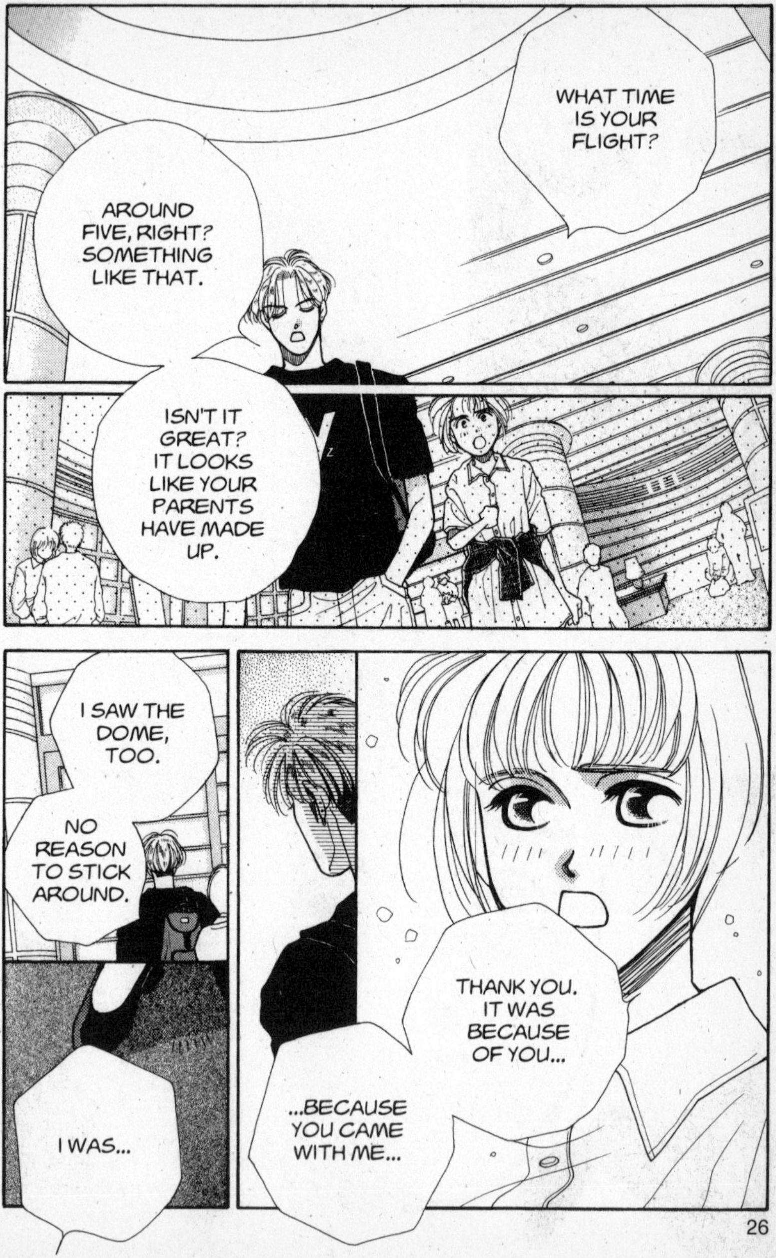
WHAT TIME IS YOUR FLIGHT?
AROUND FIVE, RIGHT? SOMETHING LIKE THAT.
ISN'T IT GREAT? IT LOOKS LIKE YOUR PARENTS HAVE MADE UP.
THANK YOU. IT WAS BECAUSE OF YOU...
...BECAUSE YOU CAME WITH ME...
I SAW THE DOME, TOO.
NO REASON TO STICK AROUND.
I WAS...

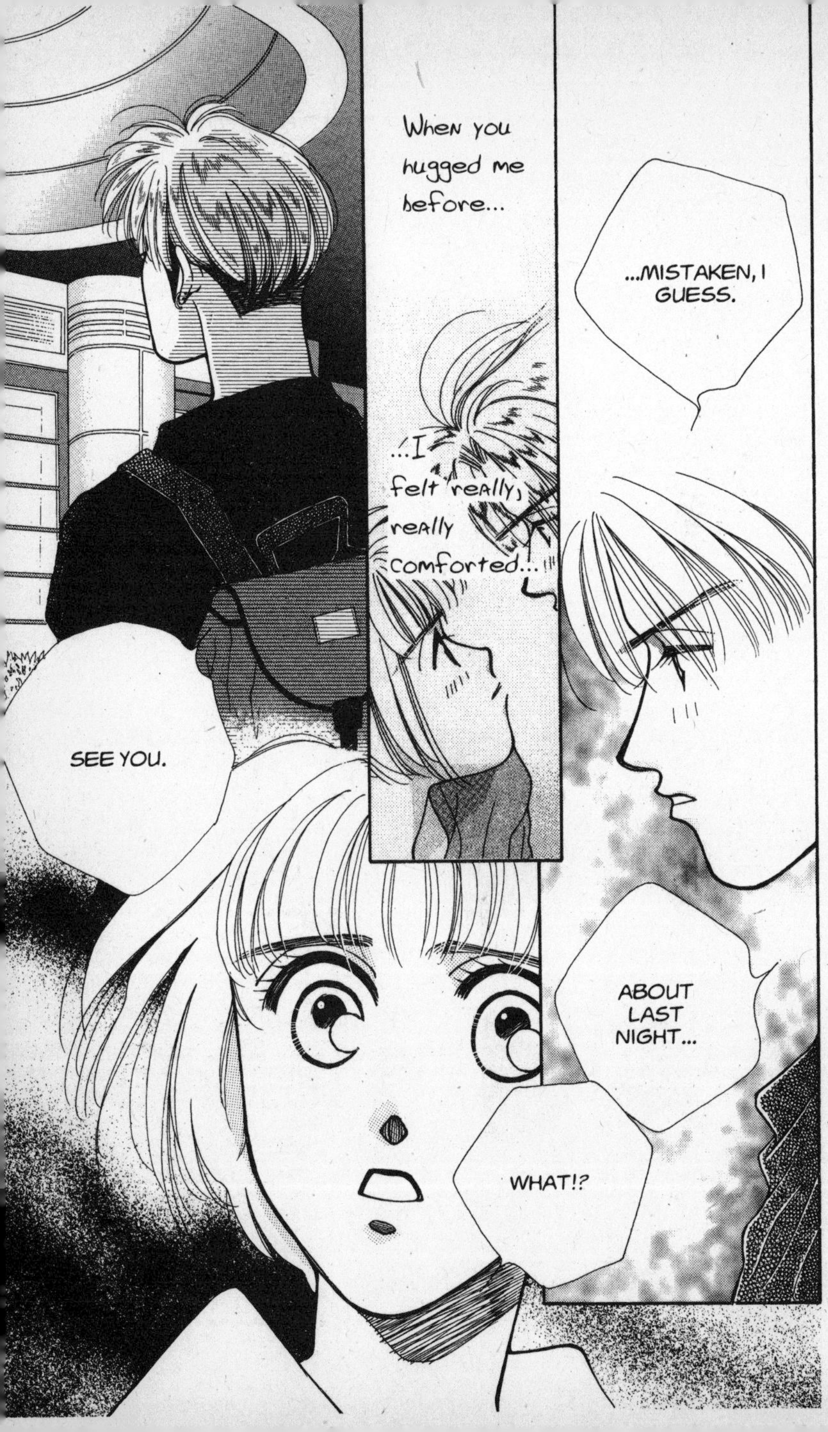
...MISTAKEN, I GUESS.
ABOUT LAST NIGHT...
When you hugged me before...
...I felt really, really comforted...
SEE YOU.
WHAT!?

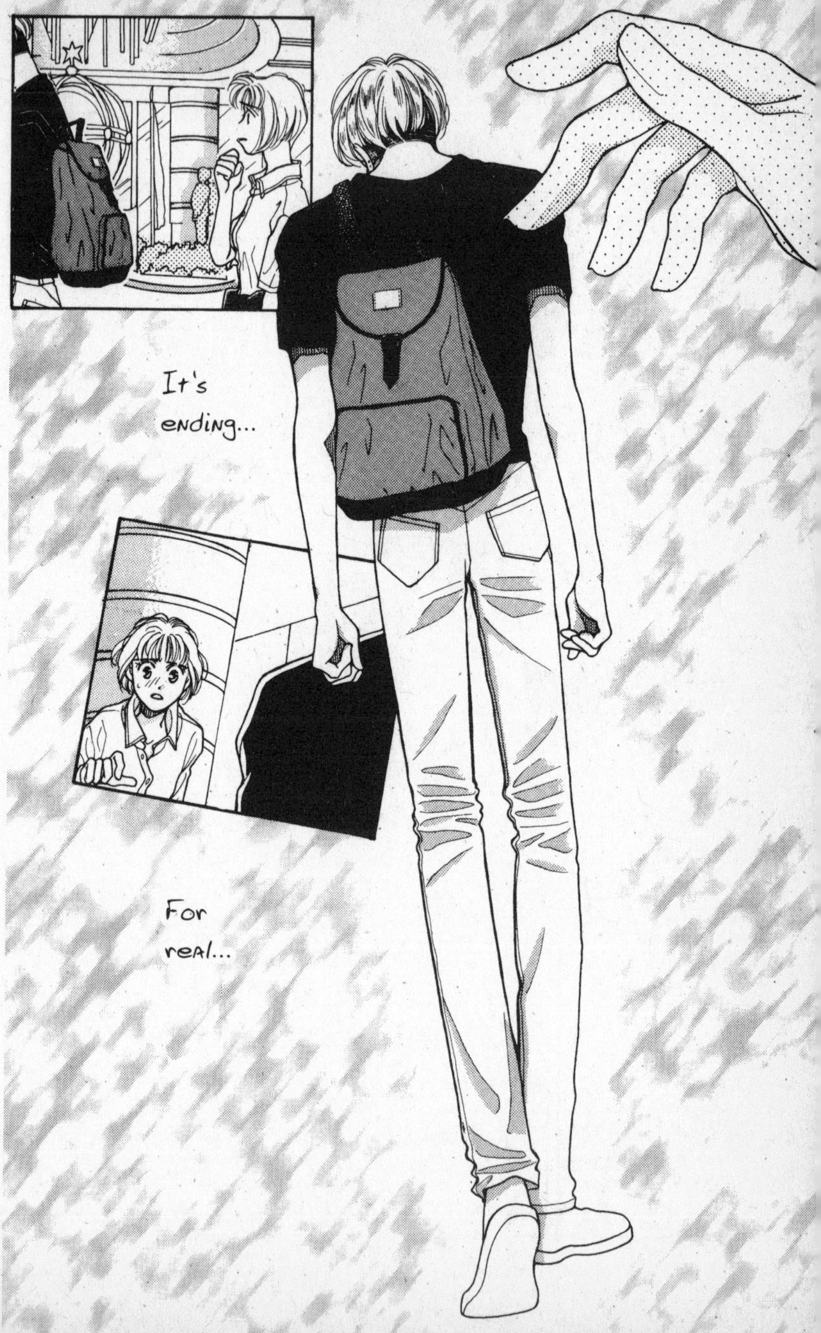
It's ending...
For real...

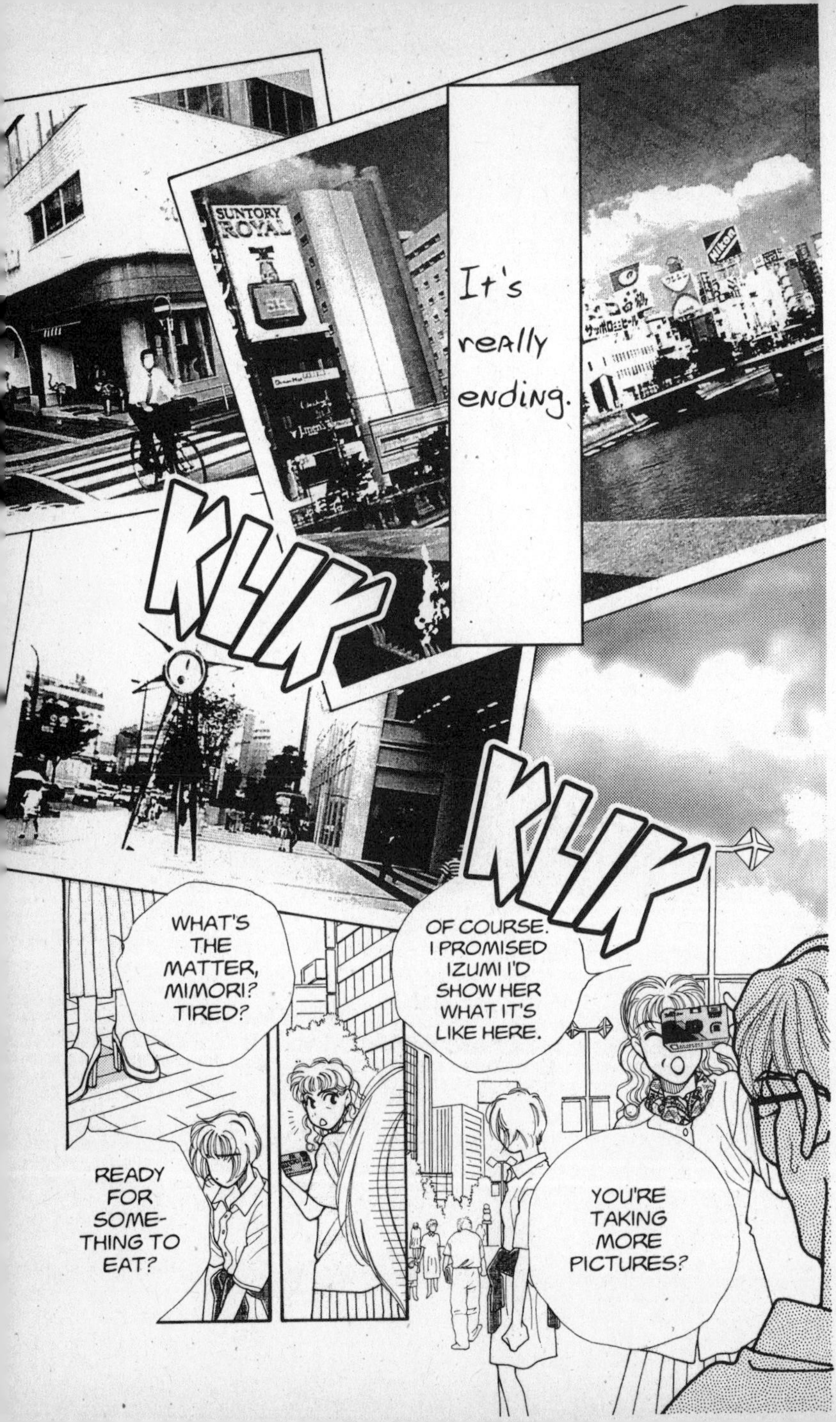
It's really ending.
KLIK
KLIK
YOU'RE TAKING MORE PICTURES?
OF COURSE. I PROMISED IZUMI I'D SHOW HER WHAT IT'S LIKE HERE.
WHAT'S THE MATTER, MIMORI? TIRED?
READY FOR SOME-THING TO EAT?

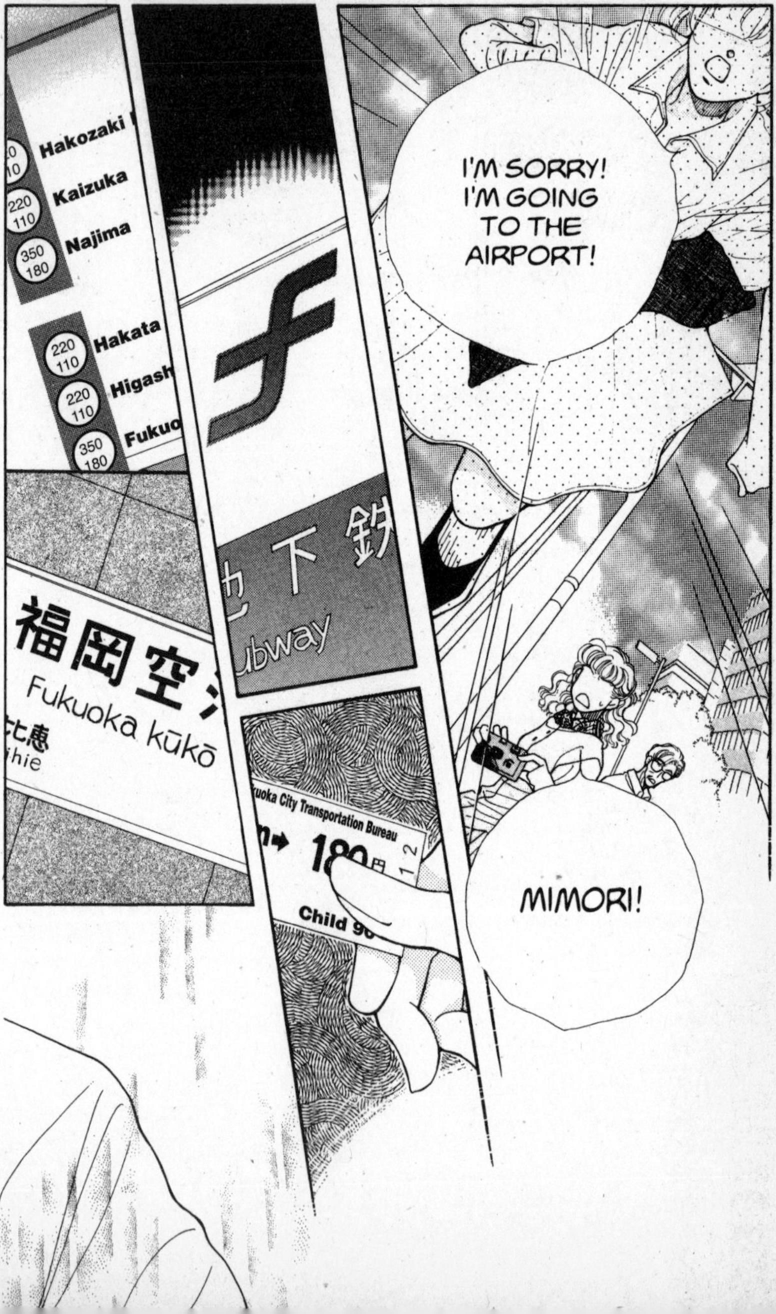
I'M SORRY! I'M GOING TO THE AIRPORT!
MIMORI!
地下鉄
ubway
uoka City Transportation Bureau
180円
Child 90
Hakozaki
Kaizuka
Najima
Hakata
Higash
Fukuo
福岡空
Fukuoka kūkō

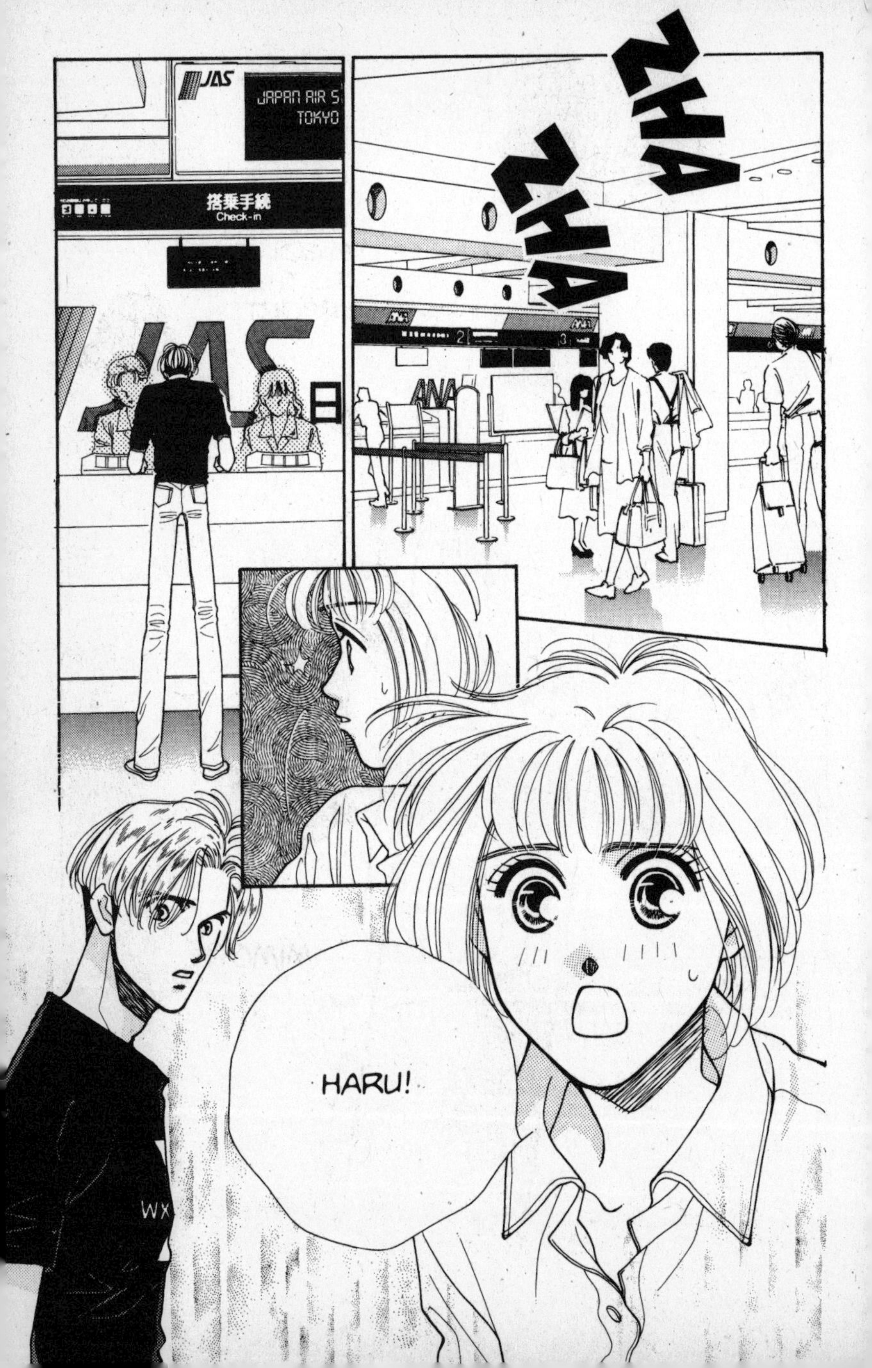
ZHA ZHA
ANA
JAS
JAPAN AIR S
TOKYO
搭乗手続
Check-in
HARU!

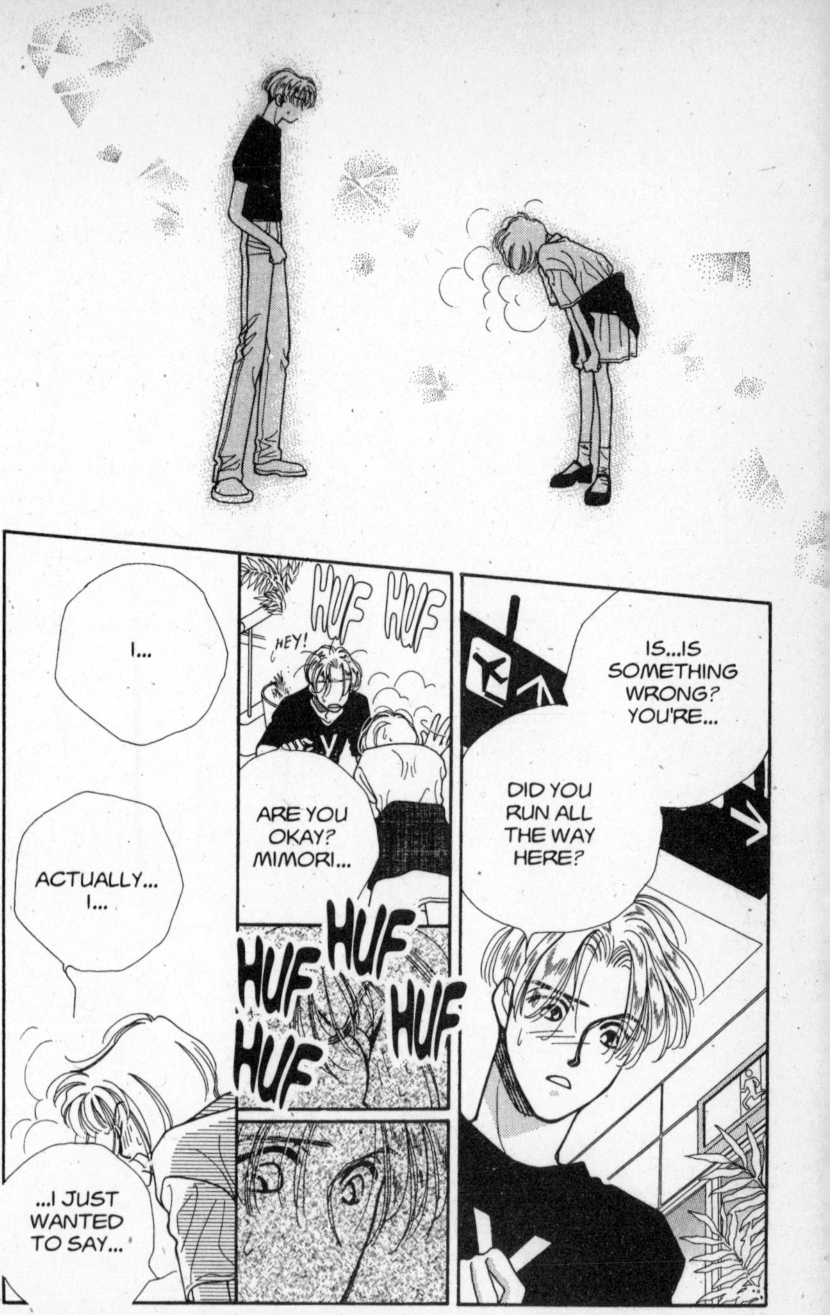
IS...IS SOMETHING WRONG? YOU'RE...
DID YOU RUN ALL THE WAY HERE?
HUF HUF
HEY!
ARE YOU OKAY? MIMORI...
HUF HUF HUF HUF
I...
ACTUALLY... I...
...I JUST WANTED TO SAY...

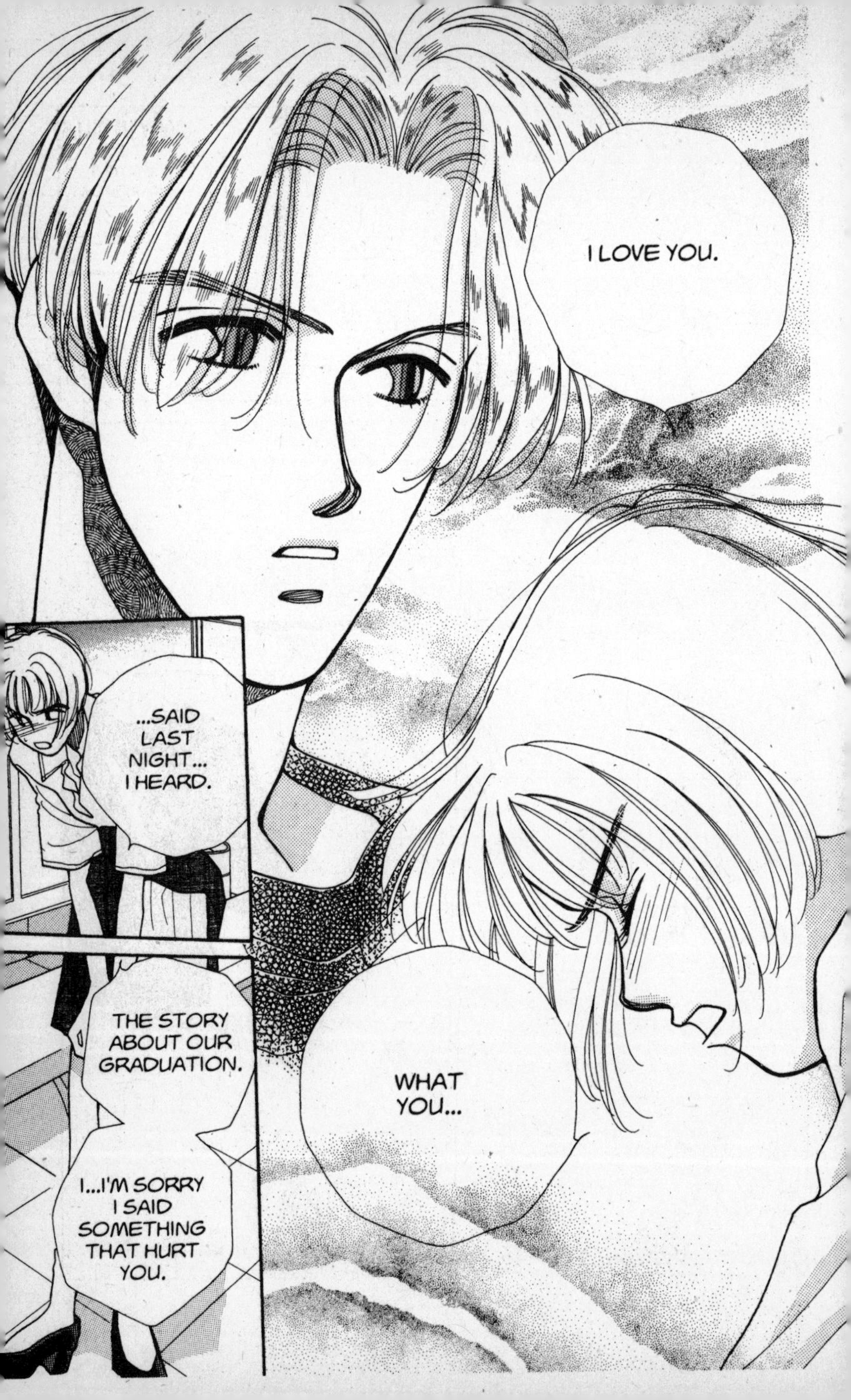
I LOVE YOU.
WHAT YOU...
...SAID LAST NIGHT... I HEARD.
THE STORY ABOUT OUR GRADUATION.
I...I'M SORRY I SAID SOMETHING THAT HURT YOU.

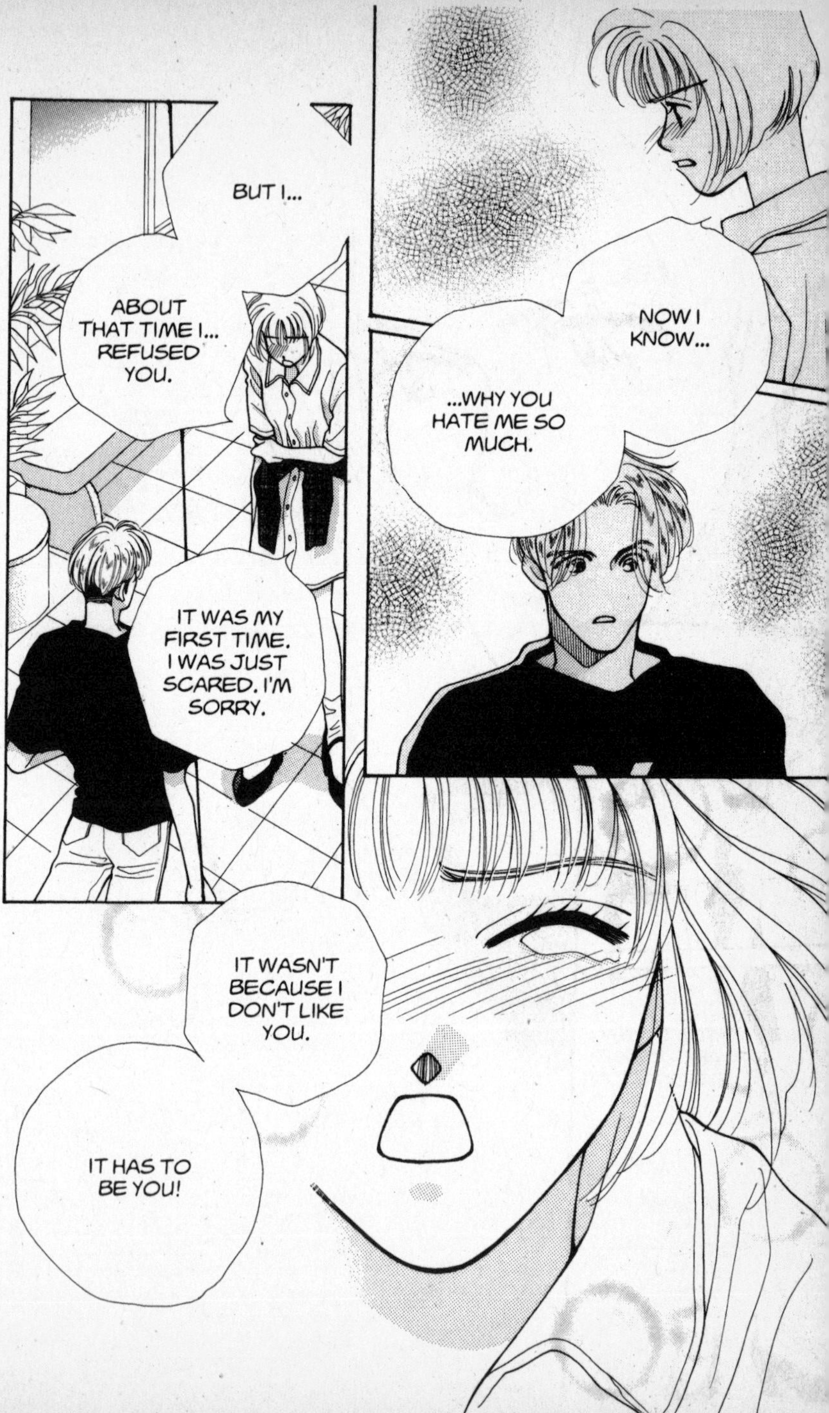
NOW I KNOW...
...WHY YOU HATE ME SO MUCH.
BUT I...
ABOUT THAT TIME I... REFUSED YOU.
IT WAS MY FIRST TIME. I WAS JUST SCARED. I'M SORRY.
IT WASN'T BECAUSE I DON'T LIKE YOU.
IT HAS TO BE YOU!

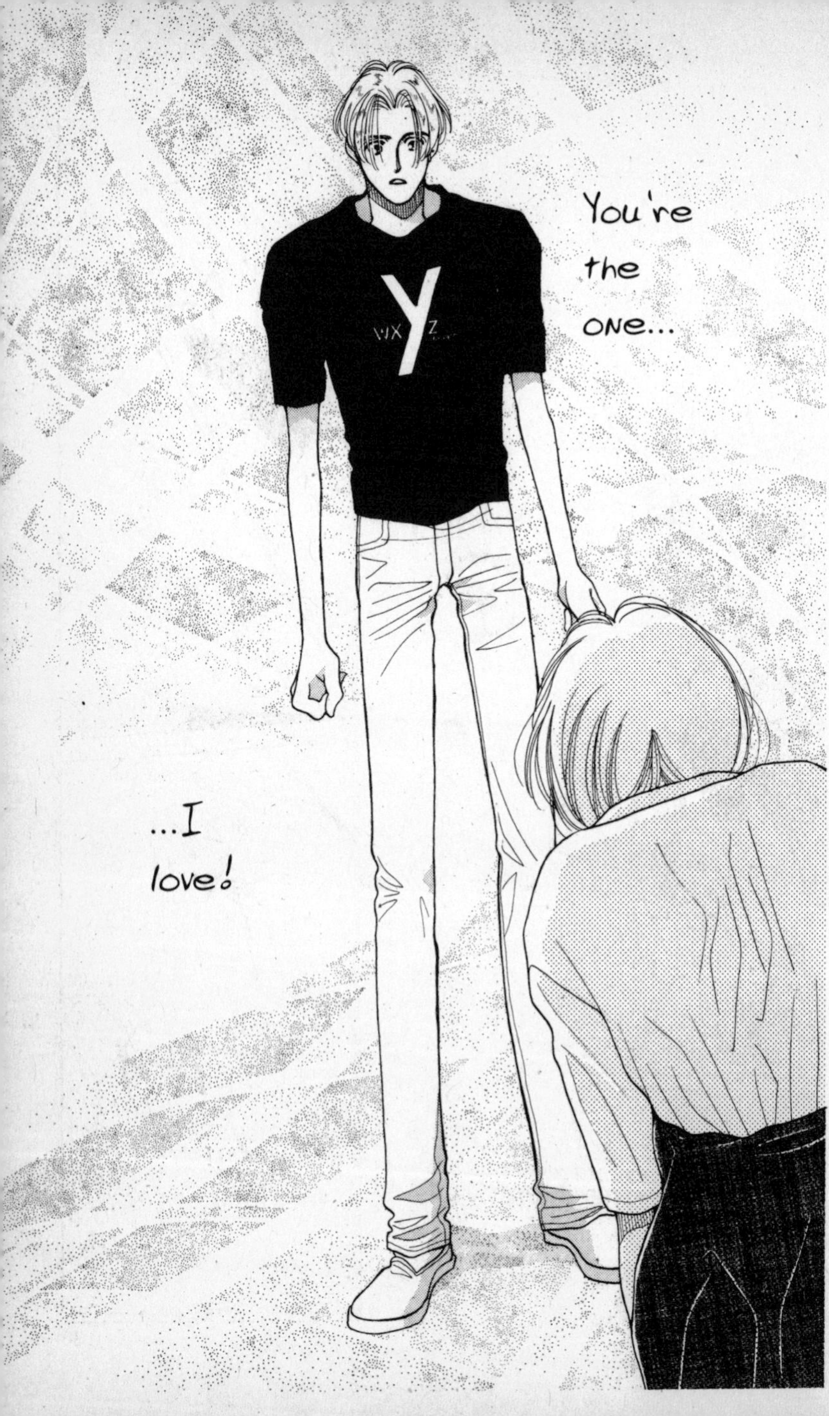
You're the one...
...I love!

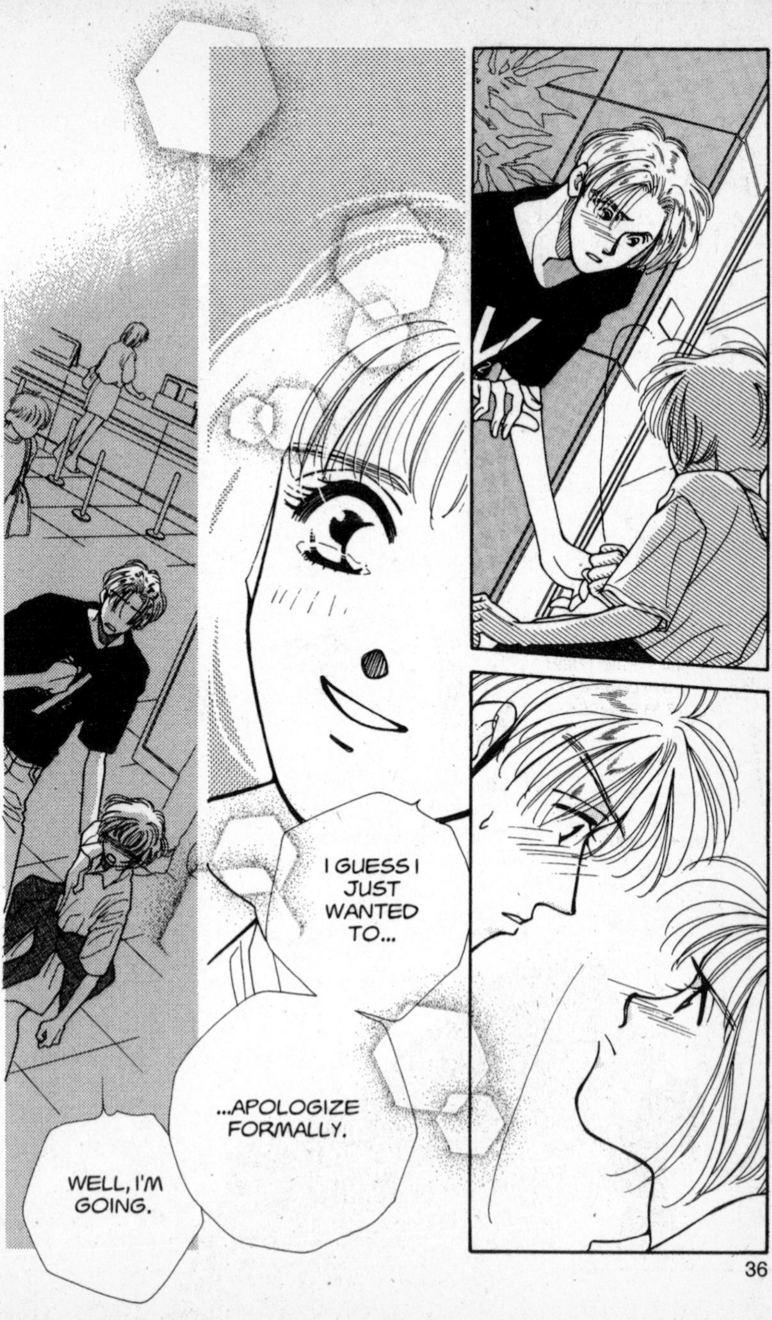
I GUESS I JUST WANTED TO...
...APOLOGIZE FORMALLY.
WELL, I'M GOING.

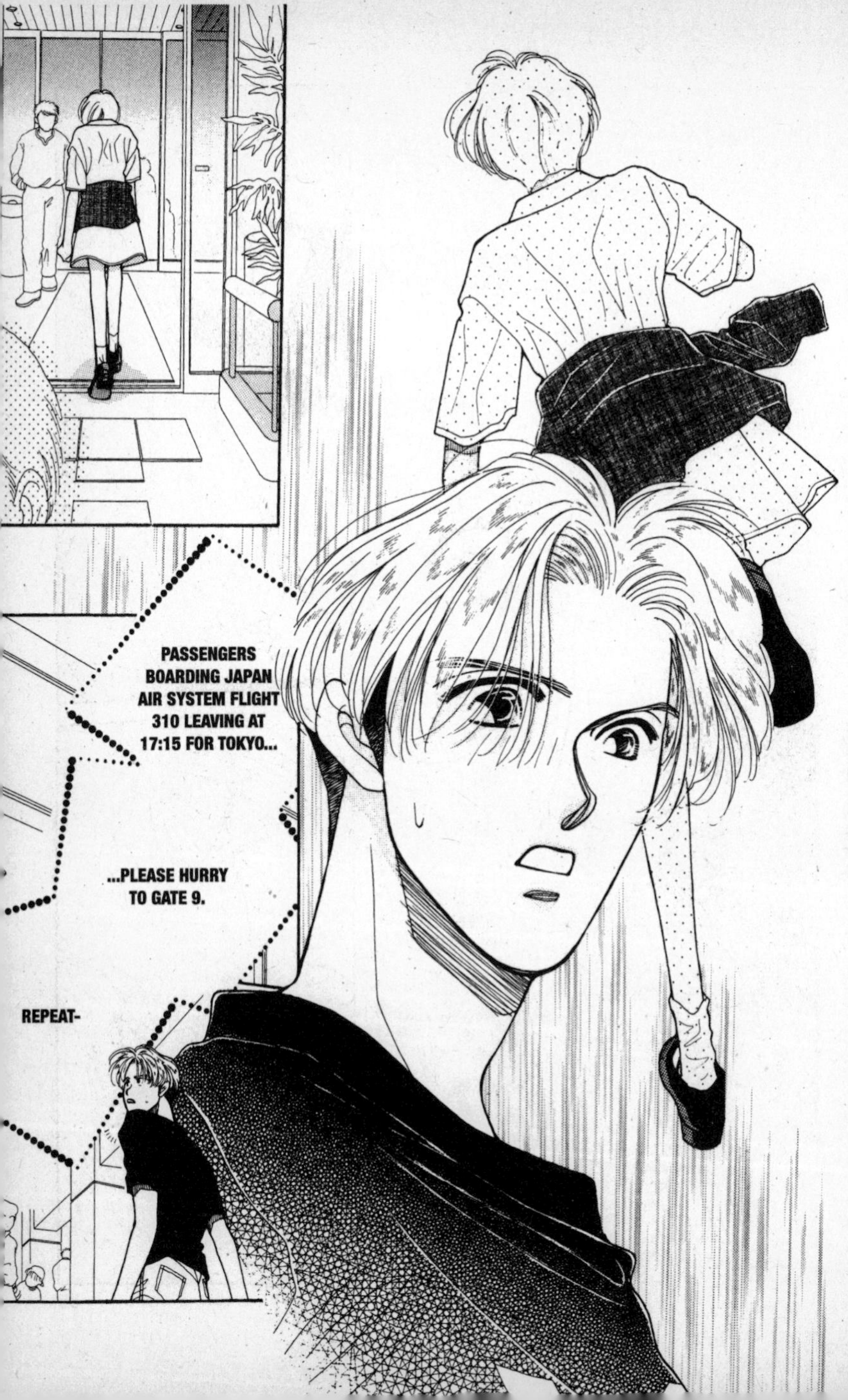
PASSENGERS BOARDING JAPAN AIR SYSTEM FLIGHT 310 LEAVING AT 17:15 FOR TOKYO...
...PLEASE HURRY TO GATE 9.
REPEAT-

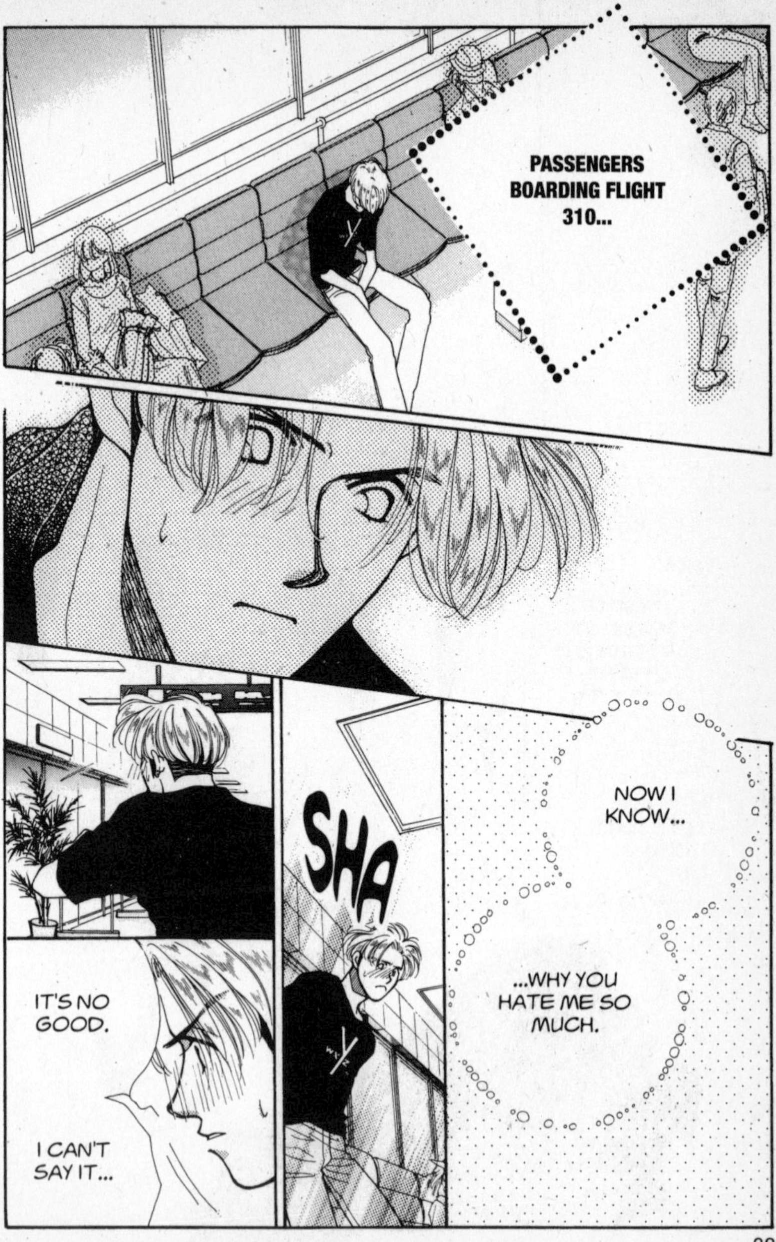
PASSENGERS BOARDING FLIGHT 310...
NOW I KNOW...
...WHY YOU HATE ME SO MUCH.
SHA
IT'S NO GOOD.
I CAN'T SAY IT...

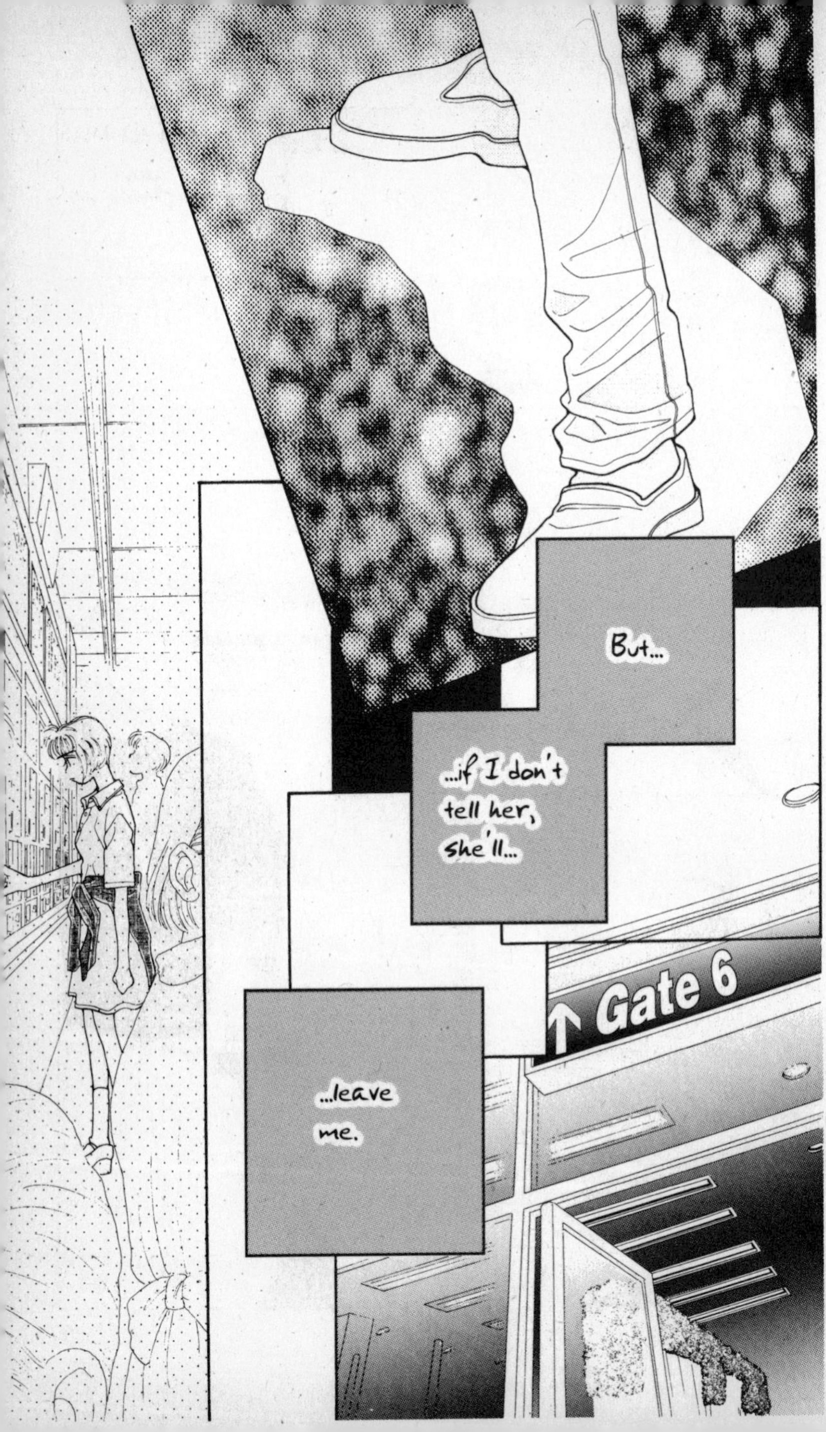

But...
...if I don't tell her, she'll...
Gate 6
...leave me.

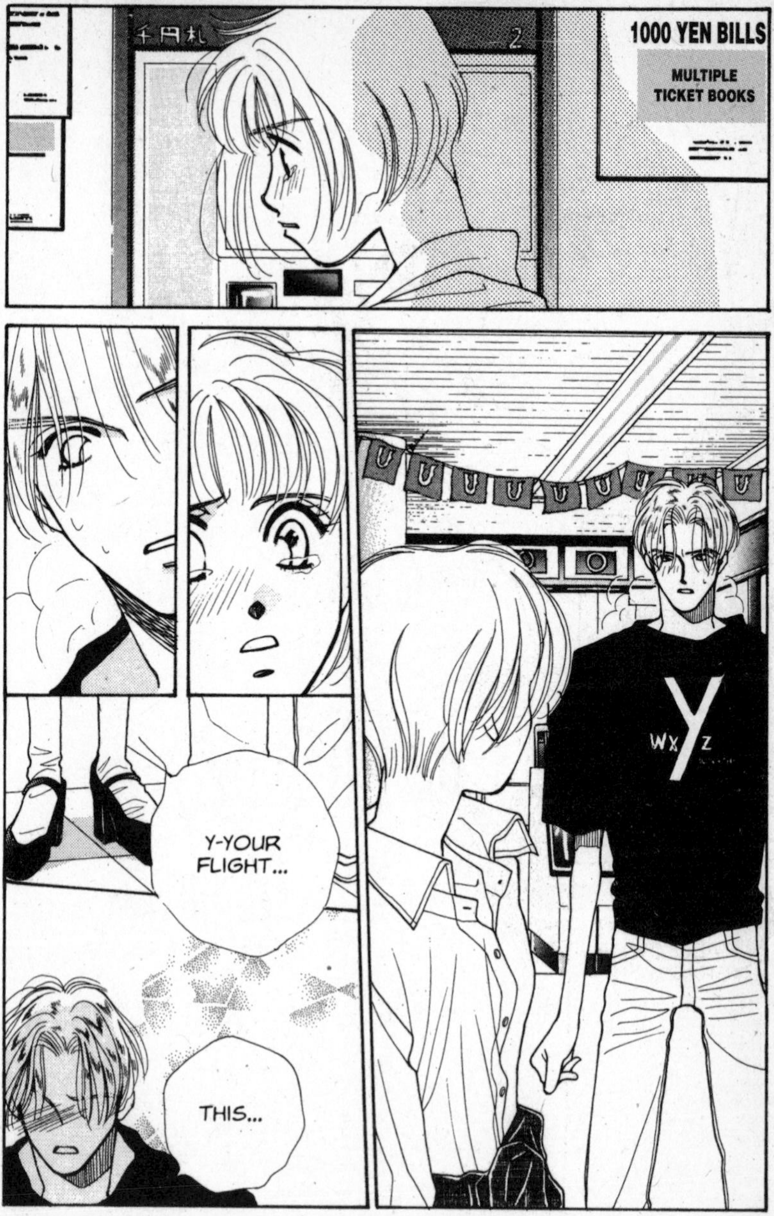
千円札
1000 YEN BILLS
MULTIPLE TICKET BOOKS
Y-YOUR FLIGHT...
THIS...

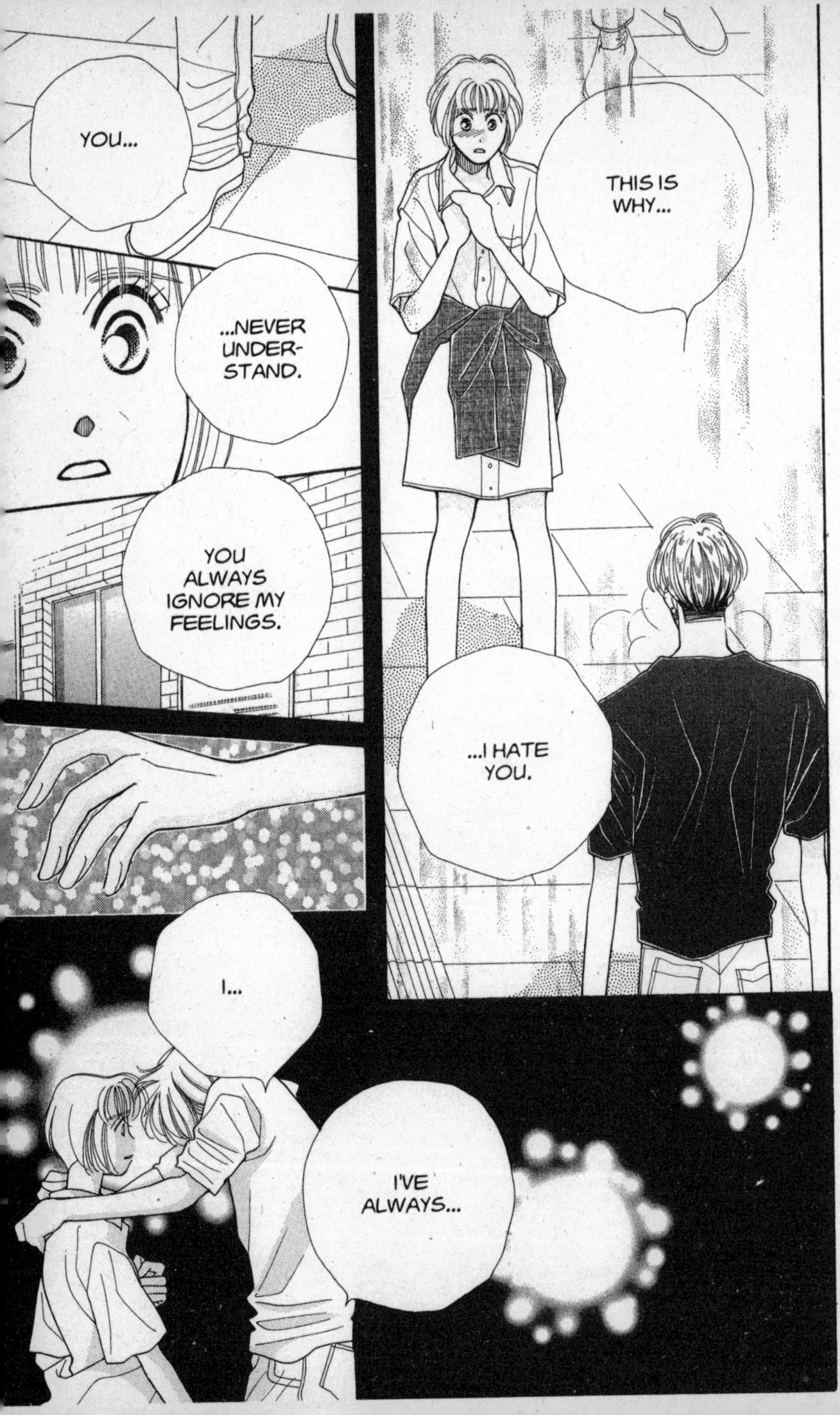
THIS IS WHY...
...I HATE YOU.
YOU...
...NEVER UNDER-STAND.
YOU ALWAYS IGNORE MY FEELINGS.
I...
I'VE ALWAYS...

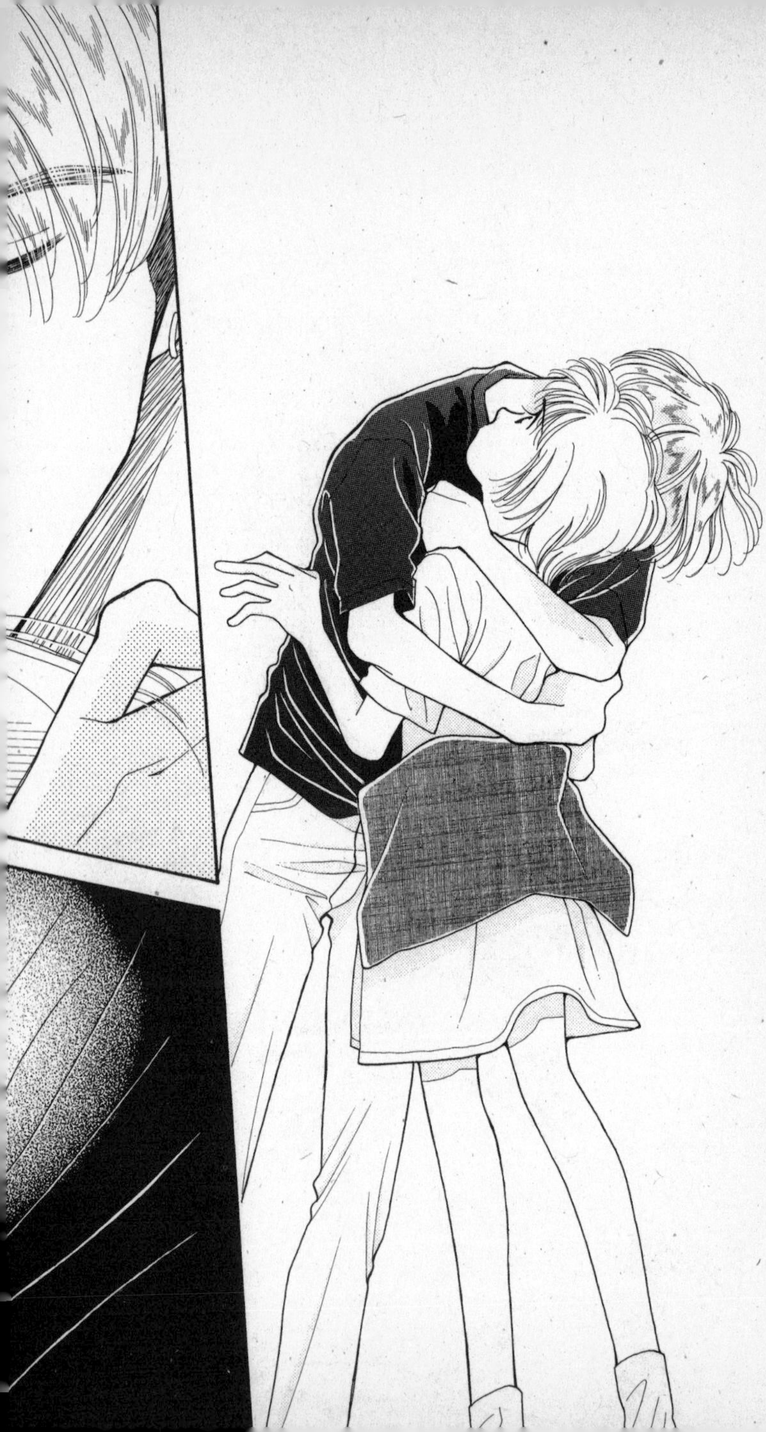

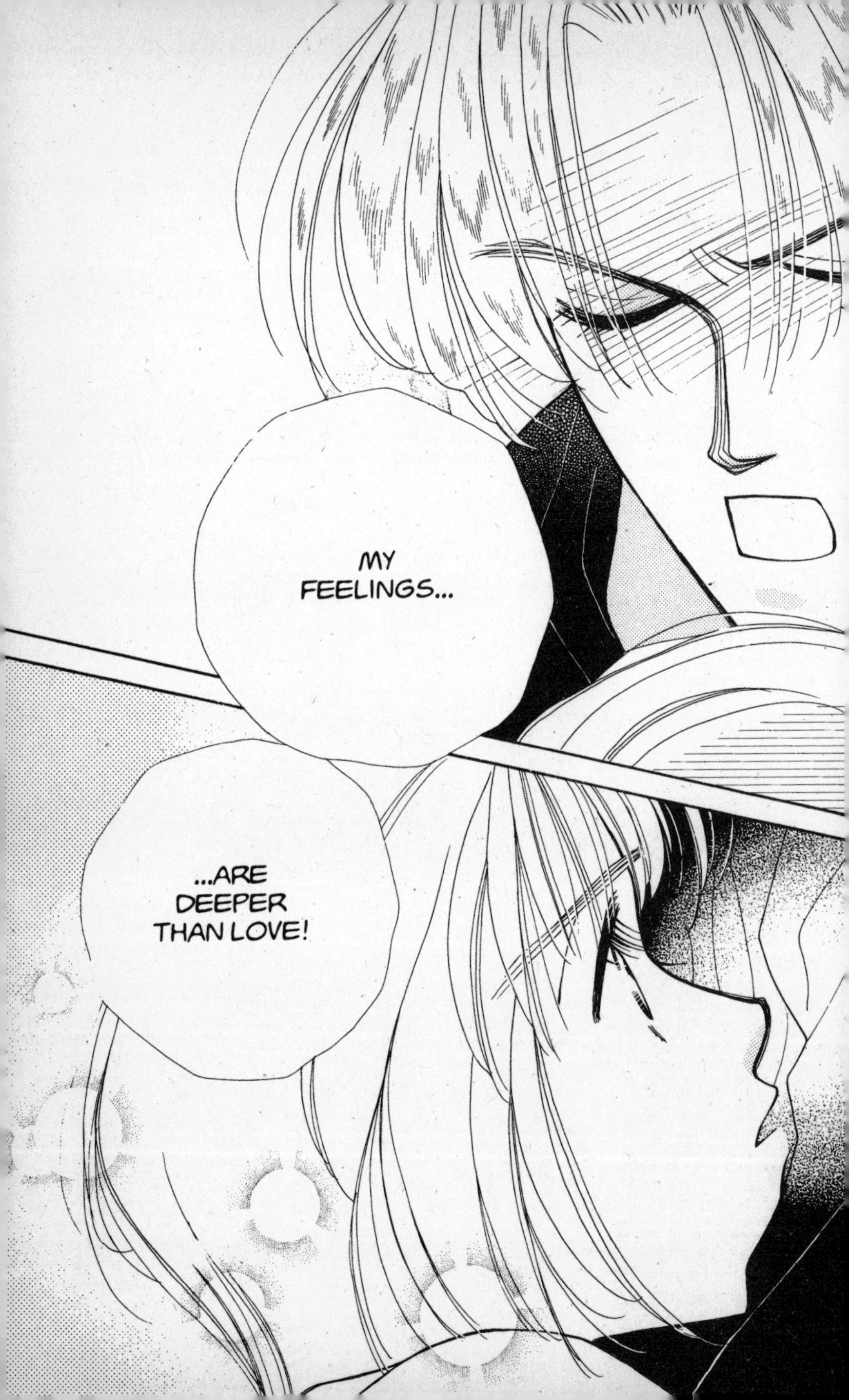
MY FEELINGS...
...ARE DEEPER THAN LOVE!

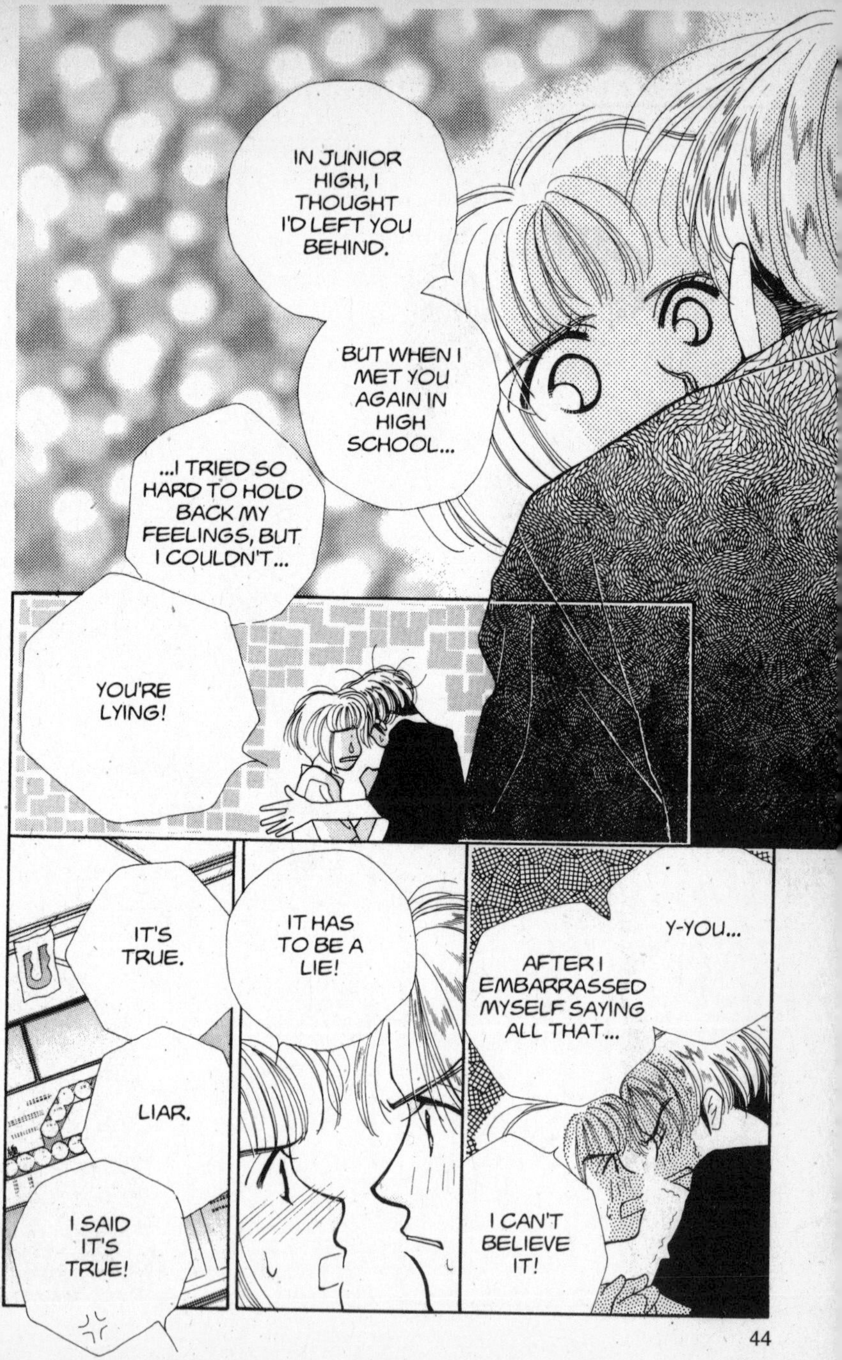
IN JUNIOR HIGH, I THOUGHT I'D LEFT YOU BEHIND.
BUT WHEN I MET YOU AGAIN IN HIGH SCHOOL...
...I TRIED SO HARD TO HOLD BACK MY FEELINGS, BUT I COULDN'T...
YOU'RE LYING!
Y-YOU...
AFTER I EMBARRASSED MYSELF SAYING ALL THAT...
I CAN'T BELIEVE IT!
IT HAS TO BE A LIE!
IT'S TRUE.
LIAR.
I SAID IT'S TRUE!

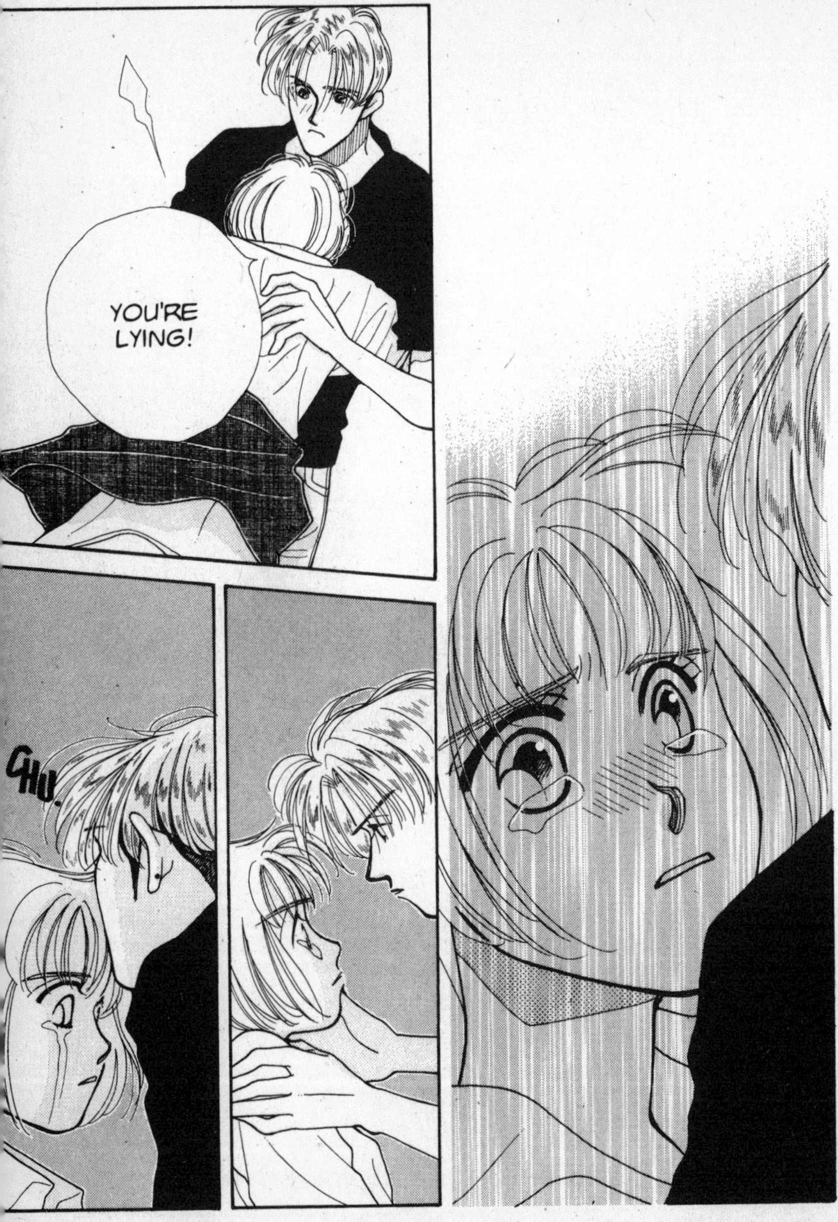
YOU'RE LYING!
CHU

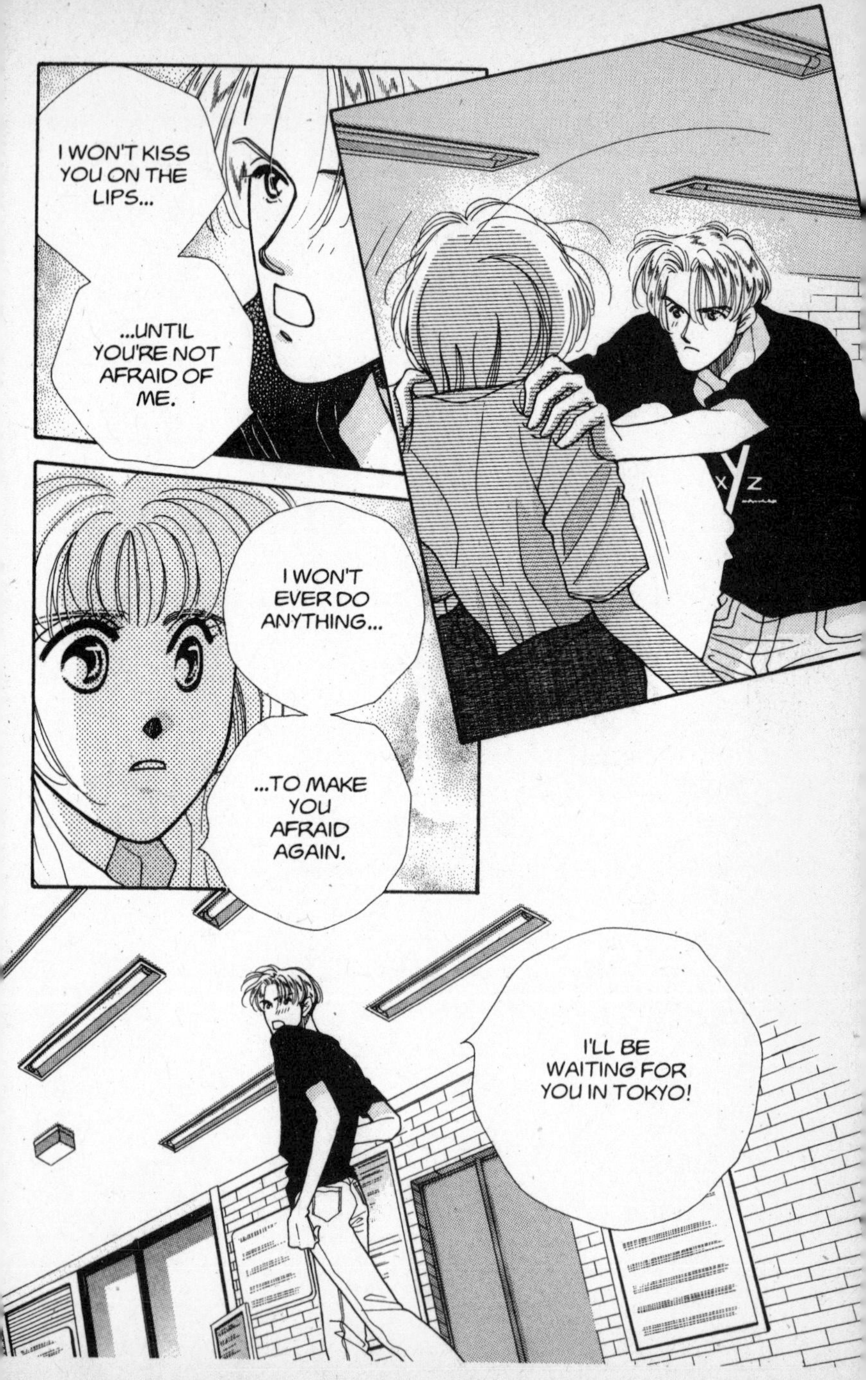
I WON'T KISS YOU ON THE LIPS...
...UNTIL YOU'RE NOT AFRAID OF ME.
I WON'T EVER DO ANYTHING...
...TO MAKE YOU AFRAID AGAIN.
I'LL BE WAITING FOR YOU IN TOKYO!

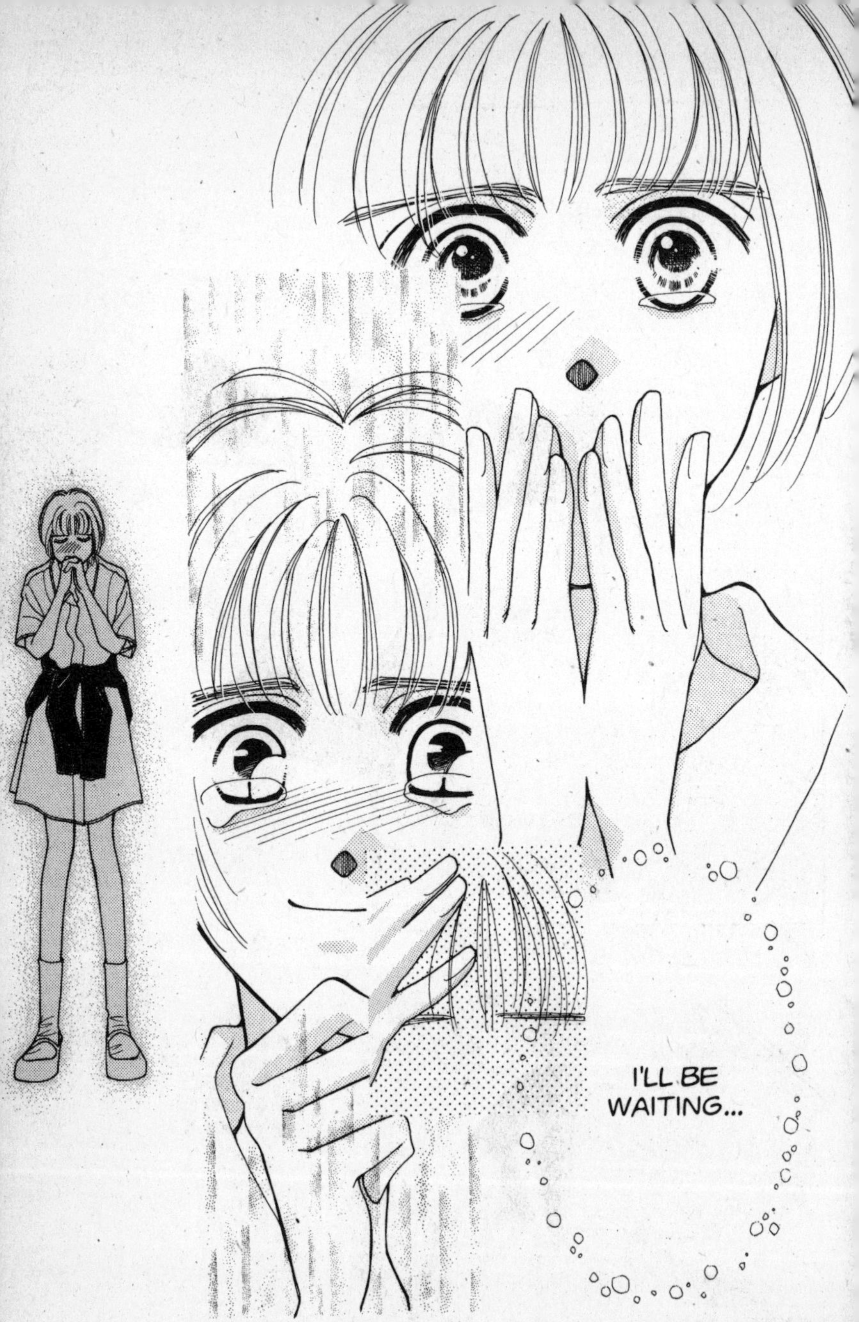
I'LL BE WAITING...

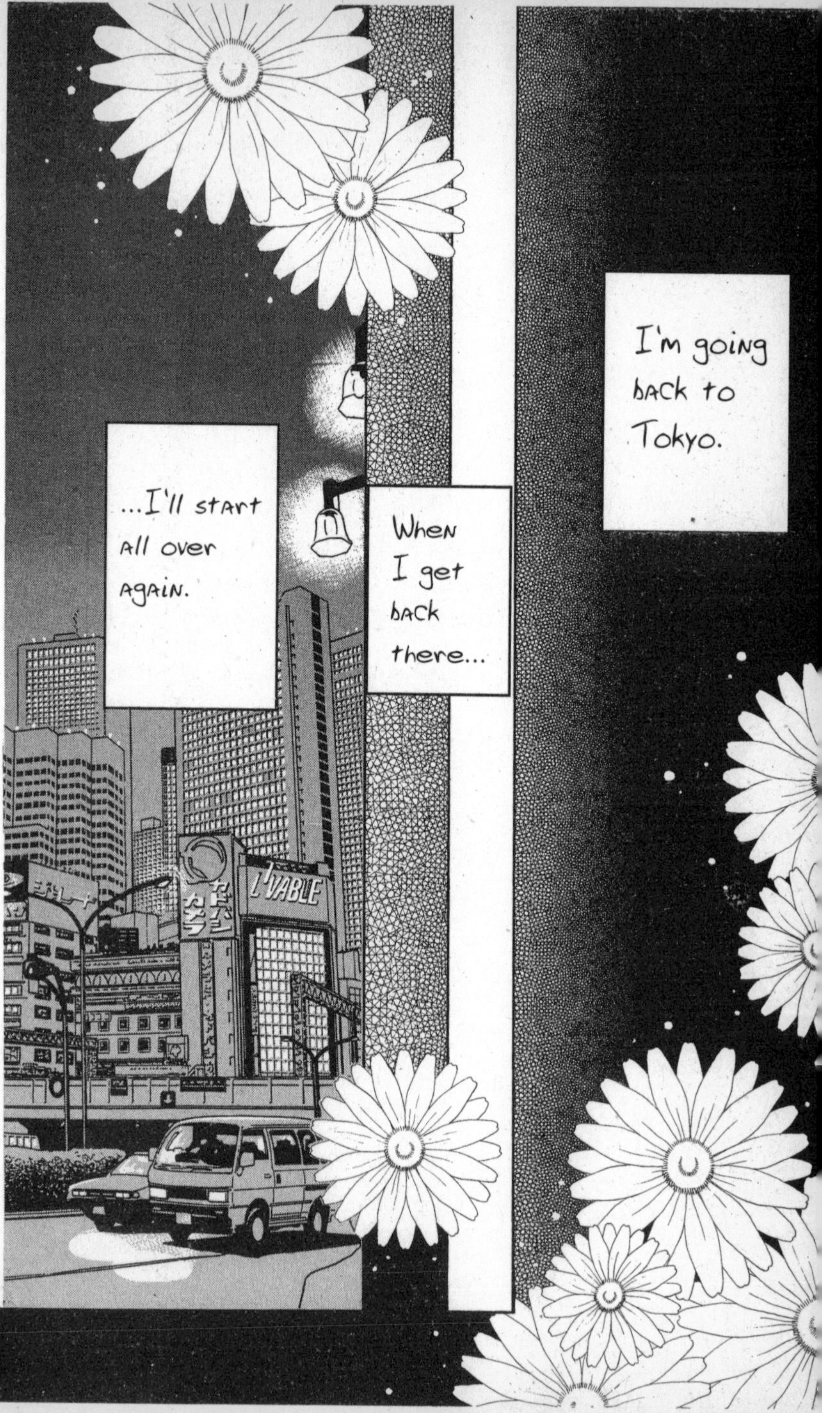
I'm going back to Tokyo.
When I get back there...
...I'll start all over again.
L'VABLE

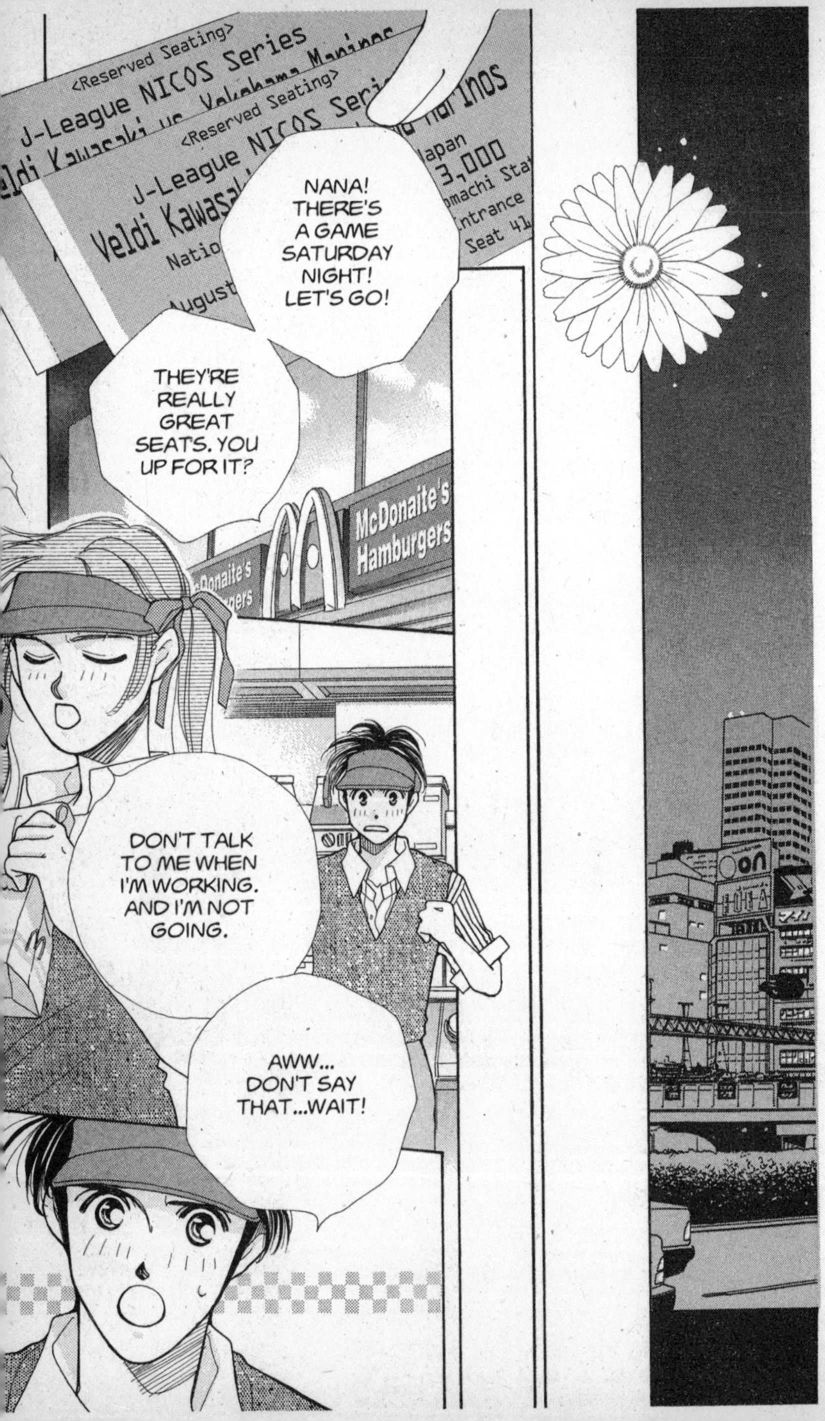
<Reserved Seating>
J-League NICOS Series
NANA! THERE'S A GAME SATURDAY NIGHT! LET'S GO!
THEY'RE REALLY GREAT SEATS. YOU UP FOR IT?
McDonaite's Hamburgers
DON'T TALK TO ME WHEN I'M WORKING. AND I'M NOT GOING.
AWW... DON'T SAY THAT...WAIT!

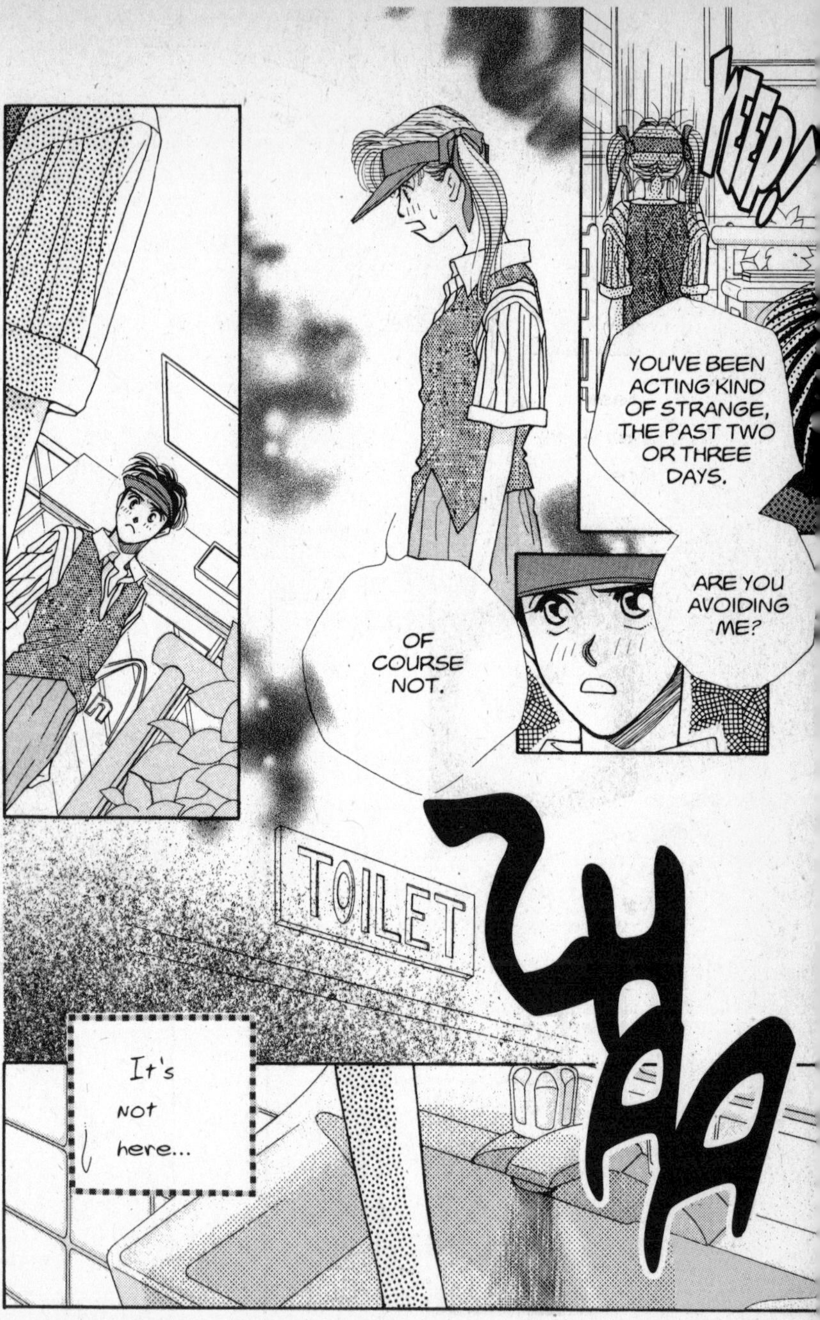
YEEP!
YOU'VE BEEN ACTING KIND OF STRANGE, THE PAST TWO OR THREE DAYS.
ARE YOU AVOIDING ME?
OF COURSE NOT.
TOILET
It's not here...

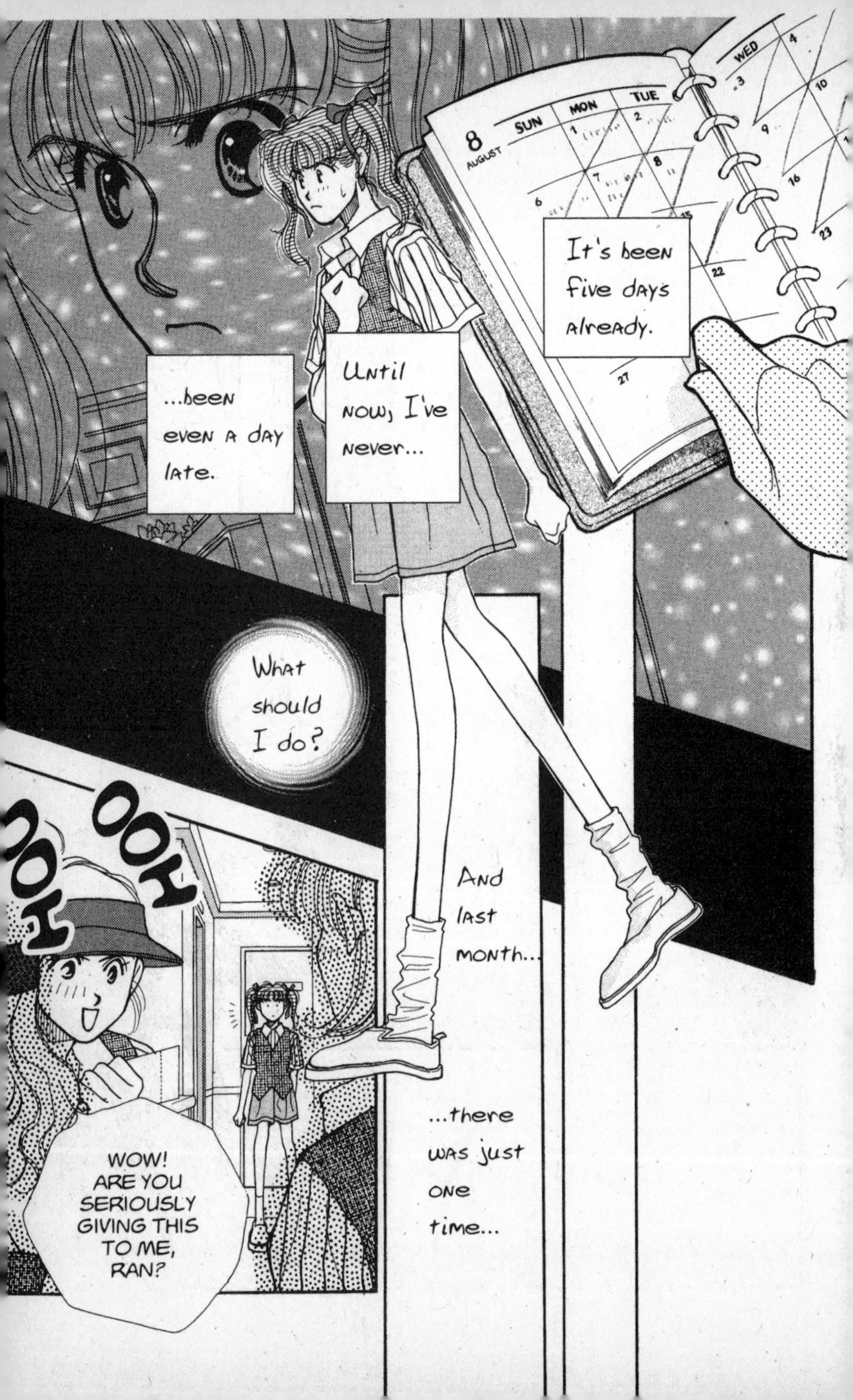
It's been five days already.
Until now, I've never...
...been even a day late.
What should I do?
And last month...
...there was just one time...
WOW! ARE YOU SERIOUSLY GIVING THIS TO ME, RAN?

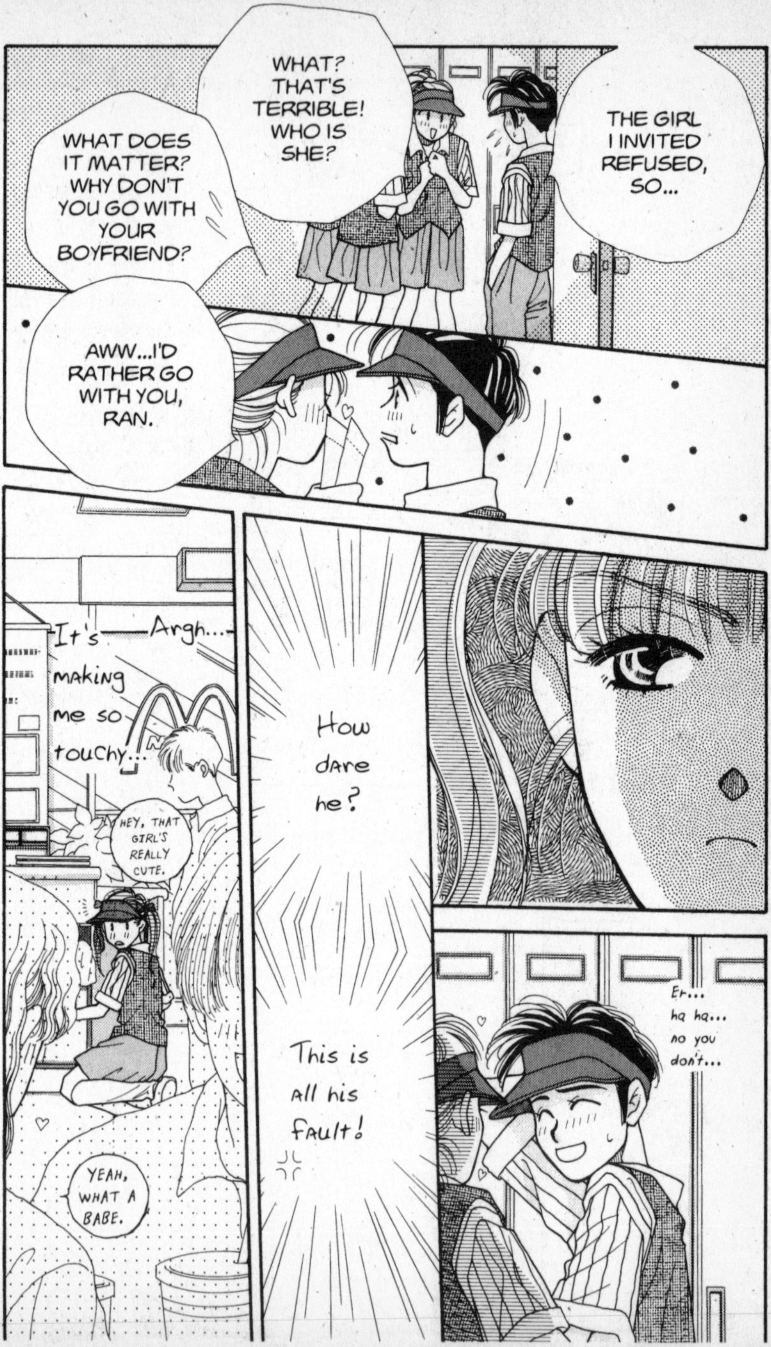
THE GIRL I INVITED REFUSED, SO...
WHAT? THAT'S TERRIBLE! WHO IS SHE?
WHAT DOES IT MATTER? WHY DON'T YOU GO WITH YOUR BOYFRIEND?
AWW...I'D RATHER GO WITH YOU, RAN.
Er... ha ha... no you don't...
How dare he?
This is all his fault!
It's ——Argh... making me so touchy...
HEY, THAT GIRL'S REALLY CUTE.
YEAH, WHAT A BABE.

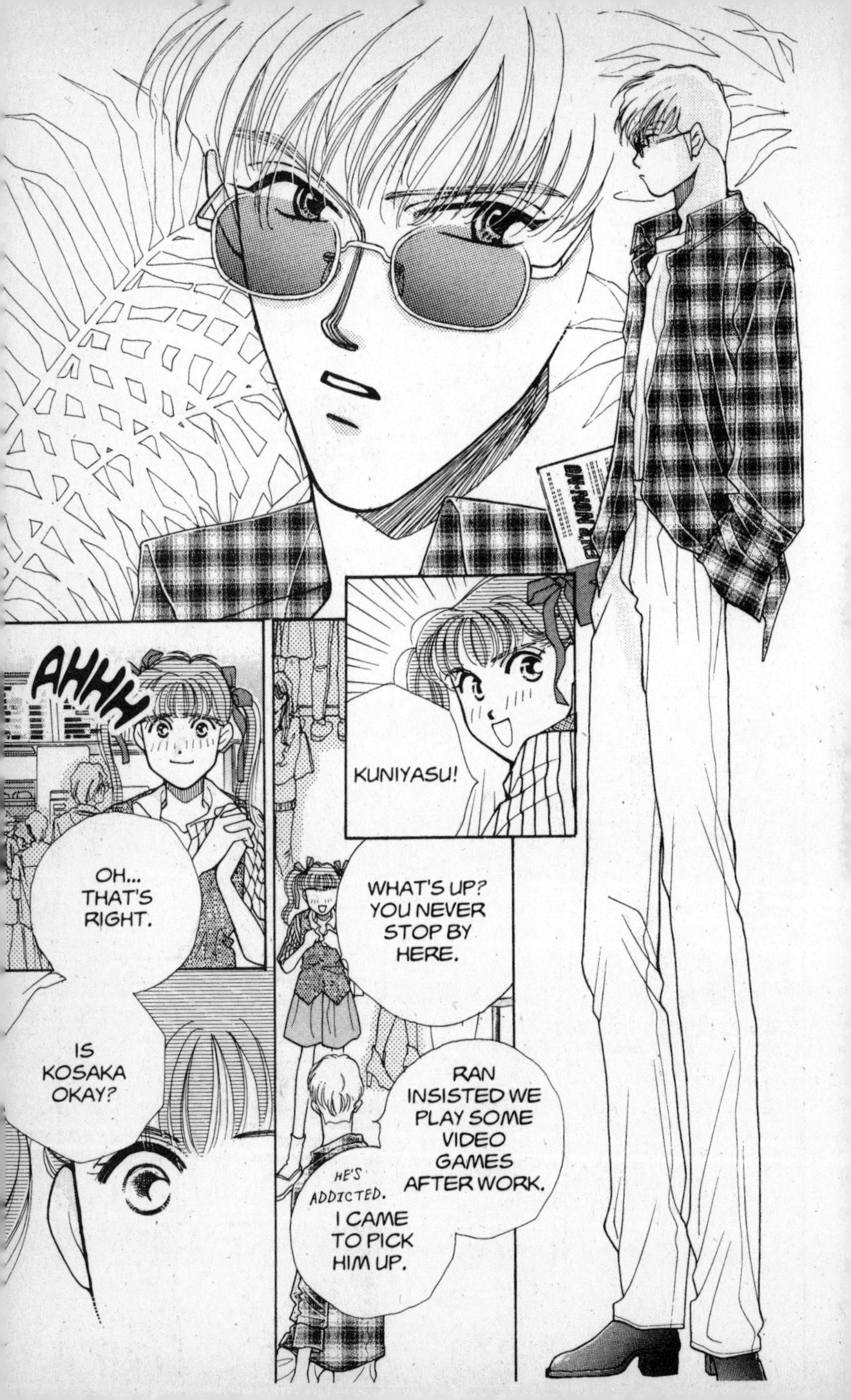
KUNIYASU!
WHAT'S UP? YOU NEVER STOP BY HERE.
RAN INSISTED WE PLAY SOME VIDEO GAMES AFTER WORK.
HE'S ADDICTED.
I CAME TO PICK HIM UP.
AHHH
OH... THAT'S RIGHT.
IS KOSAKA OKAY?

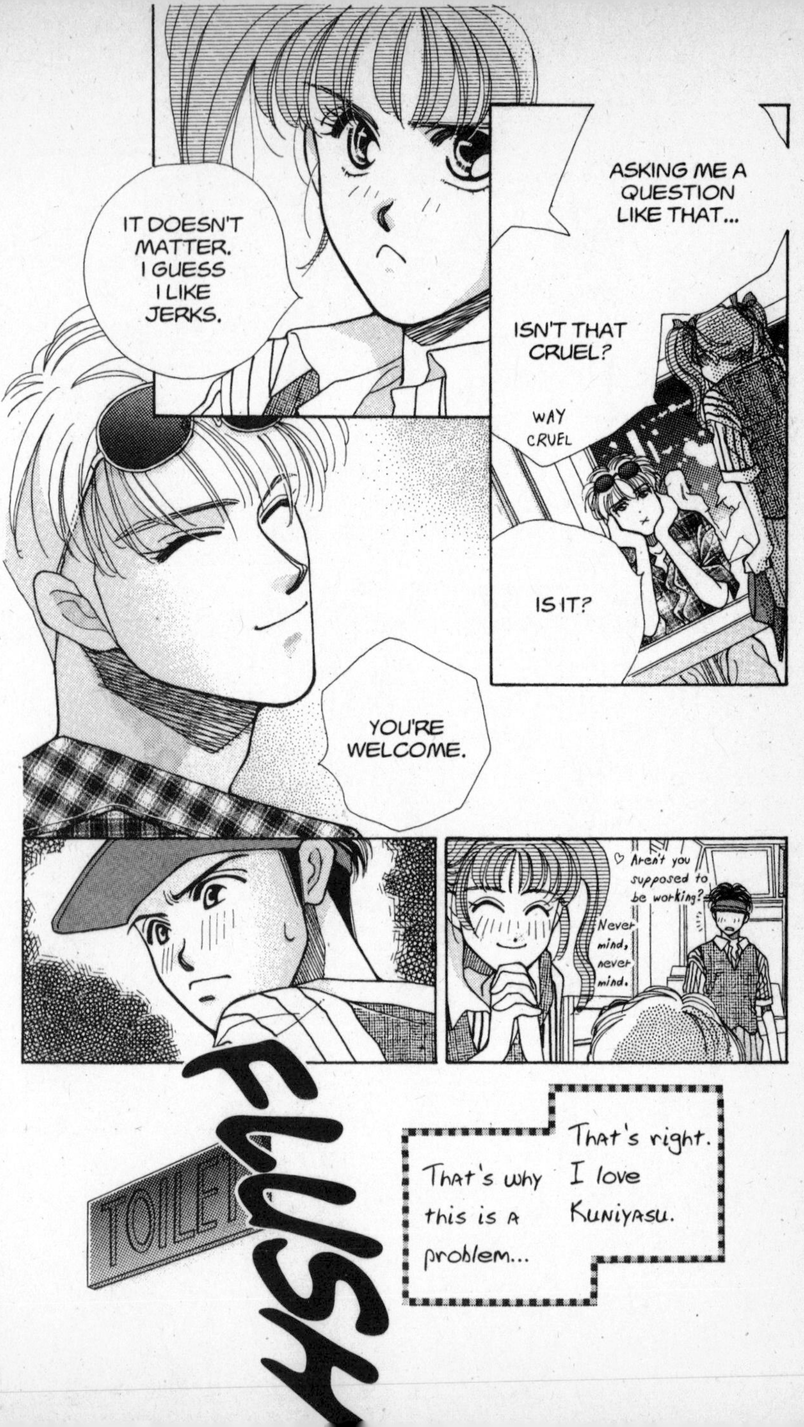
ASKING ME A QUESTION LIKE THAT...
ISN'T THAT CRUEL?
WAY CRUEL
IS IT?
IT DOESN'T MATTER. I GUESS I LIKE JERKS.
YOU'RE WELCOME.
♡ Aren't you supposed to be working?
Never mind, never mind.
FLUSH
TOILET
That's right. I love Kuniyasu.
That's why this is a problem...

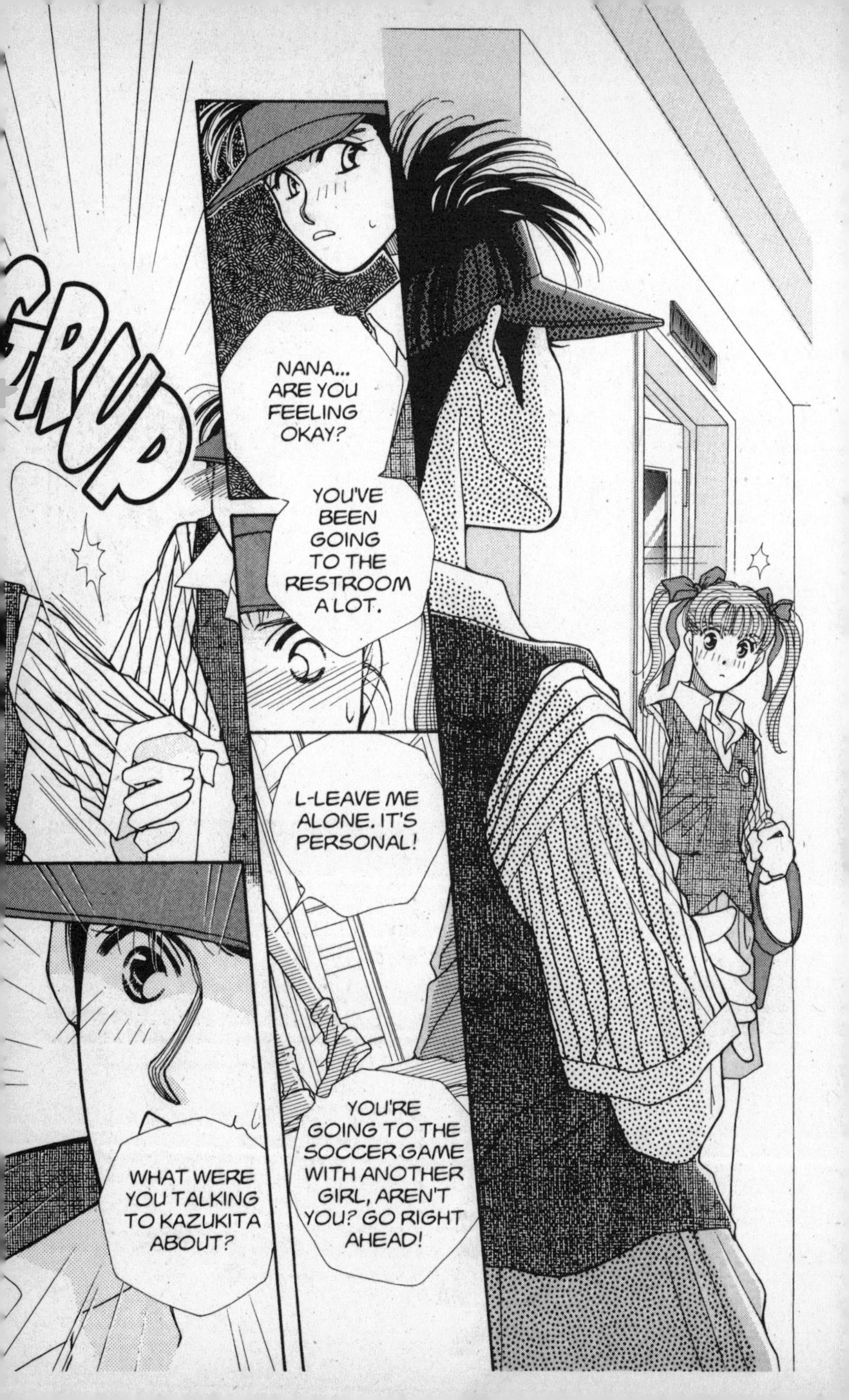
NANA... ARE YOU FEELING OKAY?
YOU'VE BEEN GOING TO THE RESTROOM A LOT.
GRUP
L-LEAVE ME ALONE. IT'S PERSONAL!
YOU'RE GOING TO THE SOCCER GAME WITH ANOTHER GIRL, AREN'T YOU? GO RIGHT AHEAD!
WHAT WERE YOU TALKING TO KAZUKITA ABOUT?

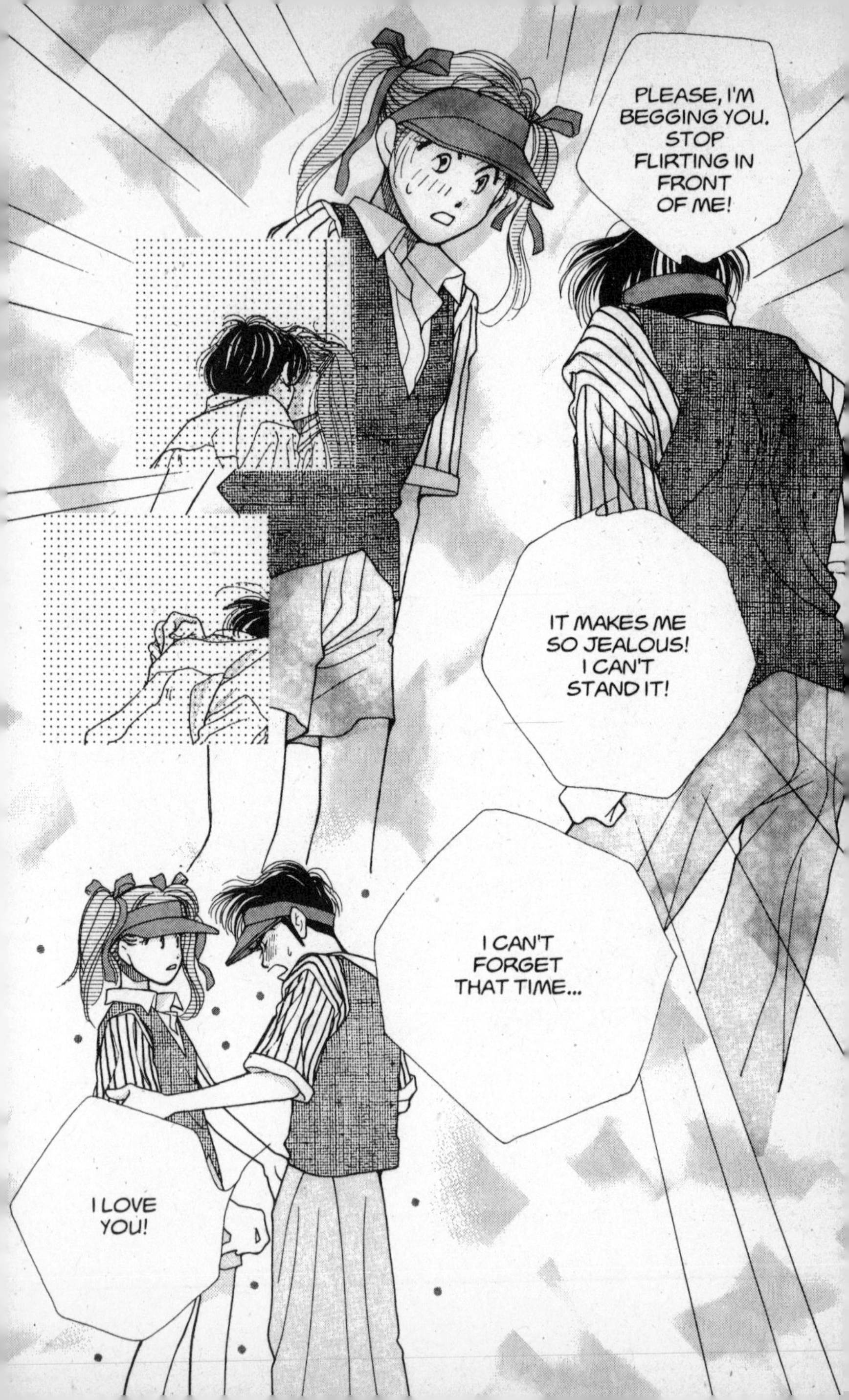
PLEASE, I'M BEGGING YOU. STOP FLIRTING IN FRONT OF ME!
IT MAKES ME SO JEALOUS! I CAN'T STAND IT!
I CAN'T FORGET THAT TIME...
I LOVE YOU!

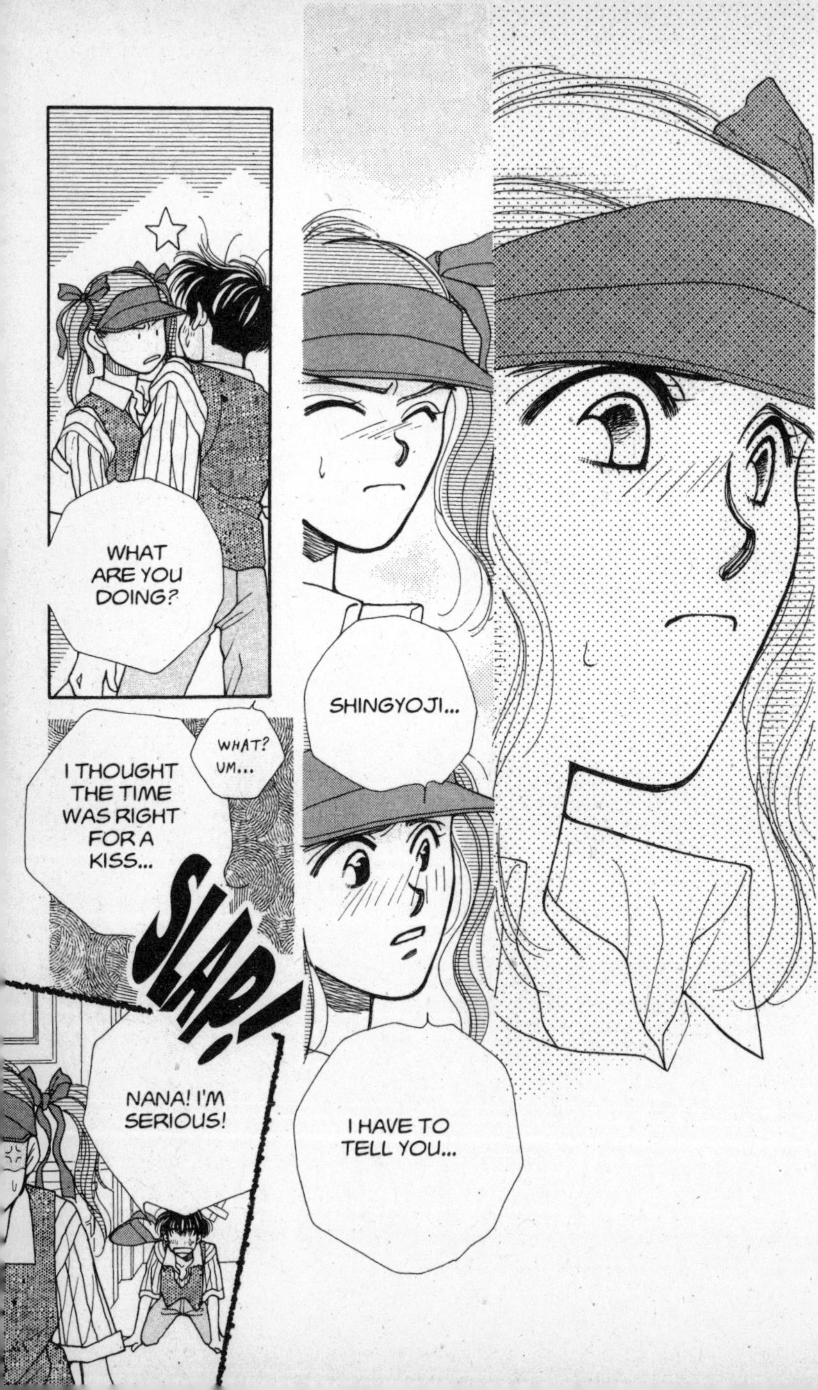
SHINGYOJI...
I HAVE TO TELL YOU...
WHAT ARE YOU DOING?
WHAT? UM...
I THOUGHT THE TIME WAS RIGHT FOR A KISS...
SLAP!
NANA! I'M SERIOUS!

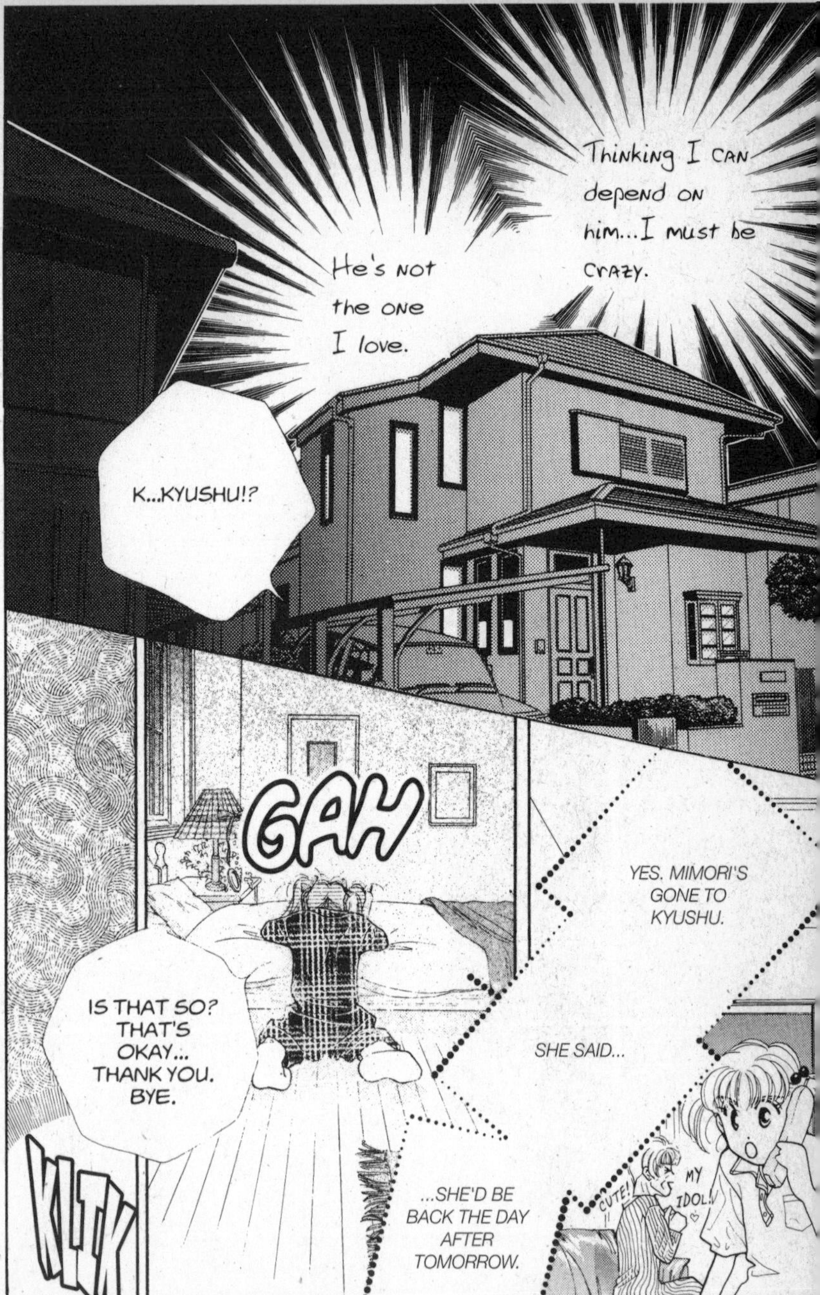
Thinking I can depend on him...I must be crazy.
He's not the one I love.
K...KYUSHU!?
YES. MIMORI'S GONE TO KYUSHU.
SHE SAID...
...SHE'D BE BACK THE DAY AFTER TOMORROW.
MY IDOL!
CUTE!
GAH
IS THAT SO? THAT'S OKAY... THANK YOU. BYE.
KLIK

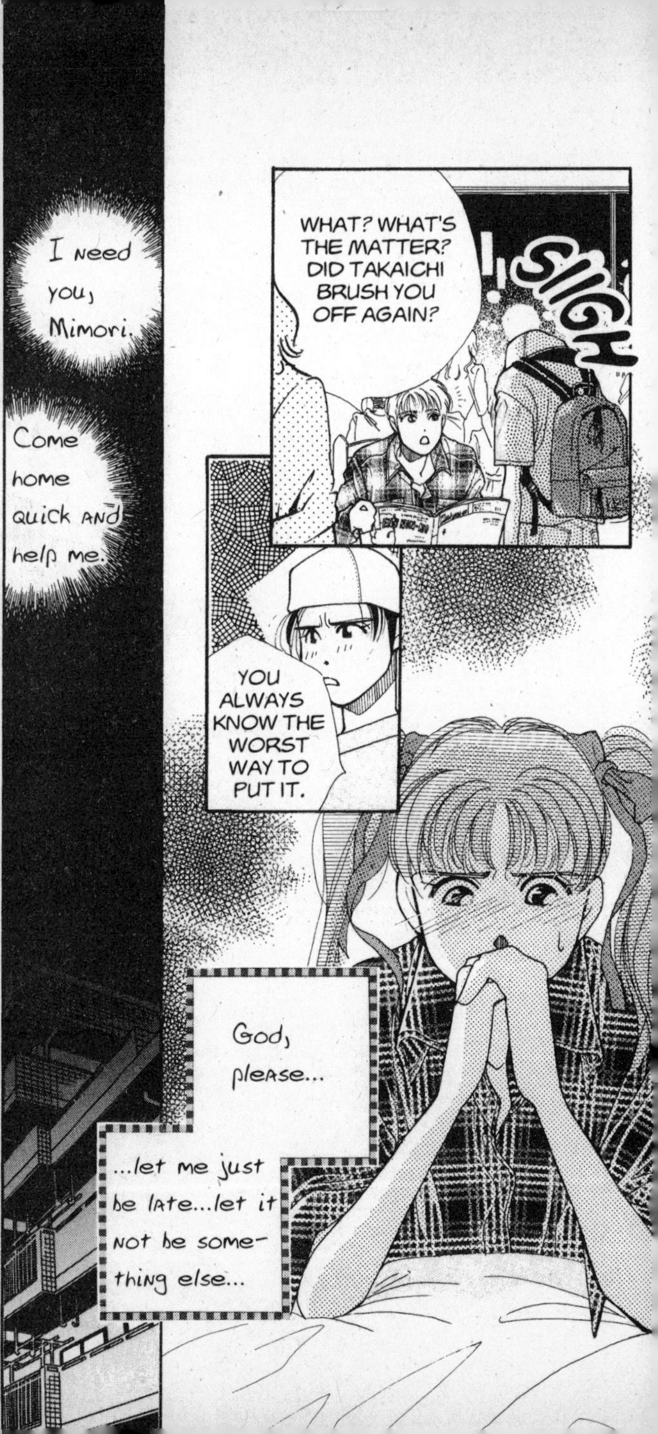
SIGH
WHAT? WHAT'S THE MATTER? DID TAKAICHI BRUSH YOU OFF AGAIN?
YOU ALWAYS KNOW THE WORST WAY TO PUT IT.
God, please...
...let me just be late...let it not be some-thing else...
I need you, Mimori.
Come home quick and help me.

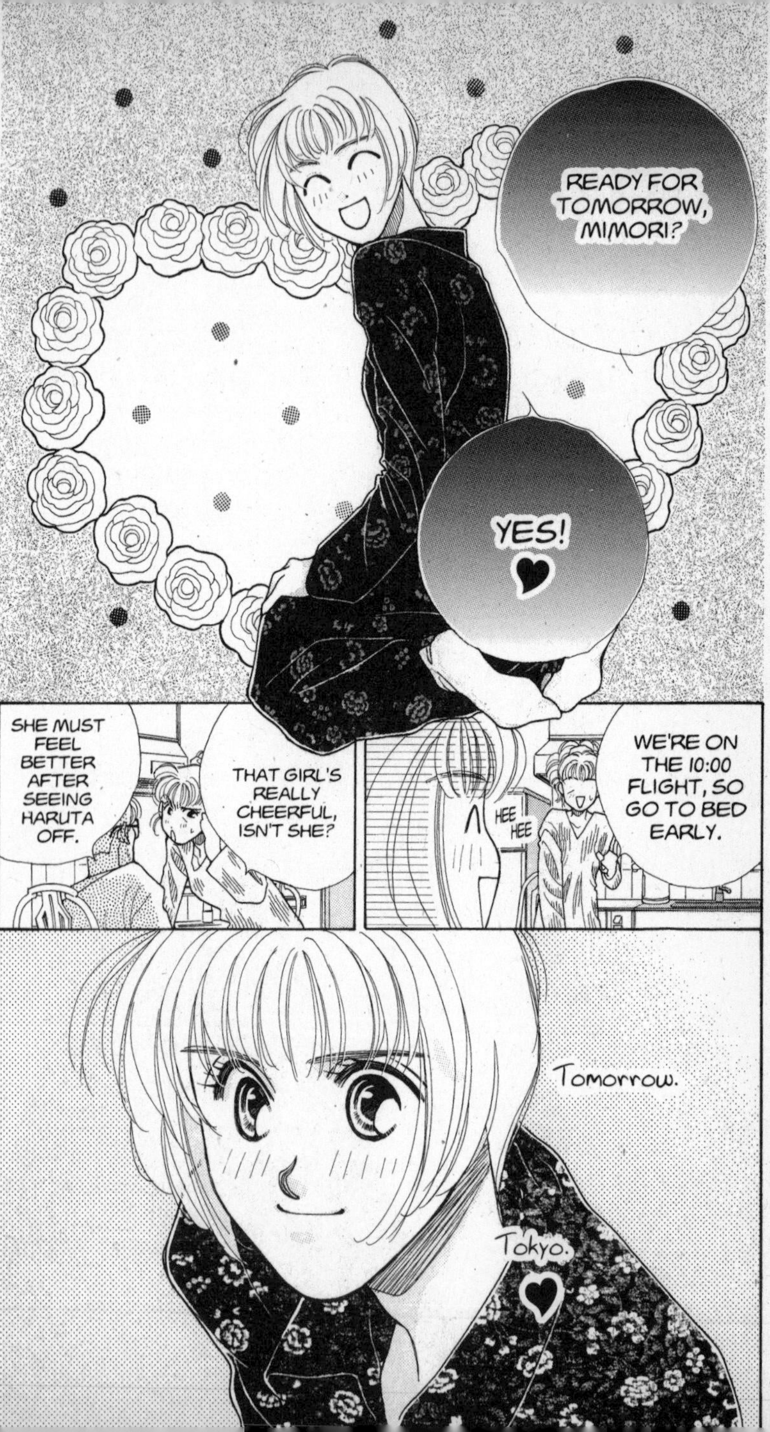
READY FOR TOMORROW, MIMORI?
YES! ♥
WE'RE ON THE 10:00 FLIGHT, SO GO TO BED EARLY.
HEE HEE
THAT GIRL'S REALLY CHEERFUL, ISN'T SHE?
SHE MUST FEEL BETTER AFTER SEEING HARUTA OFF.
Tomorrow.
Tokyo. ♥

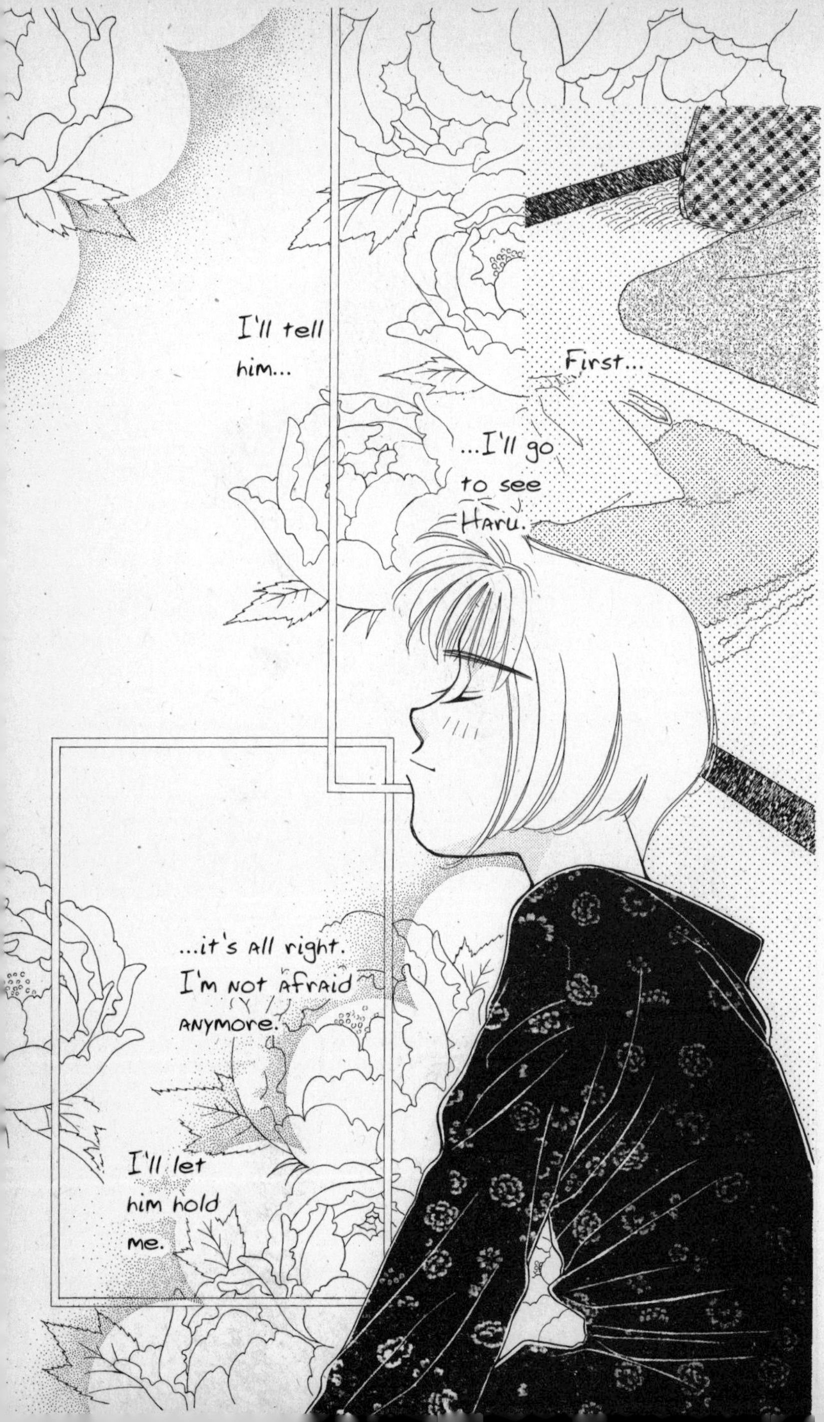
First...
...I'll go to see Haru.
I'll tell him...
...it's all right. I'm not afraid anymore.
I'll let him hold me.

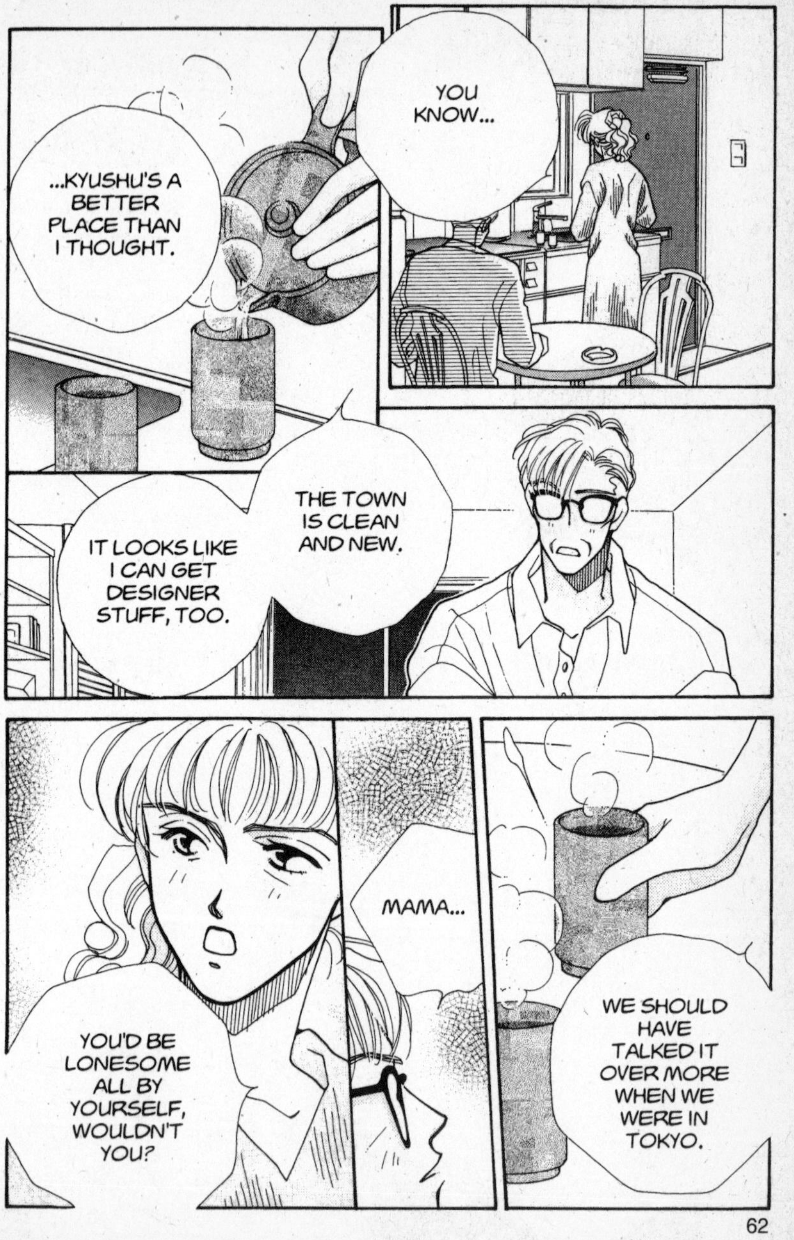
YOU KNOW...
...KYUSHU'S A BETTER PLACE THAN I THOUGHT.
THE TOWN IS CLEAN AND NEW.
IT LOOKS LIKE I CAN GET DESIGNER STUFF, TOO.
WE SHOULD HAVE TALKED IT OVER MORE WHEN WE WERE IN TOKYO.
MAMA...
YOU'D BE LONESOME ALL BY YOURSELF, WOULDN'T YOU?

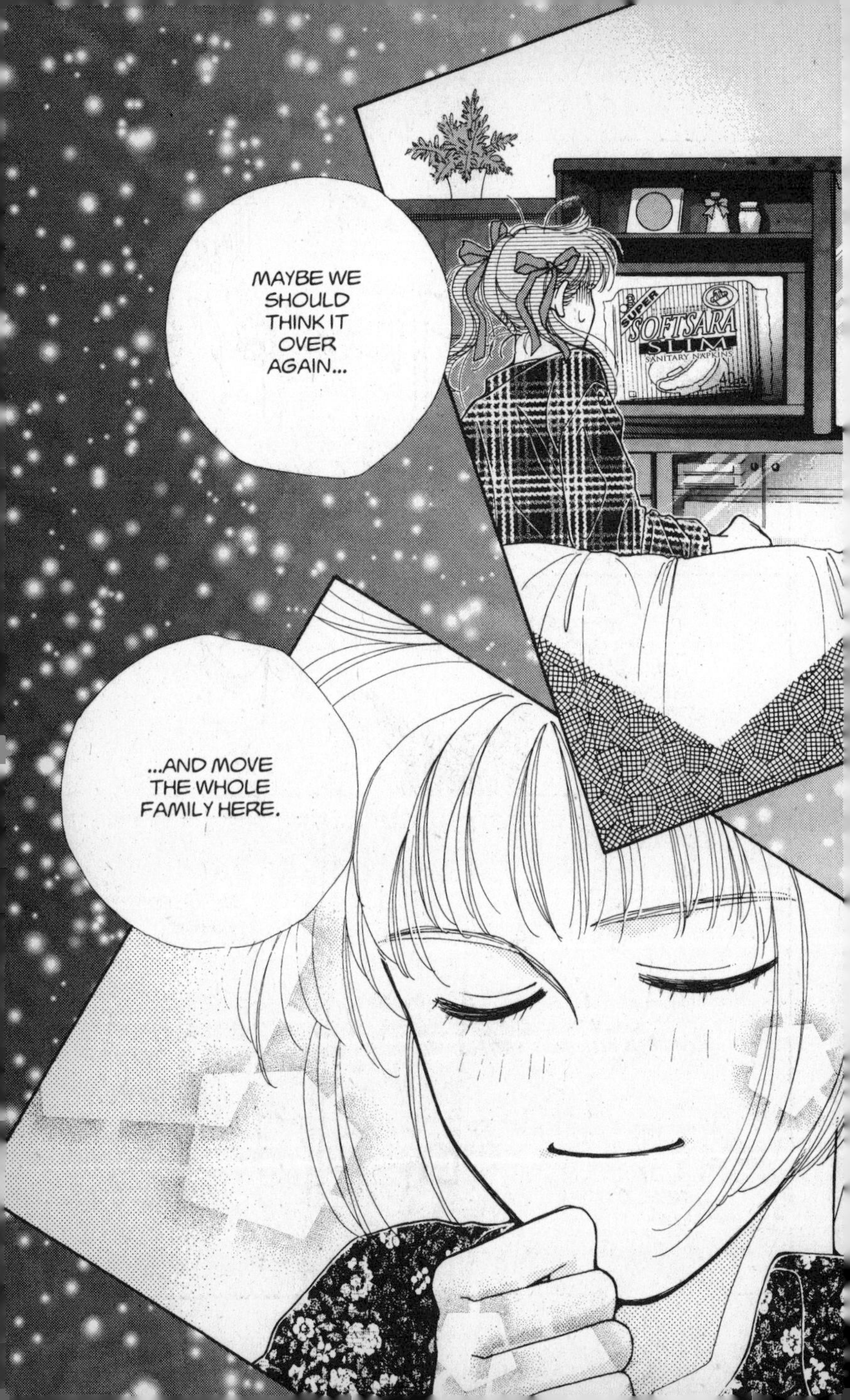
SUPER
SOFTSARA
SLIM
SANITARY NAPKINS
MAYBE WE SHOULD THINK IT OVER AGAIN...
...AND MOVE THE WHOLE FAMILY HERE.

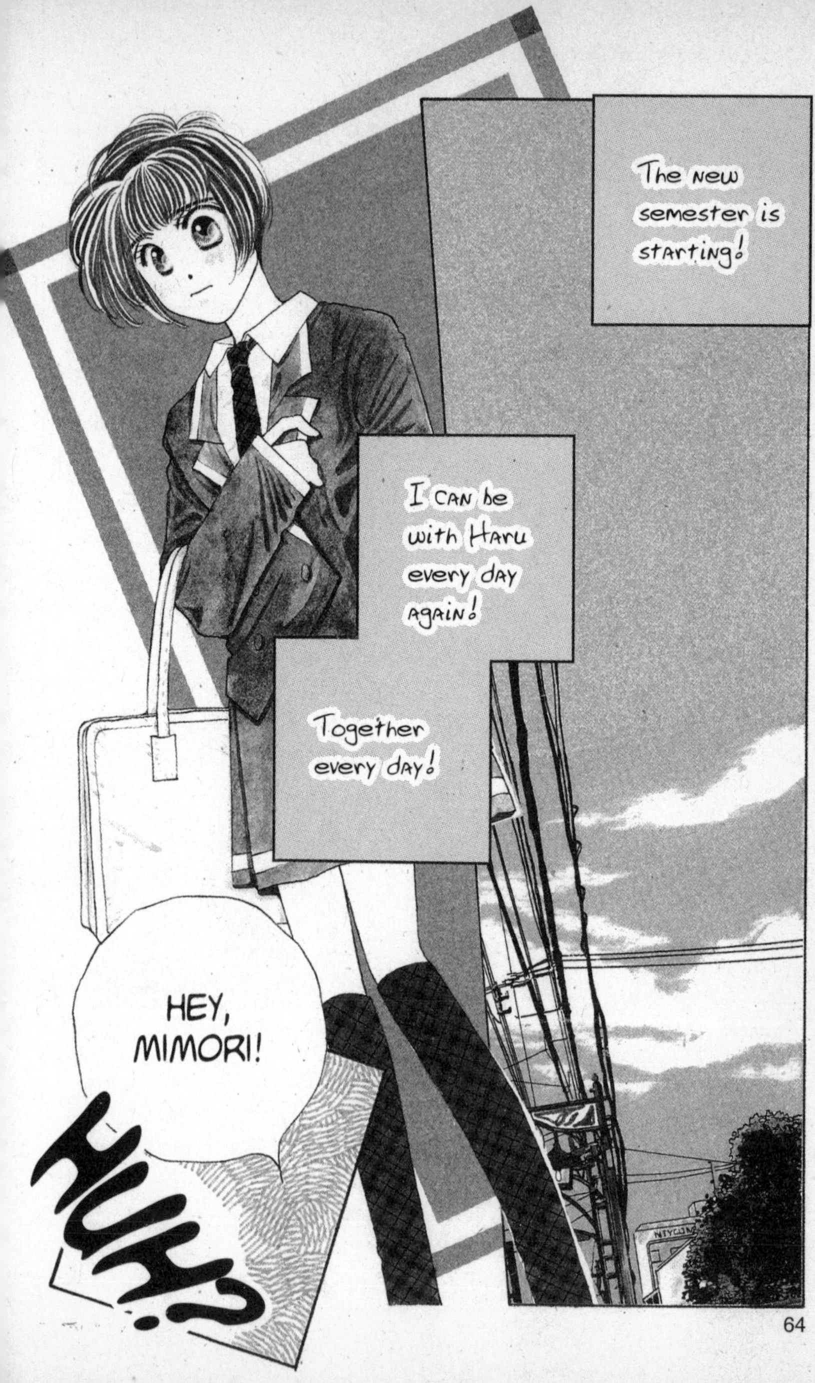
The new semester is starting!
I can be with Haru every day again!
Together every day!
HEY, MIMORI!
HUH?

I WANT TO TALK TO YOU ABOUT SOMETHING. COME STRAIGHT HOME FROM SCHOOL TODAY, OKAY?

THAT'S ALL.

Mom's acting strange.

Oh, well. What should I say when I see Haru?

What should I say first?

TAP!

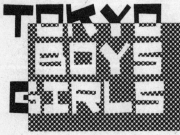

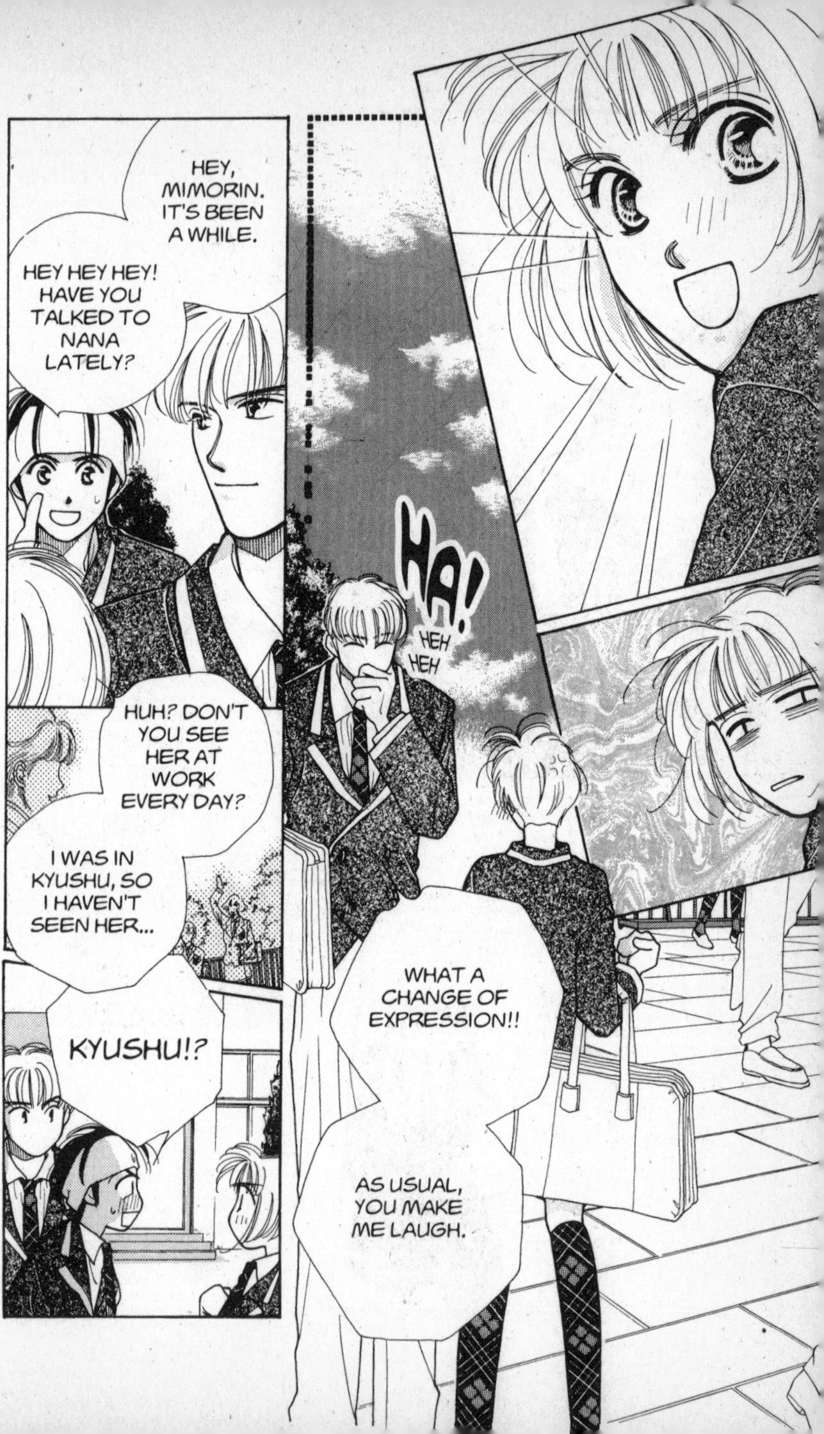
HA!
HEH HEH
WHAT A CHANGE OF EXPRESSION!!
AS USUAL, YOU MAKE ME LAUGH.
HEY, MIMORIN. IT'S BEEN A WHILE.
HEY HEY HEY! HAVE YOU TALKED TO NANA LATELY?
HUH? DON'T YOU SEE HER AT WORK EVERY DAY?
I WAS IN KYUSHU, SO I HAVEN'T SEEN HER...
KYUSHU!?

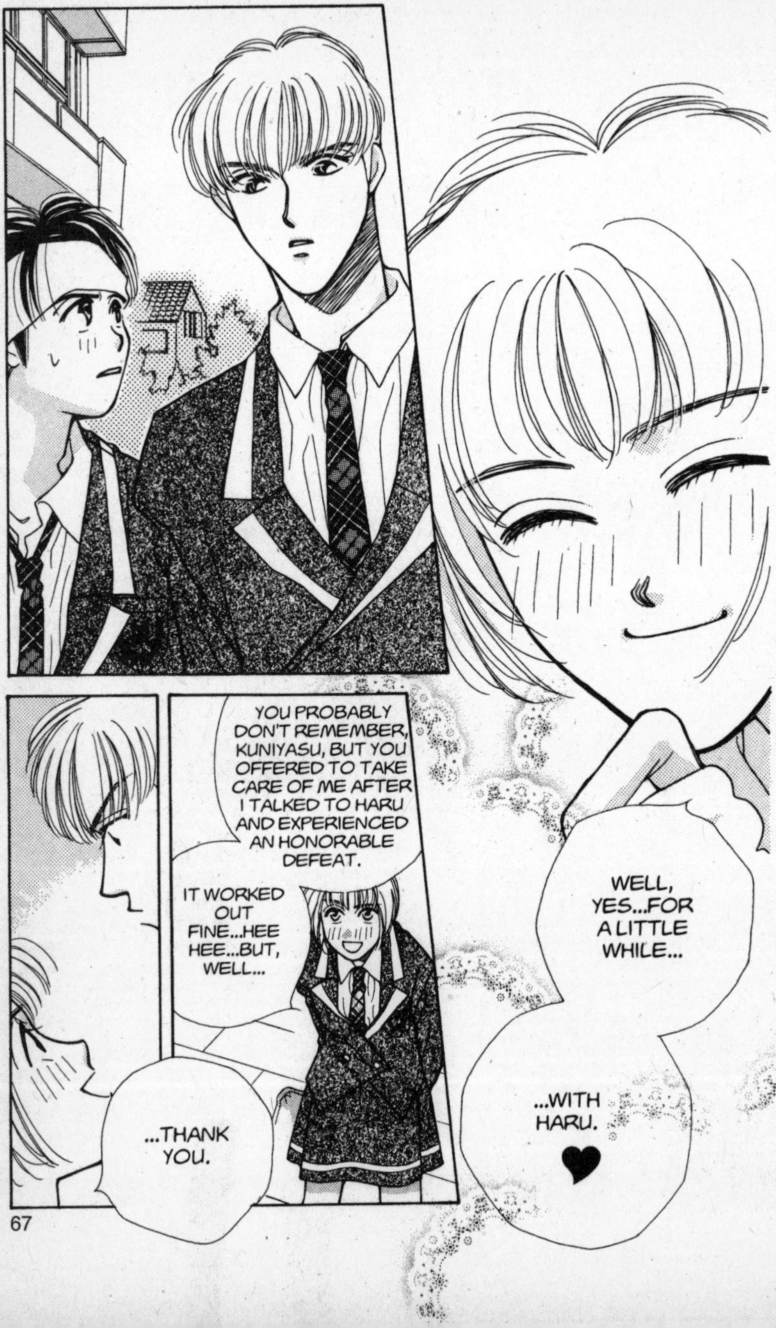
YOU PROBABLY DON'T REMEMBER, KUNIYASU, BUT YOU OFFERED TO TAKE CARE OF ME AFTER I TALKED TO HARU AND EXPERIENCED AN HONORABLE DEFEAT.
IT WORKED OUT FINE...HEE HEE...BUT, WELL...
...THANK YOU.
WELL, YES...FOR A LITTLE WHILE...
...WITH HARU. ♥

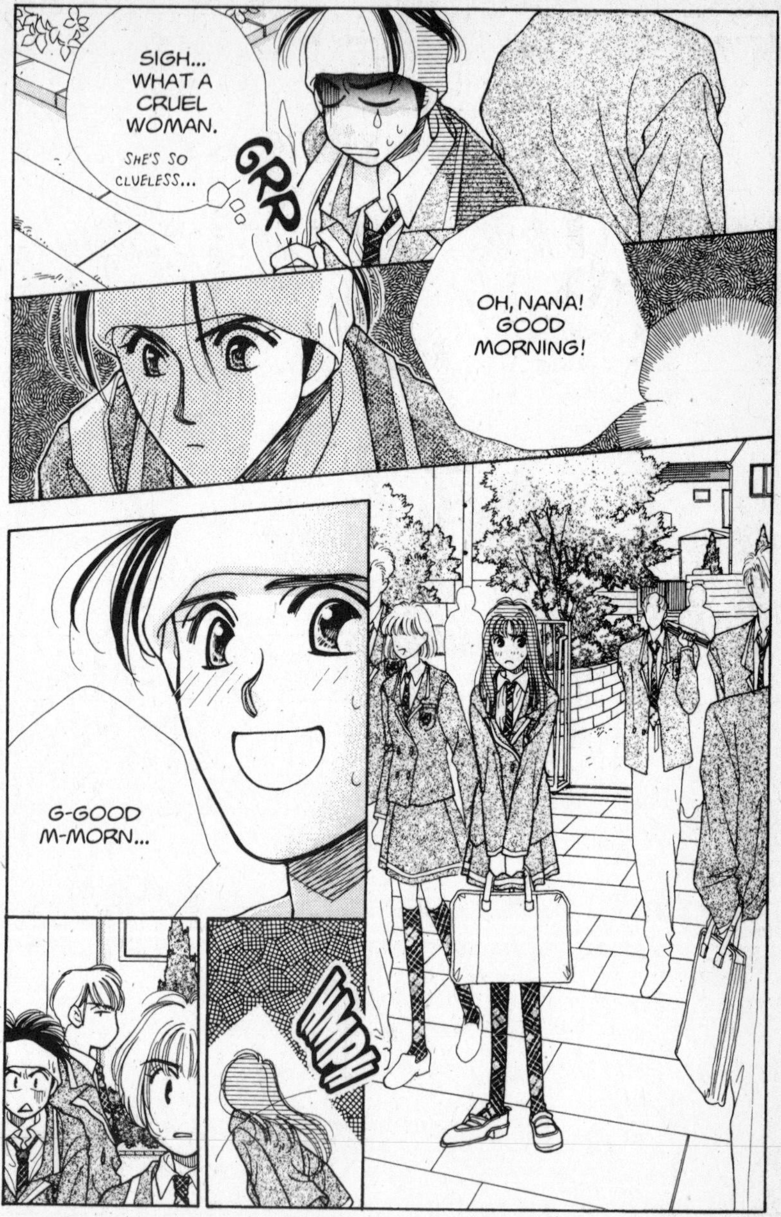
SIGH... WHAT A CRUEL WOMAN.
SHE'S SO CLUELESS...
GRR
OH, NANA! GOOD MORNING!
G-GOOD M-MORN...
HMPH

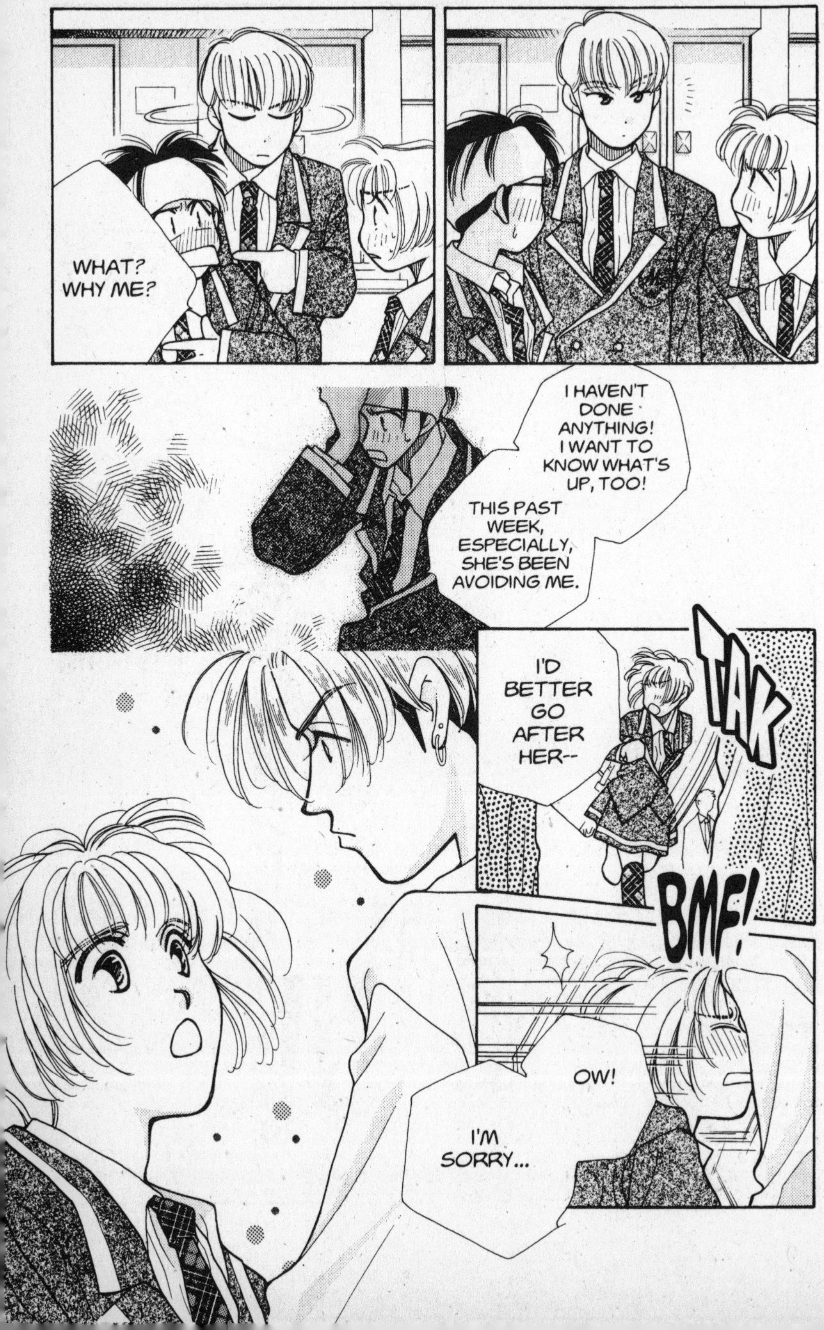
WHAT? WHY ME?
I HAVEN'T DONE ANYTHING! I WANT TO KNOW WHAT'S UP, TOO!
THIS PAST WEEK, ESPECIALLY, SHE'S BEEN AVOIDING ME.
I'D BETTER GO AFTER HER--
TAK
BMF!
OW!
I'M SORRY...

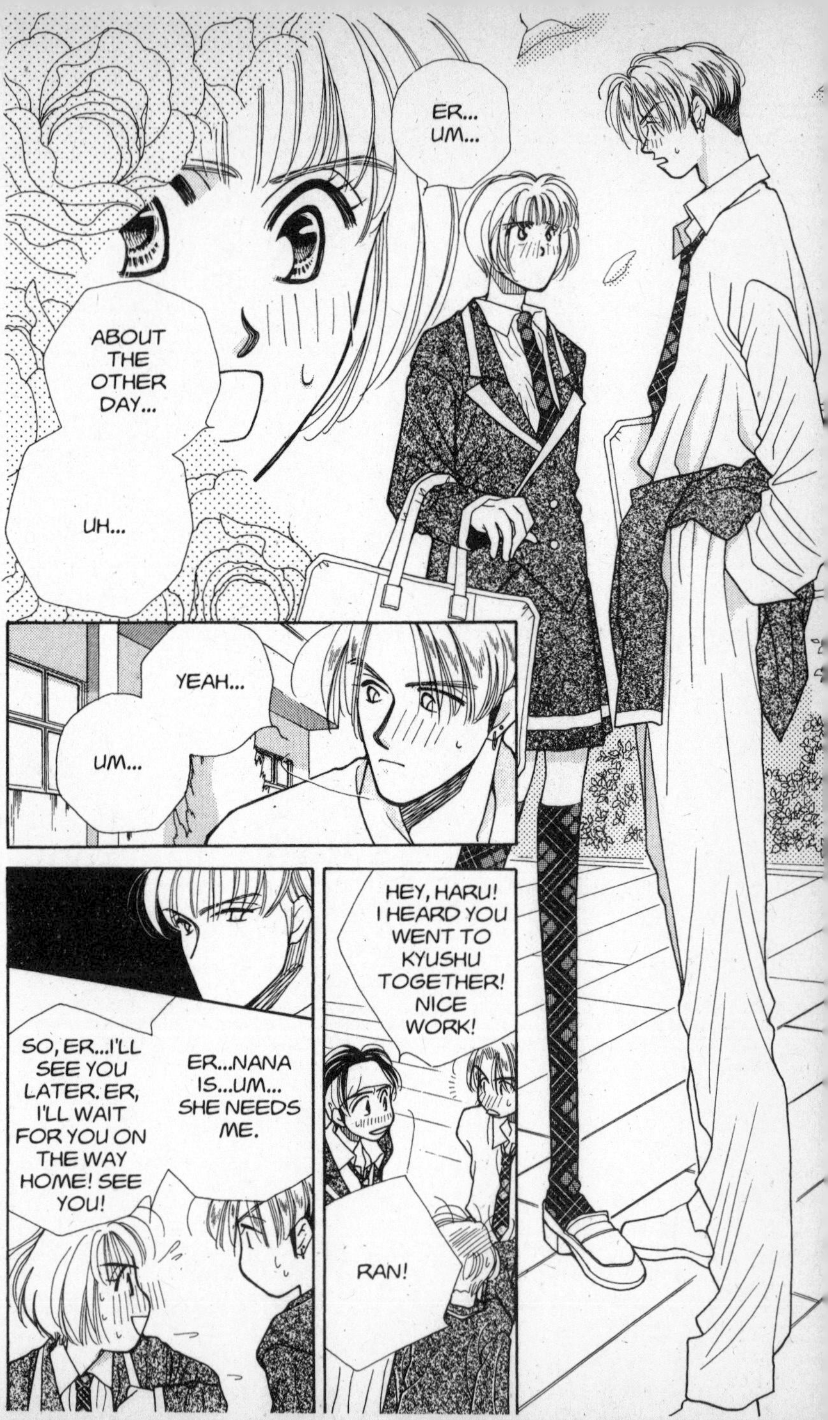
ER... UM...
ABOUT THE OTHER DAY...
UH...
YEAH...
UM...
HEY, HARU! I HEARD YOU WENT TO KYUSHU TOGETHER! NICE WORK!
RAN!
ER...NANA IS...UM... SHE NEEDS ME.
SO, ER...I'LL SEE YOU LATER. ER, I'LL WAIT FOR YOU ON THE WAY HOME! SEE YOU!

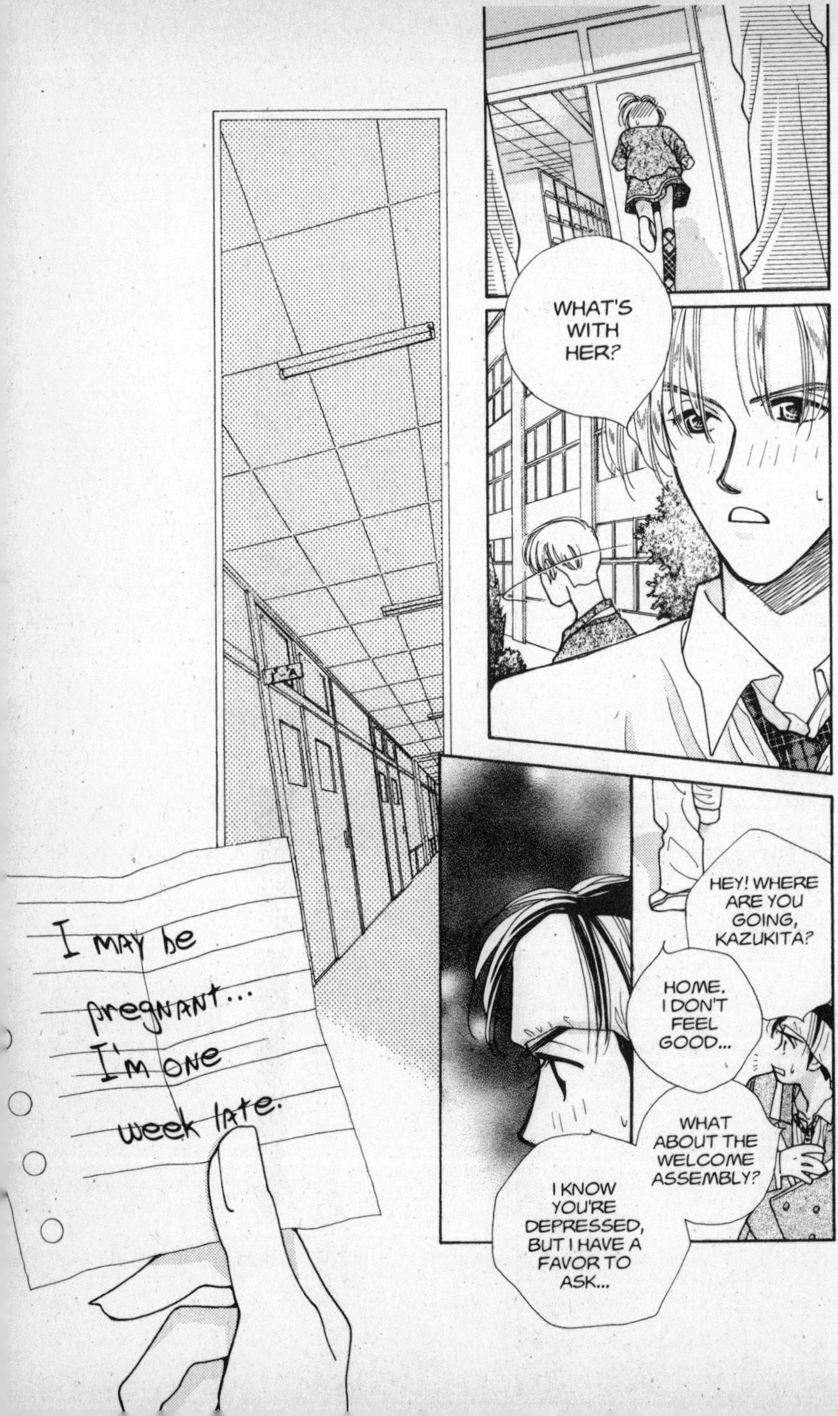
WHAT'S WITH HER?
HEY! WHERE ARE YOU GOING, KAZUKITA?
HOME. I DON'T FEEL GOOD...
WHAT ABOUT THE WELCOME ASSEMBLY?
I KNOW YOU'RE DEPRESSED, BUT I HAVE A FAVOR TO ASK...
I may be pregnant... I'm one week late.

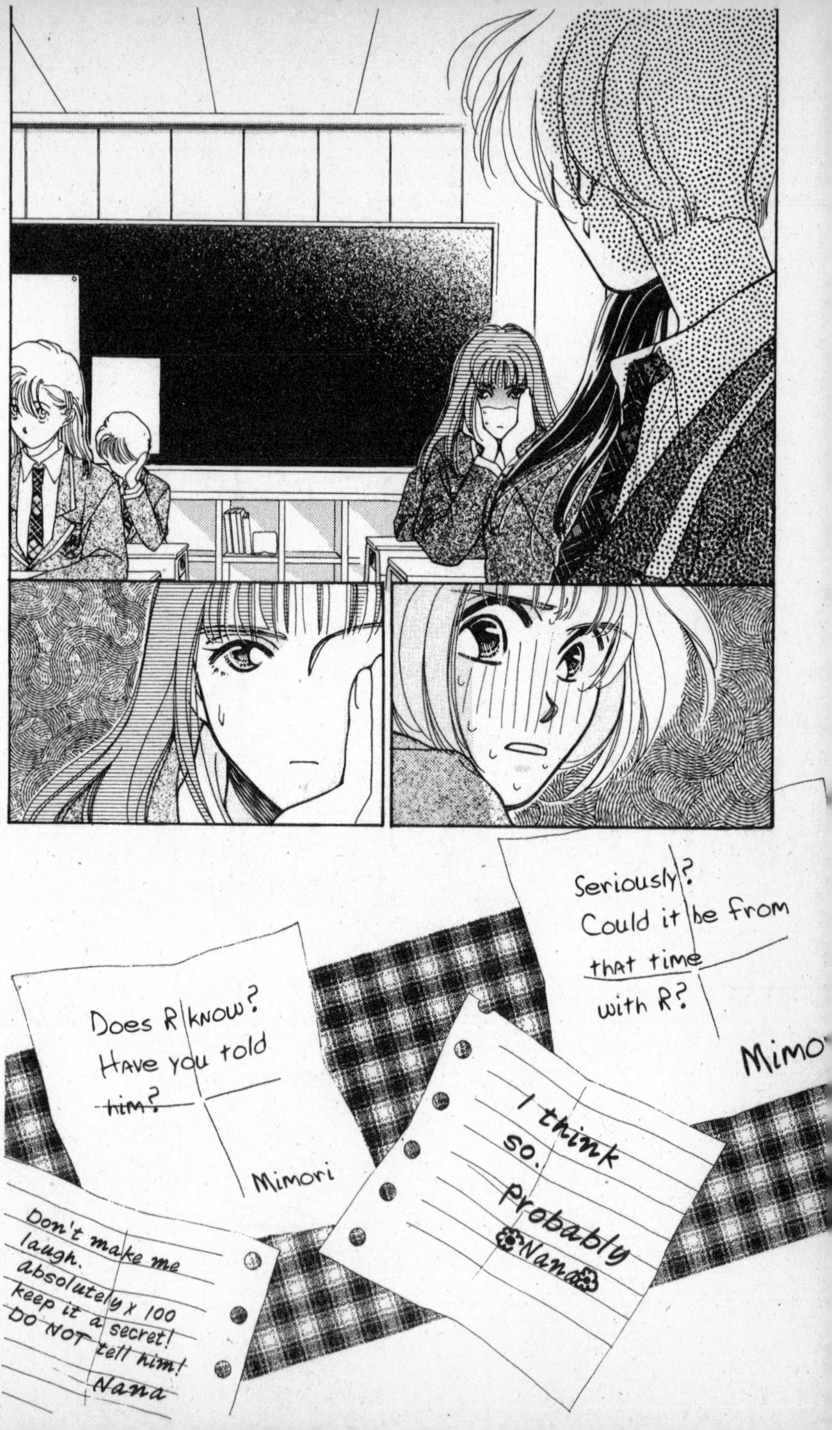
Seriously? Could it be from that time with R?
Mimo
Does R know? Have you told him?
Mimori
I think so. Probably
Nana
Don't make me laugh. absolutely x 100 keep it a secret! DO NOT tell him!
Nana

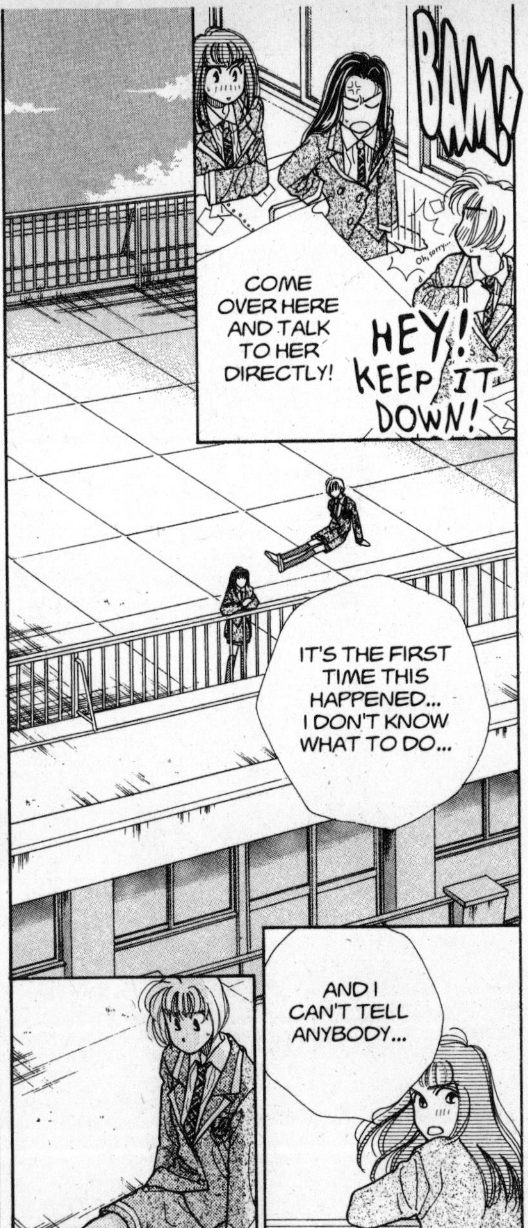
BAM!
Oh, sorry...
HEY! KEEP IT DOWN!
COME OVER HERE AND TALK TO HER DIRECTLY!
IT'S THE FIRST TIME THIS HAPPENED... I DON'T KNOW WHAT TO DO...
AND I CAN'T TELL ANYBODY...

CHARACTER RANKING

NO. 3 496 POINTS

• Mimori Kosaka •

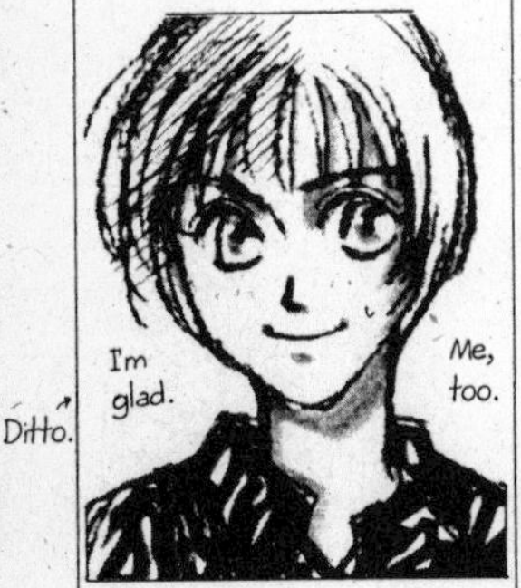
Me, too.
I'm glad.
Ditto.

I developed this character thinking how much more fun life would be if I were like her. (Her taste in boys is different, though.) I've gotten a lot of letters from people who want to be like her.

After all, her life's so interesting.

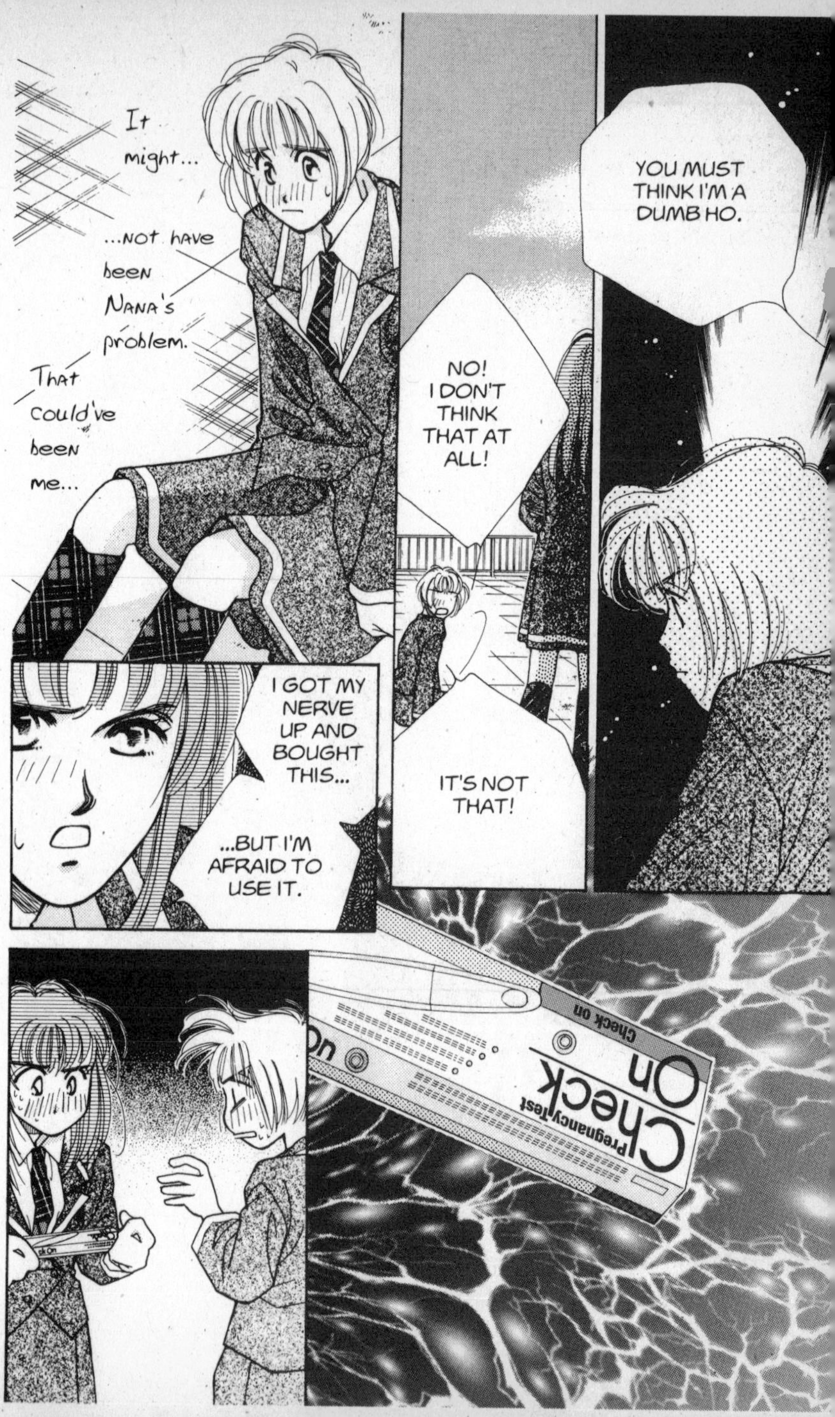
YOU MUST THINK I'M A DUMB HO.
NO! I DON'T THINK THAT AT ALL!
IT'S NOT THAT!
It might...
...not have been Nana's problem.
That could've been me...
I GOT MY NERVE UP AND BOUGHT THIS...
...BUT I'M AFRAID TO USE IT.
Check On
Pregnancy Test
Check on

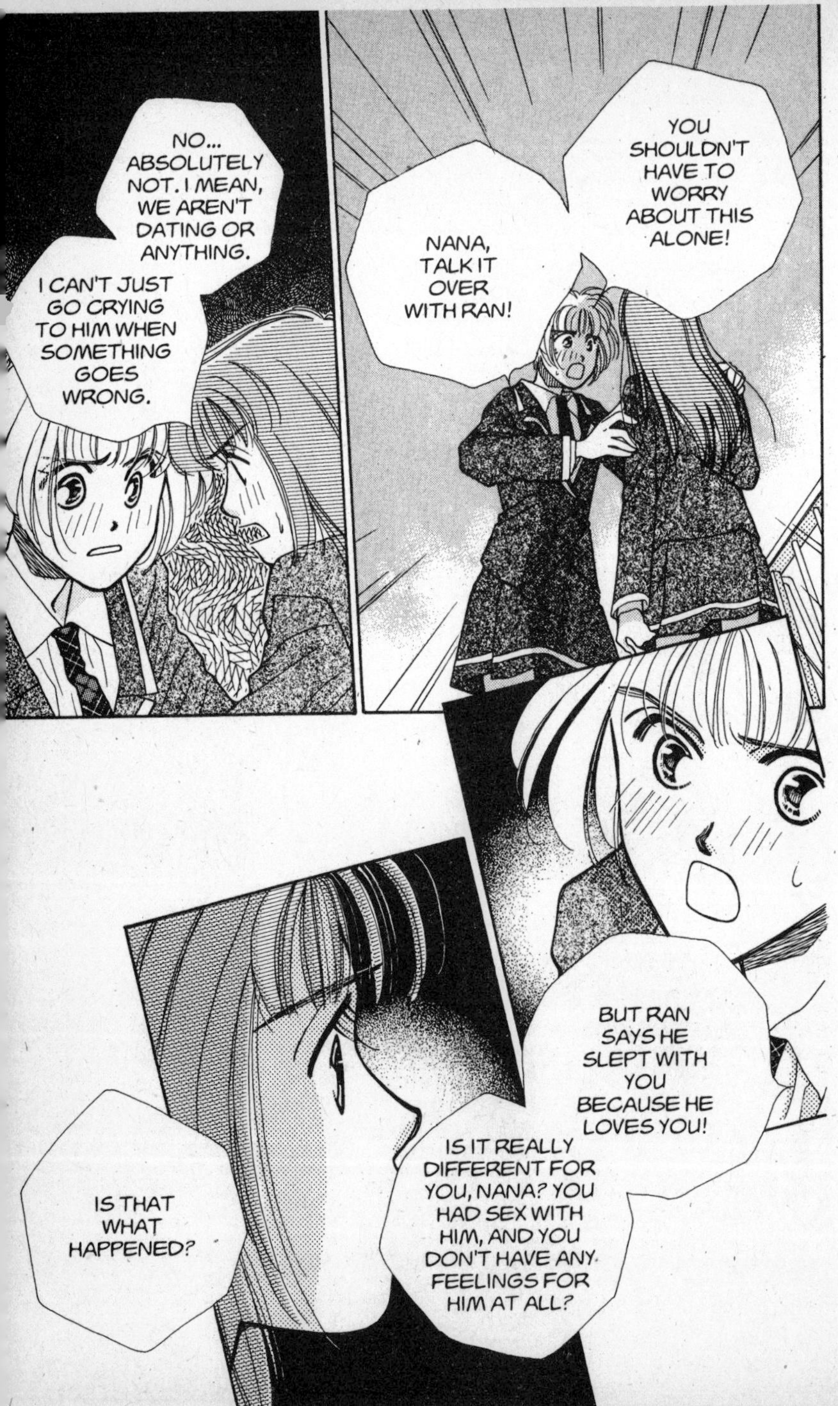
YOU SHOULDN'T HAVE TO WORRY ABOUT THIS ALONE!
NANA, TALK IT OVER WITH RAN!
NO... ABSOLUTELY NOT. I MEAN, WE AREN'T DATING OR ANYTHING.
I CAN'T JUST GO CRYING TO HIM WHEN SOMETHING GOES WRONG.
BUT RAN SAYS HE SLEPT WITH YOU BECAUSE HE LOVES YOU!
IS IT REALLY DIFFERENT FOR YOU, NANA? YOU HAD SEX WITH HIM, AND YOU DON'T HAVE ANY FEELINGS FOR HIM AT ALL?
IS THAT WHAT HAPPENED?

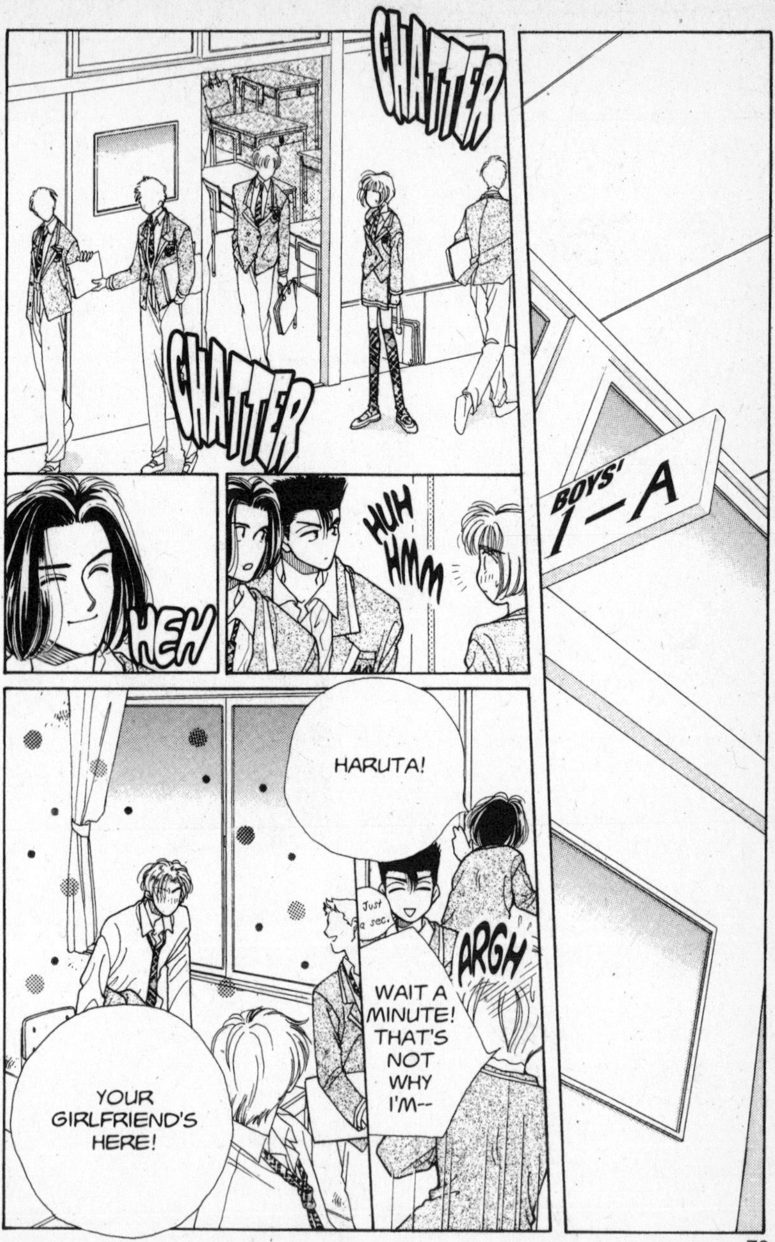
BOYS' 1-A
CHATTER
CHATTER
HUH HMM
HEH
HARUTA!
ARGH
Just a sec.
WAIT A MINUTE! THAT'S NOT WHY I'M--
YOUR GIRLFRIEND'S HERE!

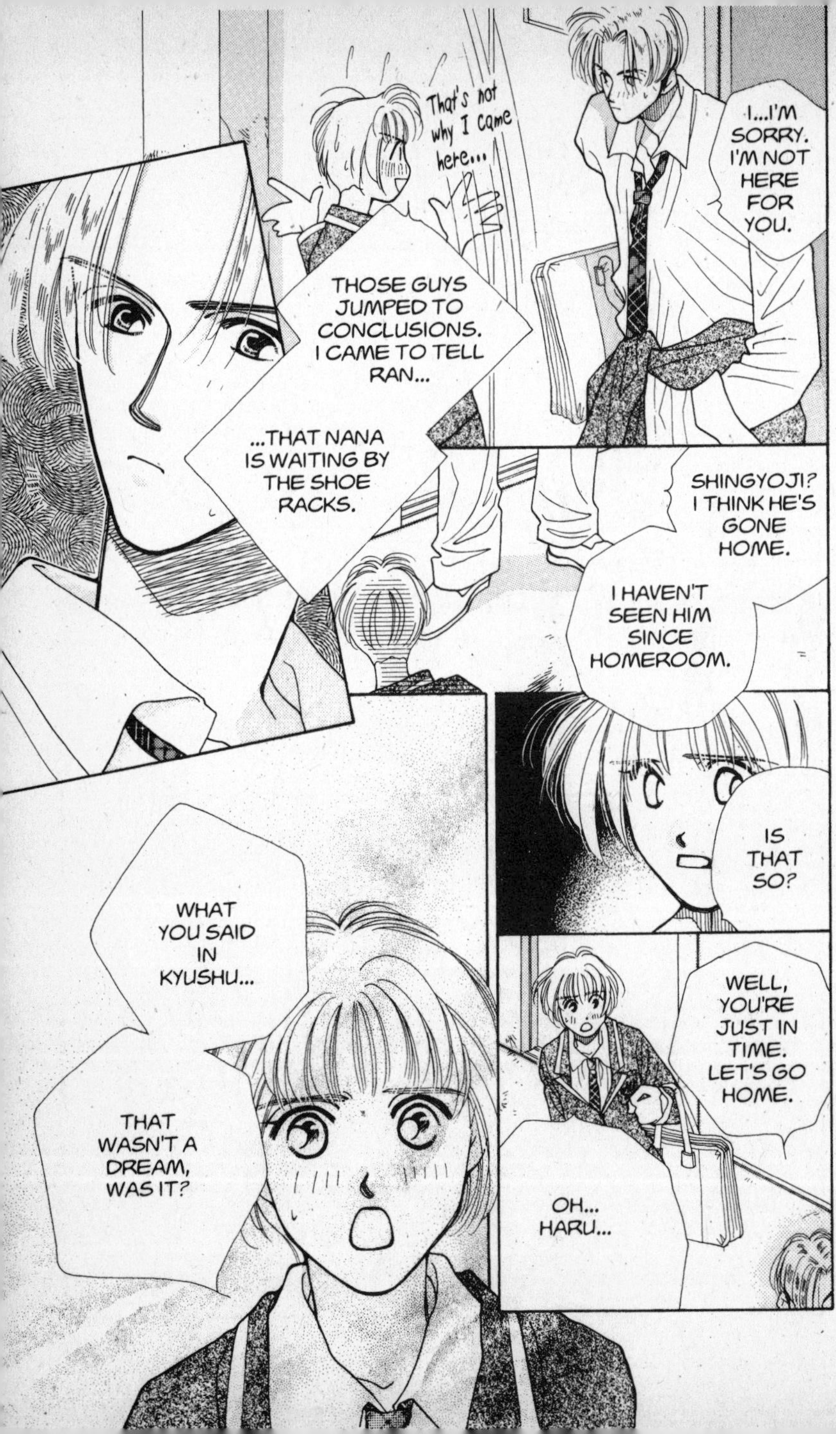
I...I'M SORRY. I'M NOT HERE FOR YOU.
That's not why I came here...
THOSE GUYS JUMPED TO CONCLUSIONS. I CAME TO TELL RAN...
...THAT NANA IS WAITING BY THE SHOE RACKS.
SHINGYOJI? I THINK HE'S GONE HOME.
I HAVEN'T SEEN HIM SINCE HOMEROOM.
IS THAT SO?
WELL, YOU'RE JUST IN TIME. LET'S GO HOME.
OH... HARU...
WHAT YOU SAID IN KYUSHU...
THAT WASN'T A DREAM, WAS IT?

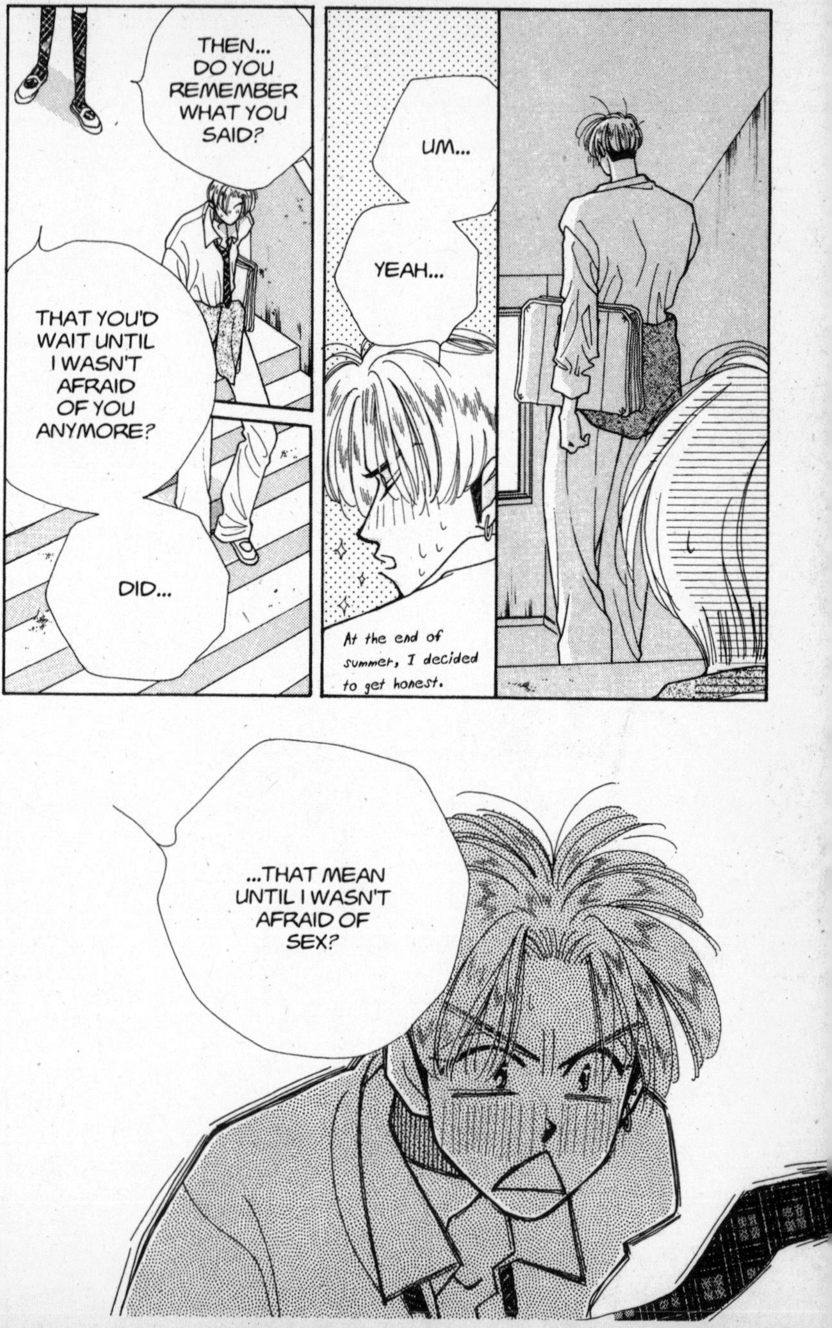
UM...
YEAH...
At the end of summer, I decided to get honest.
THEN... DO YOU REMEMBER WHAT YOU SAID?
THAT YOU'D WAIT UNTIL I WASN'T AFRAID OF YOU ANYMORE?
DID...
...THAT MEAN UNTIL I WASN'T AFRAID OF SEX?

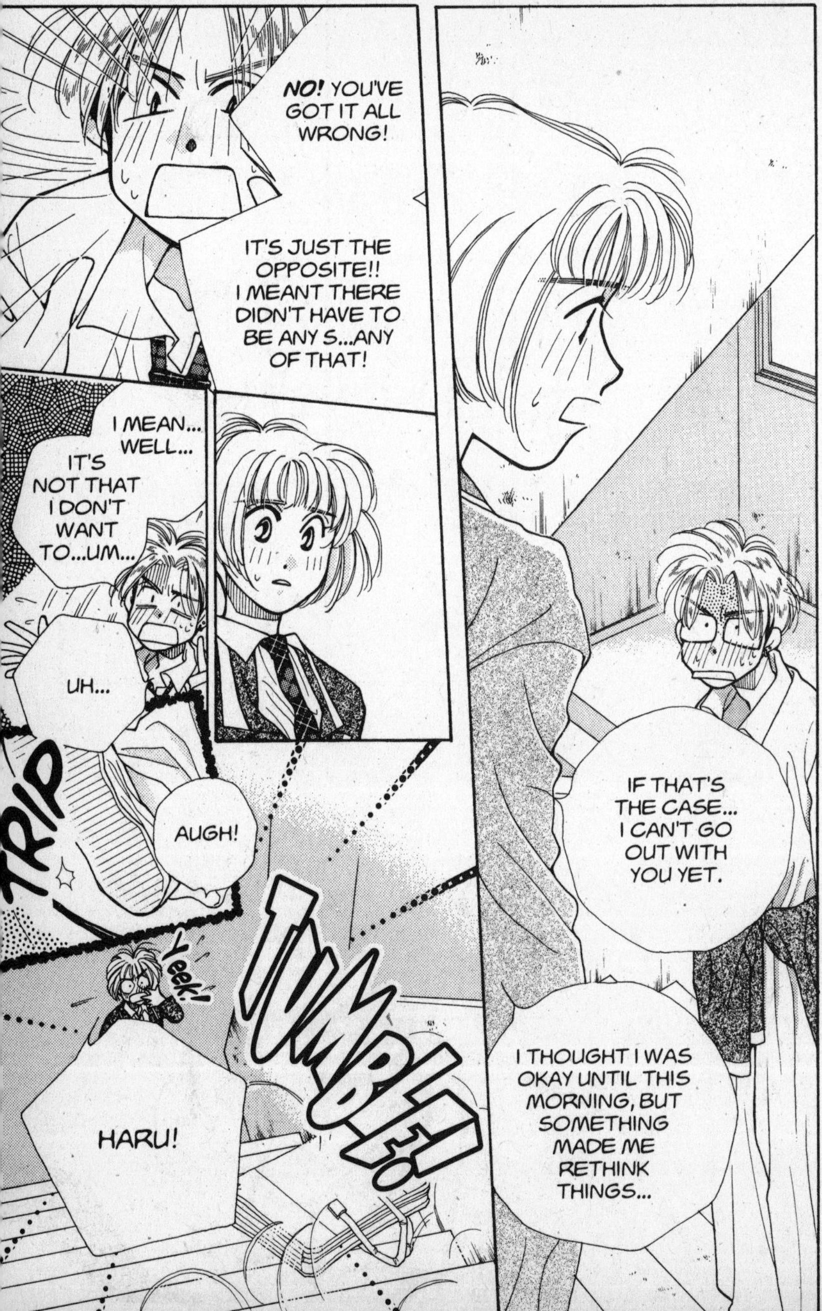
IF THAT'S THE CASE... I CAN'T GO OUT WITH YOU YET.
I THOUGHT I WAS OKAY UNTIL THIS MORNING, BUT SOMETHING MADE ME RETHINK THINGS...
NO! YOU'VE GOT IT ALL WRONG!
IT'S JUST THE OPPOSITE!! I MEANT THERE DIDN'T HAVE TO BE ANY S...ANY OF THAT!
I MEAN... WELL...
IT'S NOT THAT I DON'T WANT TO...UM...
UH...
TRIP
AUGH!
TUMBLE
Yeek!
HARU!

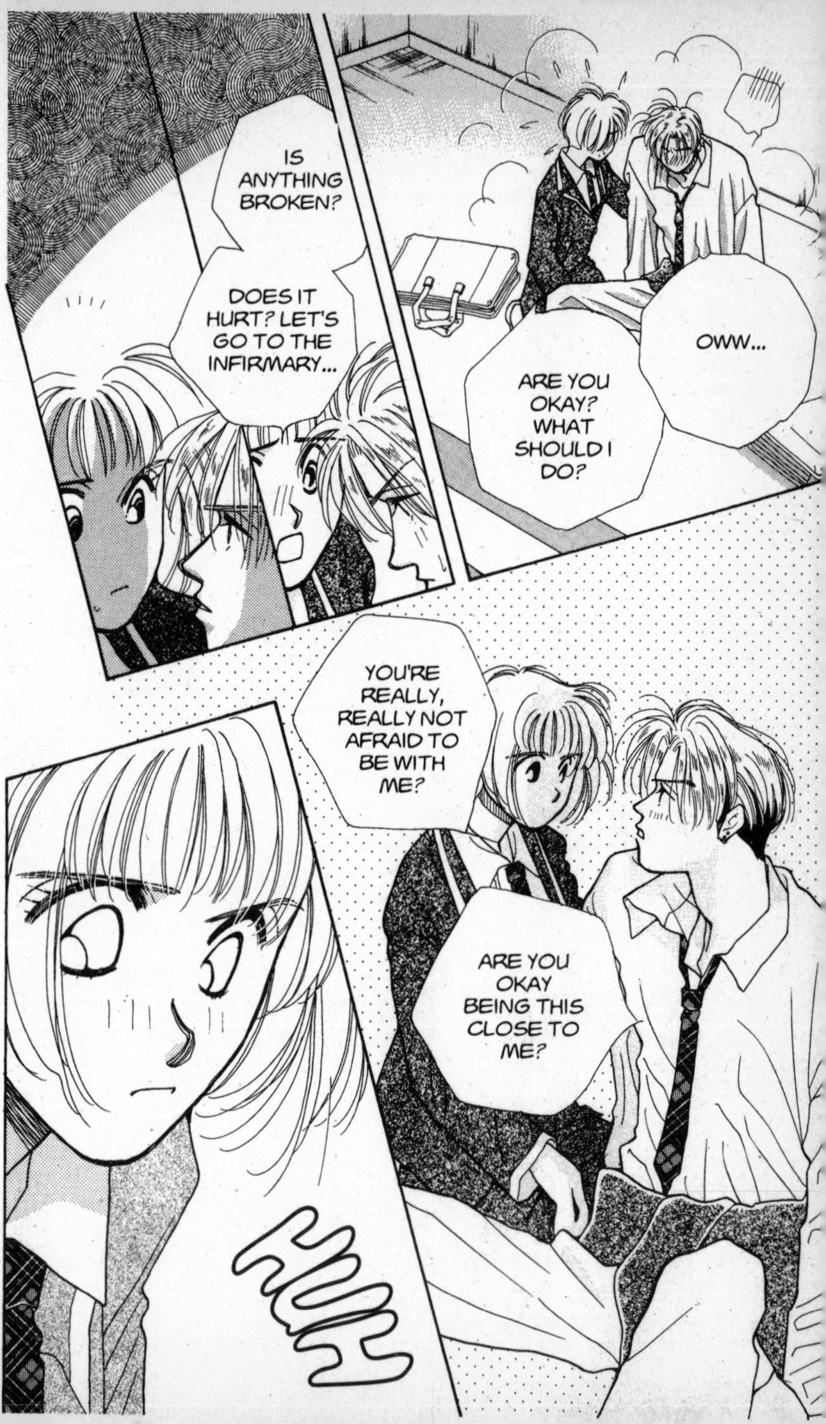
OWW...
ARE YOU OKAY? WHAT SHOULD I DO?
IS ANYTHING BROKEN?
DOES IT HURT? LET'S GO TO THE INFIRMARY...
YOU'RE REALLY, REALLY NOT AFRAID TO BE WITH ME?
ARE YOU OKAY BEING THIS CLOSE TO ME?
HUH

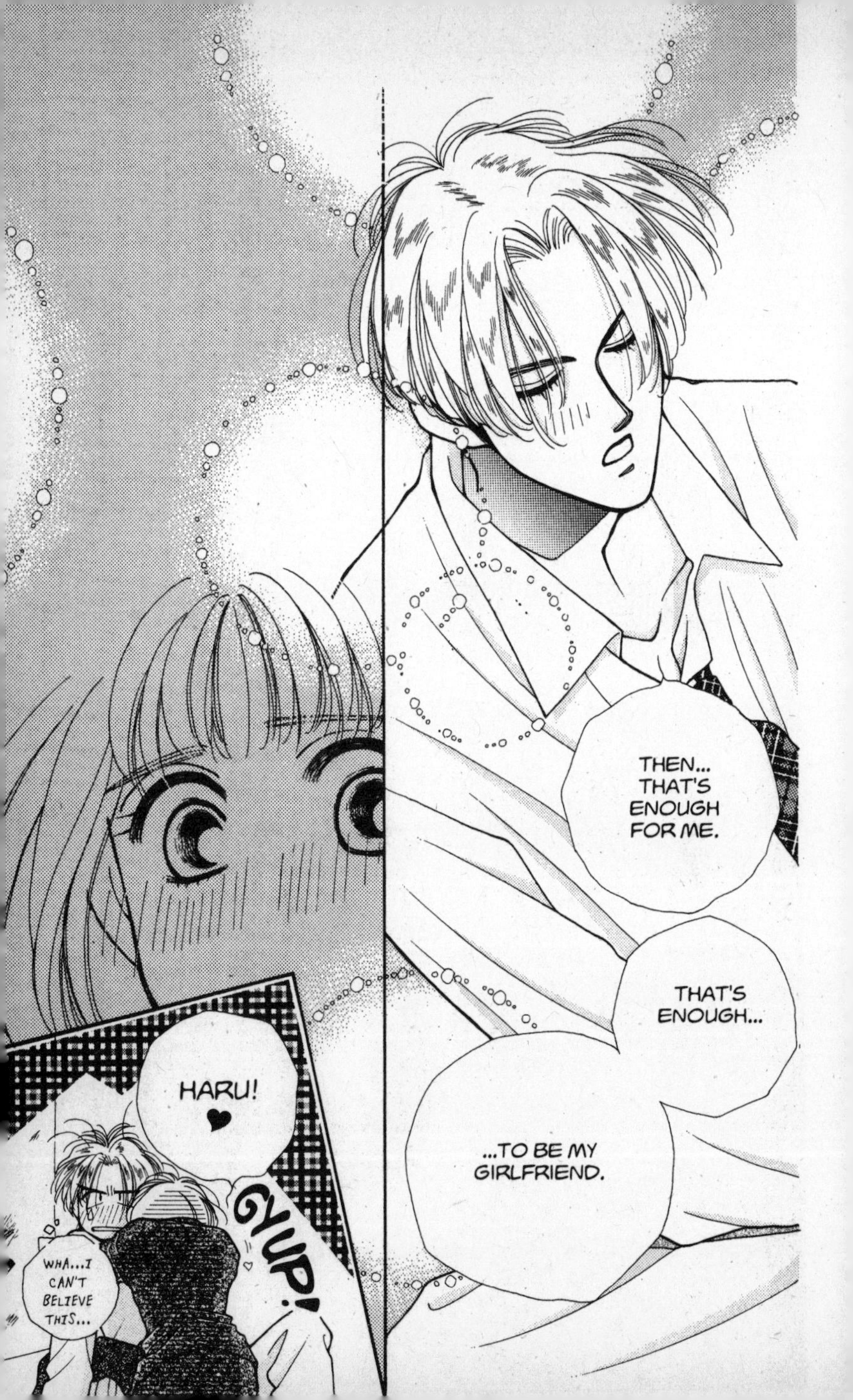
THEN... THAT'S ENOUGH FOR ME.
THAT'S ENOUGH...
...TO BE MY GIRLFRIEND.
HARU! ♥
GYUP!
WHA...I CAN'T BELIEVE THIS...

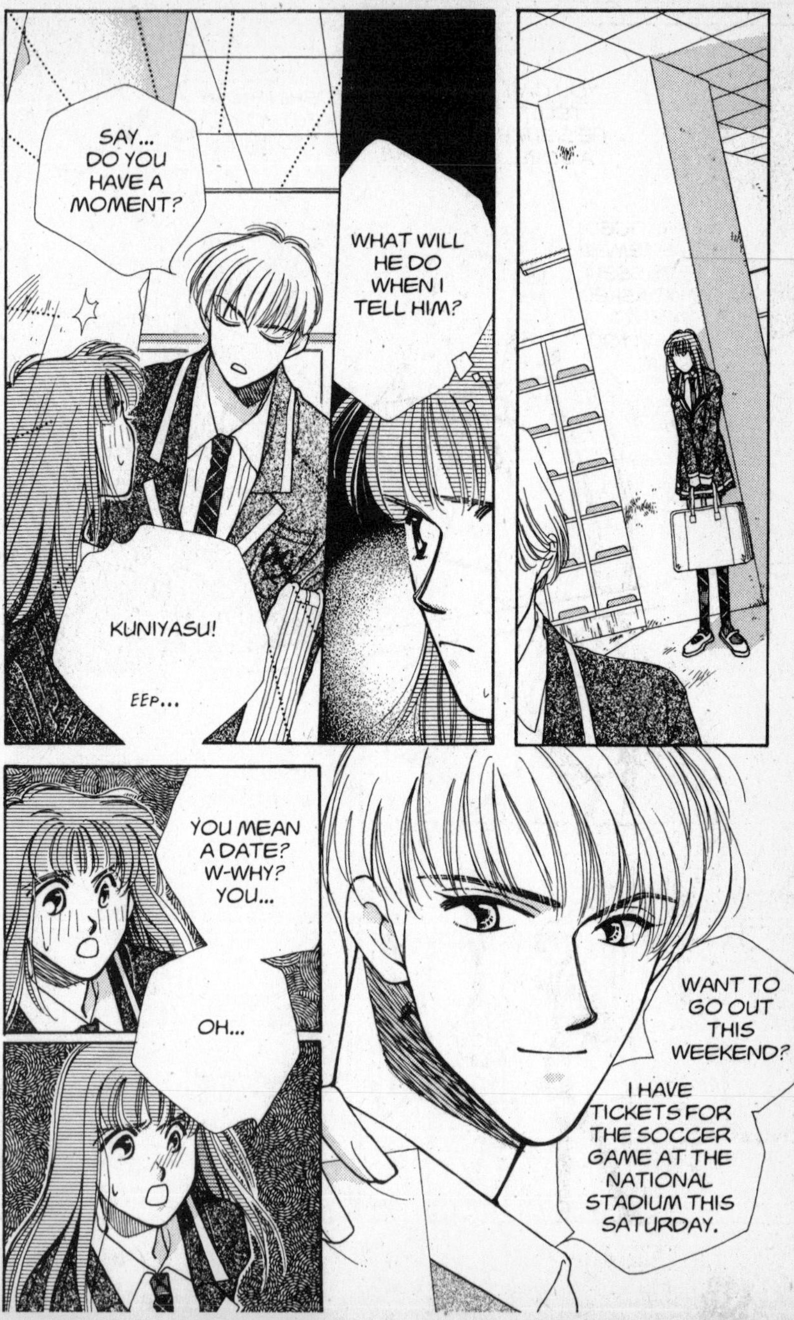
WHAT WILL HE DO WHEN I TELL HIM?
SAY... DO YOU HAVE A MOMENT?
KUNIYASU!
EEP...
WANT TO GO OUT THIS WEEKEND?
I HAVE TICKETS FOR THE SOCCER GAME AT THE NATIONAL STADIUM THIS SATURDAY.
YOU MEAN A DATE? W-WHY? YOU...
OH...

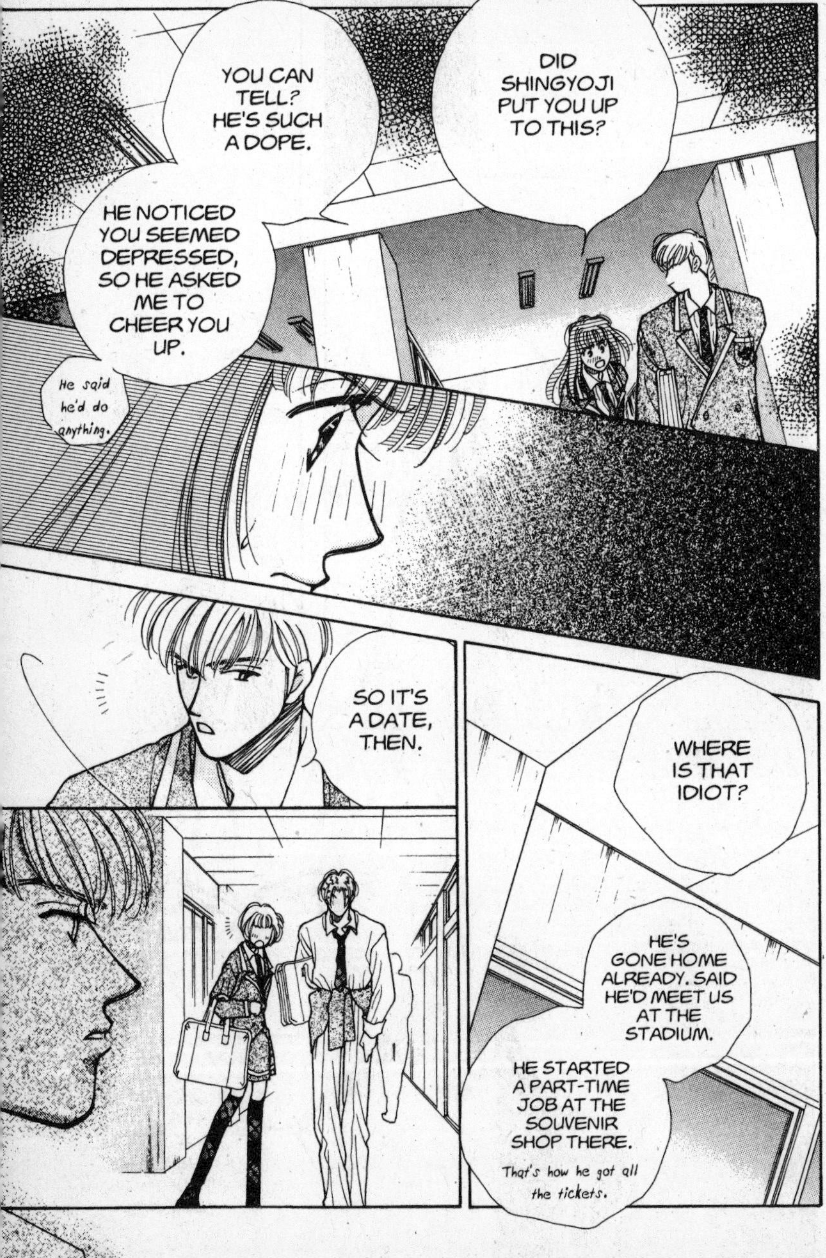
DID SHINGYOJI PUT YOU UP TO THIS?
YOU CAN TELL? HE'S SUCH A DOPE.
HE NOTICED YOU SEEMED DEPRESSED, SO HE ASKED ME TO CHEER YOU UP.
He said he'd do anything.
WHERE IS THAT IDIOT?
HE'S GONE HOME ALREADY. SAID HE'D MEET US AT THE STADIUM.
HE STARTED A PART-TIME JOB AT THE SOUVENIR SHOP THERE.
That's how he got all the tickets.
SO IT'S A DATE, THEN.

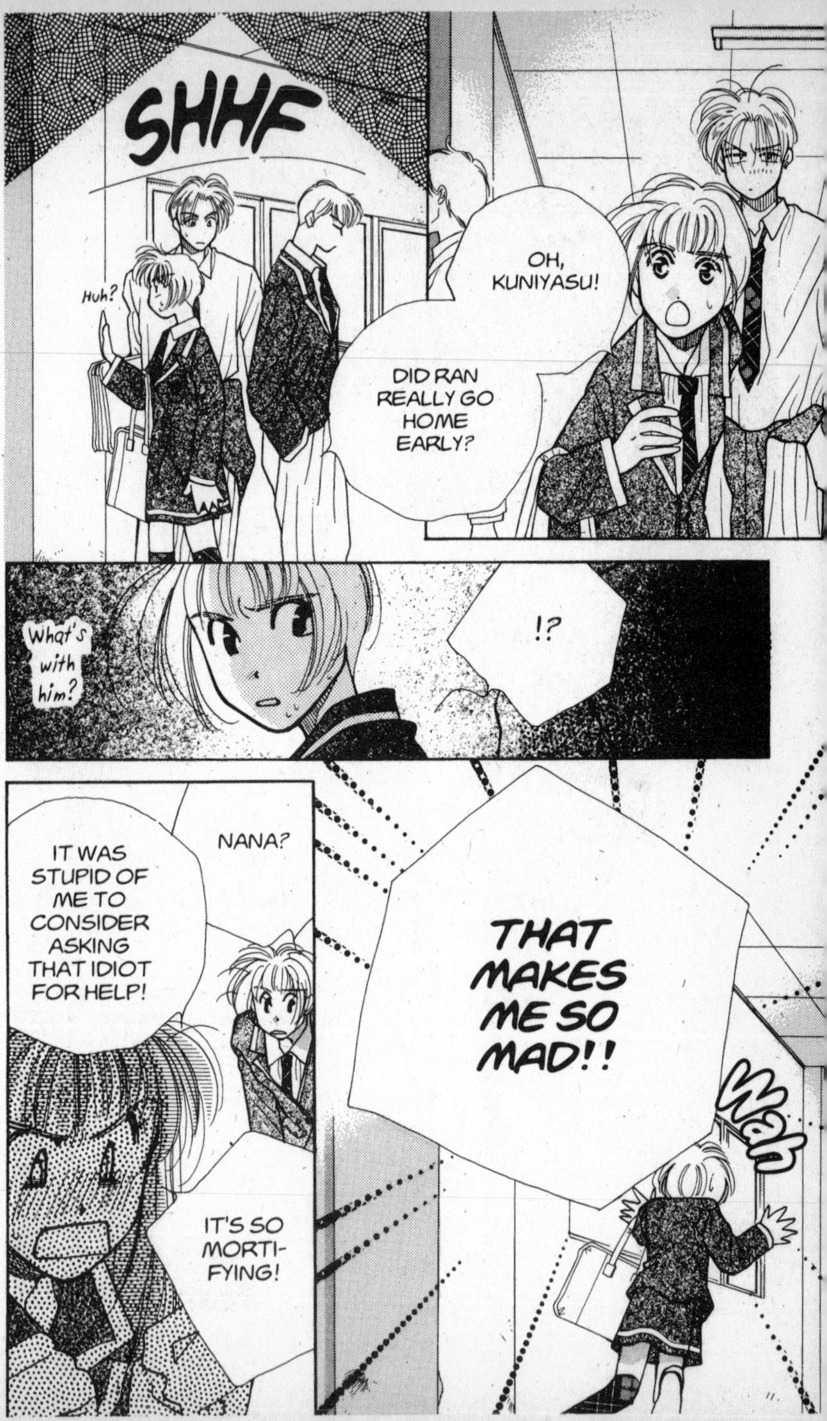
OH, KUNIYASU!
DID RAN REALLY GO HOME EARLY?
SHHF
Huh?
!?
What's with him?
THAT MAKES ME SO MAD!!
Wah
NANA?
IT WAS STUPID OF ME TO CONSIDER ASKING THAT IDIOT FOR HELP!
IT'S SO MORTI-FYING!

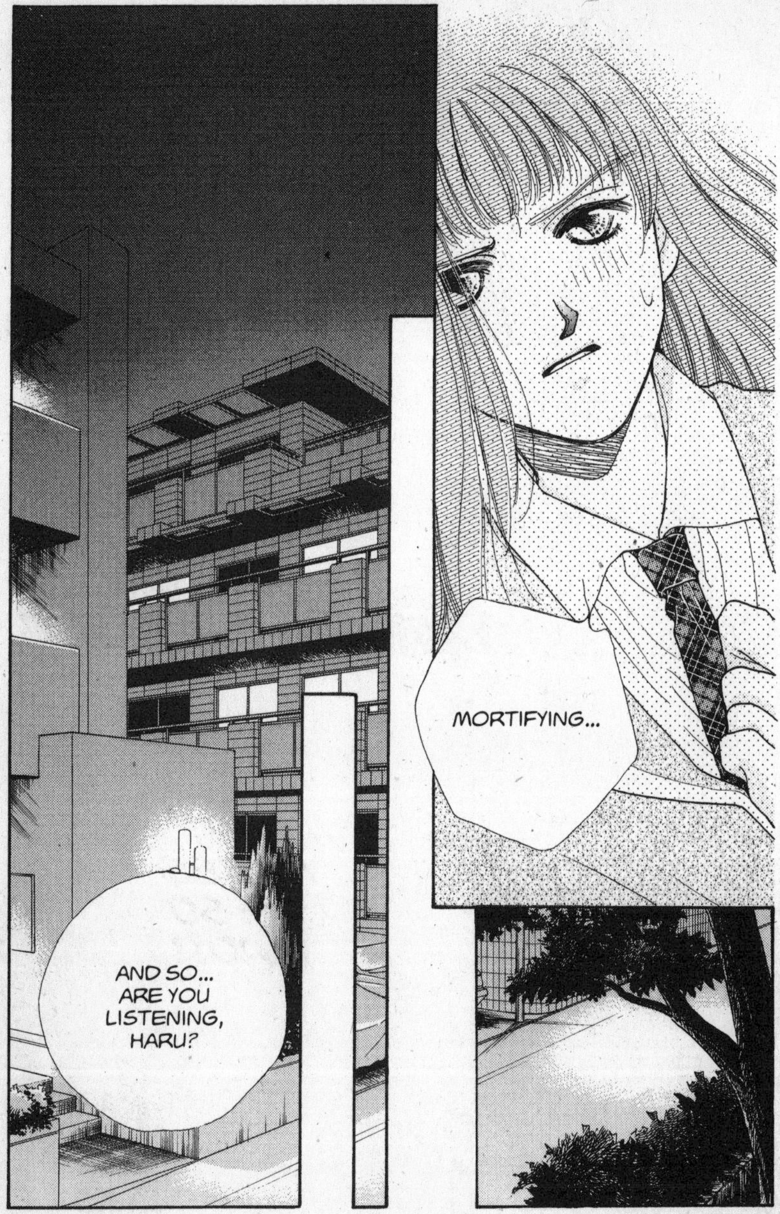
MORTIFYING...
AND SO... ARE YOU LISTENING, HARU?

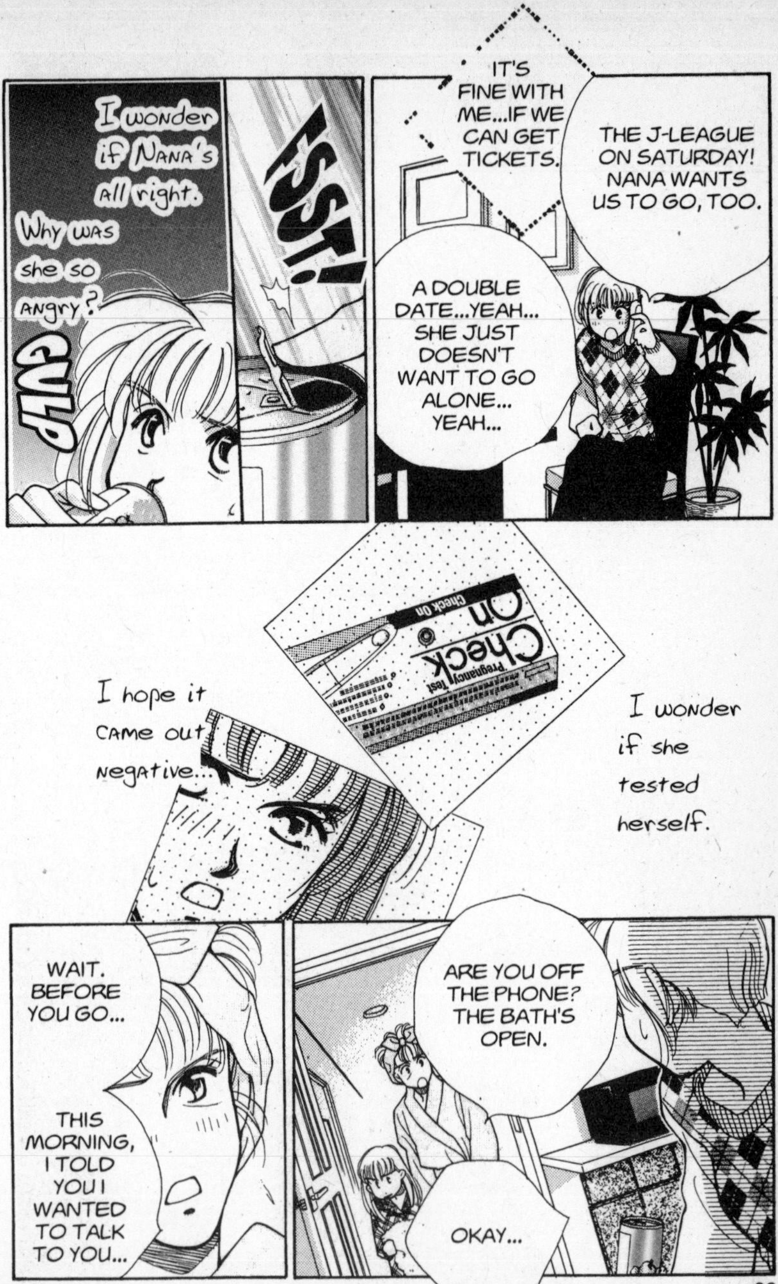
THE J-LEAGUE ON SATURDAY! NANA WANTS US TO GO, TOO.
IT'S FINE WITH ME...IF WE CAN GET TICKETS.
A DOUBLE DATE...YEAH... SHE JUST DOESN'T WANT TO GO ALONE... YEAH...
FSST!
I wonder if Nana's all right.
Why was she so angry?
GULP
I wonder if she tested herself.
Check On
Check
Pregnancy Test
I hope it came out negative...
ARE YOU OFF THE PHONE? THE BATH'S OPEN.
OKAY...
WAIT. BEFORE YOU GO...
THIS MORNING, I TOLD YOU I WANTED TO TALK TO YOU...

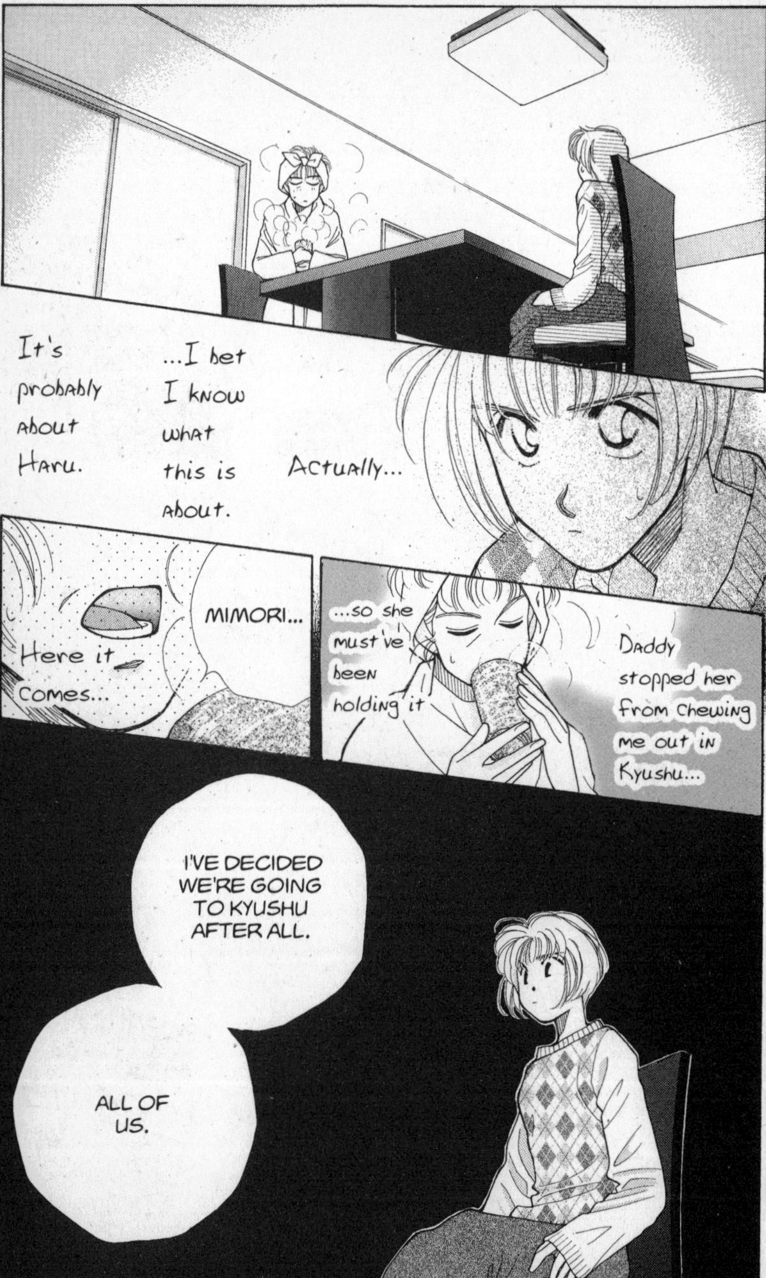
Actually...
...I bet I know what this is about.
It's probably about Haru.
Daddy stopped her from chewing me out in Kyushu...
...so she must've been holding it
MIMORI...
Here it comes...
I'VE DECIDED WE'RE GOING TO KYUSHU AFTER ALL.
ALL OF US.

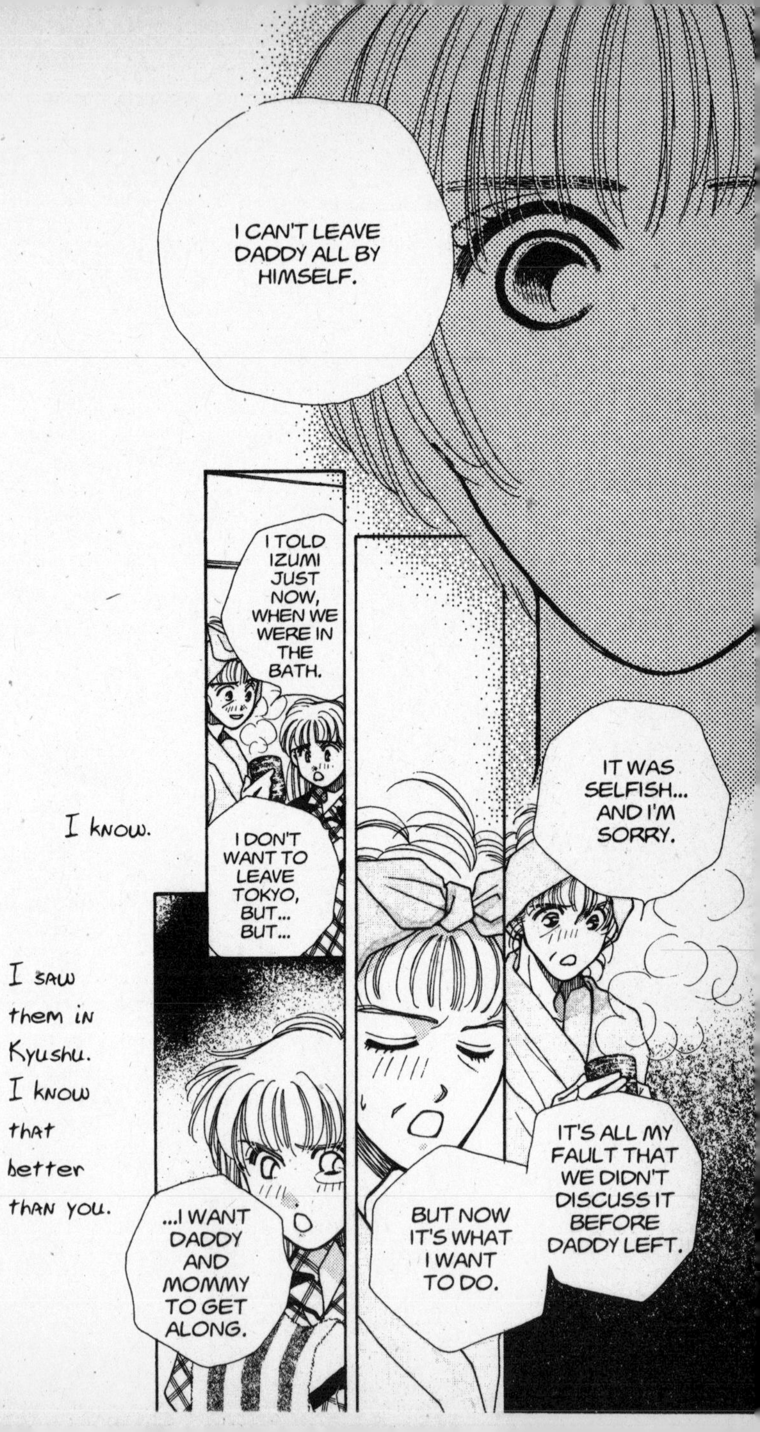
I CAN'T LEAVE DADDY ALL BY HIMSELF.
IT WAS SELFISH... AND I'M SORRY.
IT'S ALL MY FAULT THAT WE DIDN'T DISCUSS IT BEFORE DADDY LEFT.
BUT NOW IT'S WHAT I WANT TO DO.
I TOLD IZUMI JUST NOW, WHEN WE WERE IN THE BATH.
I DON'T WANT TO LEAVE TOKYO, BUT... BUT...
...I WANT DADDY AND MOMMY TO GET ALONG.
I know.
I saw them in Kyushu. I know that better than you.

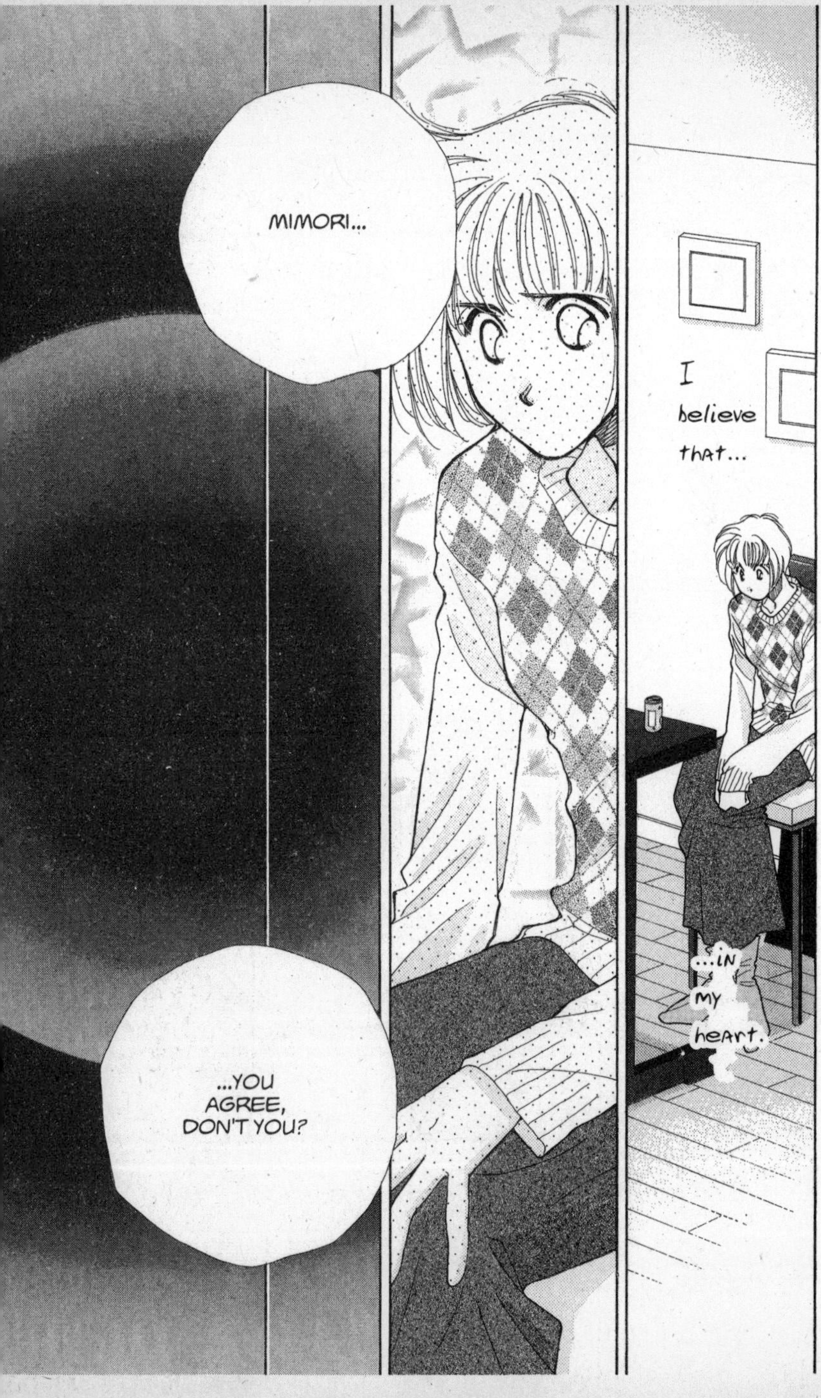

I believe that...
...in my heart.
MIMORI...
...YOU AGREE, DON'T YOU?

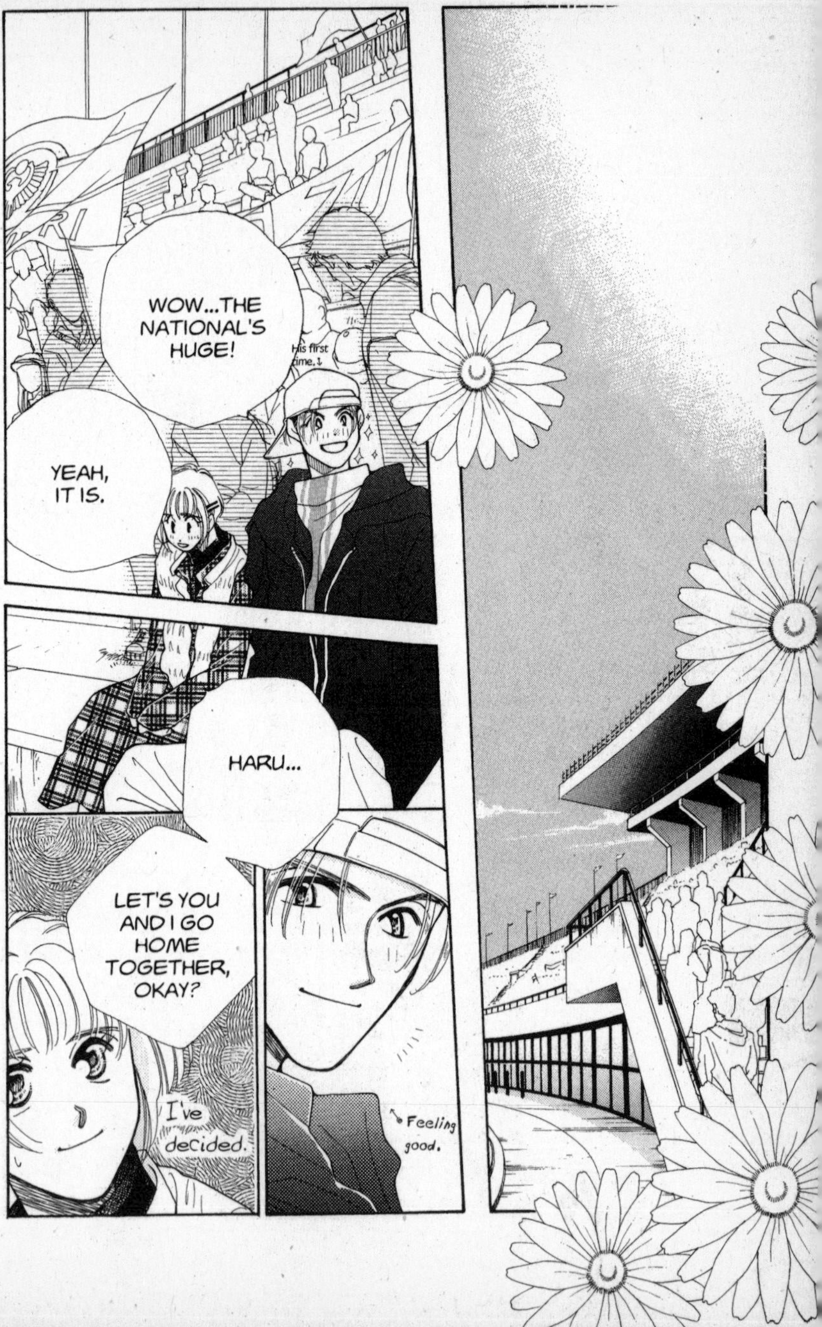
WOW...THE NATIONAL'S HUGE!
His first time.
YEAH, IT IS.
HARU...
LET'S YOU AND I GO HOME TOGETHER, OKAY?
Feeling good.
I've decided.

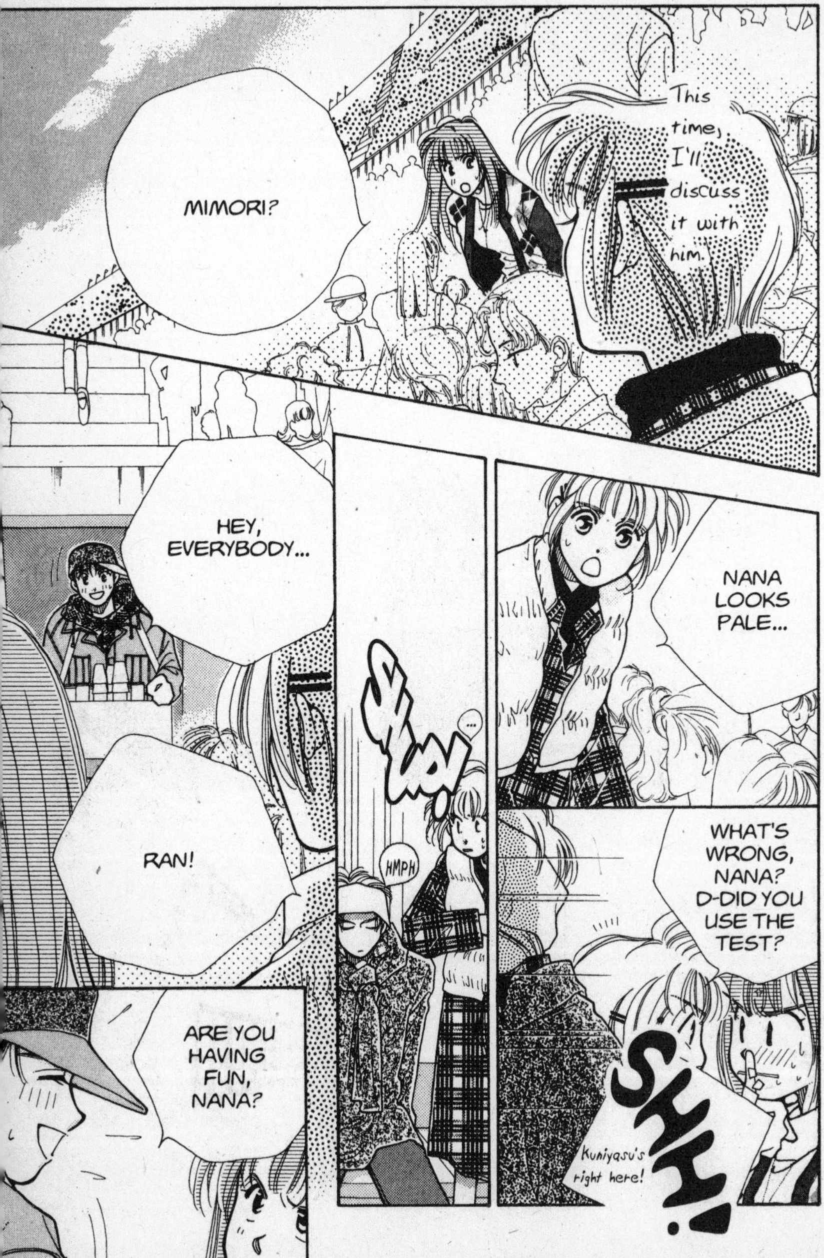
This time, I'll discuss it with him.
MIMORI?
NANA LOOKS PALE...
WHAT'S WRONG, NANA? D-DID YOU USE THE TEST?
SHH!
Kuniyasu's right here!
...
SHUP!
HMPH
HEY, EVERYBODY...
RAN!
ARE YOU HAVING FUN, NANA?

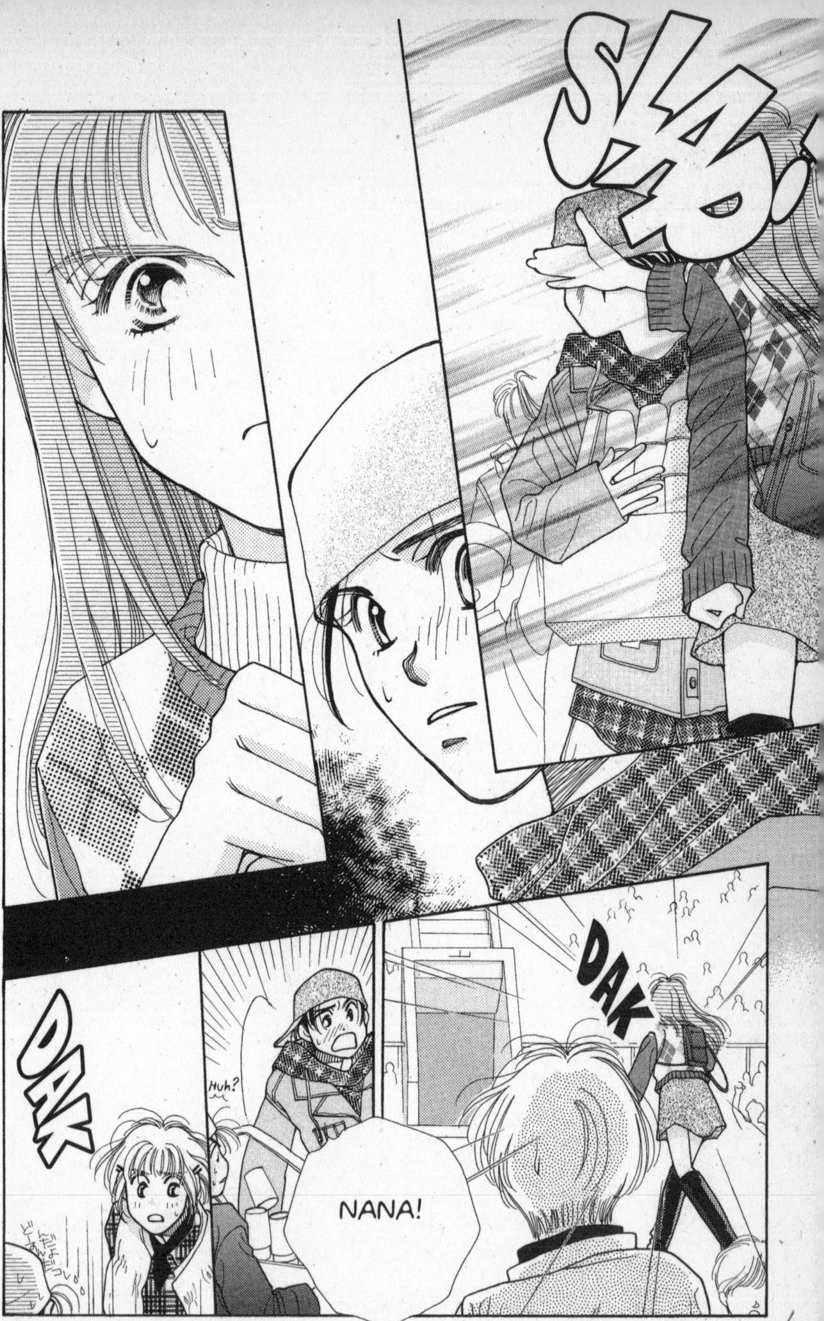
SLAP!
DAK
NANA!
Huh?
DAK

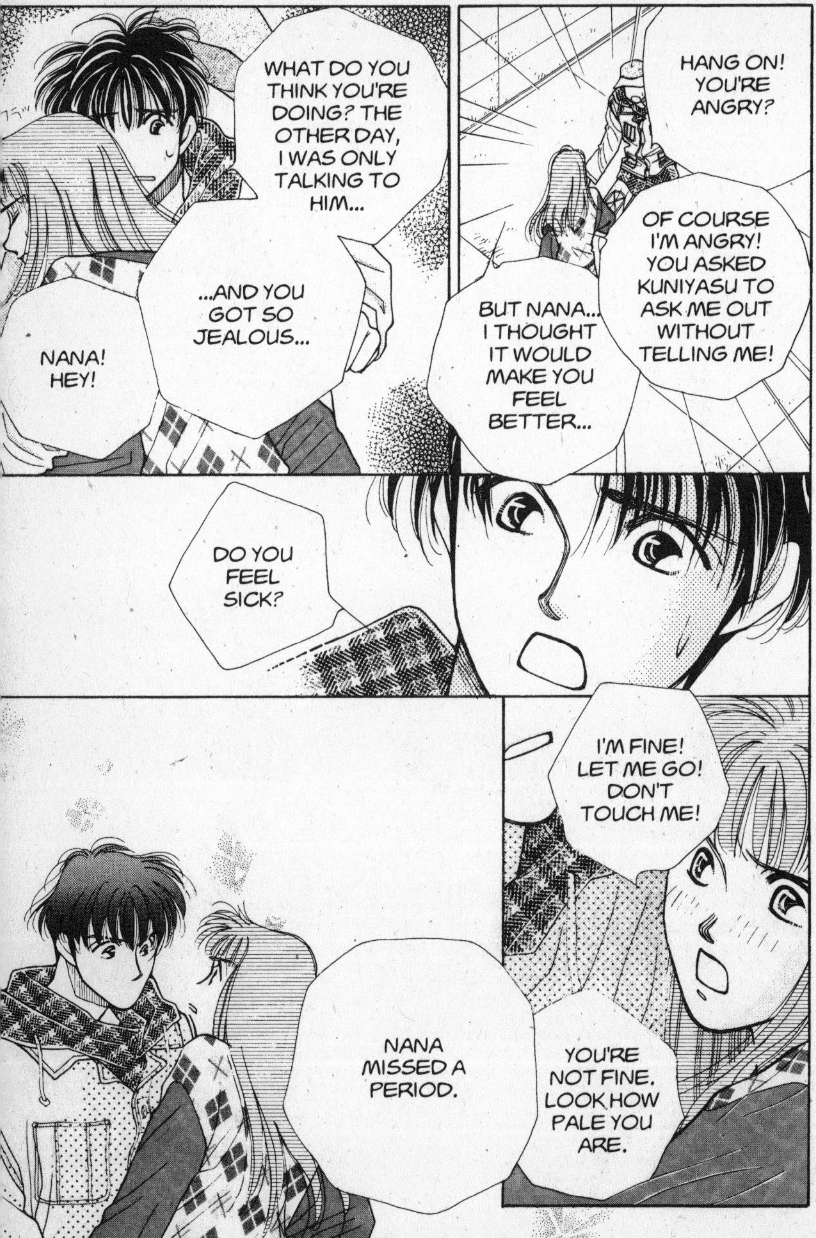
HANG ON! YOU'RE ANGRY?
OF COURSE I'M ANGRY! YOU ASKED KUNIYASU TO ASK ME OUT WITHOUT TELLING ME!
BUT NANA... I THOUGHT IT WOULD MAKE YOU FEEL BETTER...
WHAT DO YOU THINK YOU'RE DOING? THE OTHER DAY, I WAS ONLY TALKING TO HIM...
...AND YOU GOT SO JEALOUS...
NANA! HEY!
DO YOU FEEL SICK?
I'M FINE! LET ME GO! DON'T TOUCH ME!
YOU'RE NOT FINE. LOOK HOW PALE YOU ARE.
NANA MISSED A PERIOD.

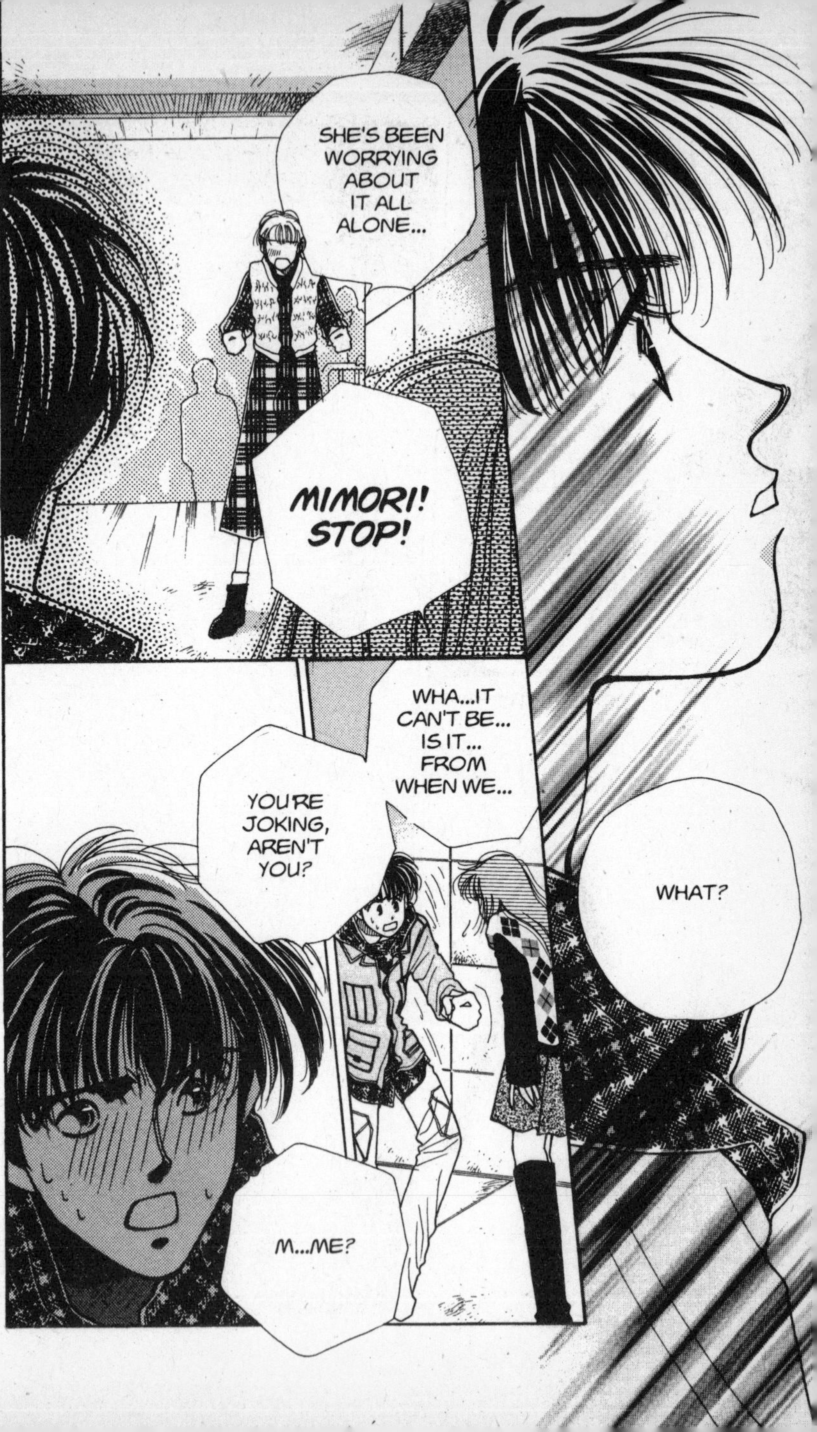
WHAT?
SHE'S BEEN WORRYING ABOUT IT ALL ALONE...
MIMORI! STOP!
WHA...IT CAN'T BE... IS IT... FROM WHEN WE...
YOU'RE JOKING, AREN'T YOU?
M...ME?

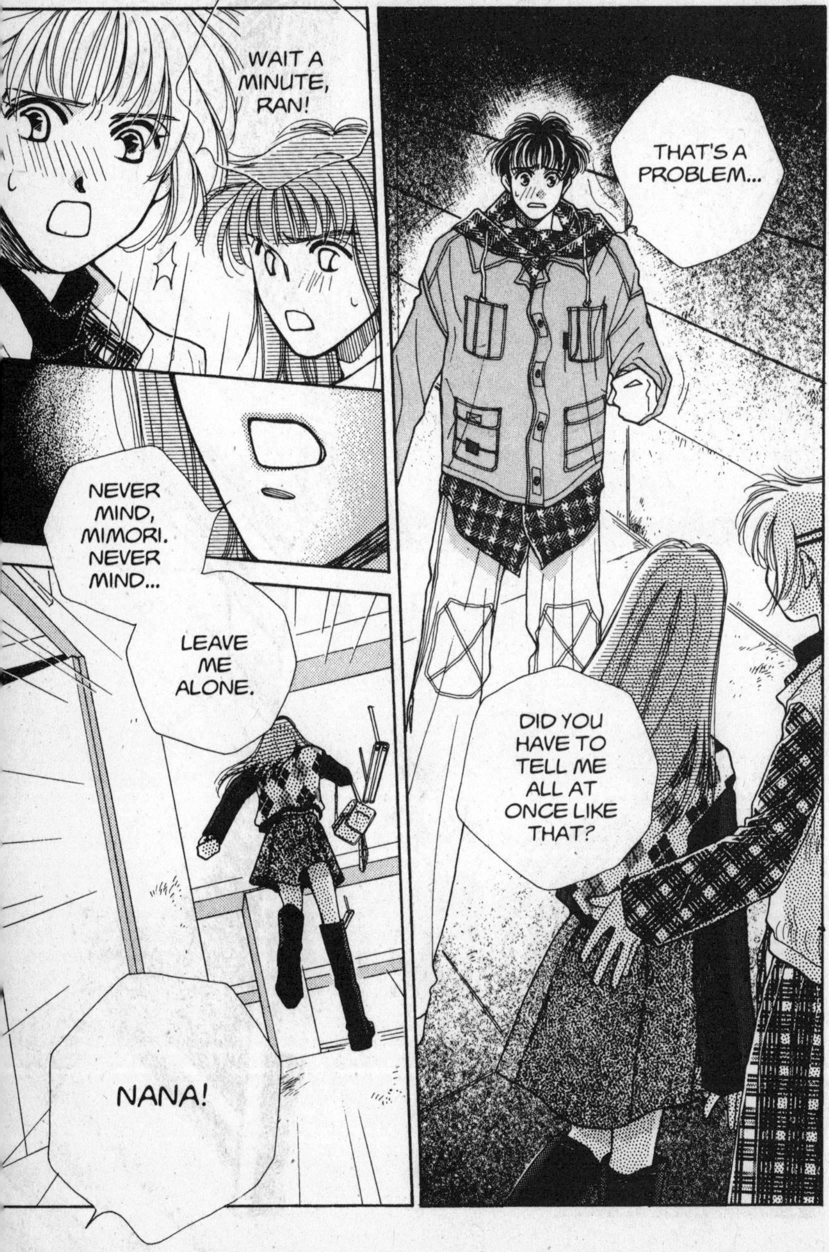
THAT'S A PROBLEM...
DID YOU HAVE TO TELL ME ALL AT ONCE LIKE THAT?
WAIT A MINUTE, RAN!
NEVER MIND, MIMORI. NEVER MIND...
LEAVE ME ALONE.
NANA!

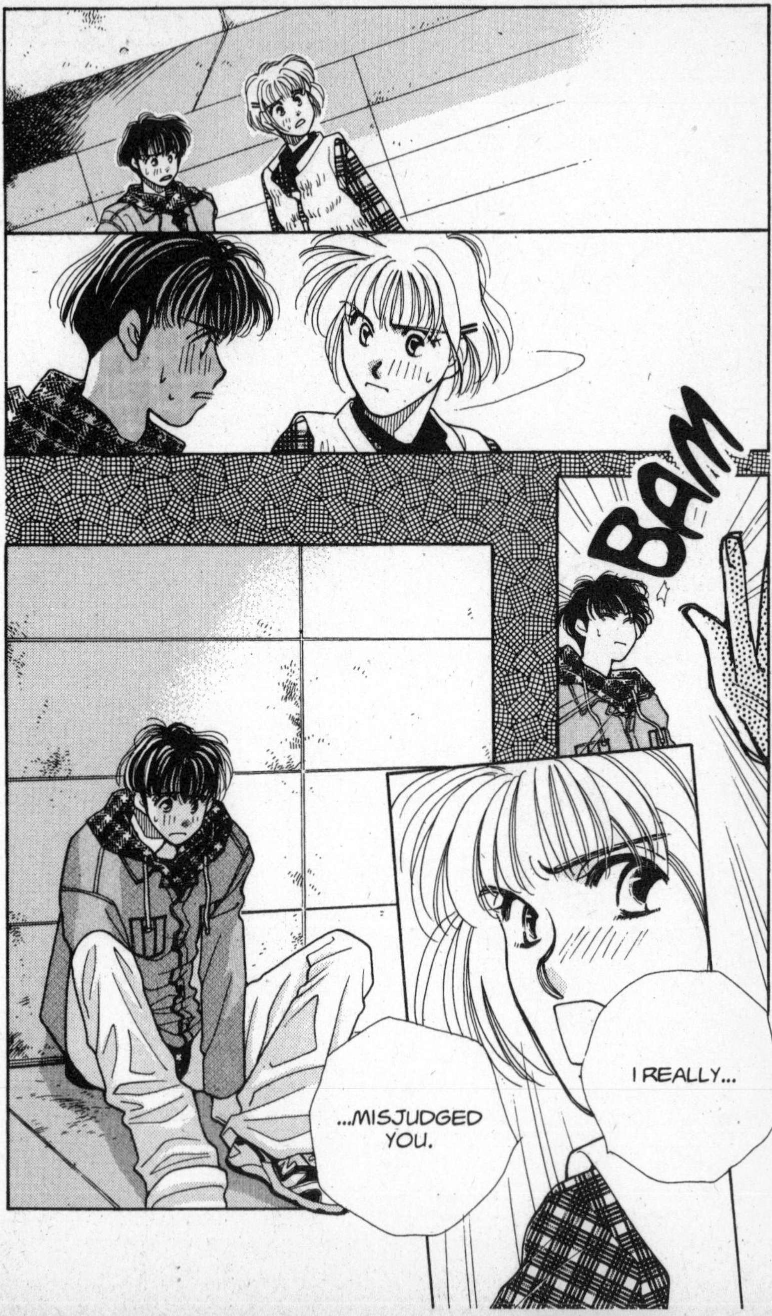
BAM
I REALLY...
...MISJUDGED YOU.

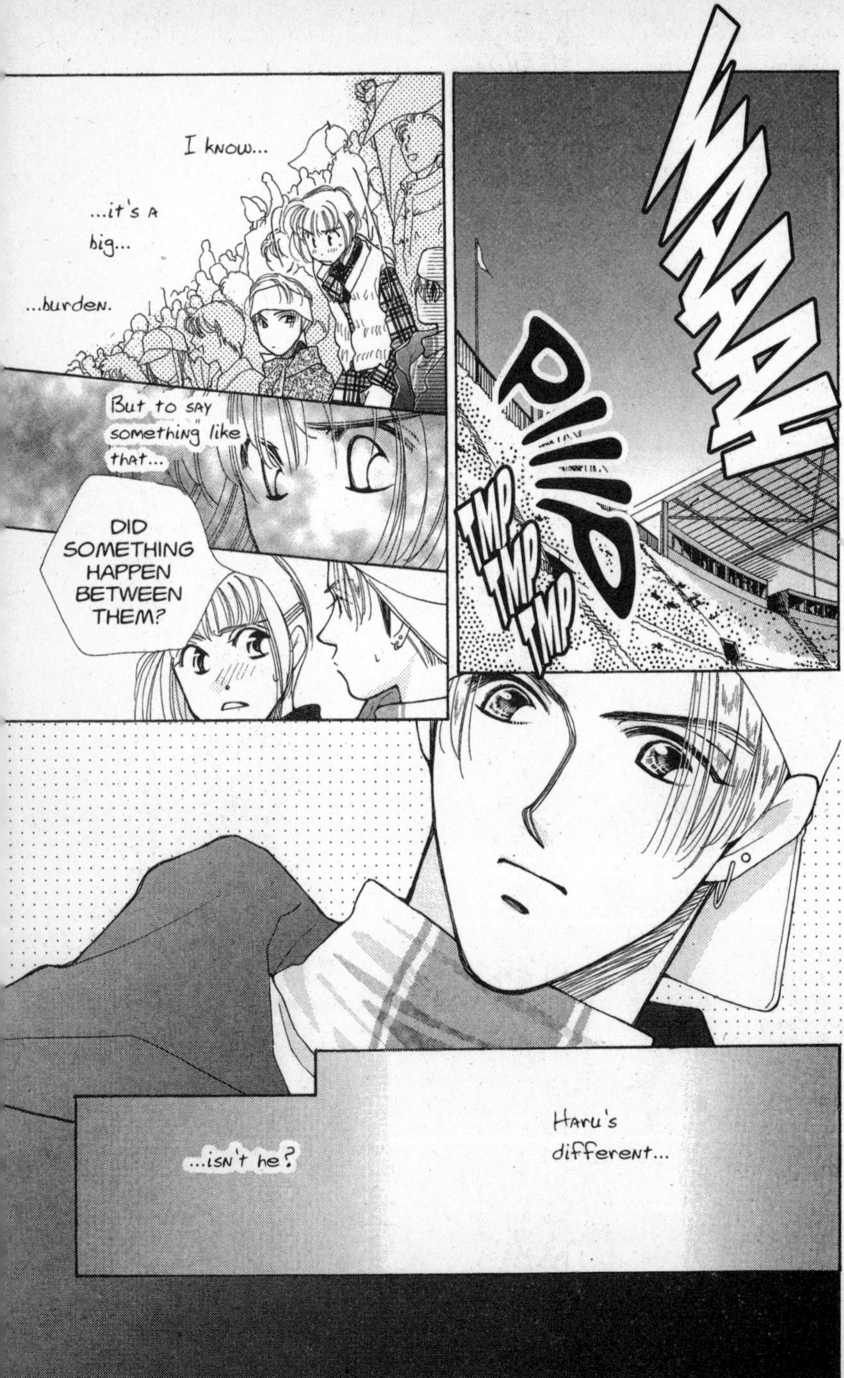
WAAAAH
PIIIP
TMP TMP TMP
I know...
...it's a big...
...burden.
But to say something like that...
DID SOMETHING HAPPEN BETWEEN THEM?
Haru's different...
...isn't he?

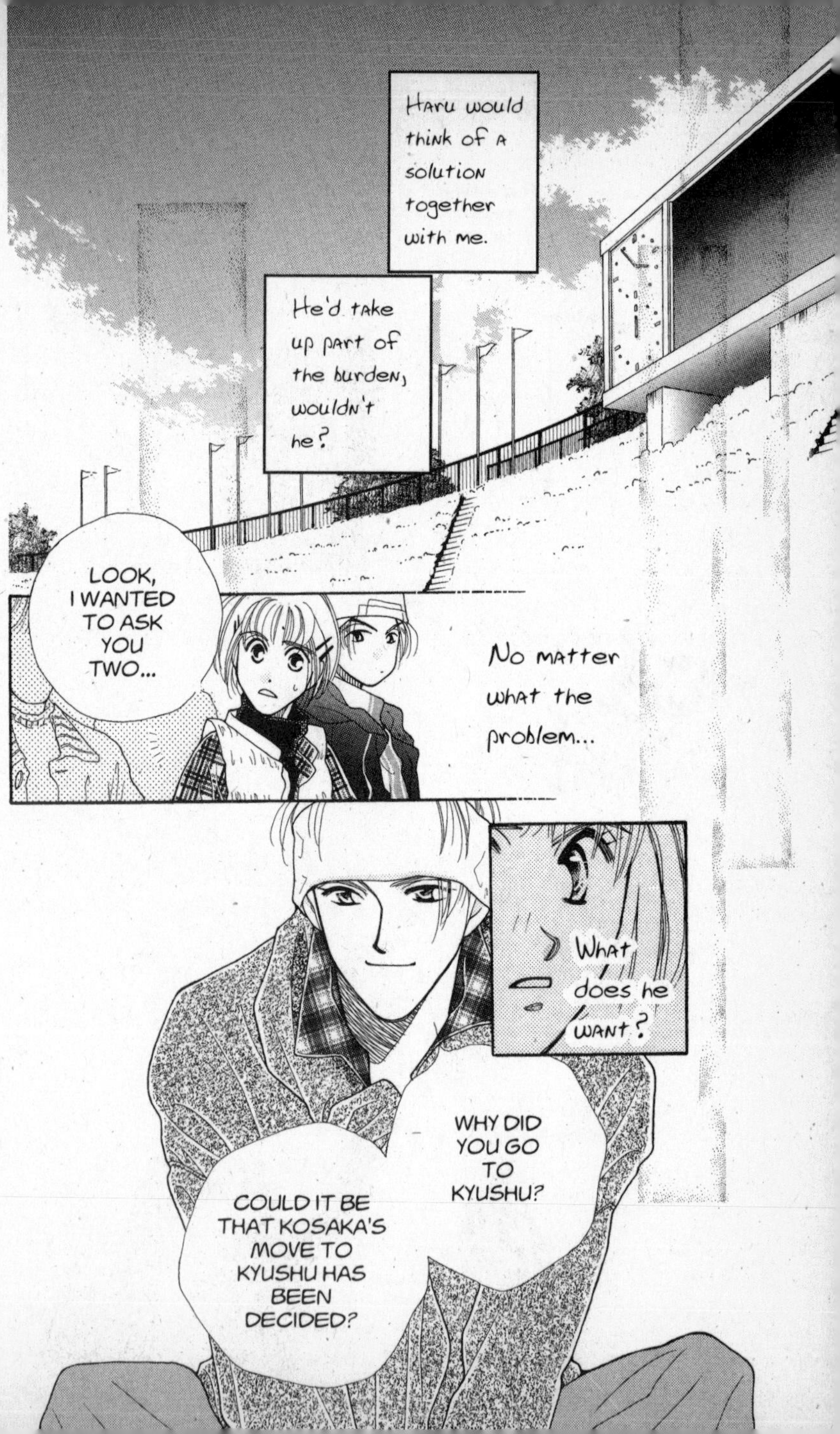
Haru would think of a solution together with me.
He'd take up part of the burden, wouldn't he?
No matter what the problem...
LOOK, I WANTED TO ASK YOU TWO...
What does he want?
WHY DID YOU GO TO KYUSHU?
COULD IT BE THAT KOSAKA'S MOVE TO KYUSHU HAS BEEN DECIDED?

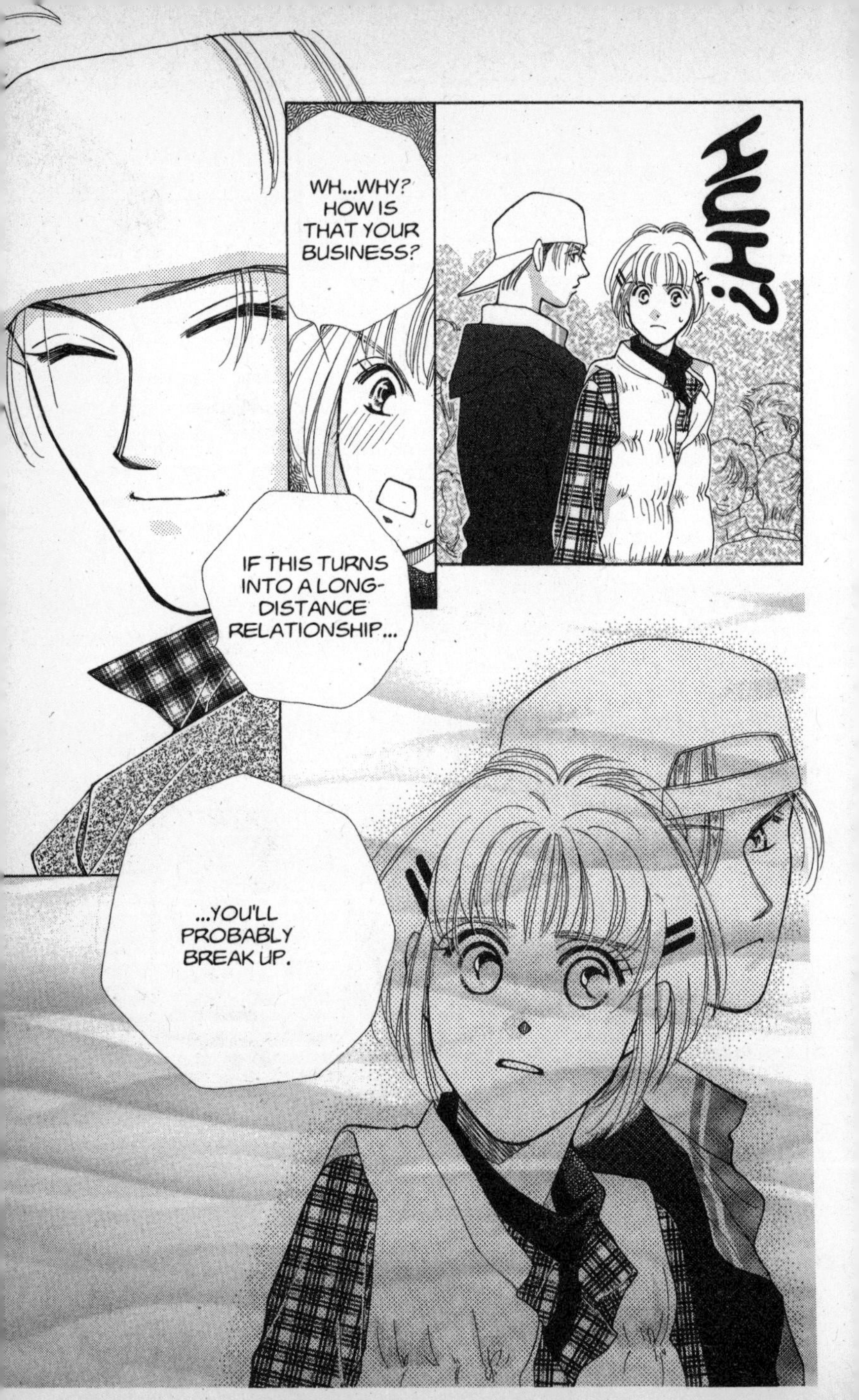
HUH?!
WH...WHY? HOW IS THAT YOUR BUSINESS?
IF THIS TURNS INTO A LONG-DISTANCE RELATIONSHIP...
...YOU'LL PROBABLY BREAK UP.

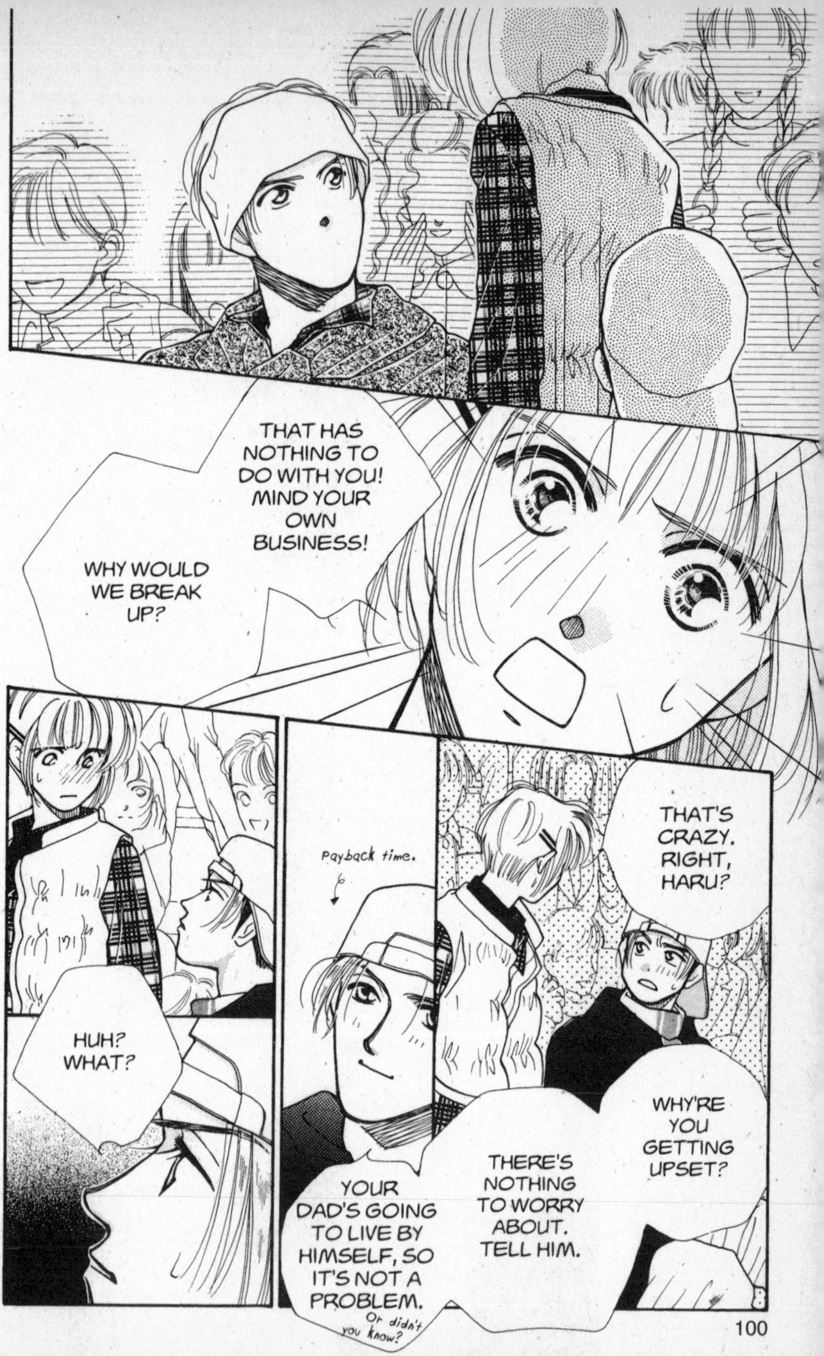
THAT HAS NOTHING TO DO WITH YOU! MIND YOUR OWN BUSINESS!
WHY WOULD WE BREAK UP?
THAT'S CRAZY. RIGHT, HARU?
WHY'RE YOU GETTING UPSET?
THERE'S NOTHING TO WORRY ABOUT. TELL HIM.
Payback time.
YOUR DAD'S GOING TO LIVE BY HIMSELF, SO IT'S NOT A PROBLEM.
Or didn't you know?
HUH? WHAT?

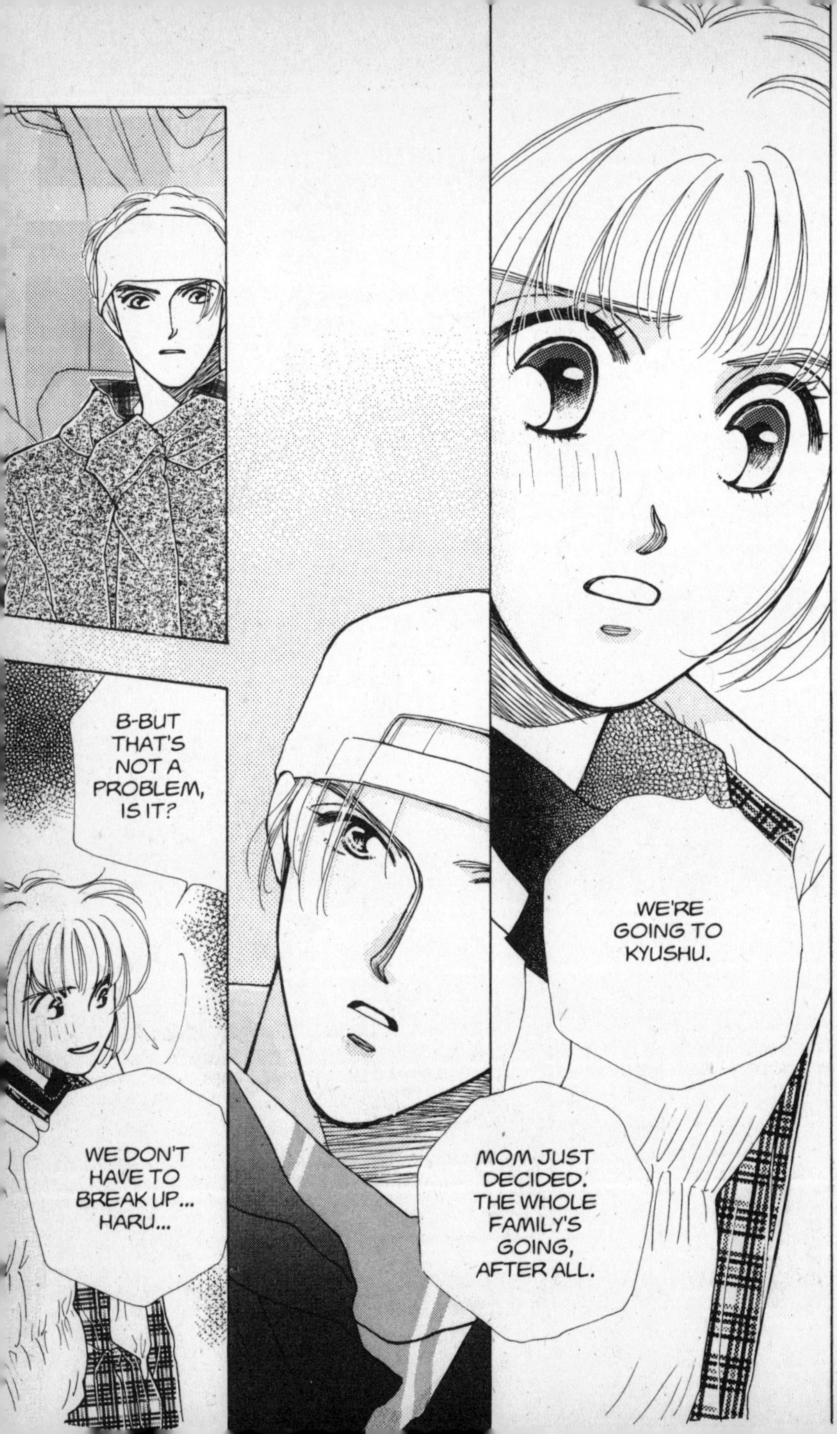
WE'RE GOING TO KYUSHU.
MOM JUST DECIDED. THE WHOLE FAMILY'S GOING, AFTER ALL.
B-BUT THAT'S NOT A PROBLEM, IS IT?
WE DON'T HAVE TO BREAK UP... HARU...

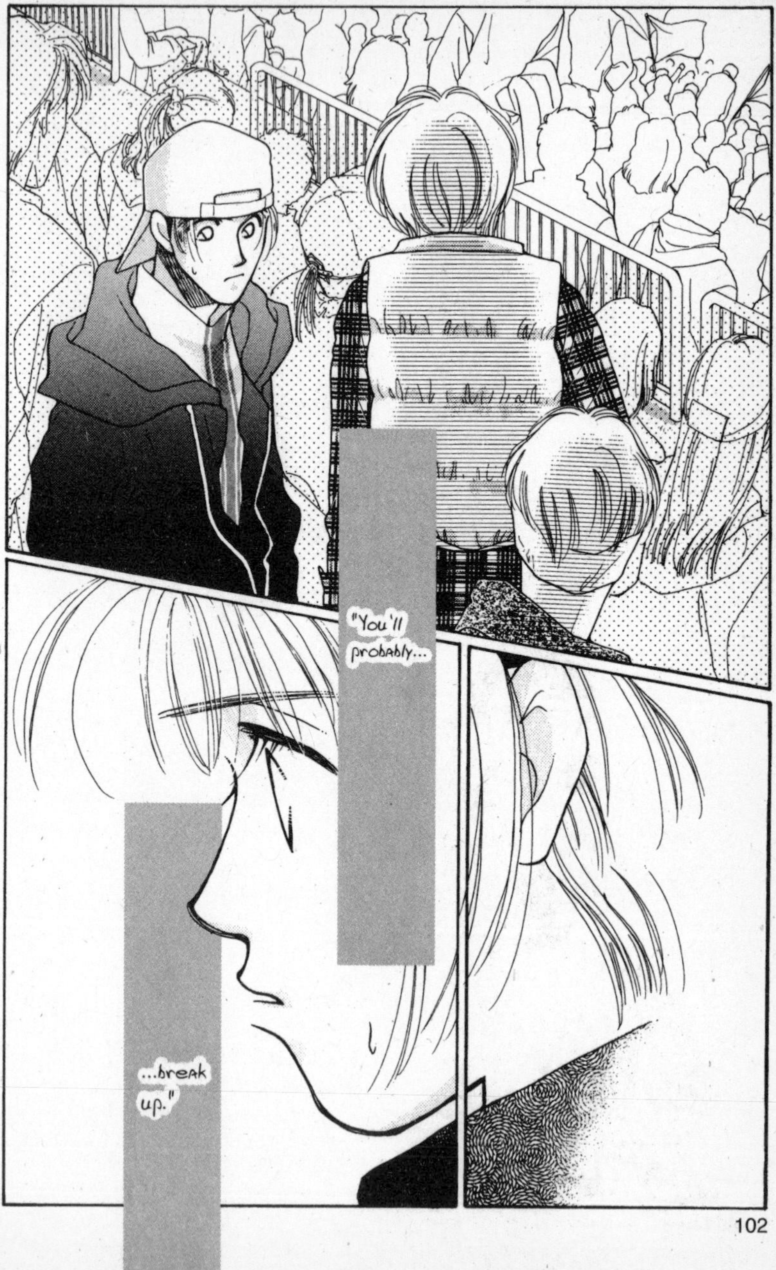
"You'll probably...
...break up."

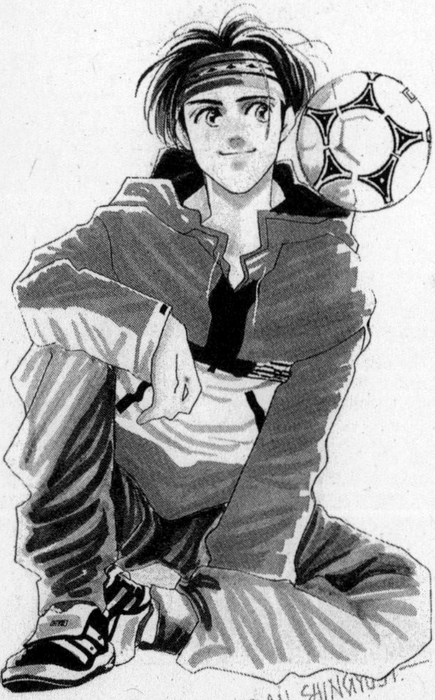
RAN. SHINGYOJI.

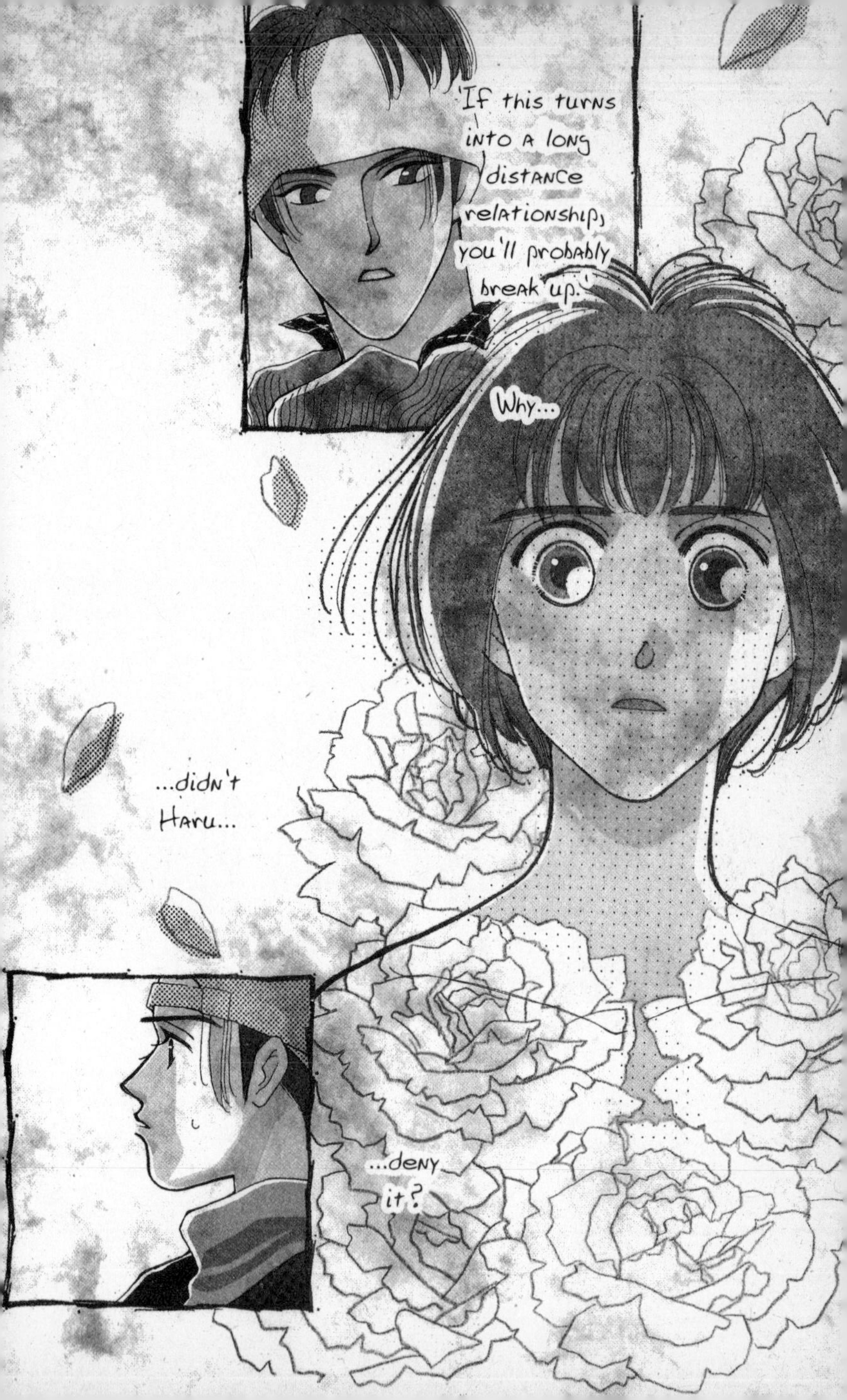
'If this turns into a long distance relationship, you'll probably break up.'
Why...
...didn't Haru...
...deny it?

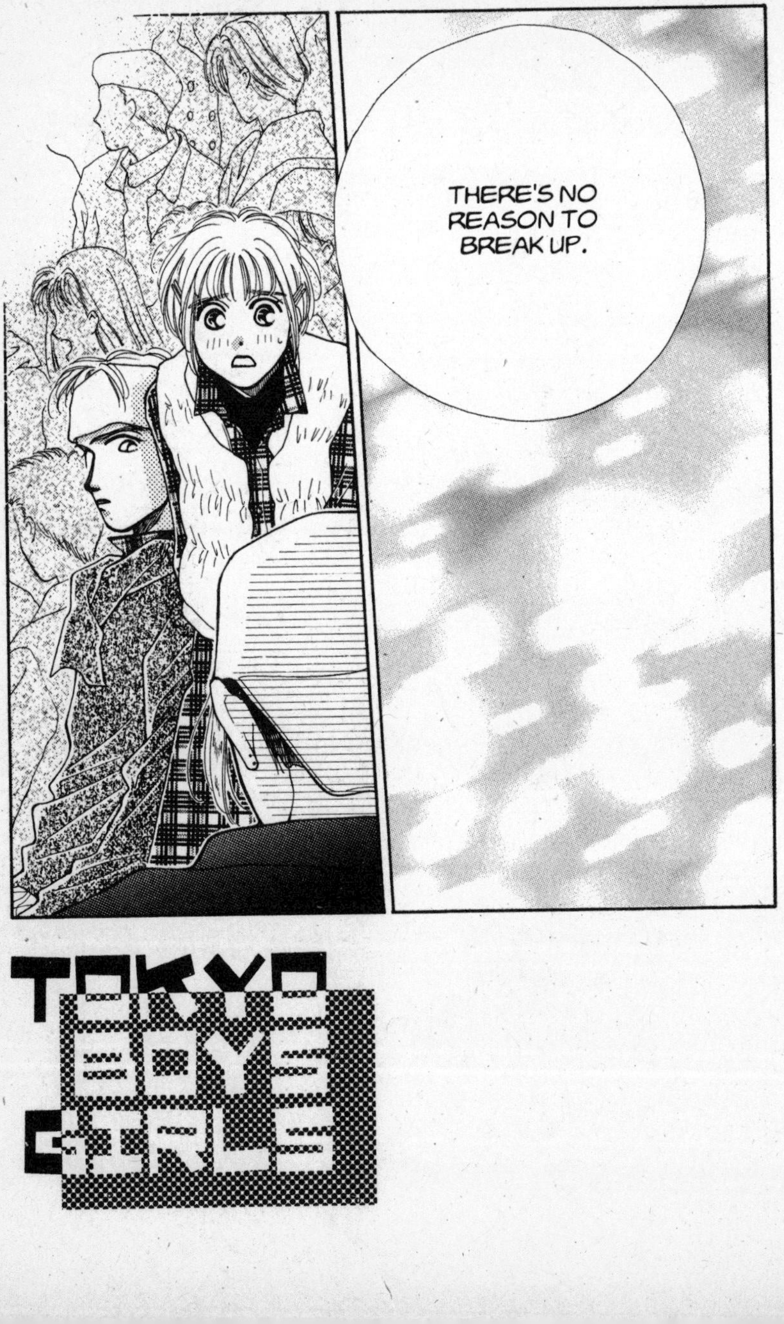
THERE'S NO REASON TO BREAK UP.

TOKYO BOYS GIRLS

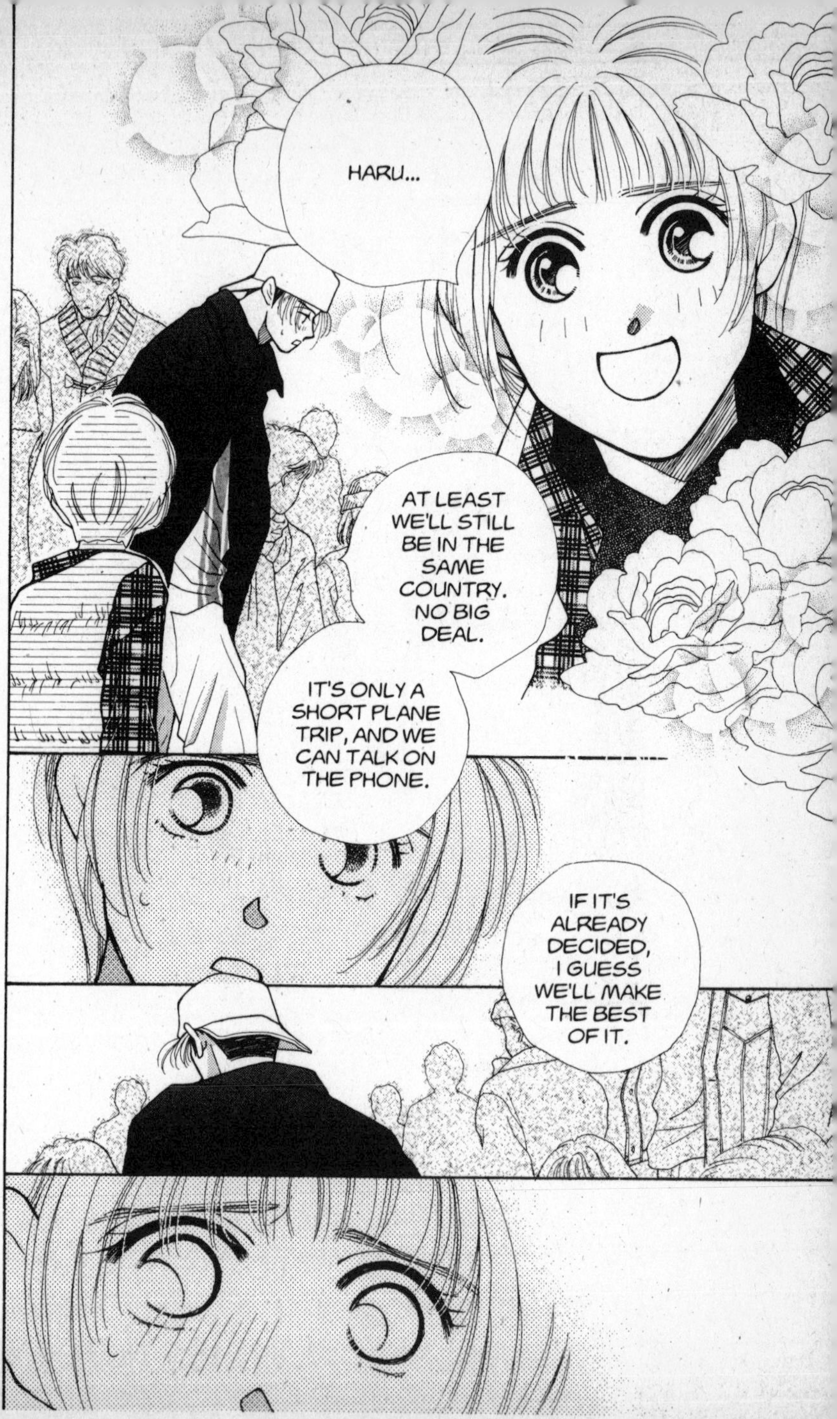
HARU...
AT LEAST WE'LL STILL BE IN THE SAME COUNTRY. NO BIG DEAL.
IT'S ONLY A SHORT PLANE TRIP, AND WE CAN TALK ON THE PHONE.
IF IT'S ALREADY DECIDED, I GUESS WE'LL MAKE THE BEST OF IT.

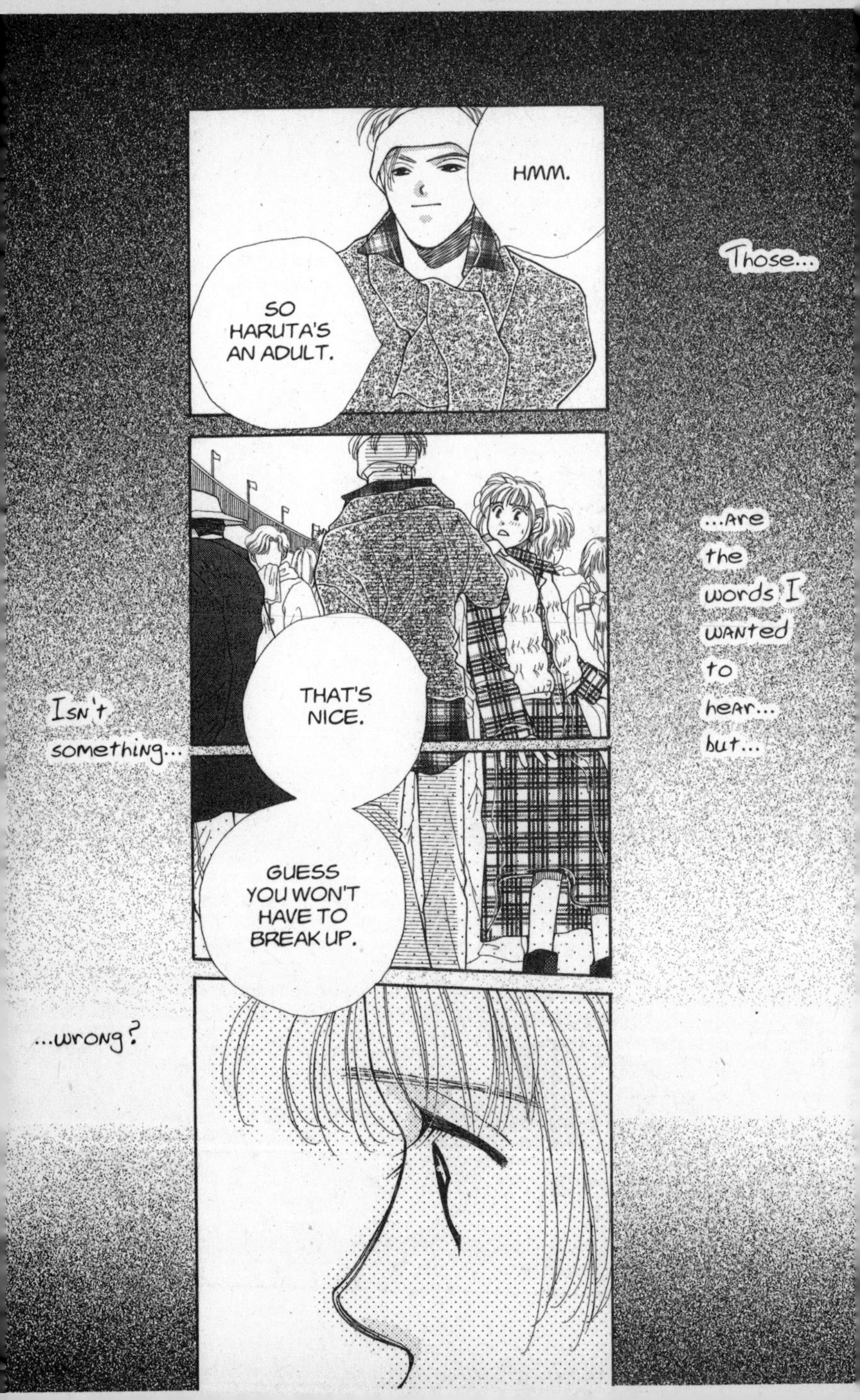
HMM.
SO HARUTA'S AN ADULT.
Those...
...are the words I wanted to hear... but...
THAT'S NICE.
GUESS YOU WON'T HAVE TO BREAK UP.
Isn't something...
...wrong?

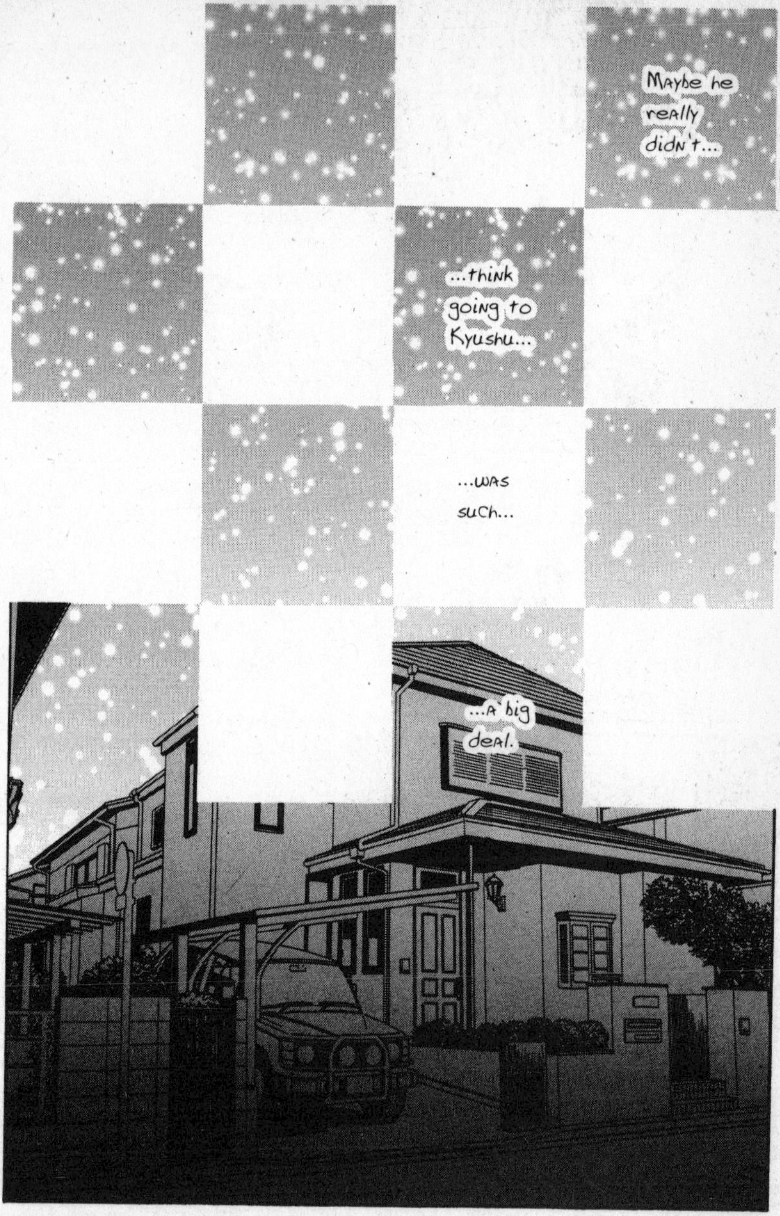
Maybe he really didn't...
...think going to Kyushu...
...was such...
...a big deal.

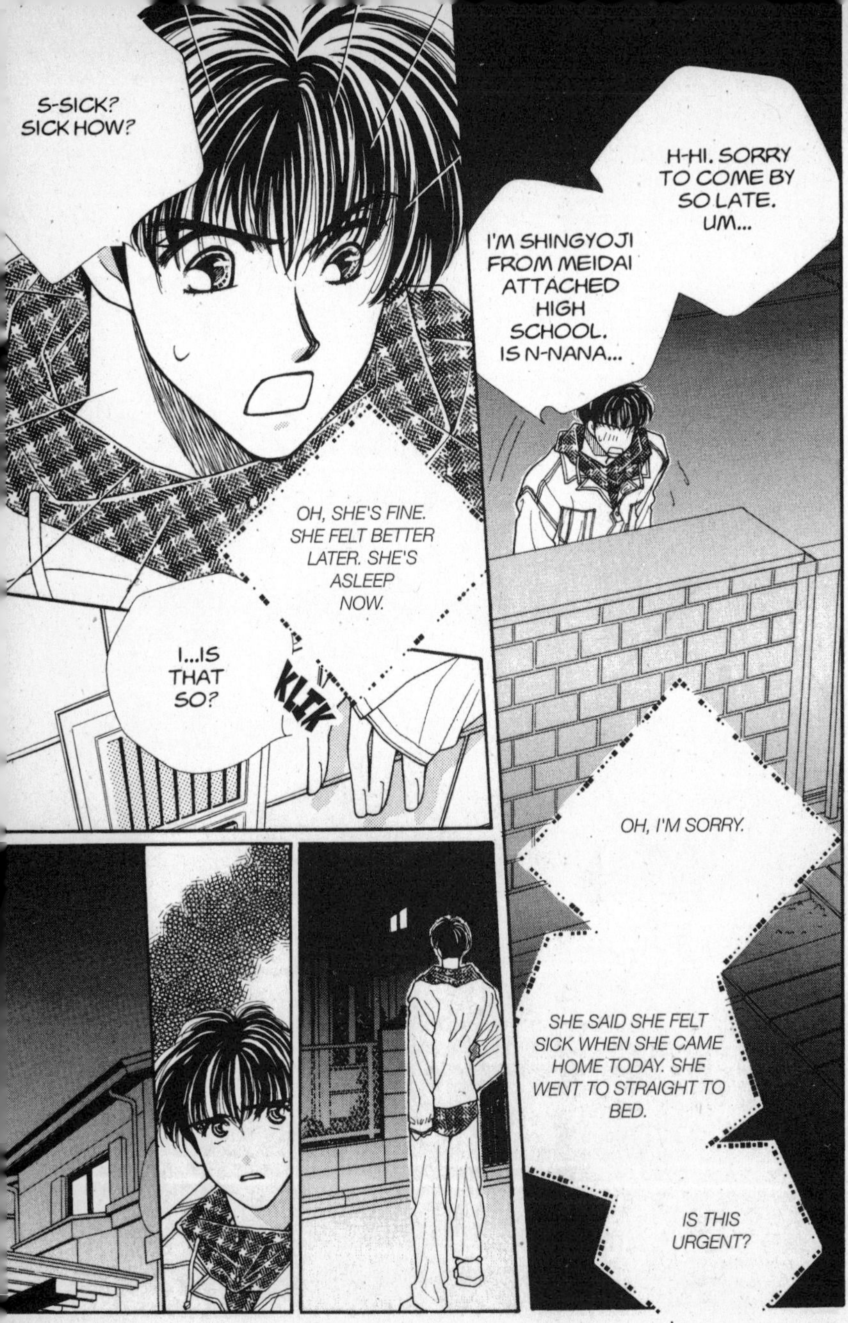
H-HI. SORRY TO COME BY SO LATE. UM...
I'M SHINGYOJI FROM MEIDAI ATTACHED HIGH SCHOOL. IS N-NANA...
OH, I'M SORRY.
SHE SAID SHE FELT SICK WHEN SHE CAME HOME TODAY. SHE WENT TO STRAIGHT TO BED.
IS THIS URGENT?
S-SICK? SICK HOW?
OH, SHE'S FINE. SHE FELT BETTER LATER. SHE'S ASLEEP NOW.
I...IS THAT SO?
KLIK

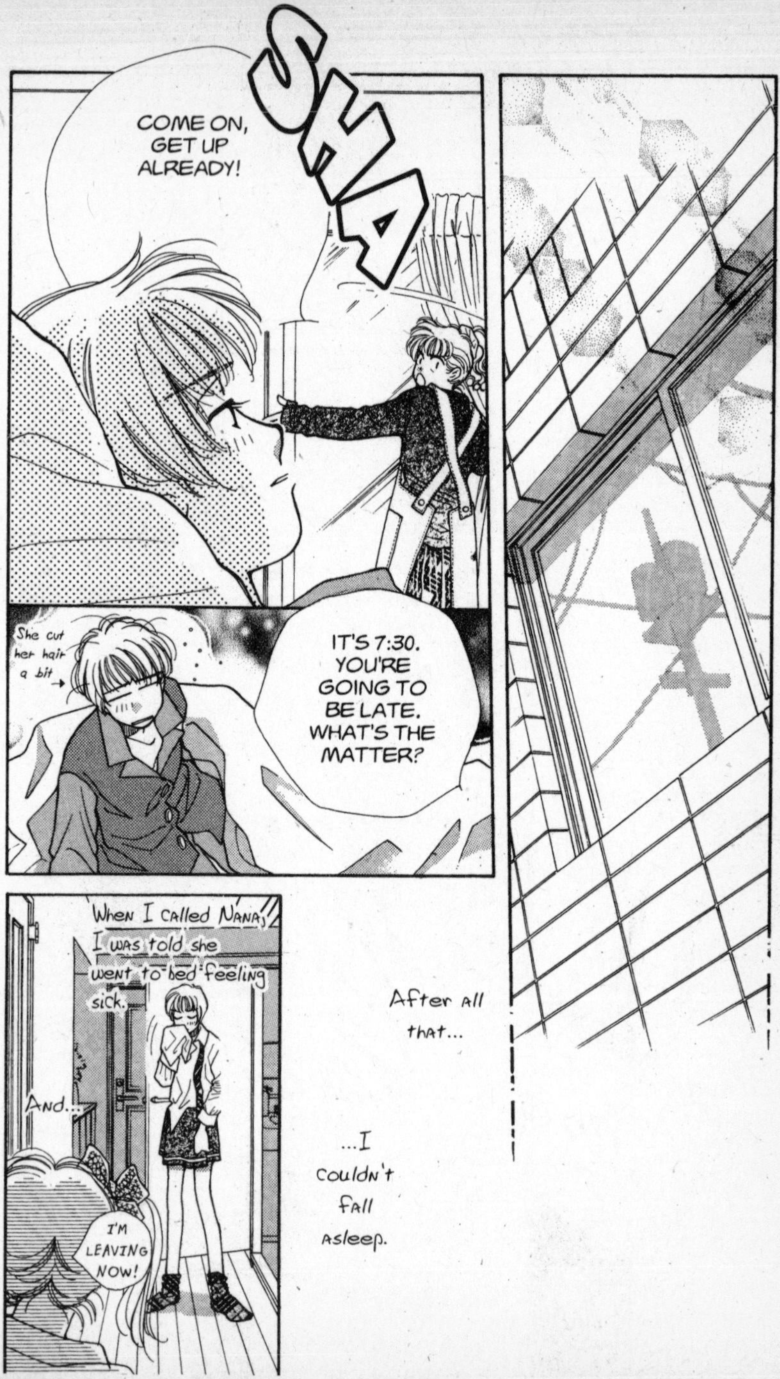
After all that...
...I couldn't fall asleep.
SHA
COME ON, GET UP ALREADY!
IT'S 7:30. YOU'RE GOING TO BE LATE. WHAT'S THE MATTER?
She cut her hair a bit
When I called Nana, I was told she went to bed feeling sick.
And...
I'M LEAVING NOW!

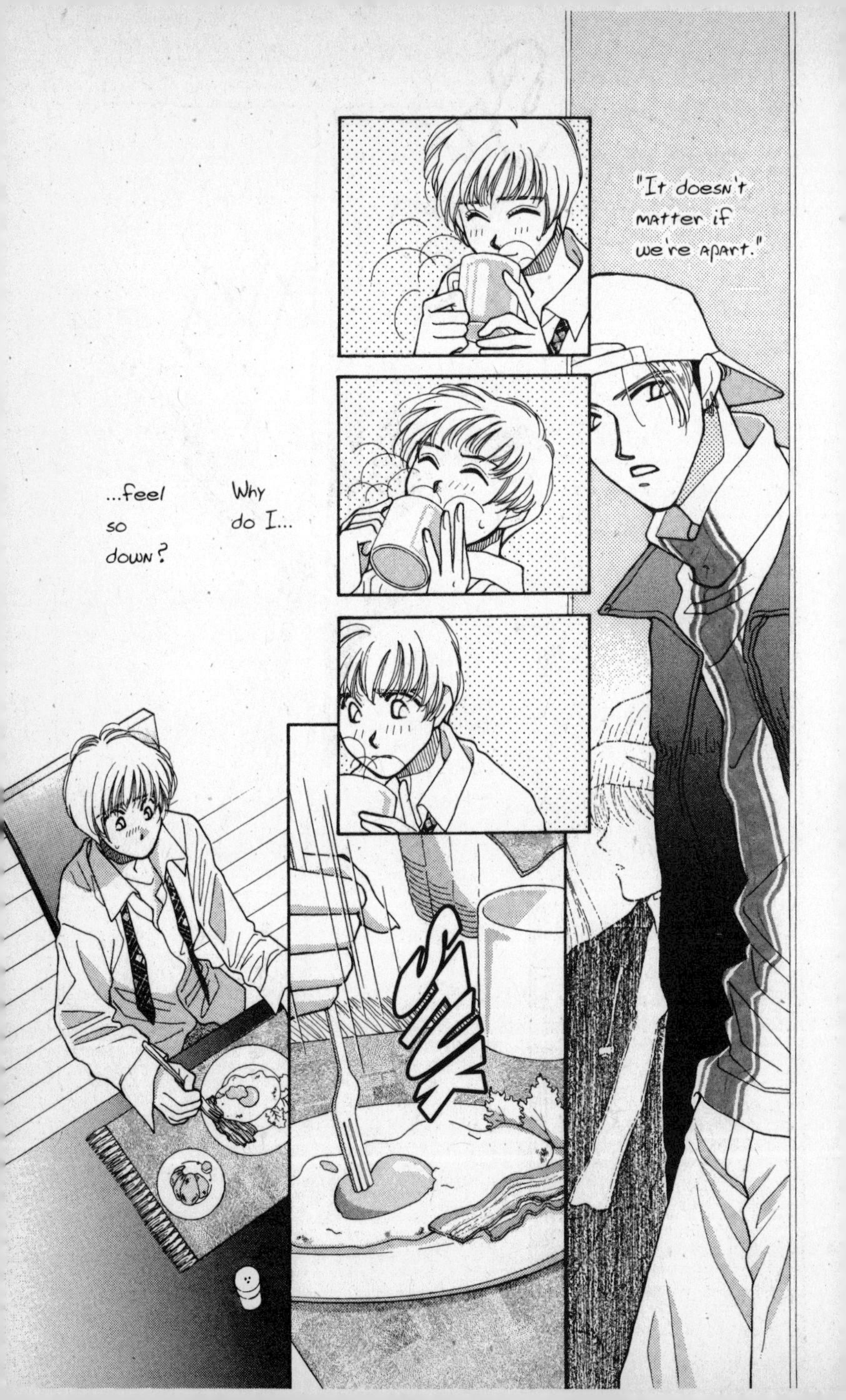
"It doesn't matter if we're apart."
STICK
Why do I...
...feel so down?

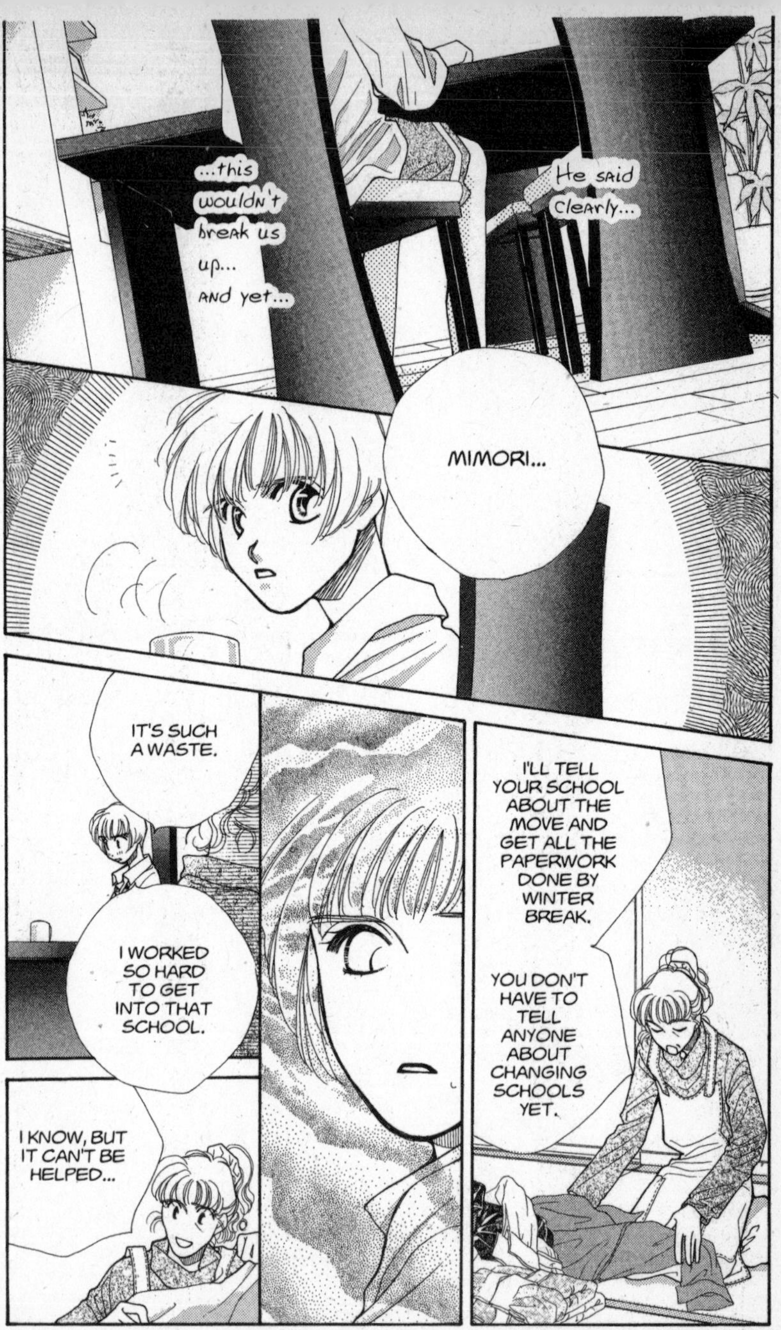
He said clearly...
...this wouldn't break us up... and yet...
MIMORI...
I'LL TELL YOUR SCHOOL ABOUT THE MOVE AND GET ALL THE PAPERWORK DONE BY WINTER BREAK.
YOU DON'T HAVE TO TELL ANYONE ABOUT CHANGING SCHOOLS YET.
IT'S SUCH A WASTE.
I WORKED SO HARD TO GET INTO THAT SCHOOL.
I KNOW, BUT IT CAN'T BE HELPED...

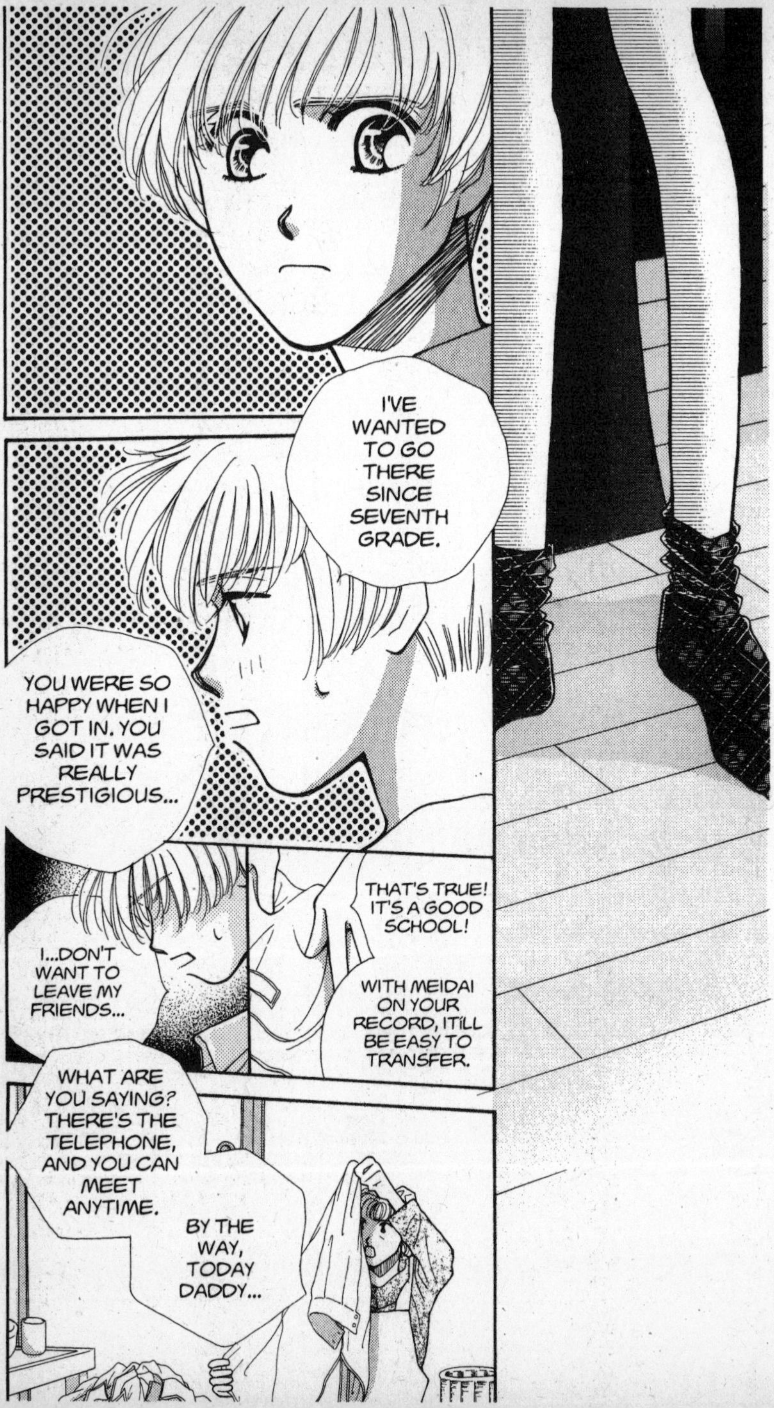
I'VE WANTED TO GO THERE SINCE SEVENTH GRADE.
YOU WERE SO HAPPY WHEN I GOT IN. YOU SAID IT WAS REALLY PRESTIGIOUS...
THAT'S TRUE! IT'S A GOOD SCHOOL!
WITH MEIDAI ON YOUR RECORD, IT'LL BE EASY TO TRANSFER.
I...DON'T WANT TO LEAVE MY FRIENDS...
WHAT ARE YOU SAYING? THERE'S THE TELEPHONE, AND YOU CAN MEET ANYTIME.
BY THE WAY, TODAY DADDY...

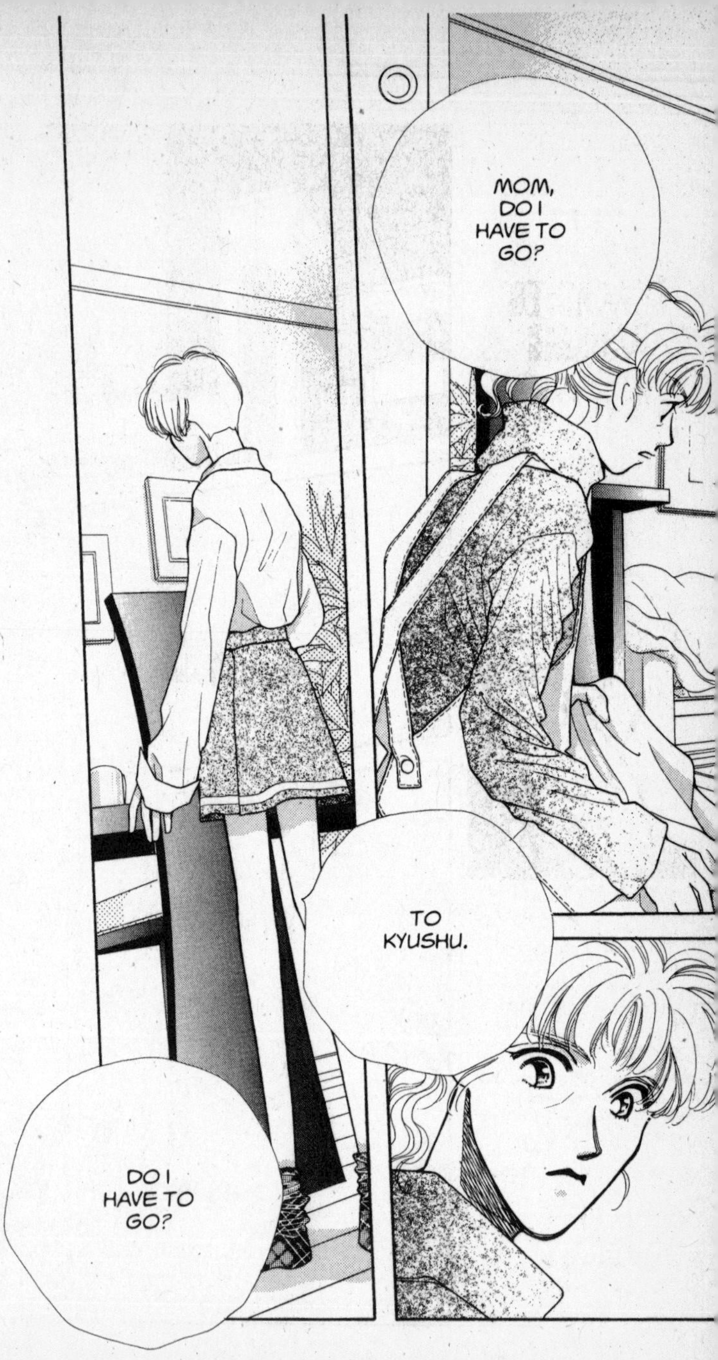
MOM, DO I HAVE TO GO?
TO KYUSHU.
DO I HAVE TO GO?

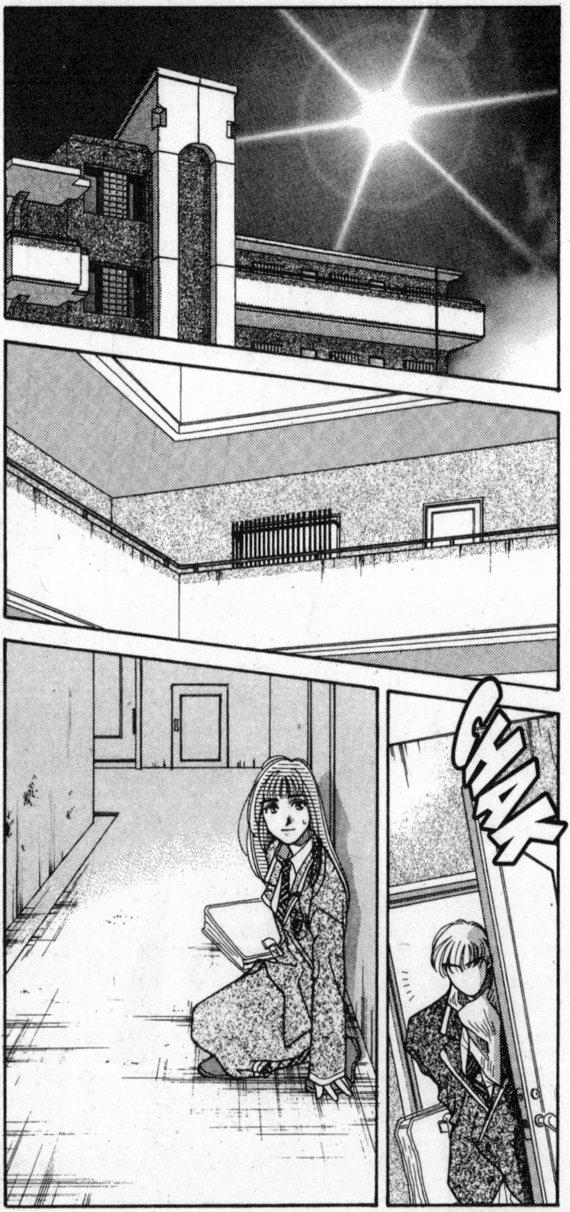
CHAK

CHARACTER RANKING

NO, 2 661 POINTS

• Kazukita Kuniyasu •

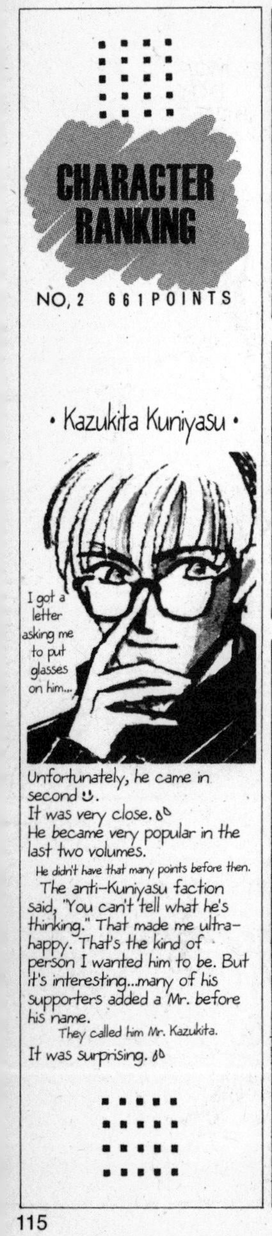
I got a letter asking me to put glasses on him...

Unfortunately, he came in second. It was very close. He became very popular in the last two volumes.

He didn't have that many points before then.

The anti-Kuniyasu faction said, "You can't tell what he's thinking." That made me ultra-happy. That's the kind of person I wanted him to be. But it's interesting...many of his supporters added a Mr. before his name.

They called him Mr. Kazukita.

It was surprising.

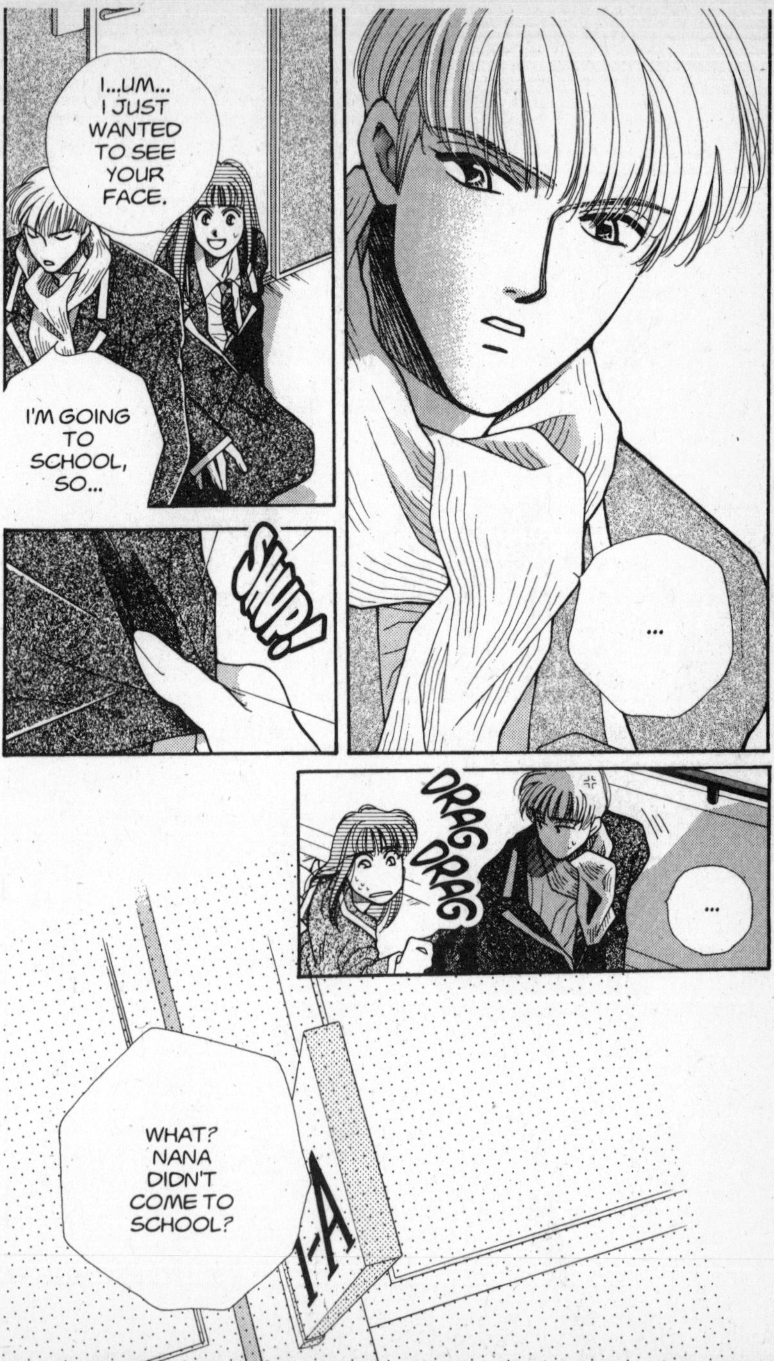
...
I...UM... I JUST WANTED TO SEE YOUR FACE.
I'M GOING TO SCHOOL, SO...
SHUP!
...
DRAG DRAG
1-A
WHAT? NANA DIDN'T COME TO SCHOOL?

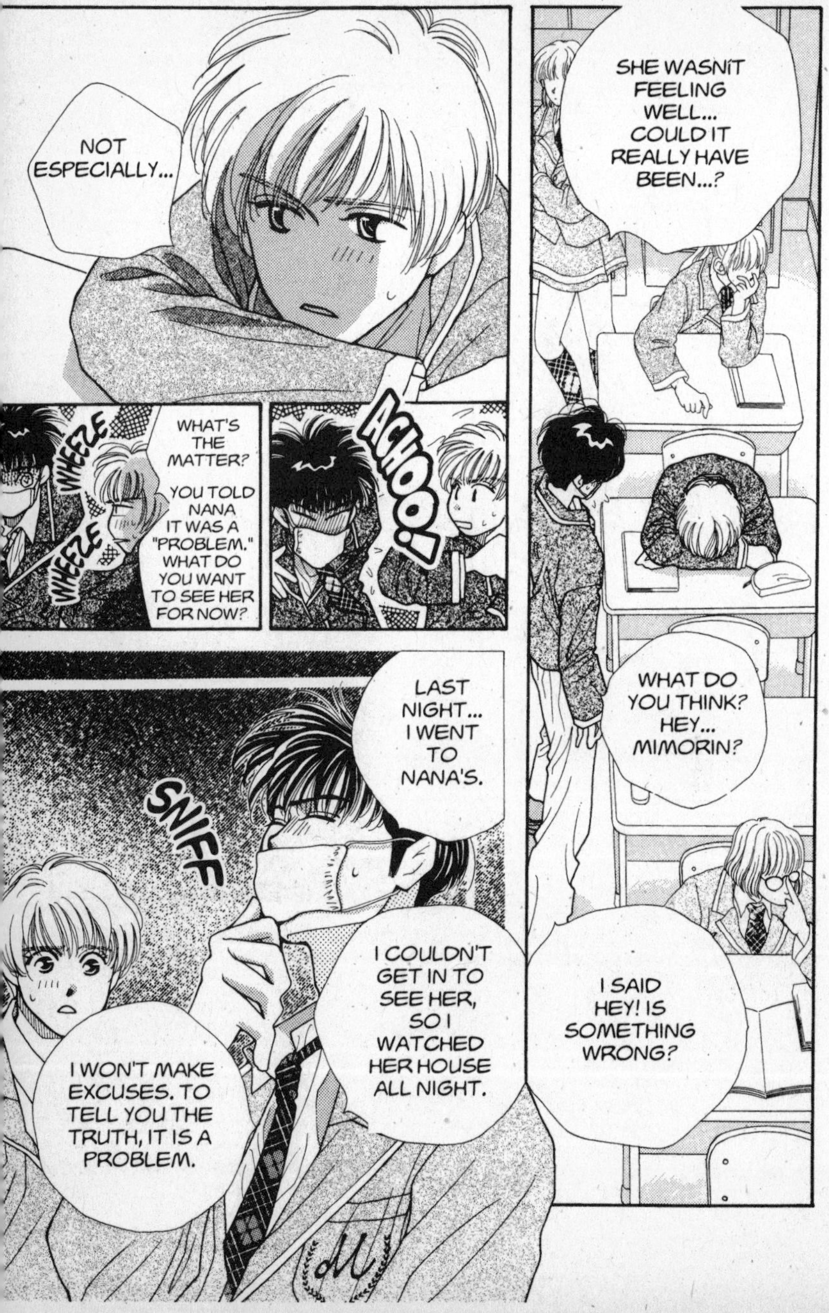
SHE WASN'T FEELING WELL... COULD IT REALLY HAVE BEEN...?
WHAT DO YOU THINK? HEY... MIMORIN?
I SAID HEY! IS SOMETHING WRONG?
NOT ESPECIALLY...
ACHOO!
WHEEZE
WHEEZE
WHAT'S THE MATTER?
YOU TOLD NANA IT WAS A "PROBLEM." WHAT DO YOU WANT TO SEE HER FOR NOW?
LAST NIGHT... I WENT TO NANA'S.
SNIFF
I COULDN'T GET IN TO SEE HER, SO I WATCHED HER HOUSE ALL NIGHT.
I WON'T MAKE EXCUSES. TO TELL YOU THE TRUTH, IT IS A PROBLEM.

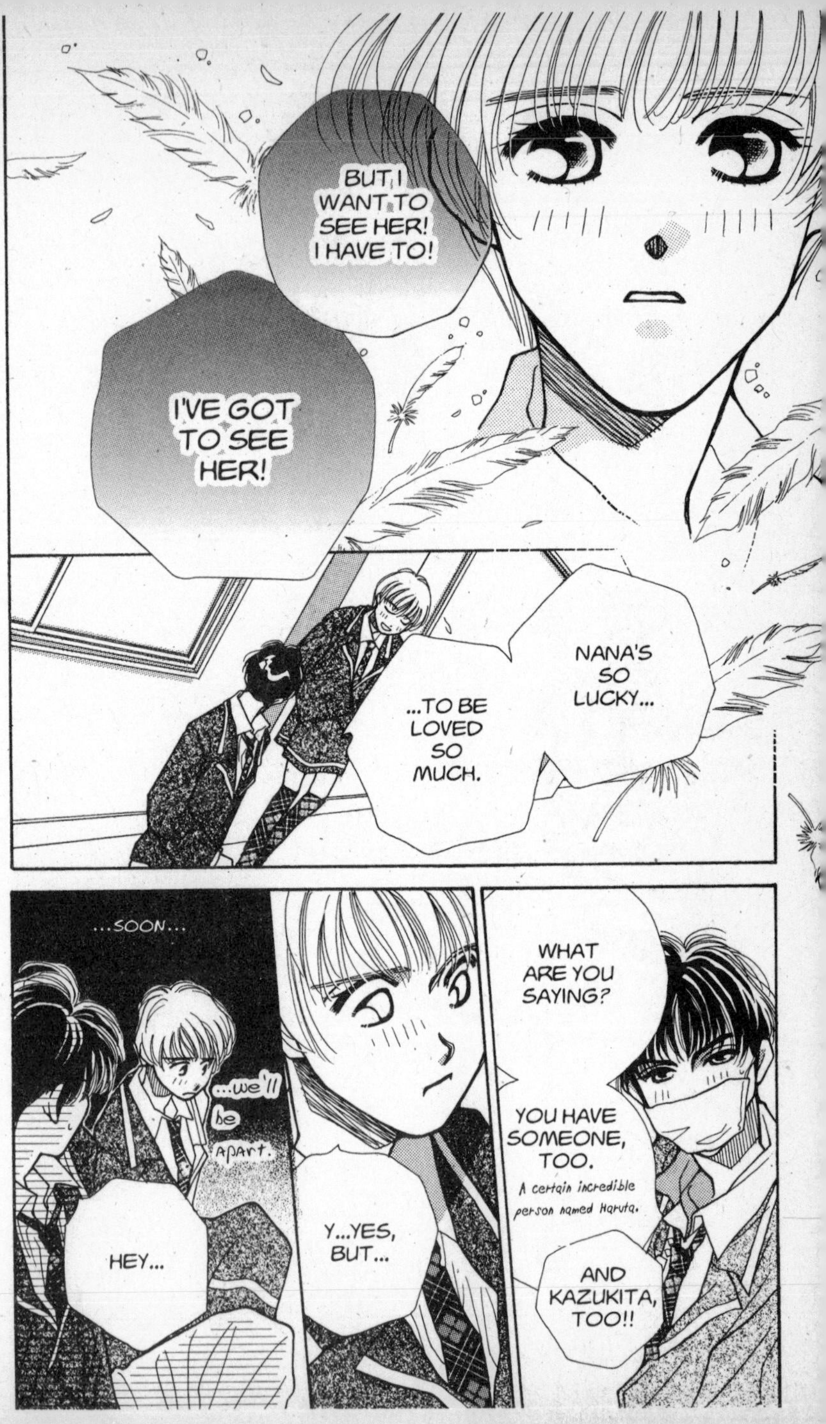
BUT I WANT TO SEE HER! I HAVE TO!
I'VE GOT TO SEE HER!
NANA'S SO LUCKY...
...TO BE LOVED SO MUCH.
WHAT ARE YOU SAYING?
YOU HAVE SOMEONE, TOO.
A certain incredible person named Haruta.
AND KAZUKITA, TOO!!
Y...YES, BUT...
...SOON...
...we'll be apart.
HEY...

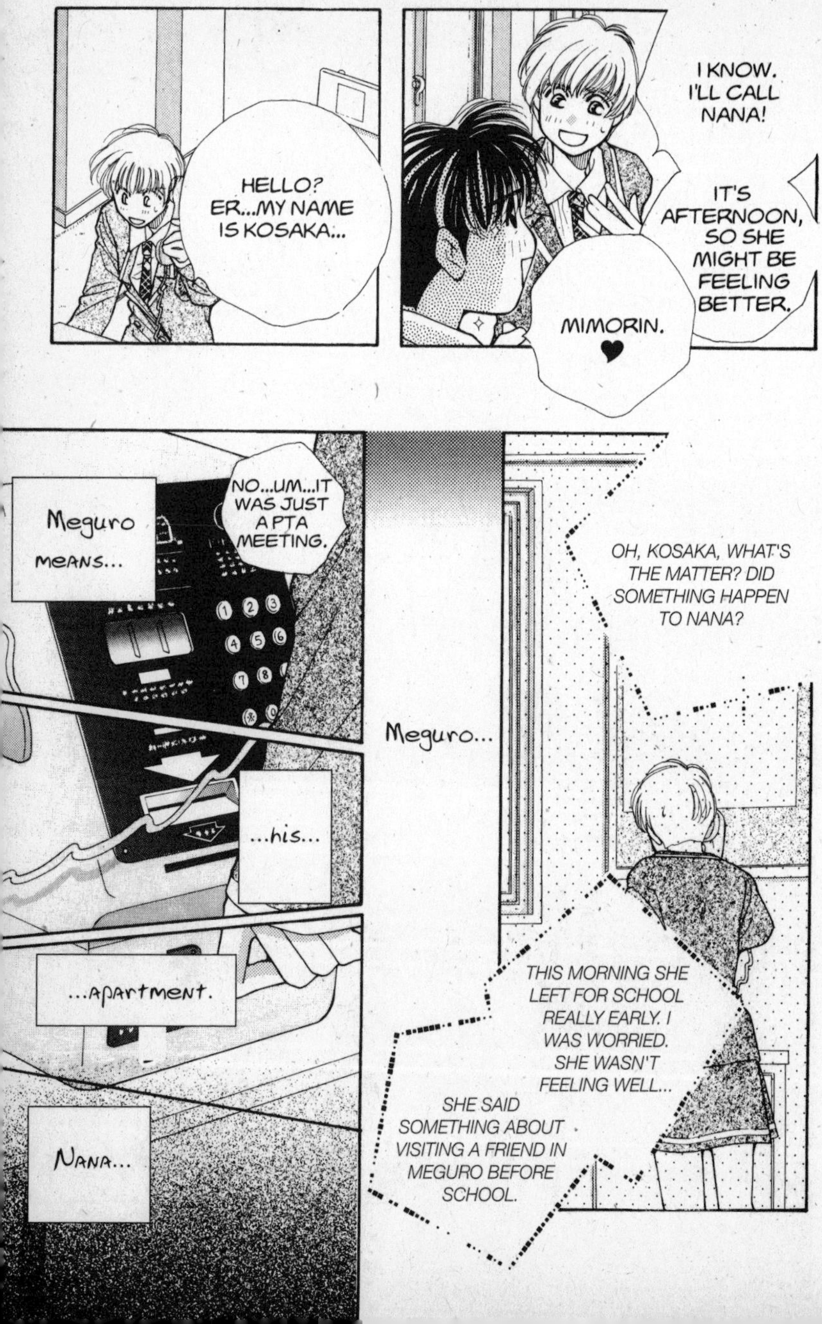
I KNOW. I'LL CALL NANA!
IT'S AFTERNOON, SO SHE MIGHT BE FEELING BETTER.
MIMORIN. ♥
HELLO? ER...MY NAME IS KOSAKA...
OH, KOSAKA, WHAT'S THE MATTER? DID SOMETHING HAPPEN TO NANA?
THIS MORNING SHE LEFT FOR SCHOOL REALLY EARLY. I WAS WORRIED. SHE WASN'T FEELING WELL...
SHE SAID SOMETHING ABOUT VISITING A FRIEND IN MEGURO BEFORE SCHOOL.
Meguro...
NO...UM...IT WAS JUST A PTA MEETING.
Meguro means...
...his...
...apartment.
Nana...

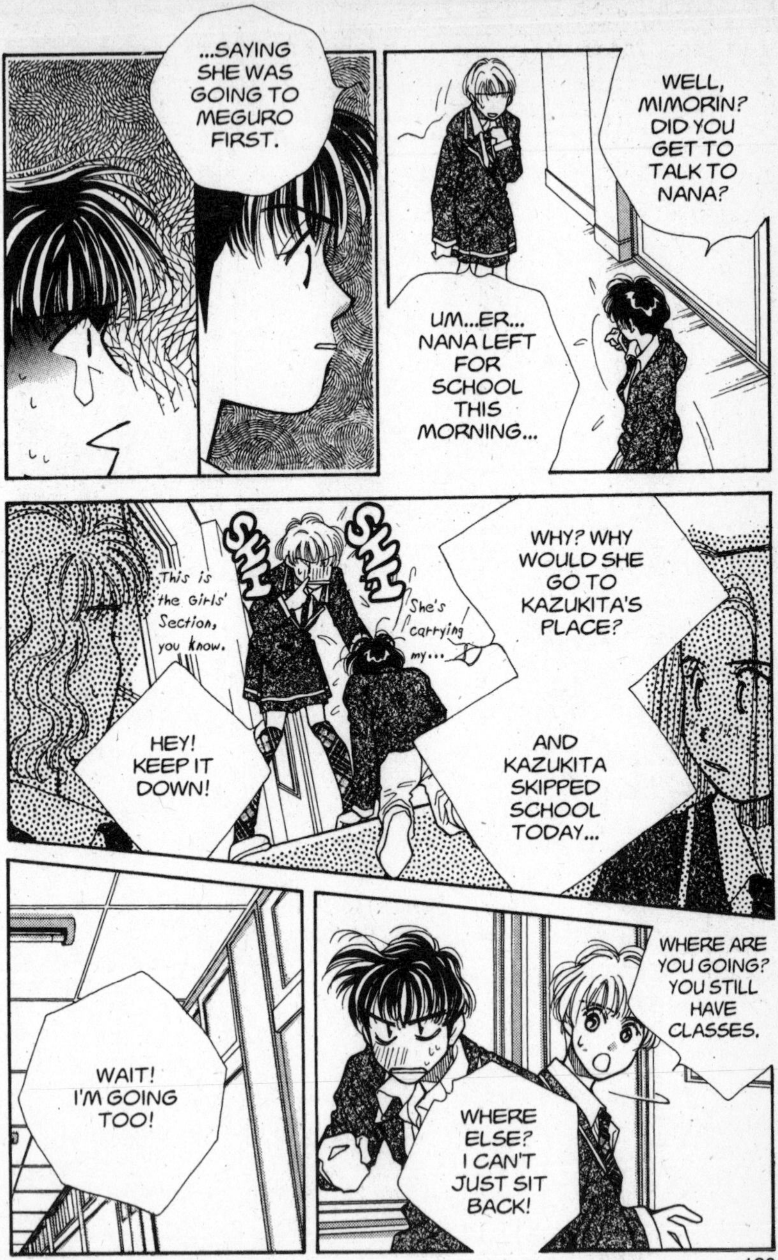
WELL, MIMORIN? DID YOU GET TO TALK TO NANA?
UM...ER... NANA LEFT FOR SCHOOL THIS MORNING...
...SAYING SHE WAS GOING TO MEGURO FIRST.
WHY? WHY WOULD SHE GO TO KAZUKITA'S PLACE?
AND KAZUKITA SKIPPED SCHOOL TODAY...
She's carrying my...
SH
SH
This is the Girls' Section, you know.
HEY! KEEP IT DOWN!
WHERE ARE YOU GOING? YOU STILL HAVE CLASSES.
WHERE ELSE? I CAN'T JUST SIT BACK!
WAIT! I'M GOING TOO!

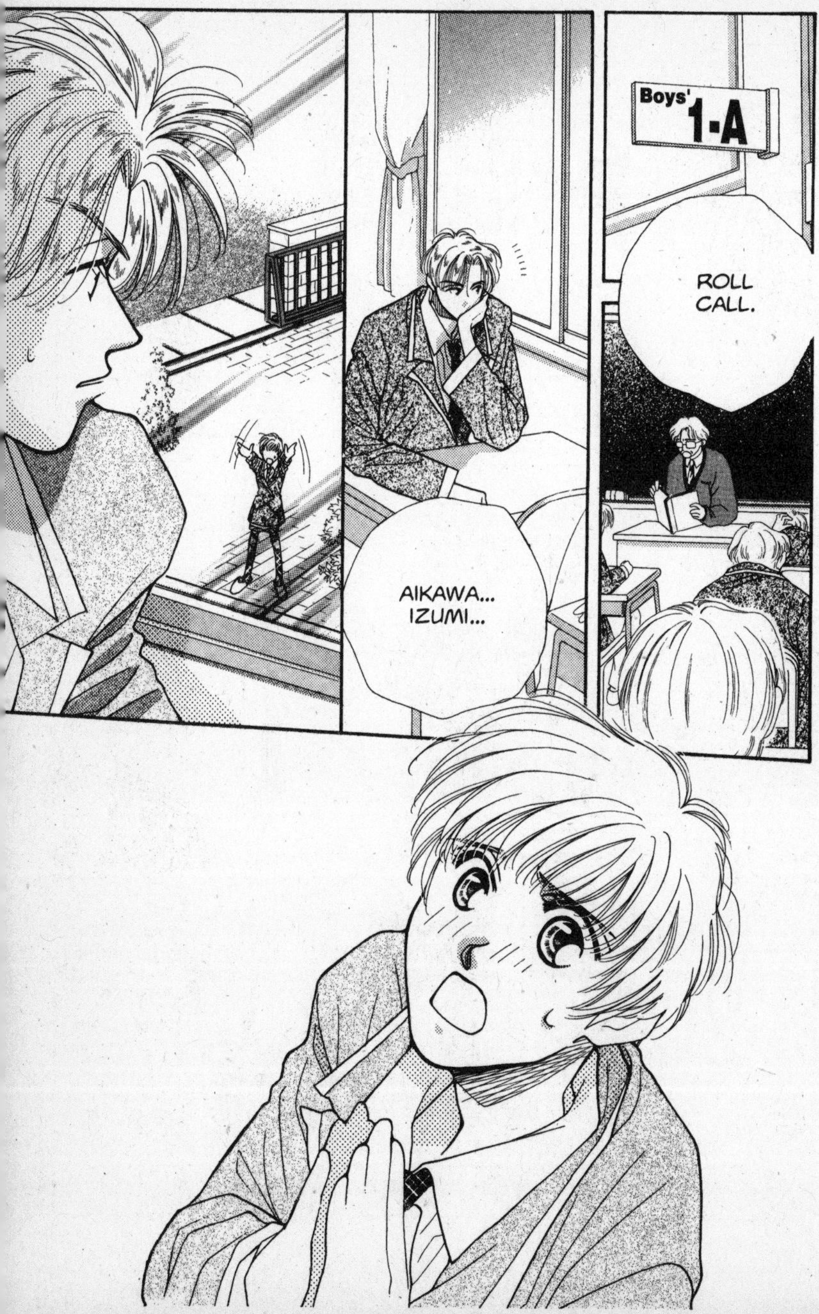
Boys' 1-A
ROLL CALL.
AIKAWA... IZUMI...

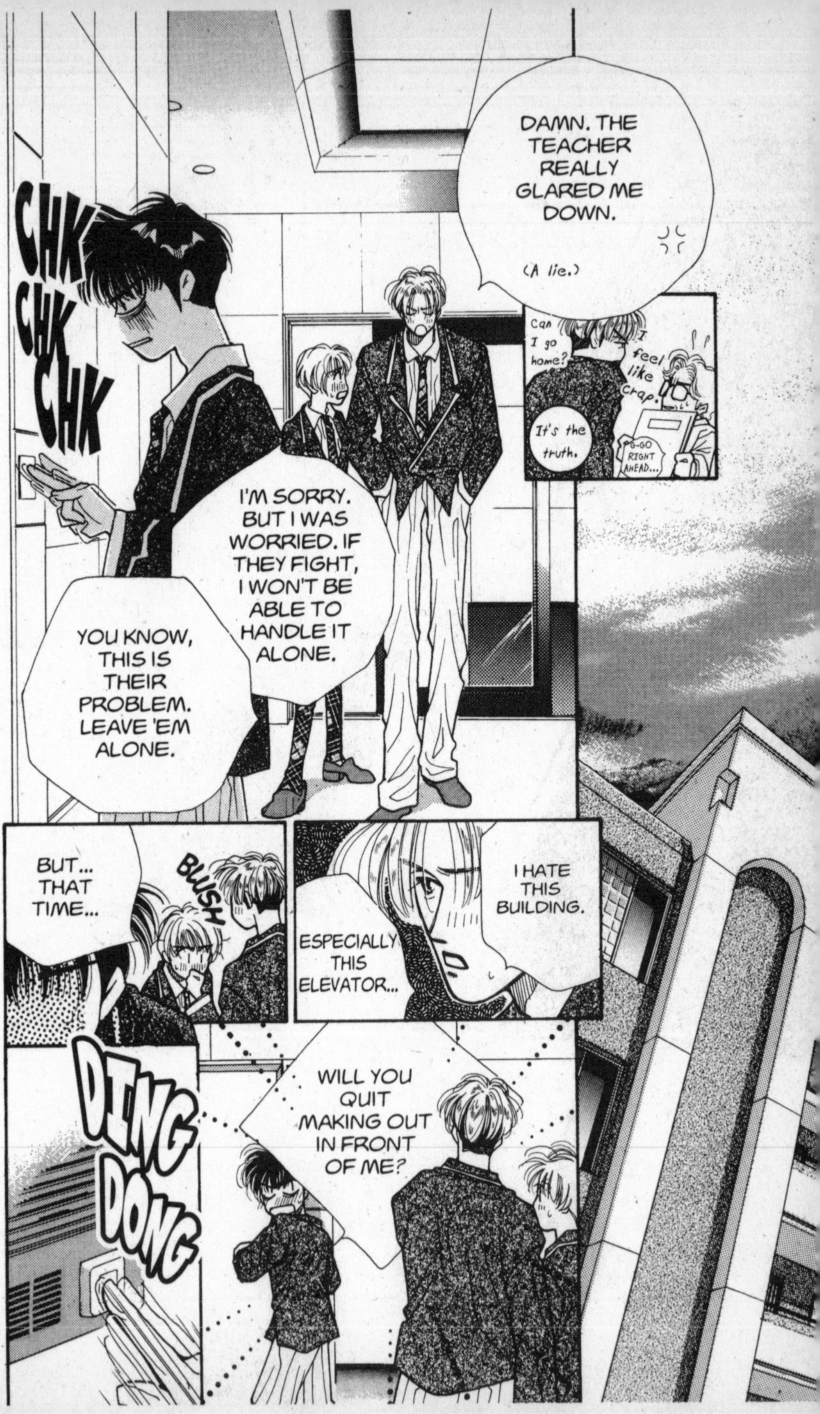
DAMN. THE TEACHER REALLY GLARED ME DOWN.
(A lie.)
Can I go home?
I feel like crap.
It's the truth.
G-GO RIGHT AHEAD...
CHK CHK CHK
I'M SORRY. BUT I WAS WORRIED. IF THEY FIGHT, I WON'T BE ABLE TO HANDLE IT ALONE.
YOU KNOW, THIS IS THEIR PROBLEM. LEAVE 'EM ALONE.
I HATE THIS BUILDING.
ESPECIALLY THIS ELEVATOR...
BUT... THAT TIME...
BLUSH
WILL YOU QUIT MAKING OUT IN FRONT OF ME?
DING DONG

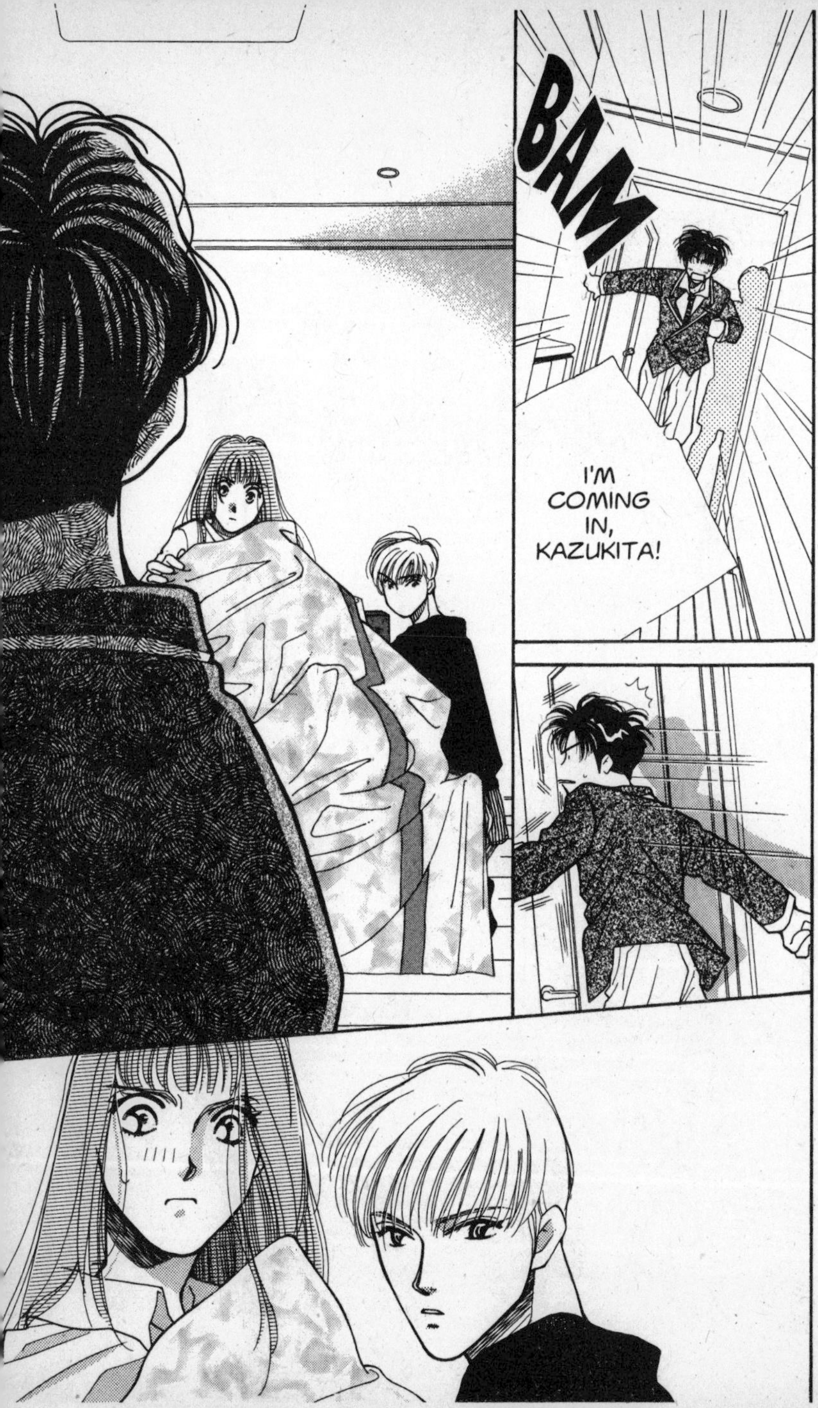
BAM
I'M COMING IN, KAZUKITA!

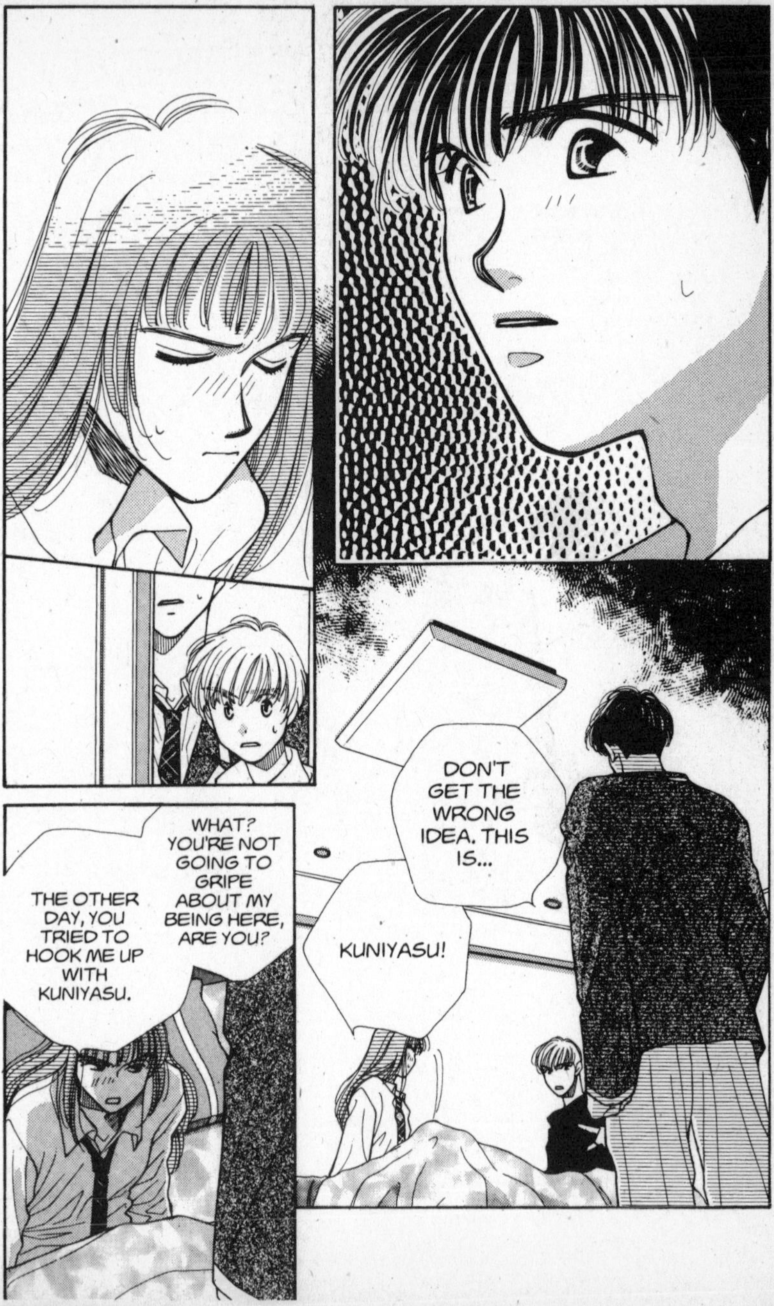
DON'T GET THE WRONG IDEA. THIS IS...
KUNIYASU!
WHAT? YOU'RE NOT GOING TO GRIPE ABOUT MY BEING HERE, ARE YOU?
THE OTHER DAY, YOU TRIED TO HOOK ME UP WITH KUNIYASU.

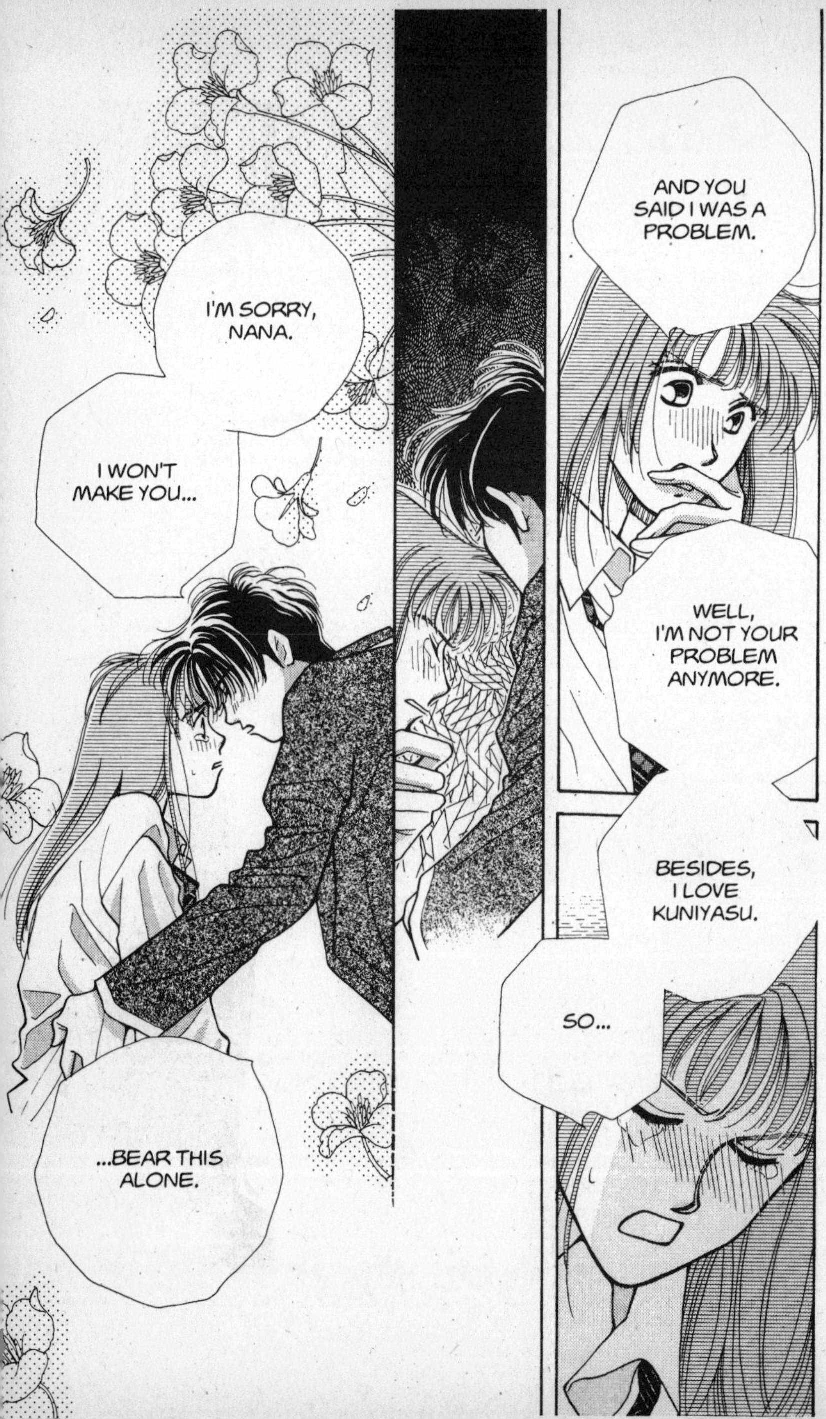
AND YOU SAID I WAS A PROBLEM.
WELL, I'M NOT YOUR PROBLEM ANYMORE.
BESIDES, I LOVE KUNIYASU.
SO...
I'M SORRY, NANA.
I WON'T MAKE YOU...
...BEAR THIS ALONE.

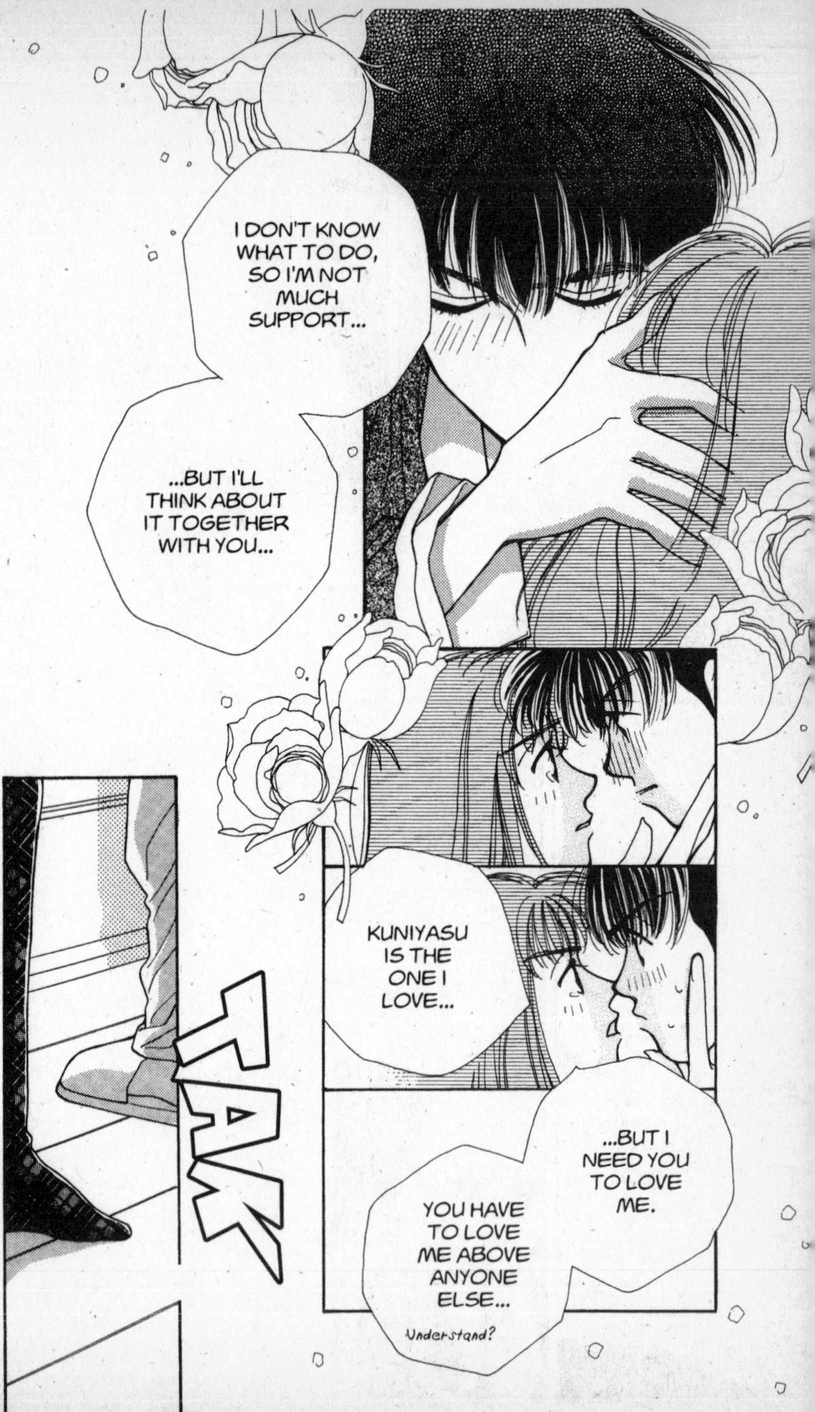
I DON'T KNOW WHAT TO DO, SO I'M NOT MUCH SUPPORT...
...BUT I'LL THINK ABOUT IT TOGETHER WITH YOU...
KUNIYASU IS THE ONE I LOVE...
...BUT I NEED YOU TO LOVE ME.
YOU HAVE TO LOVE ME ABOVE ANYONE ELSE...
Understand?
TAK

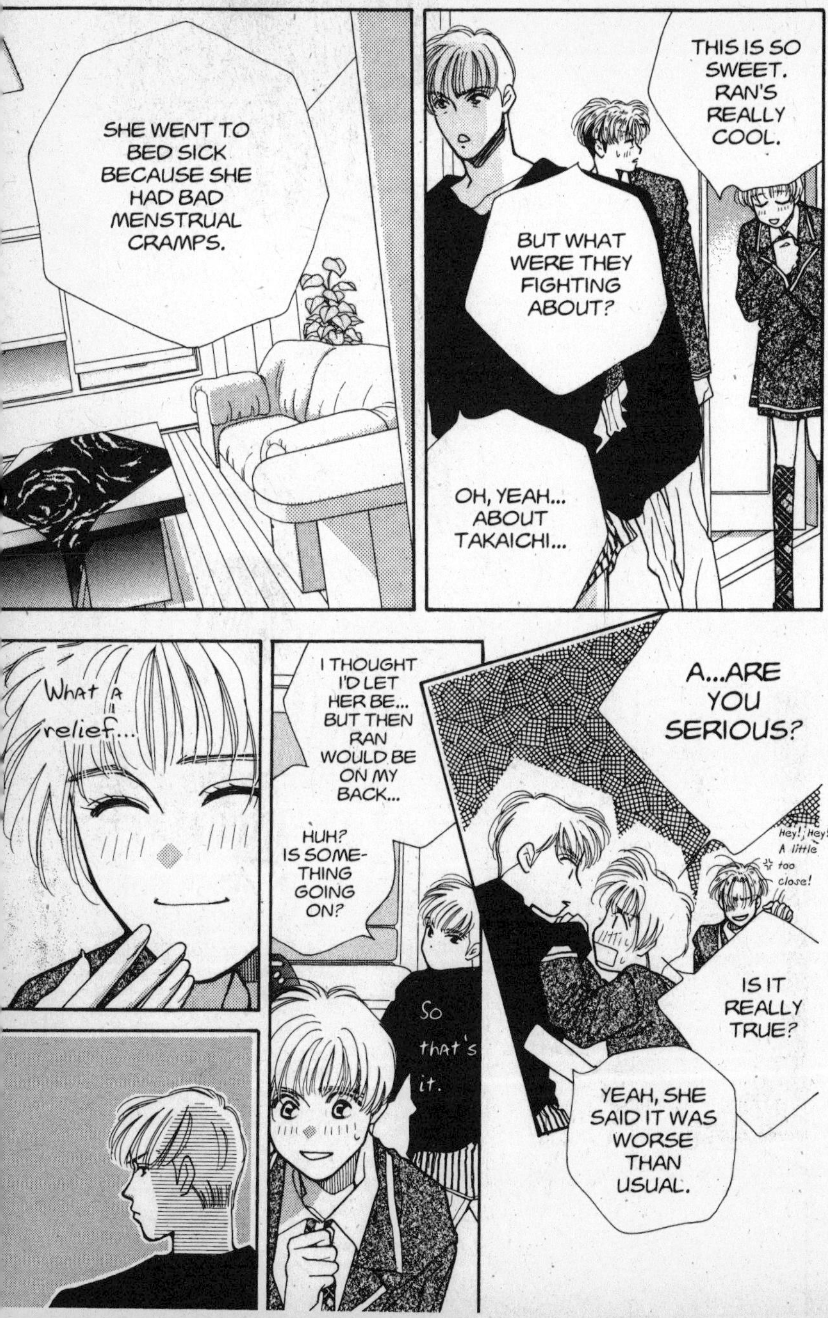
THIS IS SO SWEET. RAN'S REALLY COOL.
BUT WHAT WERE THEY FIGHTING ABOUT?
OH, YEAH... ABOUT TAKAICHI...
SHE WENT TO BED SICK BECAUSE SHE HAD BAD MENSTRUAL CRAMPS.
A...ARE YOU SERIOUS?
Hey! Hey! A little too close!
IS IT REALLY TRUE?
YEAH, SHE SAID IT WAS WORSE THAN USUAL.
I THOUGHT I'D LET HER BE... BUT THEN RAN WOULD BE ON MY BACK...
HUH? IS SOME-THING GOING ON?
So that's it.
What a relief...

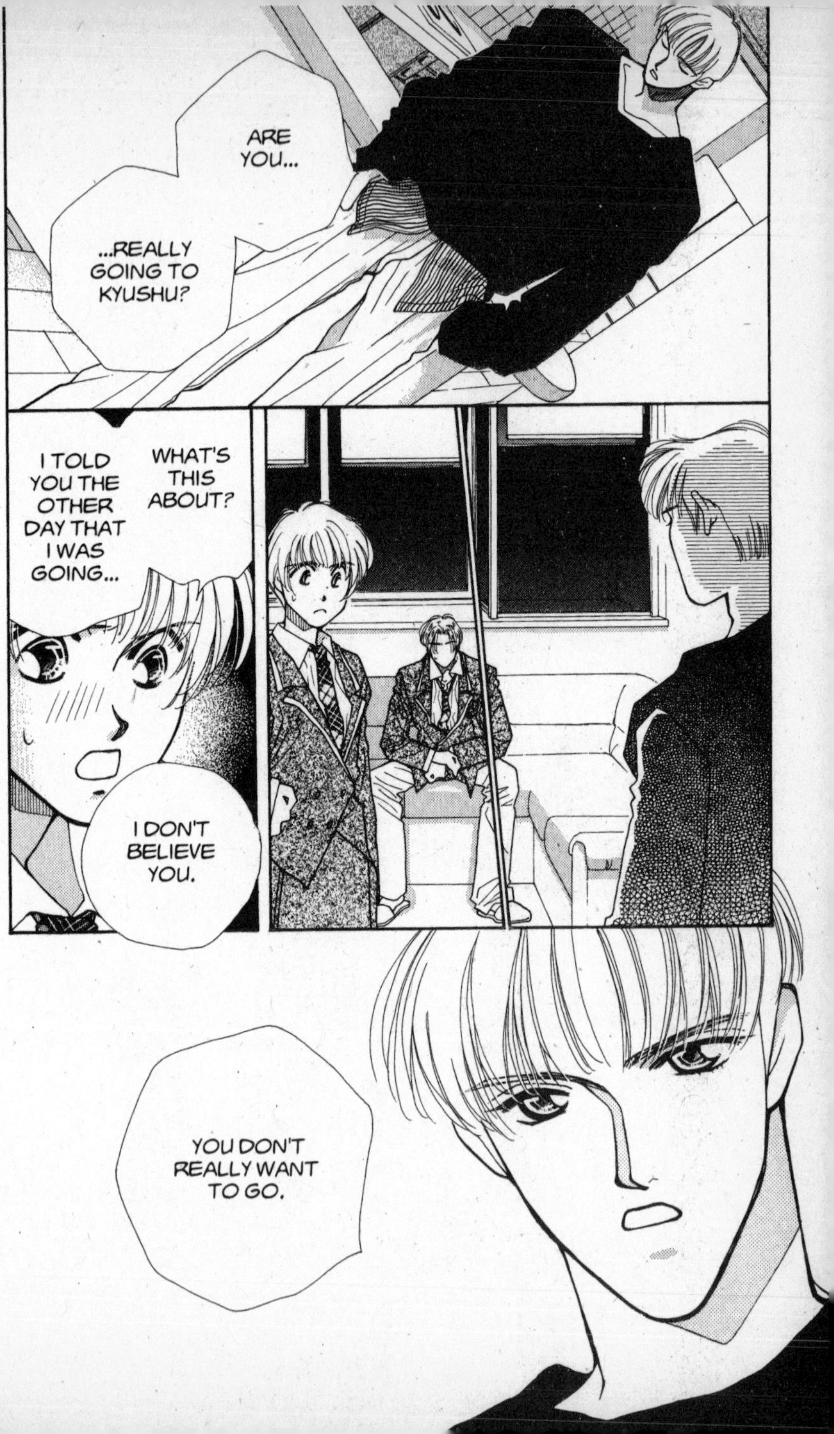
ARE YOU...
...REALLY GOING TO KYUSHU?
WHAT'S THIS ABOUT?
I TOLD YOU THE OTHER DAY THAT I WAS GOING...
I DON'T BELIEVE YOU.
YOU DON'T REALLY WANT TO GO.

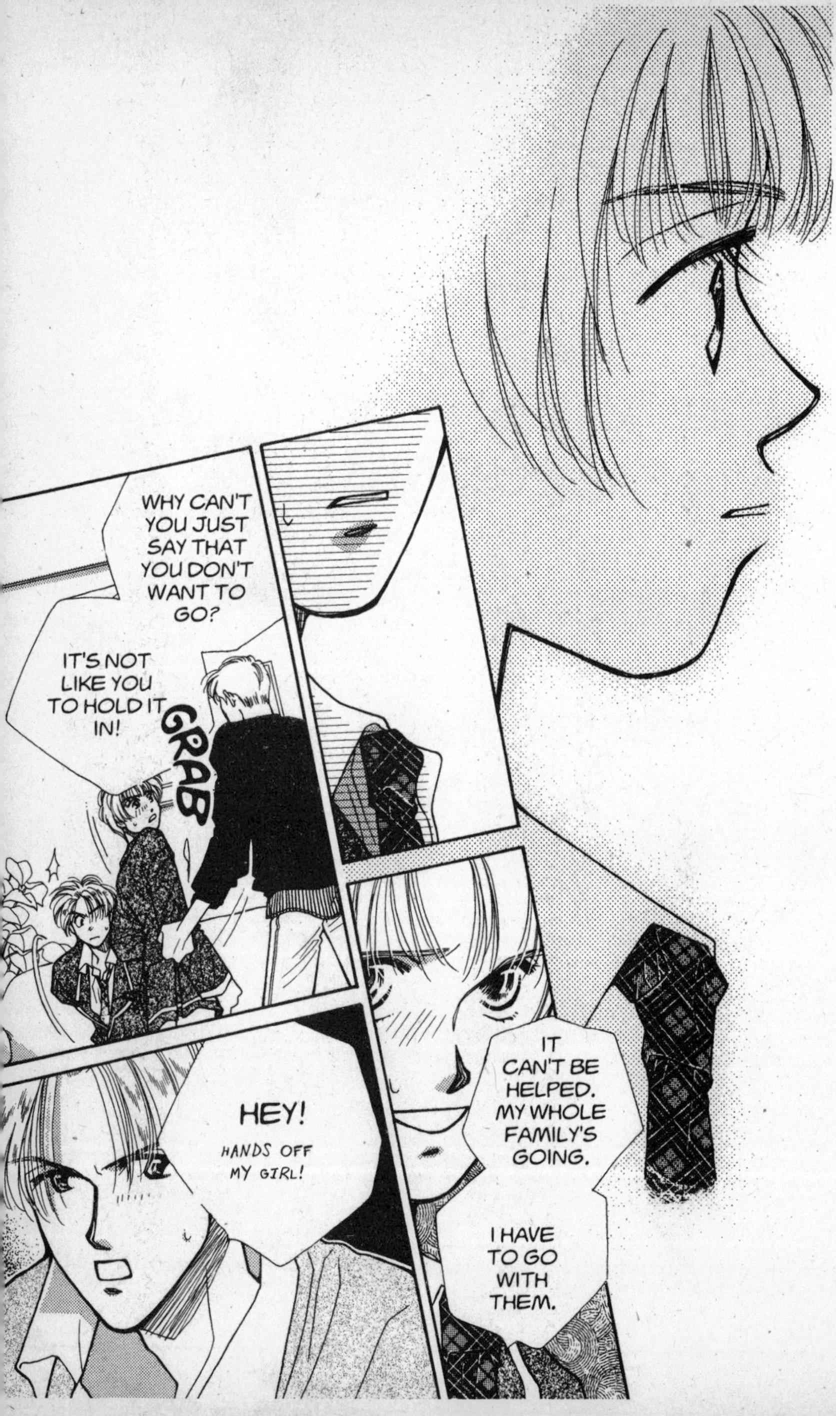
WHY CAN'T YOU JUST SAY THAT YOU DON'T WANT TO GO?
IT'S NOT LIKE YOU TO HOLD IT IN!
GRAB
IT CAN'T BE HELPED. MY WHOLE FAMILY'S GOING.
I HAVE TO GO WITH THEM.
HEY!
HANDS OFF MY GIRL!

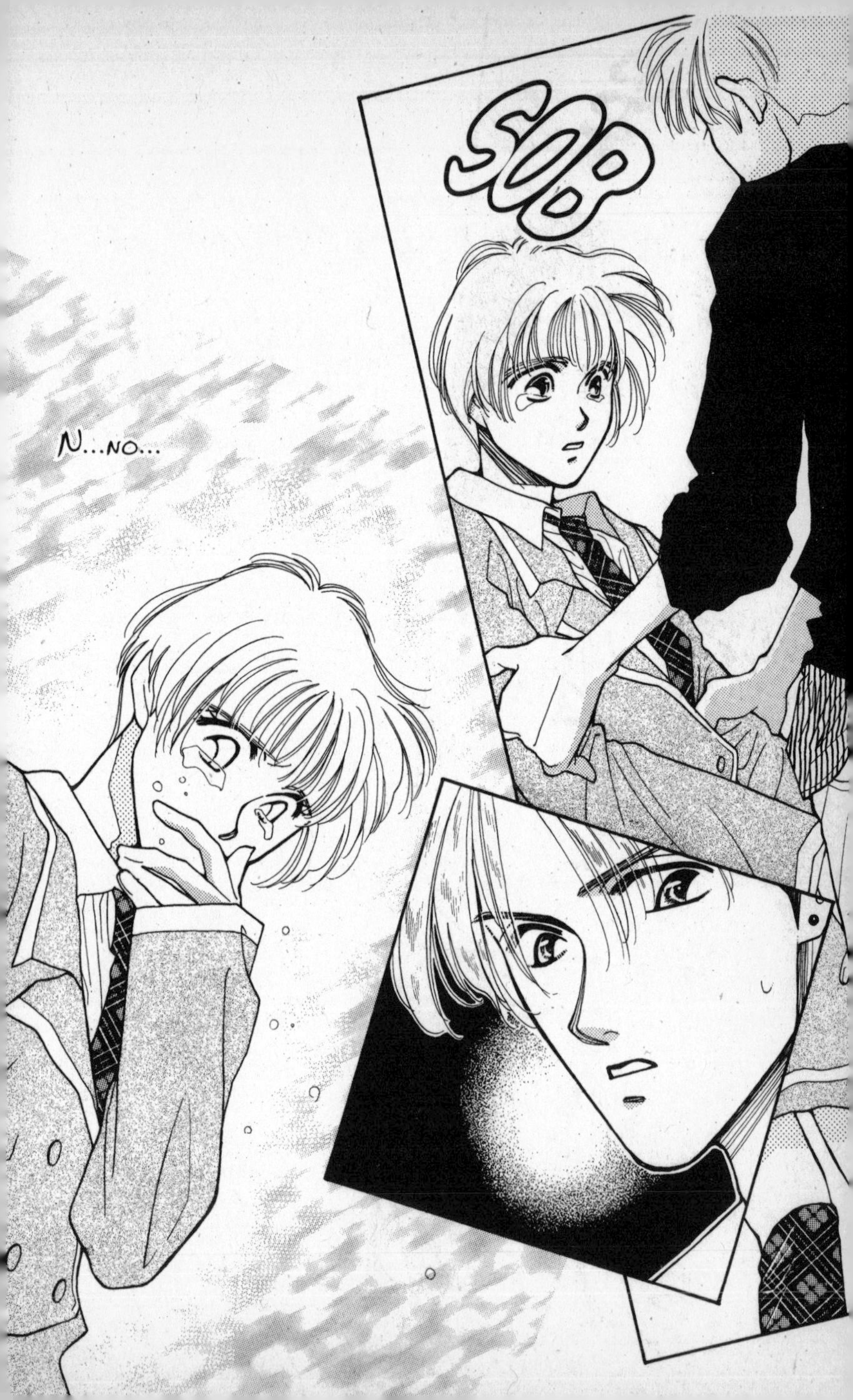
SOB
N...NO...

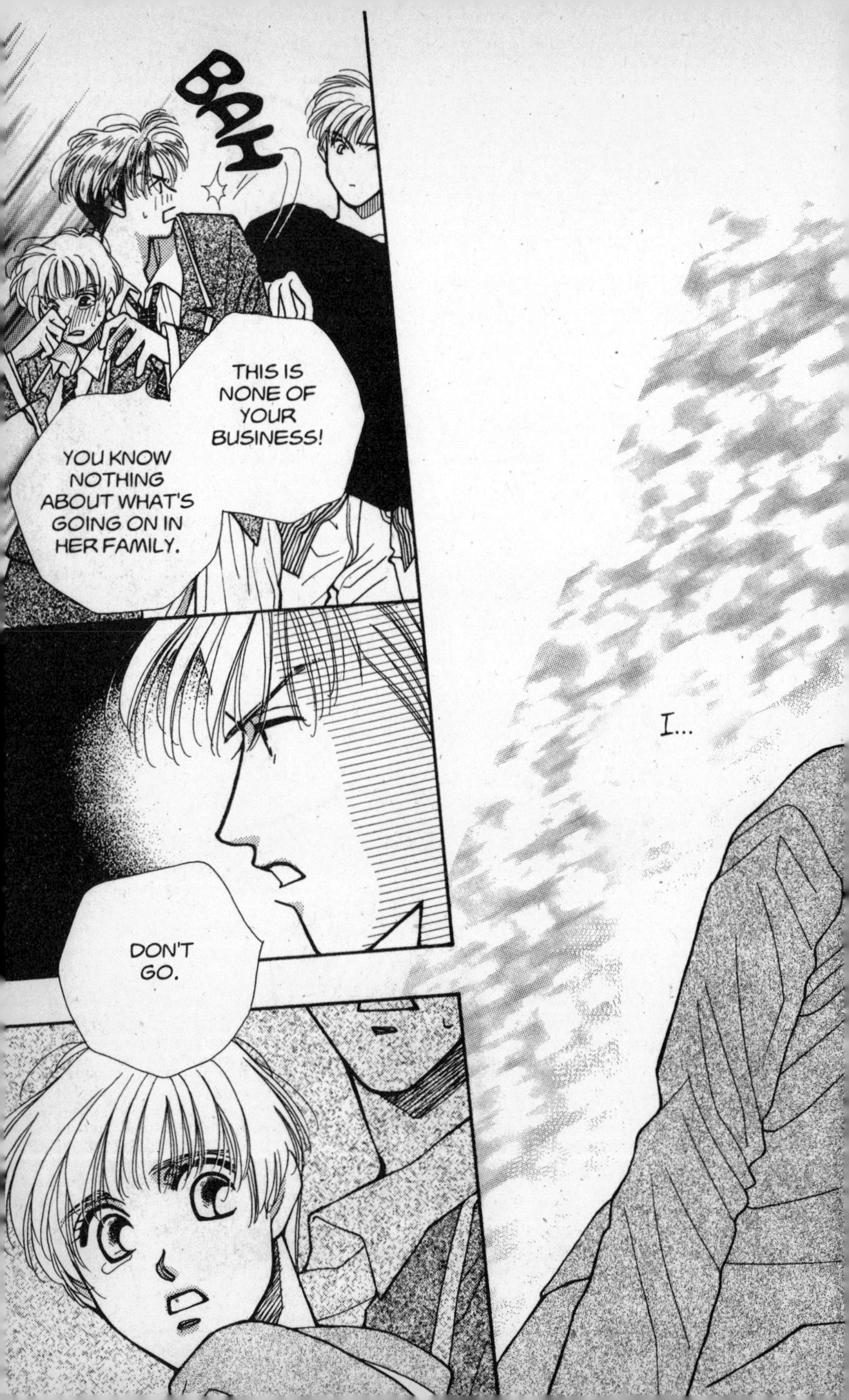
I...
BAH
THIS IS NONE OF YOUR BUSINESS!
YOU KNOW NOTHING ABOUT WHAT'S GOING ON IN HER FAMILY.
DON'T GO.

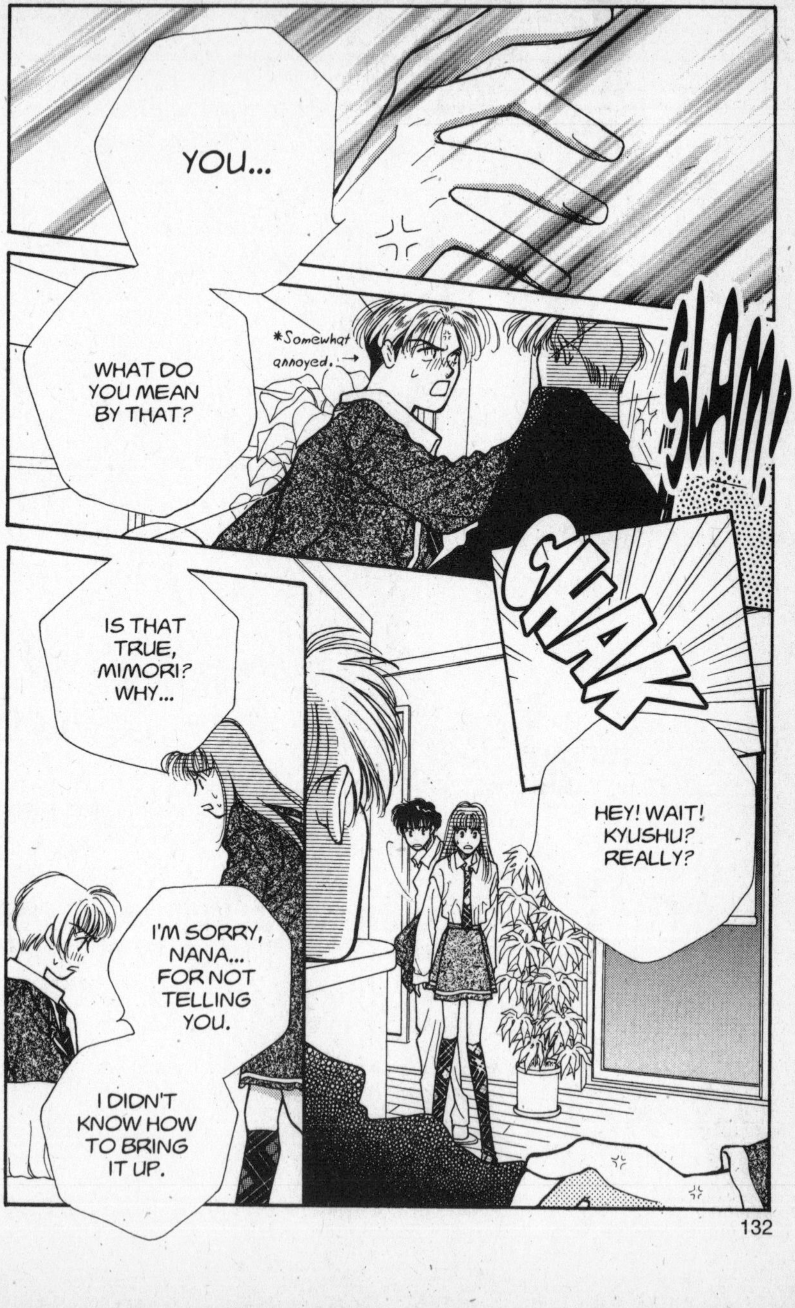
YOU...
SLAM!
*Somewhat annoyed.
WHAT DO YOU MEAN BY THAT?
CHAK
HEY! WAIT! KYUSHU? REALLY?
IS THAT TRUE, MIMORI? WHY...
I'M SORRY, NANA... FOR NOT TELLING YOU.
I DIDN'T KNOW HOW TO BRING IT UP.

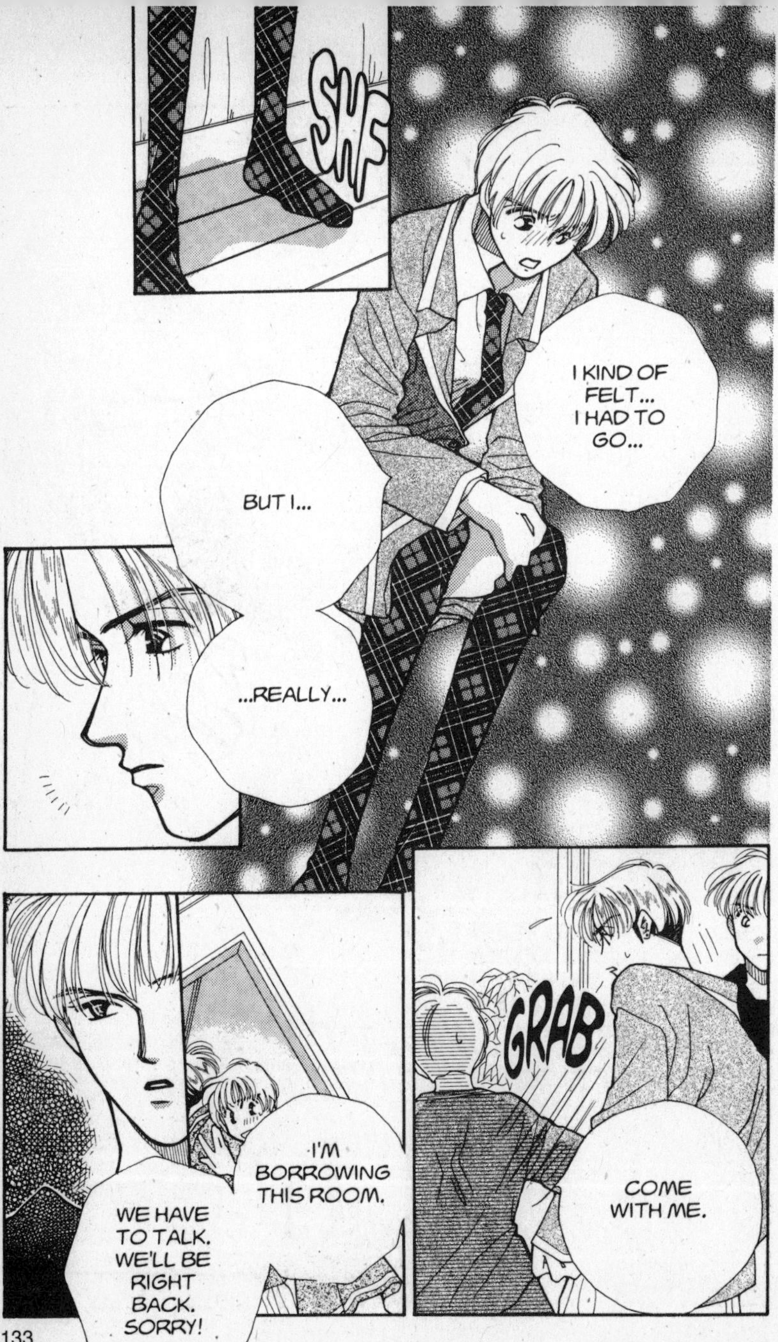
I KIND OF FELT... I HAD TO GO...
BUT I...
...REALLY...
SHF
GRAB
COME WITH ME.
I'M BORROWING THIS ROOM.
WE HAVE TO TALK. WE'LL BE RIGHT BACK. SORRY!

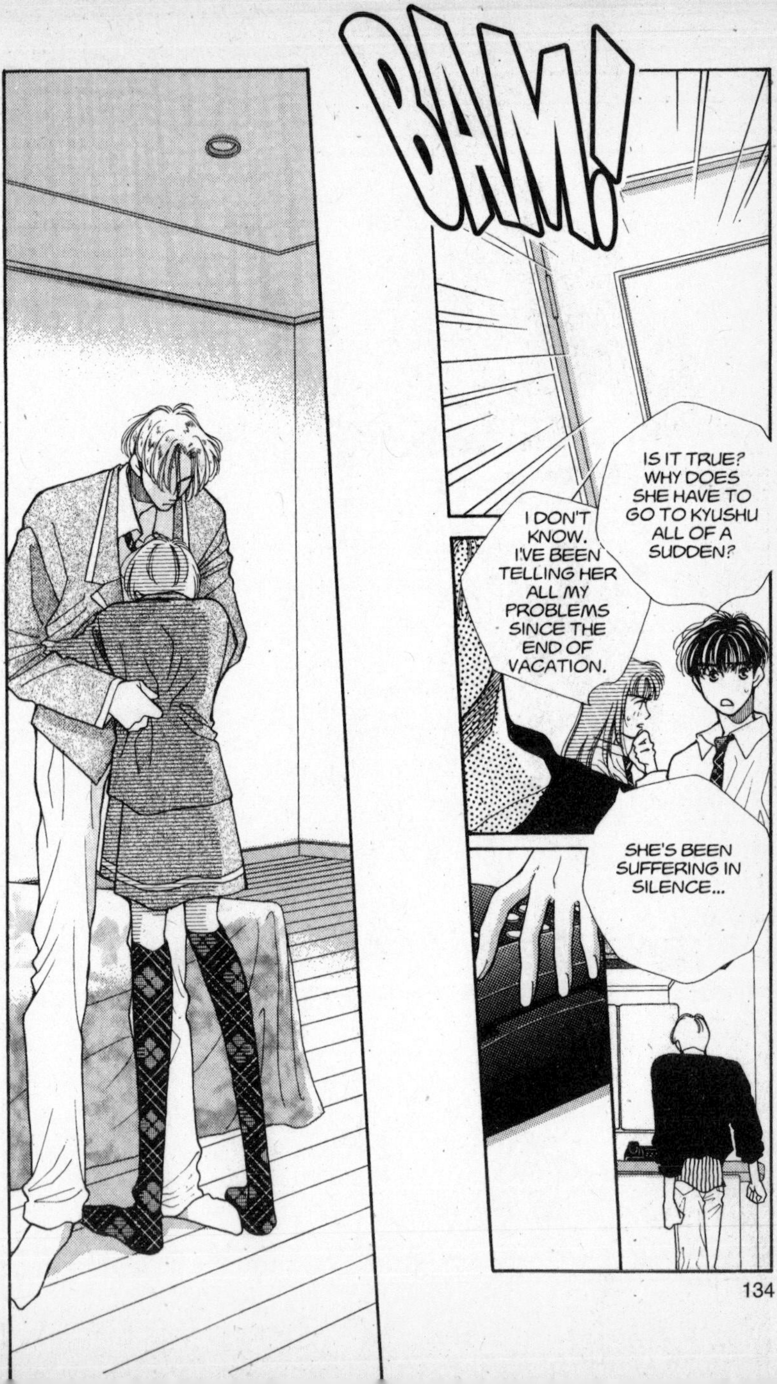
BAM!
IS IT TRUE? WHY DOES SHE HAVE TO GO TO KYUSHU ALL OF A SUDDEN?
I DON'T KNOW. I'VE BEEN TELLING HER ALL MY PROBLEMS SINCE THE END OF VACATION.
SHE'S BEEN SUFFERING IN SILENCE...

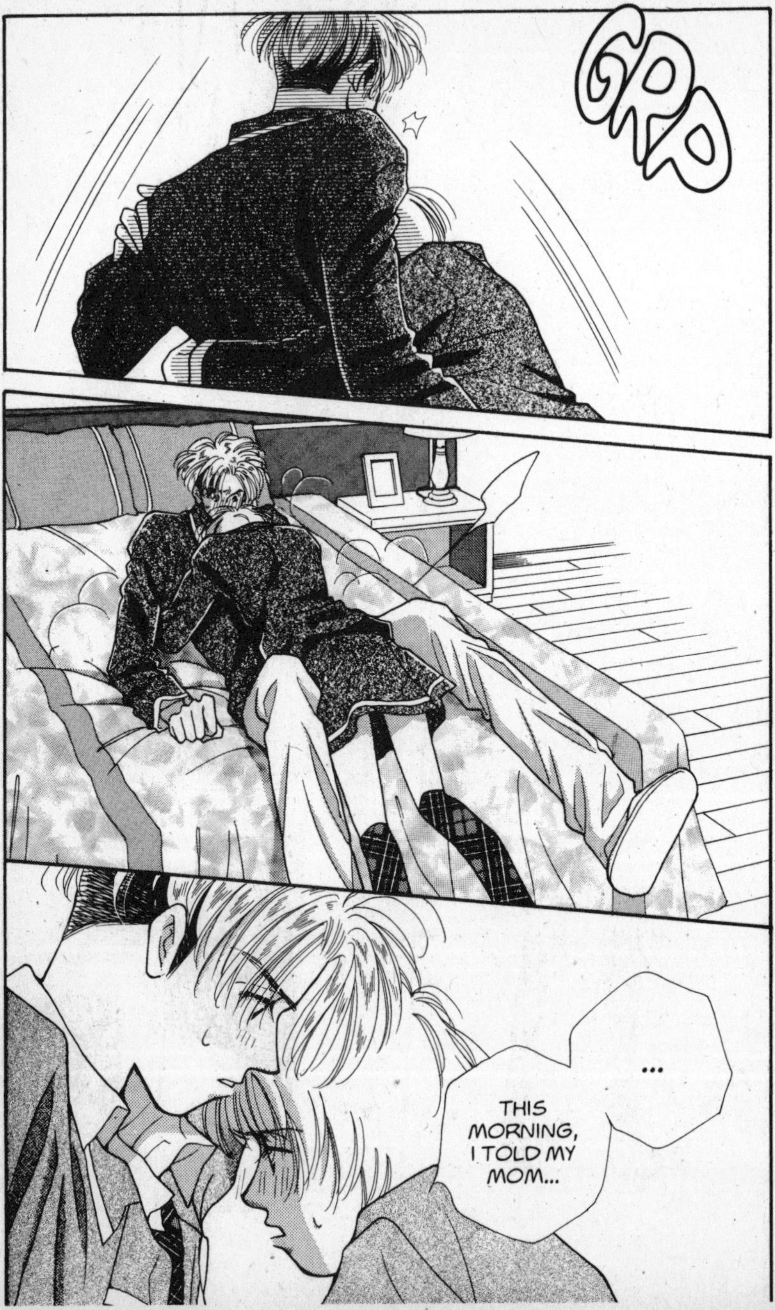
GRP
...
THIS MORNING, I TOLD MY MOM...

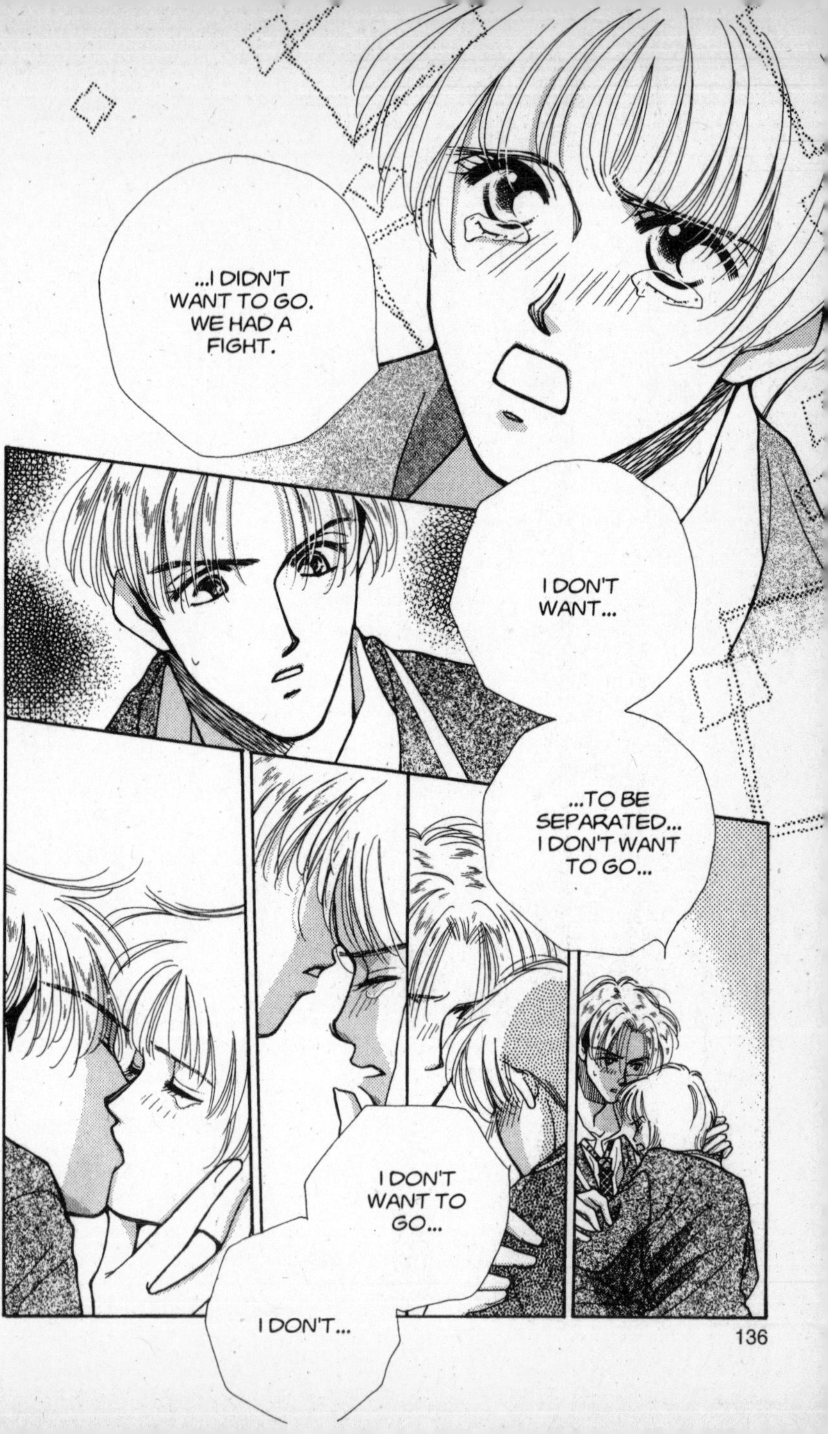
...I DIDN'T WANT TO GO. WE HAD A FIGHT.
I DON'T WANT...
...TO BE SEPARATED... I DON'T WANT TO GO...
I DON'T WANT TO GO...
I DON'T...

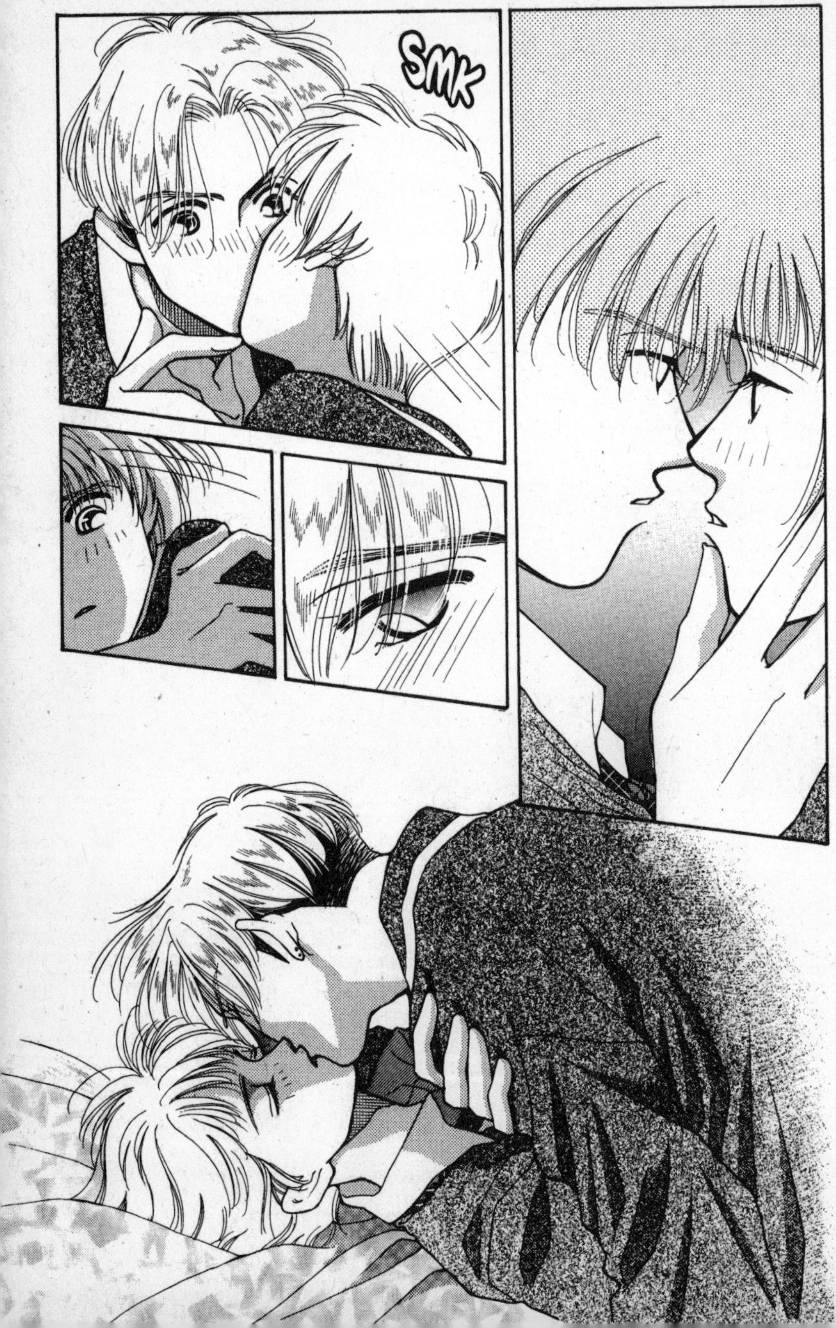
SMK

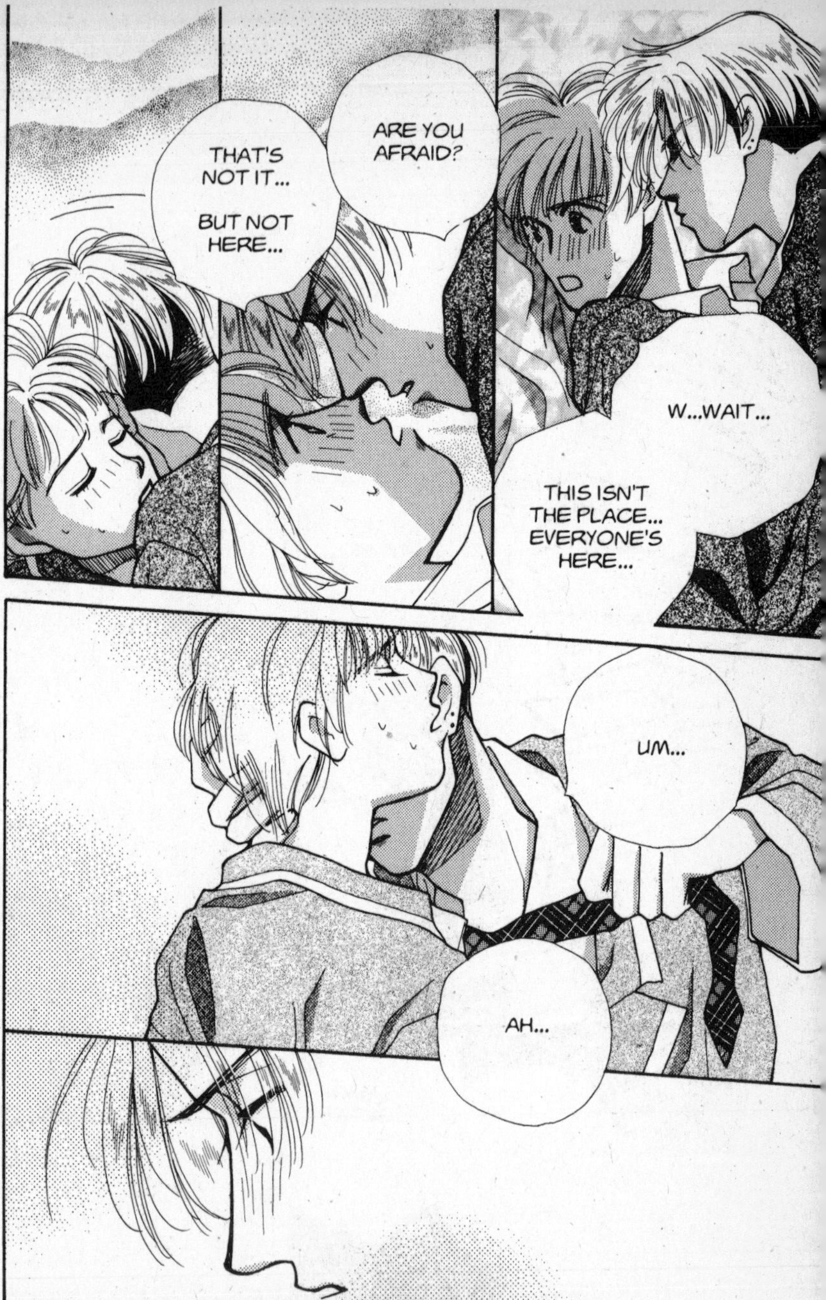
W...WAIT...
THIS ISN'T THE PLACE... EVERYONE'S HERE...
ARE YOU AFRAID?
THAT'S NOT IT...
BUT NOT HERE...
UM...
AH...

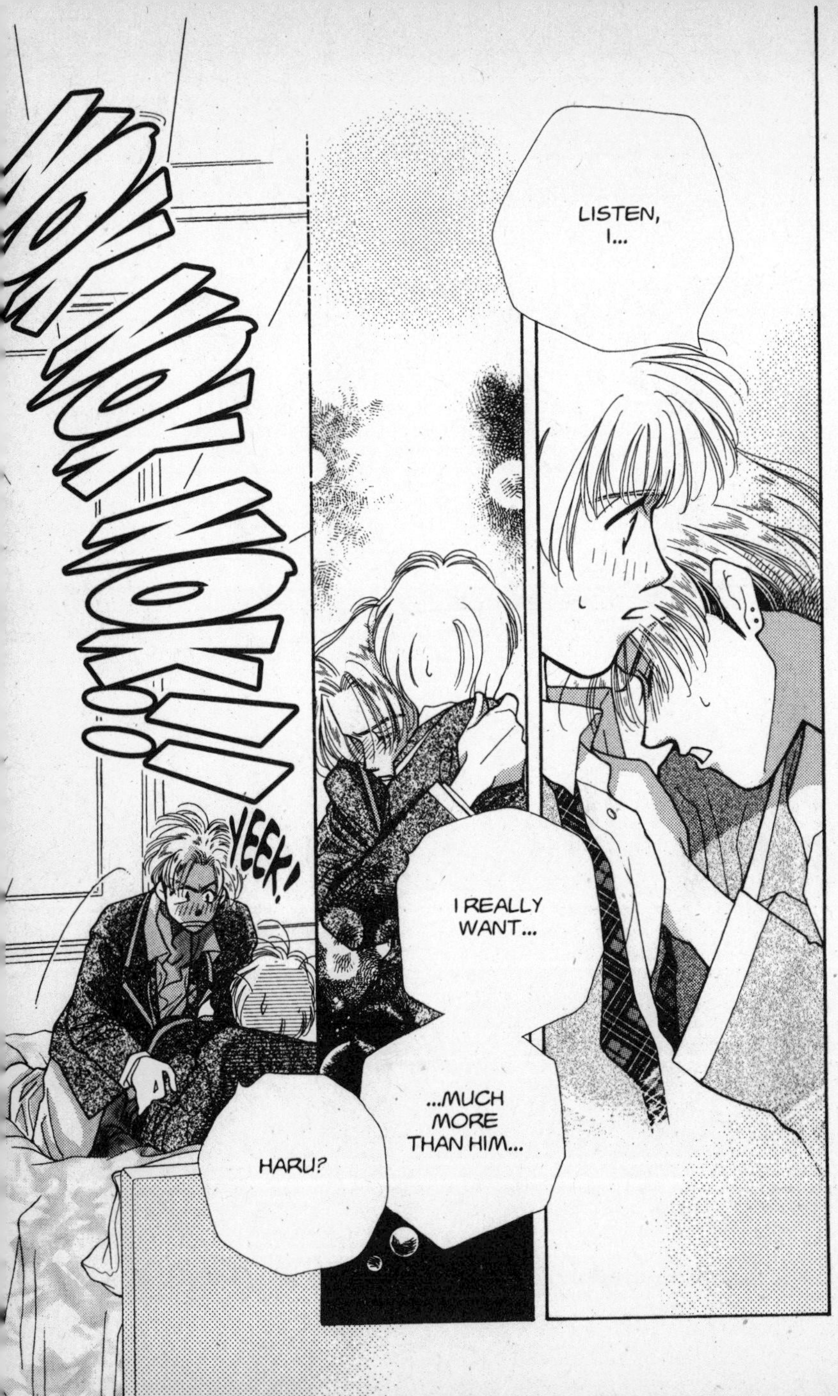
LISTEN, I...
I REALLY WANT...
...MUCH MORE THAN HIM...
HARU?
YEEK!

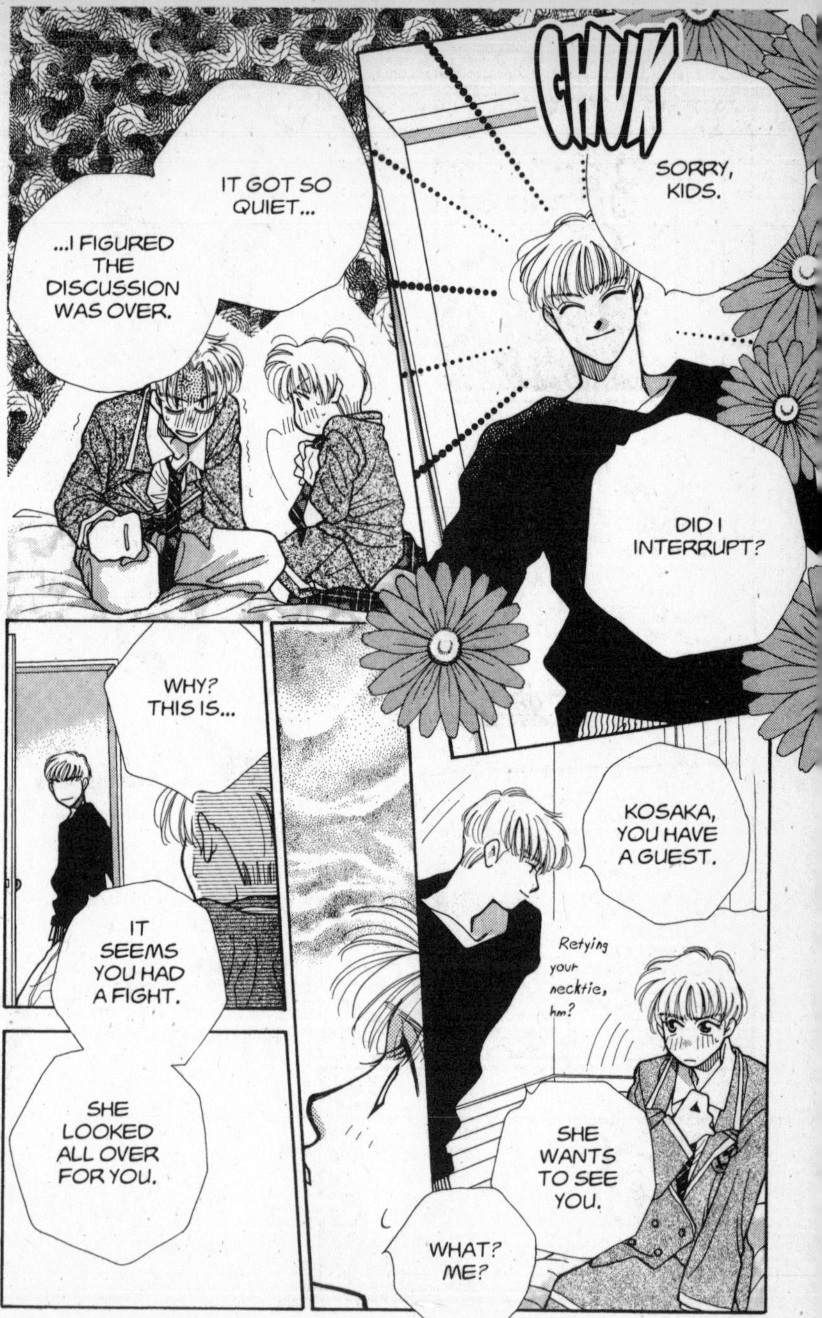
CHUK
SORRY, KIDS.
DID I INTERRUPT?
IT GOT SO QUIET...
...I FIGURED THE DISCUSSION WAS OVER.
KOSAKA, YOU HAVE A GUEST.
Retying your necktie, hm?
SHE WANTS TO SEE YOU.
WHAT? ME?
WHY? THIS IS...
IT SEEMS YOU HAD A FIGHT.
SHE LOOKED ALL OVER FOR YOU.

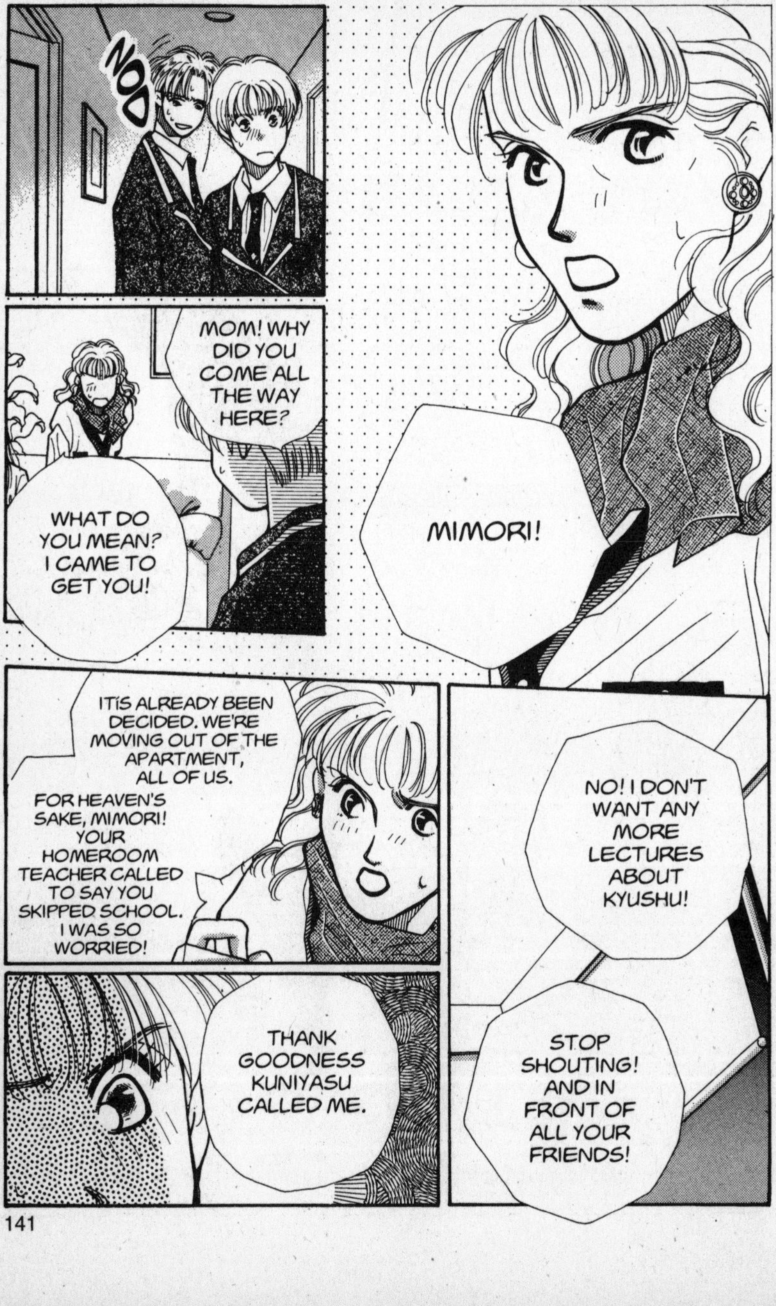
MIMORI!
NOD
MOM! WHY DID YOU COME ALL THE WAY HERE?
WHAT DO YOU MEAN? I CAME TO GET YOU!
IT'S ALREADY BEEN DECIDED. WE'RE MOVING OUT OF THE APARTMENT, ALL OF US.
FOR HEAVEN'S SAKE, MIMORI! YOUR HOMEROOM TEACHER CALLED TO SAY YOU SKIPPED SCHOOL. I WAS SO WORRIED!
THANK GOODNESS KUNIYASU CALLED ME.
NO! I DON'T WANT ANY MORE LECTURES ABOUT KYUSHU!
STOP SHOUTING! AND IN FRONT OF ALL YOUR FRIENDS!

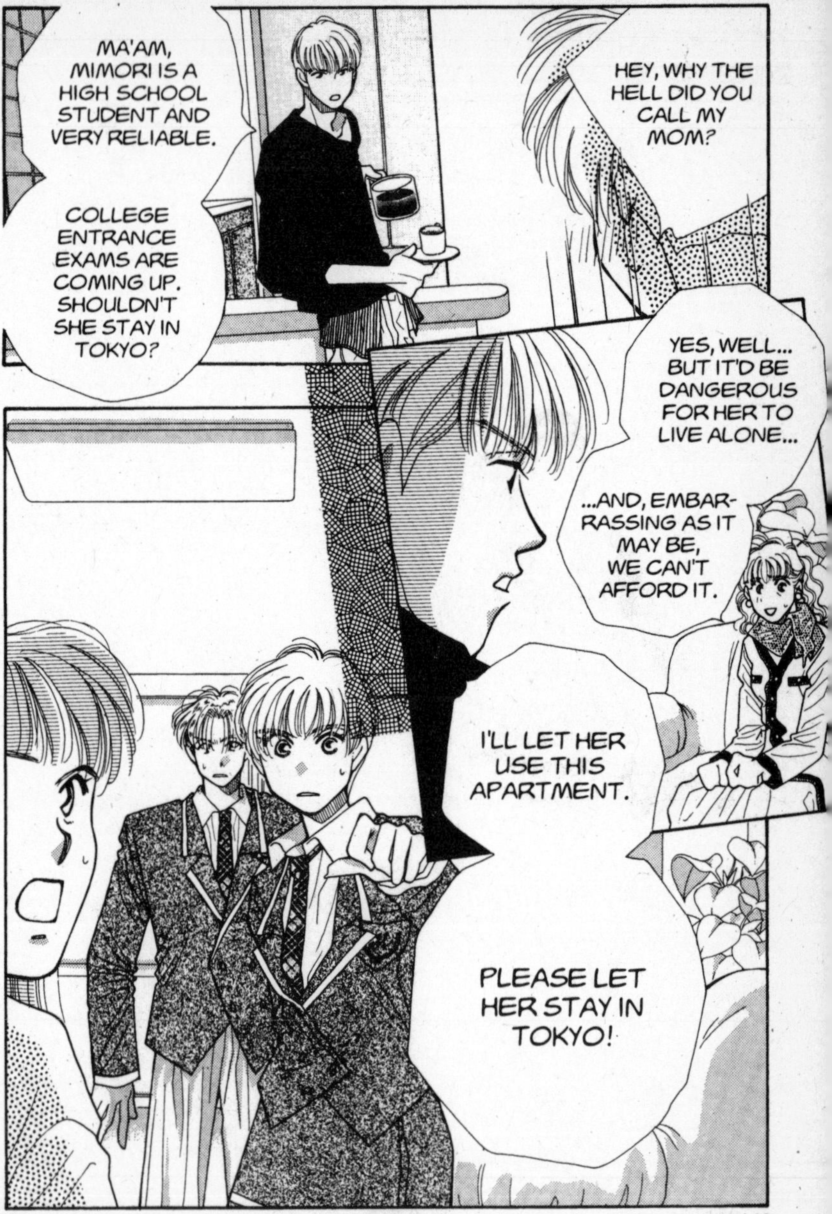
HEY, WHY THE HELL DID YOU CALL MY MOM?
MA'AM, MIMORI IS A HIGH SCHOOL STUDENT AND VERY RELIABLE.
COLLEGE ENTRANCE EXAMS ARE COMING UP. SHOULDN'T SHE STAY IN TOKYO?
YES, WELL... BUT IT'D BE DANGEROUS FOR HER TO LIVE ALONE...
...AND, EMBAR-RASSING AS IT MAY BE, WE CAN'T AFFORD IT.
I'LL LET HER USE THIS APARTMENT.
PLEASE LET HER STAY IN TOKYO!

CHARACTER RANKING

NO.1 666 POINTS

• Atsushi Haruta •

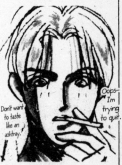

Oops— I'm trying to quit.
Don't want to taste like an ashtray.

Congratulations!
Haruta managed to maintain his lead.

Readers complained about things like his childish behavior and his small-town dress sense.

Oh, and that his legs are too long...

So what? It's a comic book!

But by page 162, his points might drop. Oh, well...I planned from the very beginning that the final episode would be like this.

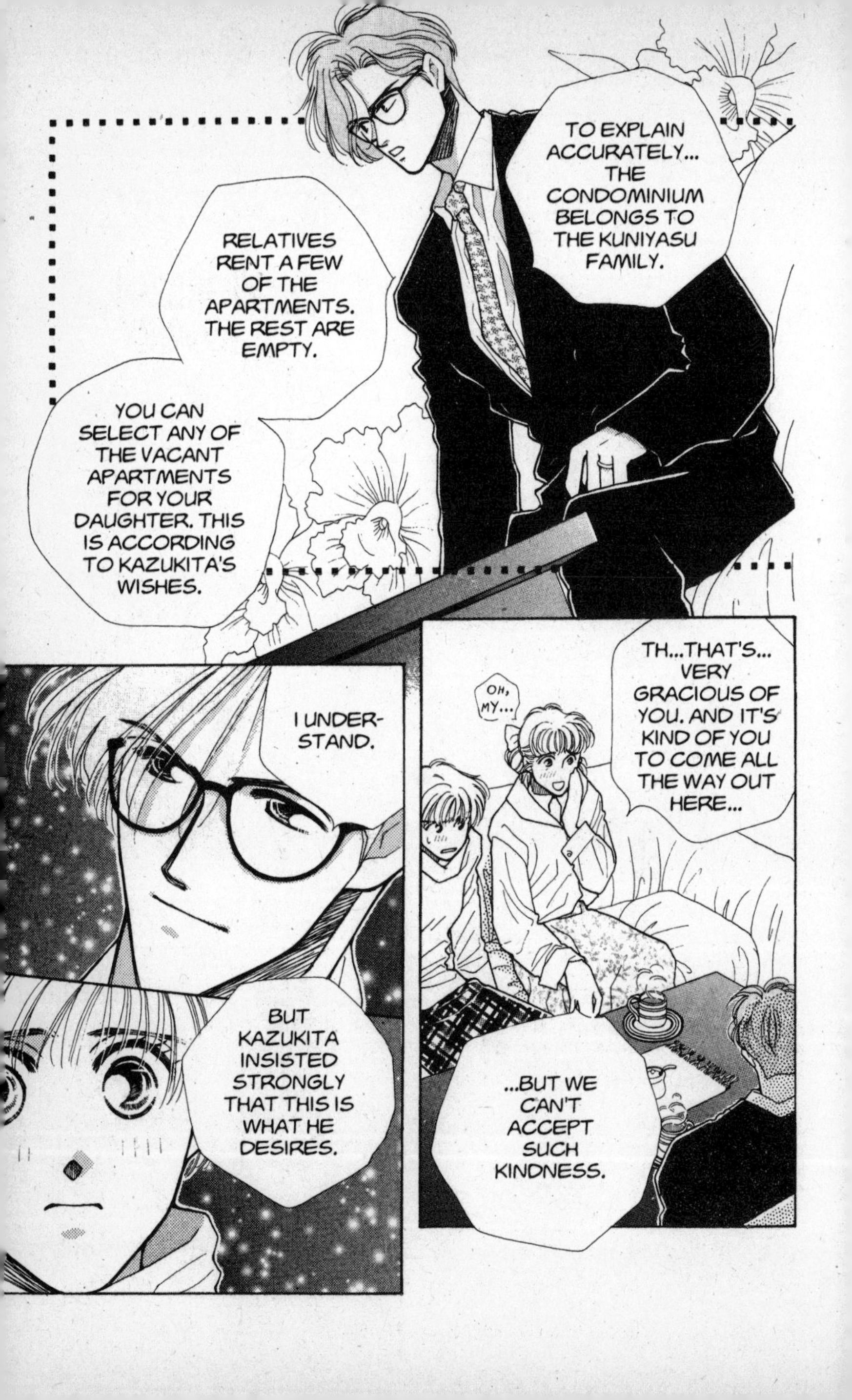
TO EXPLAIN ACCURATELY... THE CONDOMINIUM BELONGS TO THE KUNIYASU FAMILY.
RELATIVES RENT A FEW OF THE APARTMENTS. THE REST ARE EMPTY.
YOU CAN SELECT ANY OF THE VACANT APARTMENTS FOR YOUR DAUGHTER. THIS IS ACCORDING TO KAZUKITA'S WISHES.
OH, MY...
TH...THAT'S... VERY GRACIOUS OF YOU. AND IT'S KIND OF YOU TO COME ALL THE WAY OUT HERE...
...BUT WE CAN'T ACCEPT SUCH KINDNESS.
I UNDER-STAND.
BUT KAZUKITA INSISTED STRONGLY THAT THIS IS WHAT HE DESIRES.

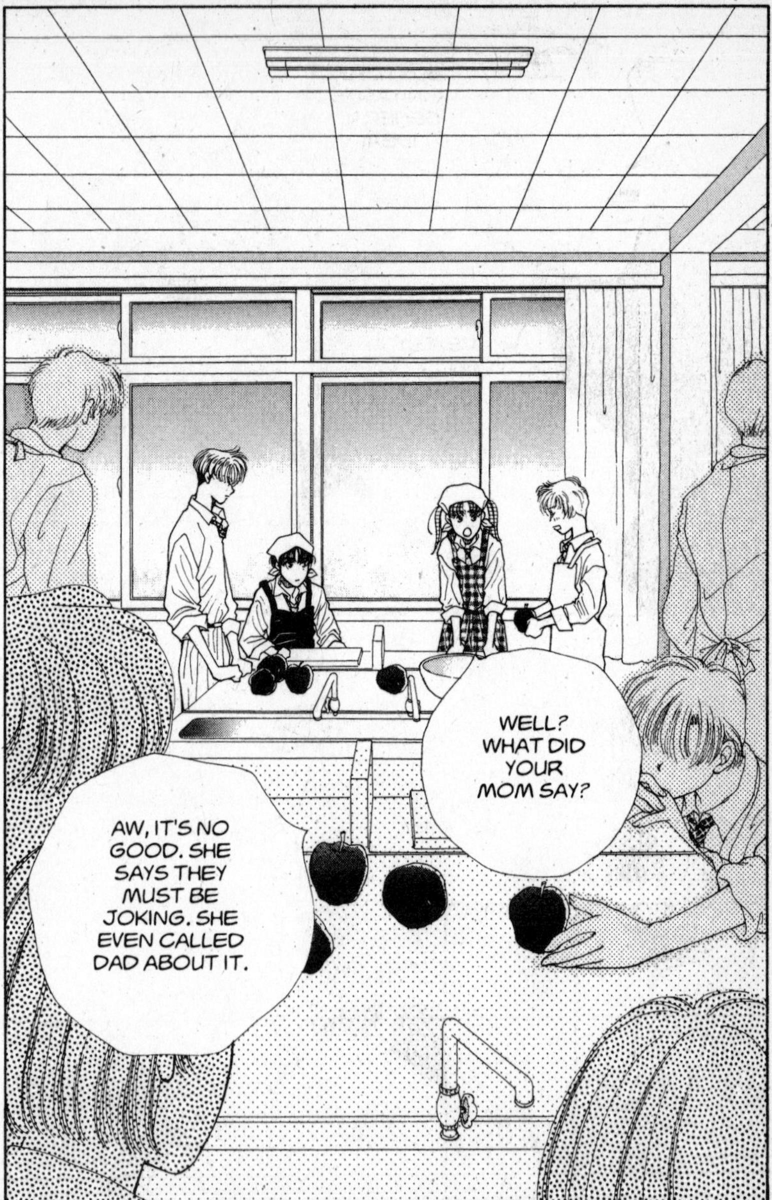
WELL? WHAT DID YOUR MOM SAY?
AW, IT'S NO GOOD. SHE SAYS THEY MUST BE JOKING. SHE EVEN CALLED DAD ABOUT IT.

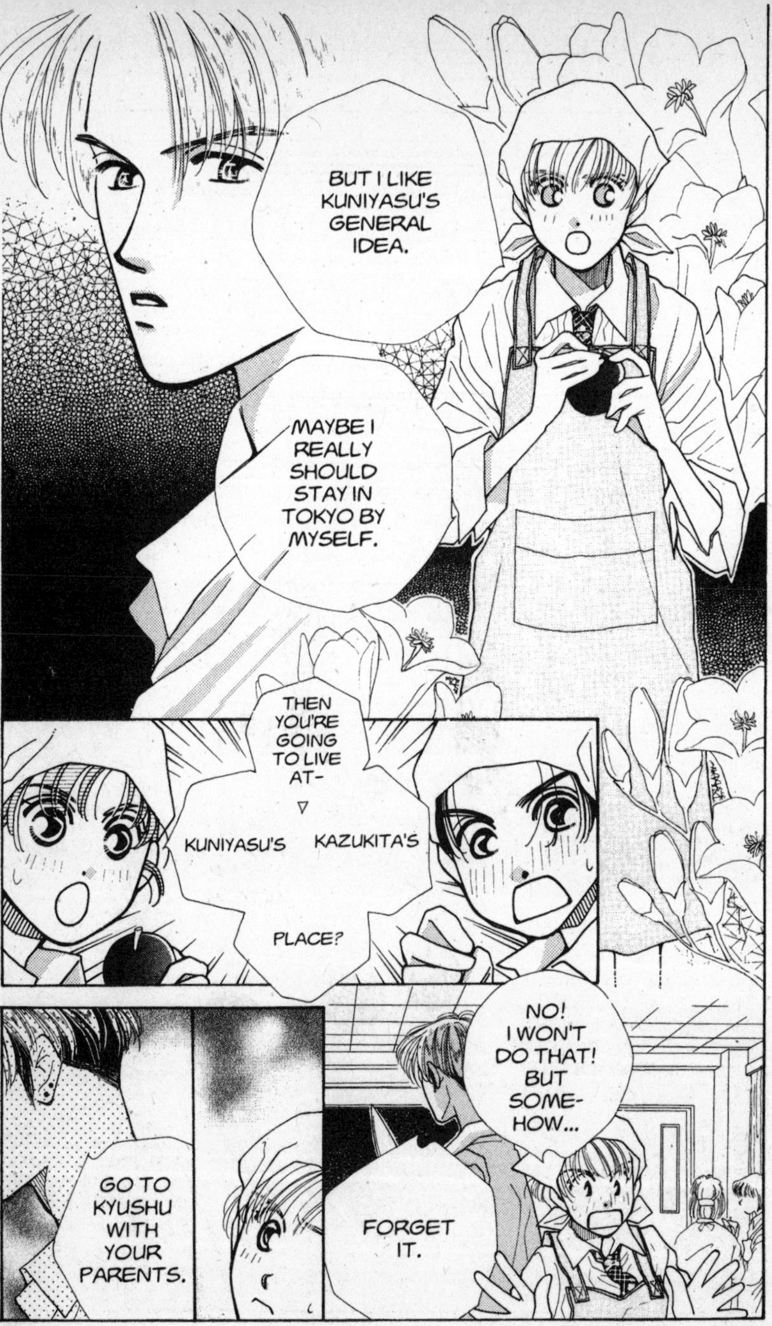
BUT I LIKE KUNIYASU'S GENERAL IDEA.
MAYBE I REALLY SHOULD STAY IN TOKYO BY MYSELF.
THEN YOU'RE GOING TO LIVE AT-
KUNIYASU'S KAZUKITA'S
PLACE?
NO! I WON'T DO THAT! BUT SOME-HOW...
FORGET IT.
GO TO KYUSHU WITH YOUR PARENTS.

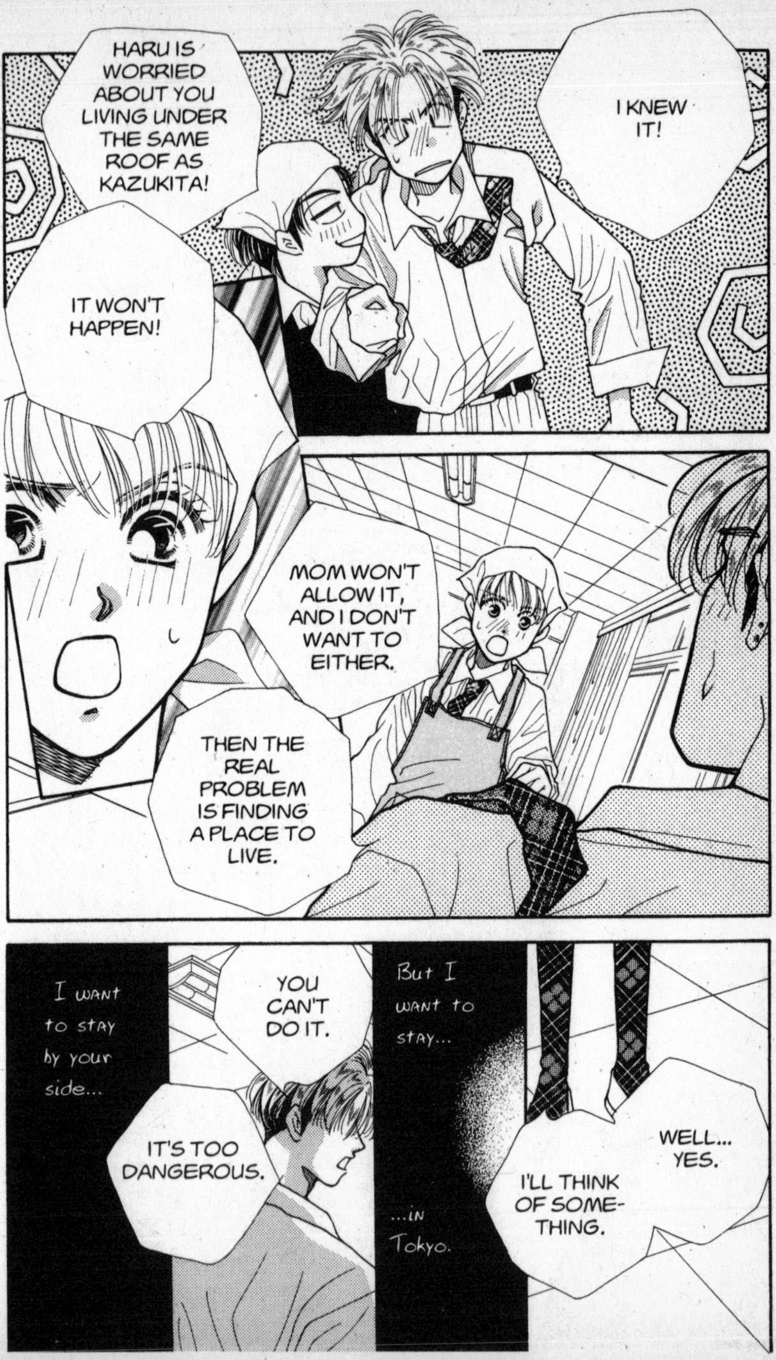
I KNEW IT!
HARU IS WORRIED ABOUT YOU LIVING UNDER THE SAME ROOF AS KAZUKITA!
IT WON'T HAPPEN!
MOM WON'T ALLOW IT, AND I DON'T WANT TO EITHER.
THEN THE REAL PROBLEM IS FINDING A PLACE TO LIVE.
WELL... YES.
I'LL THINK OF SOME-THING.
But I want to stay...
...in Tokyo.
YOU CAN'T DO IT.
IT'S TOO DANGEROUS.
I want to stay by your side...

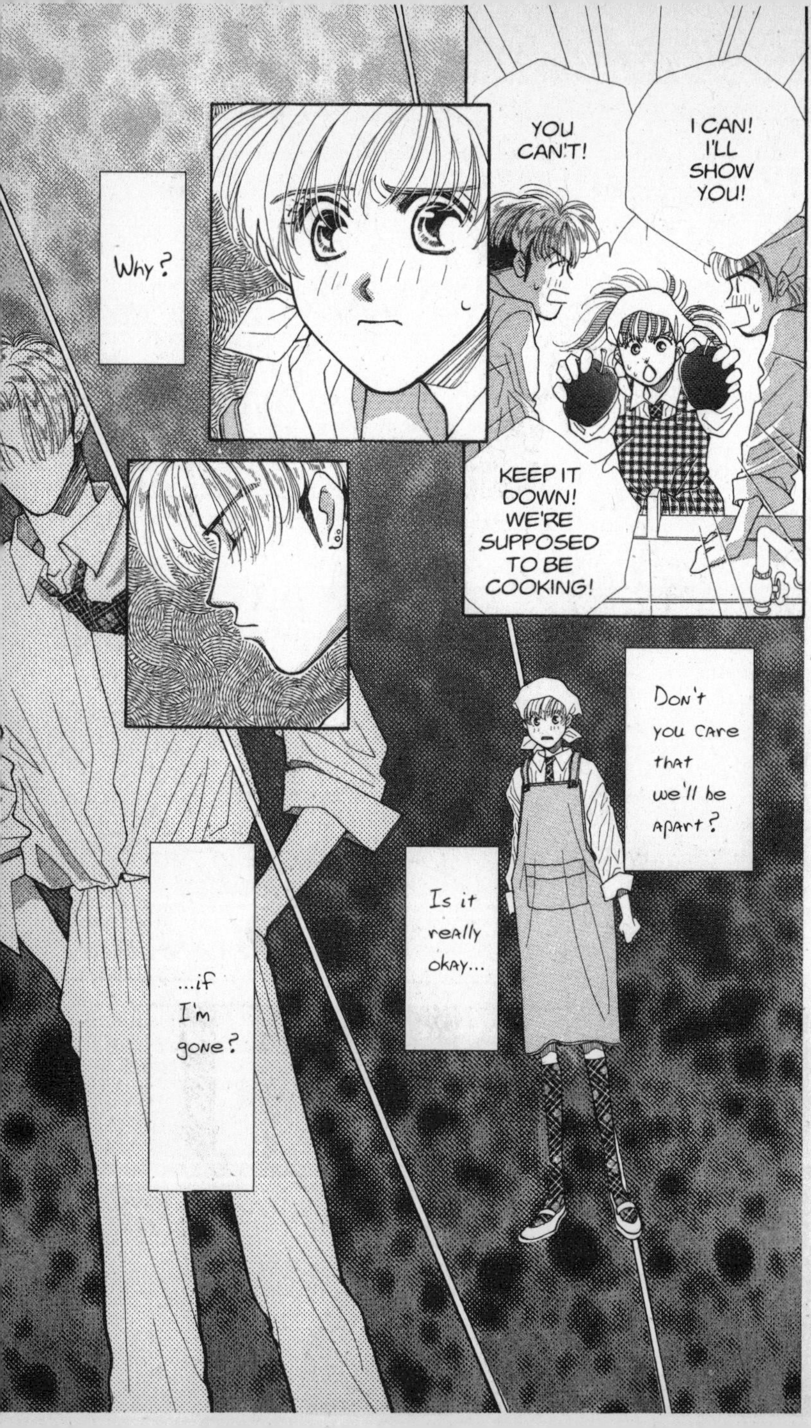
I CAN! I'LL SHOW YOU!
YOU CAN'T!
KEEP IT DOWN! WE'RE SUPPOSED TO BE COOKING!
Why?
Don't you care that we'll be apart?
Is it really okay...
...if I'm gone?

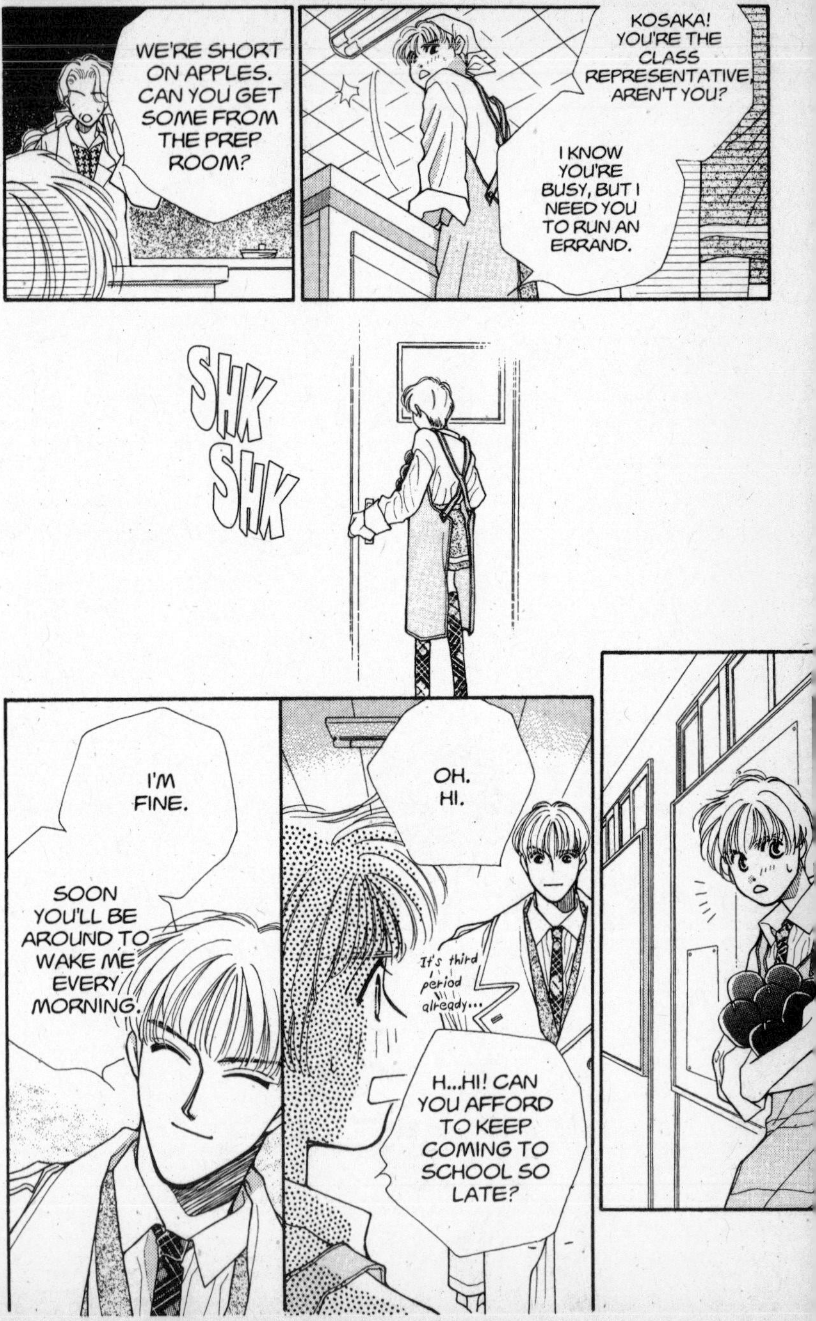
KOSAKA! YOU'RE THE CLASS REPRESENTATIVE, AREN'T YOU?
I KNOW YOU'RE BUSY, BUT I NEED YOU TO RUN AN ERRAND.
WE'RE SHORT ON APPLES. CAN YOU GET SOME FROM THE PREP ROOM?
SHK SHK
OH. HI.
It's third period already...
H...HI! CAN YOU AFFORD TO KEEP COMING TO SCHOOL SO LATE?
I'M FINE.
SOON YOU'LL BE AROUND TO WAKE ME EVERY MORNING.

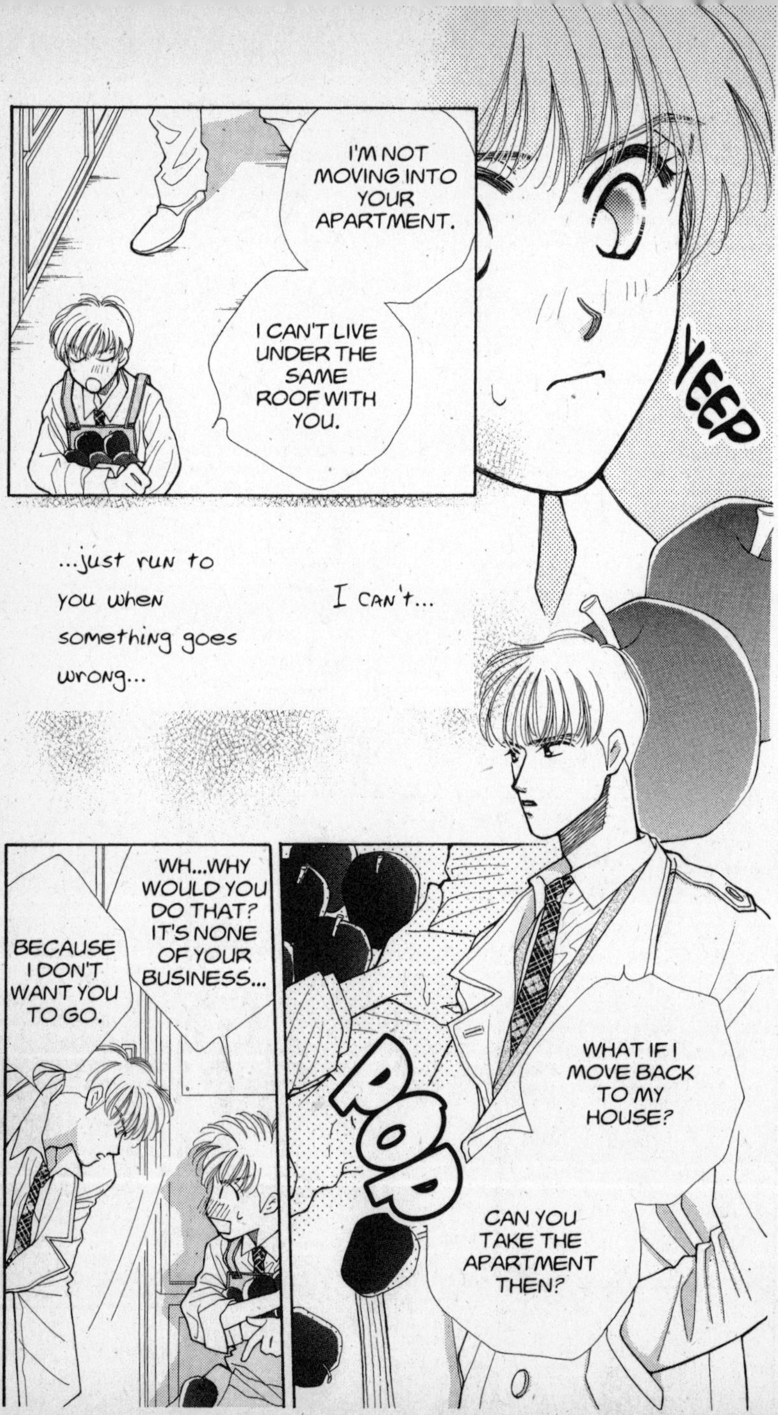
YEEP
I'M NOT MOVING INTO YOUR APARTMENT.
I CAN'T LIVE UNDER THE SAME ROOF WITH YOU.
I can't...
...just run to you when something goes wrong...
WHAT IF I MOVE BACK TO MY HOUSE?
CAN YOU TAKE THE APARTMENT THEN?
POP
WH...WHY WOULD YOU DO THAT? IT'S NONE OF YOUR BUSINESS...
BECAUSE I DON'T WANT YOU TO GO.

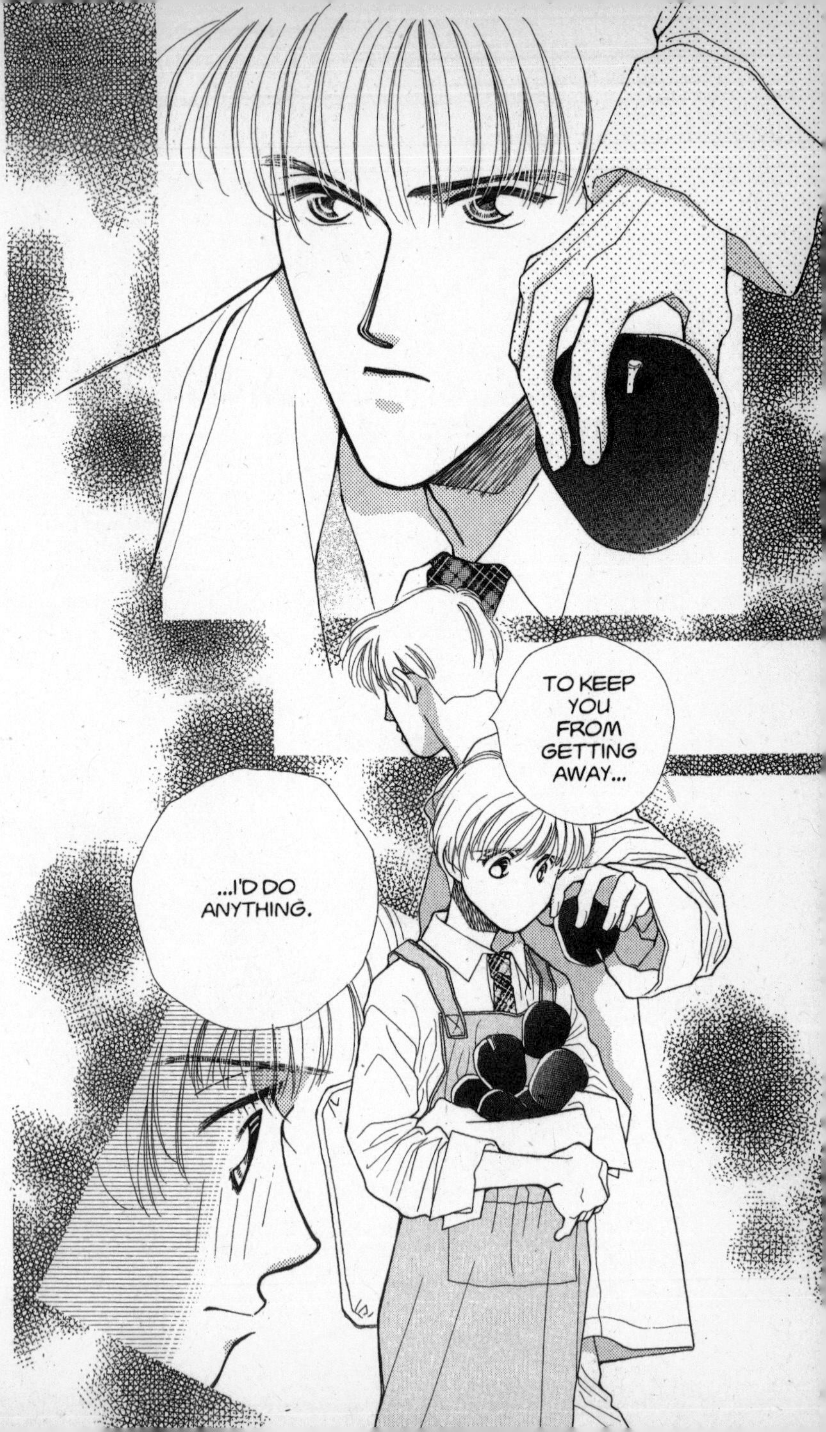
TO KEEP YOU FROM GETTING AWAY...
...I'D DO ANYTHING.

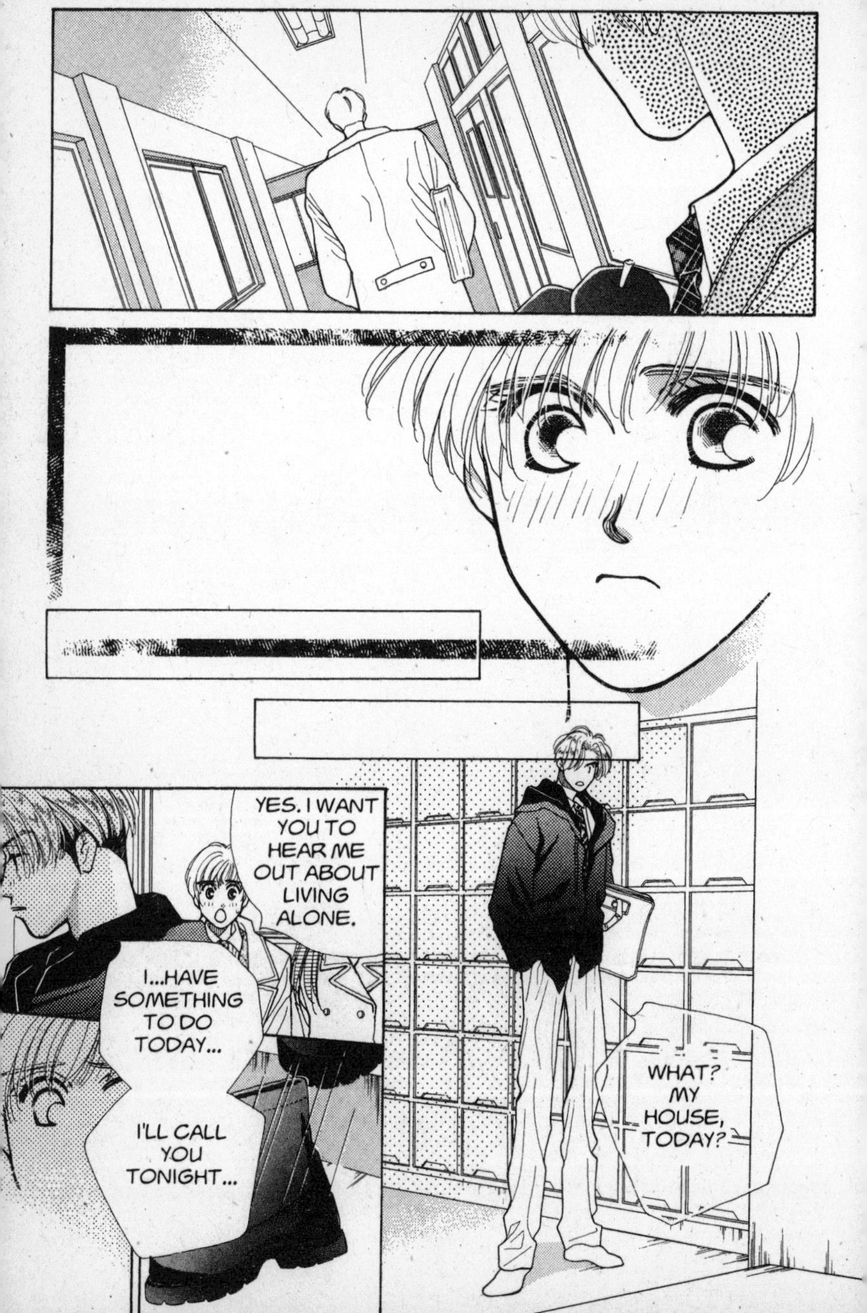
WHAT? MY HOUSE, TODAY?
YES. I WANT YOU TO HEAR ME OUT ABOUT LIVING ALONE.
I...HAVE SOMETHING TO DO TODAY...
I'LL CALL YOU TONIGHT...

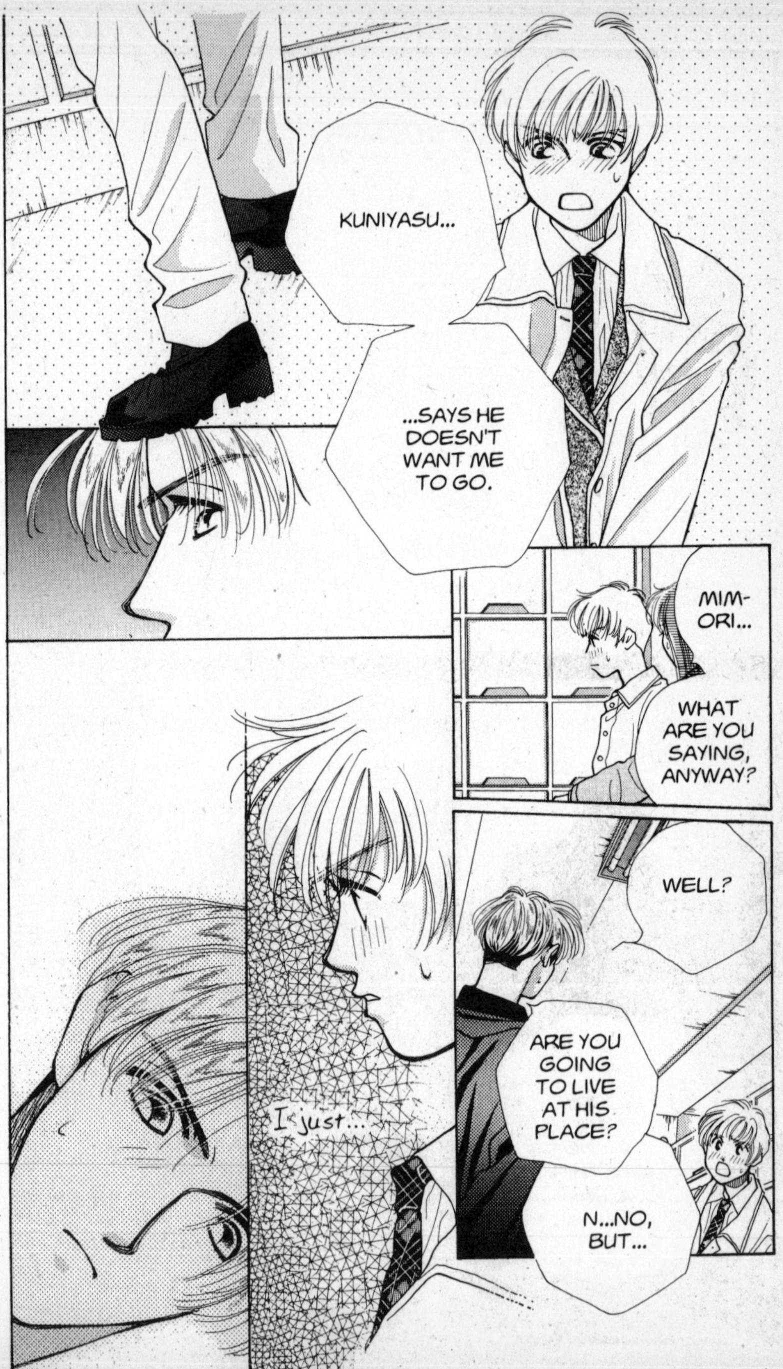
KUNIYASU...
...SAYS HE DOESN'T WANT ME TO GO.
MIM-ORI...
WHAT ARE YOU SAYING, ANYWAY?
WELL?
ARE YOU GOING TO LIVE AT HIS PLACE?
N...NO, BUT...
I just...

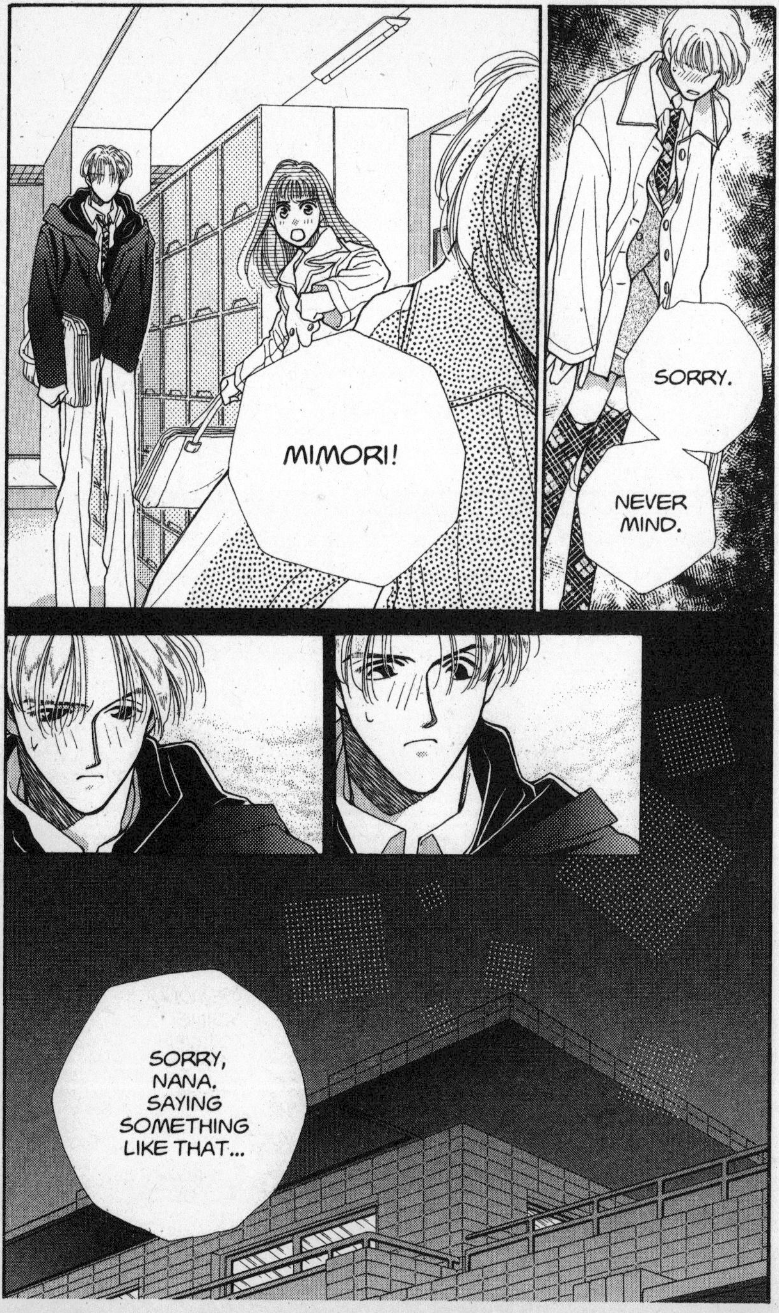
SORRY.
NEVER MIND.
MIMORI!
SORRY, NANA. SAYING SOMETHING LIKE THAT...

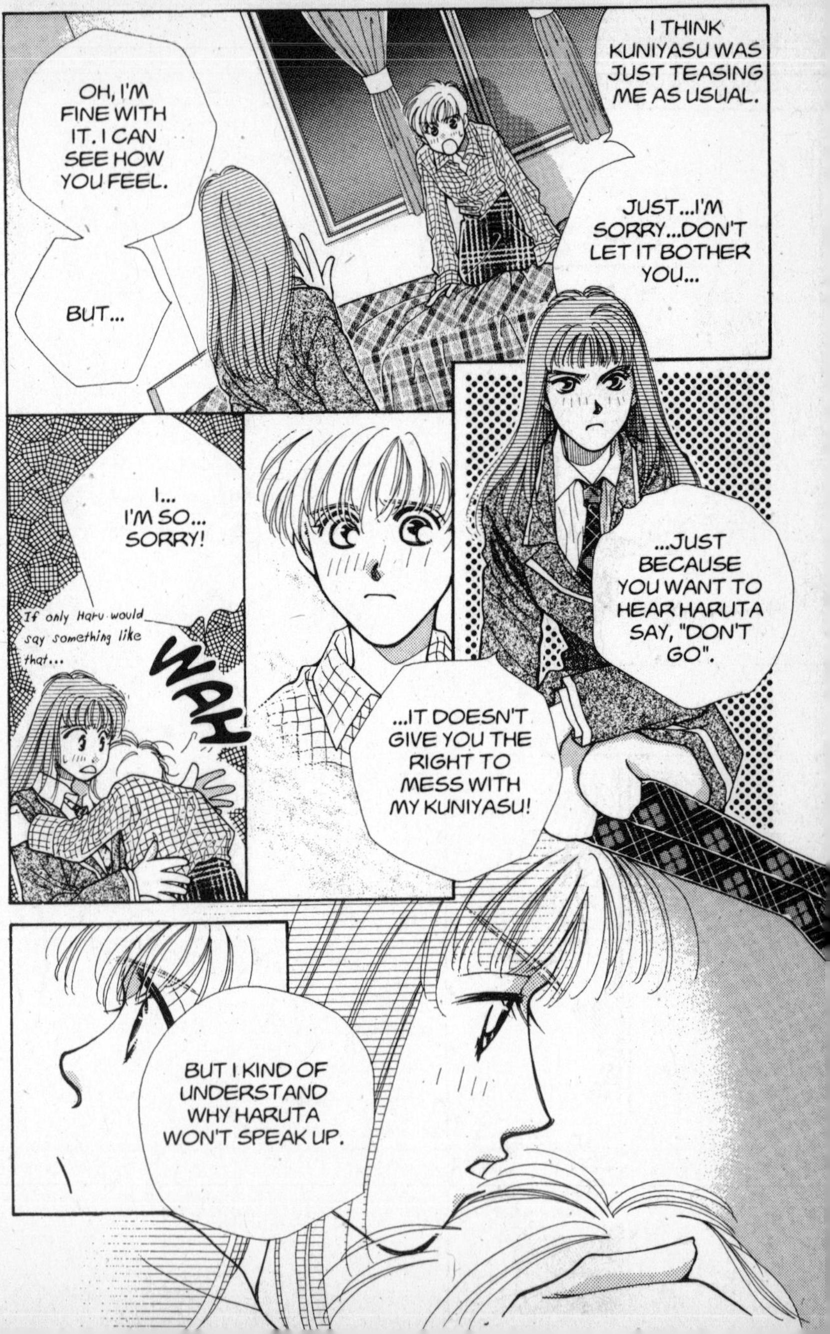
I THINK KUNIYASU WAS JUST TEASING ME AS USUAL.
JUST...I'M SORRY...DON'T LET IT BOTHER YOU...
OH, I'M FINE WITH IT. I CAN SEE HOW YOU FEEL.
BUT...
...JUST BECAUSE YOU WANT TO HEAR HARUTA SAY, "DON'T GO".
...IT DOESN'T GIVE YOU THE RIGHT TO MESS WITH MY KUNIYASU!
I... I'M SO... SORRY!
WAH
If only Haru would say something like that...
BUT I KIND OF UNDERSTAND WHY HARUTA WON'T SPEAK UP.

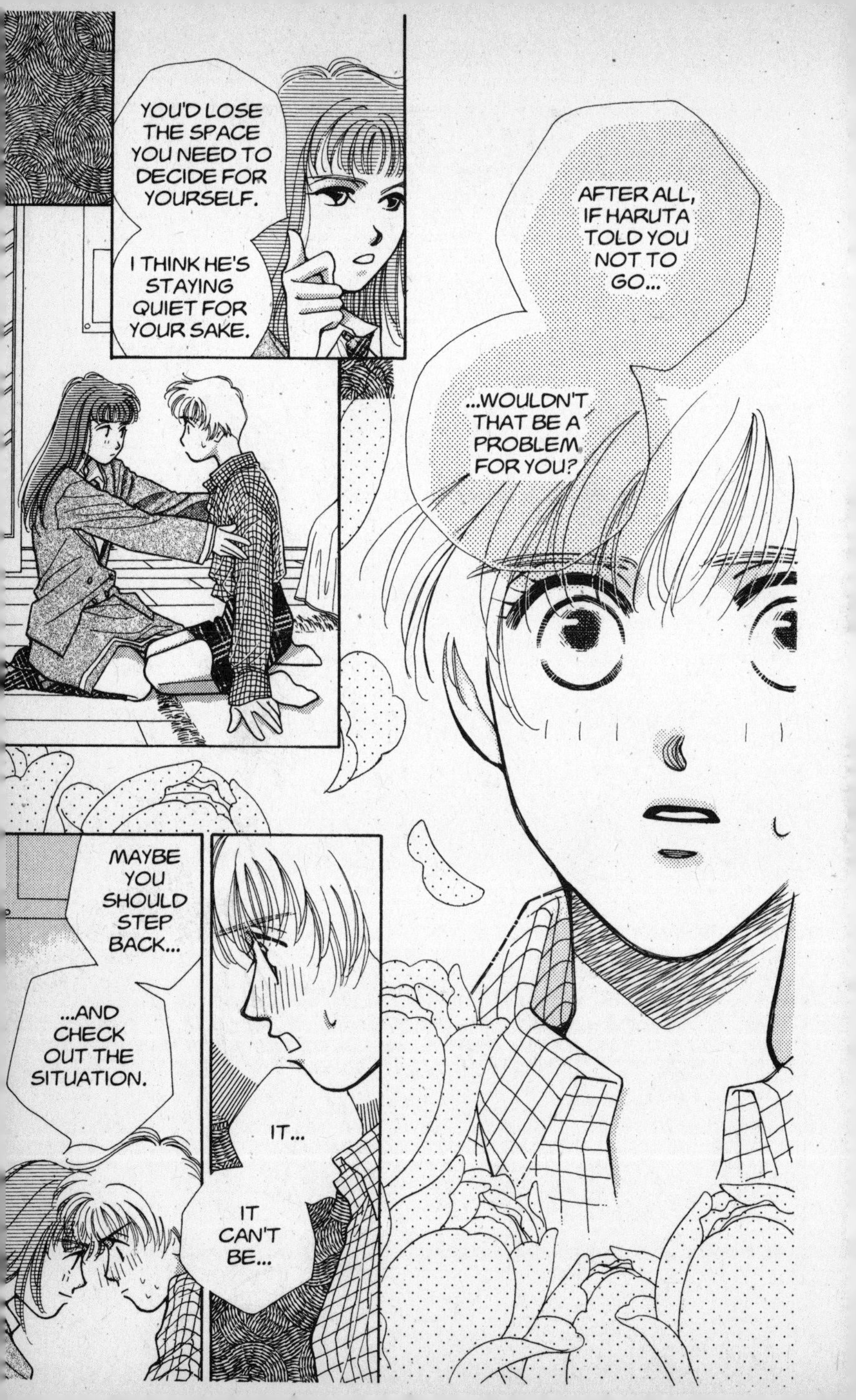
AFTER ALL, IF HARUTA TOLD YOU NOT TO GO...
...WOULDN'T THAT BE A PROBLEM FOR YOU?
YOU'D LOSE THE SPACE YOU NEED TO DECIDE FOR YOURSELF.
I THINK HE'S STAYING QUIET FOR YOUR SAKE.
IT...
IT CAN'T BE...
MAYBE YOU SHOULD STEP BACK...
...AND CHECK OUT THE SITUATION.

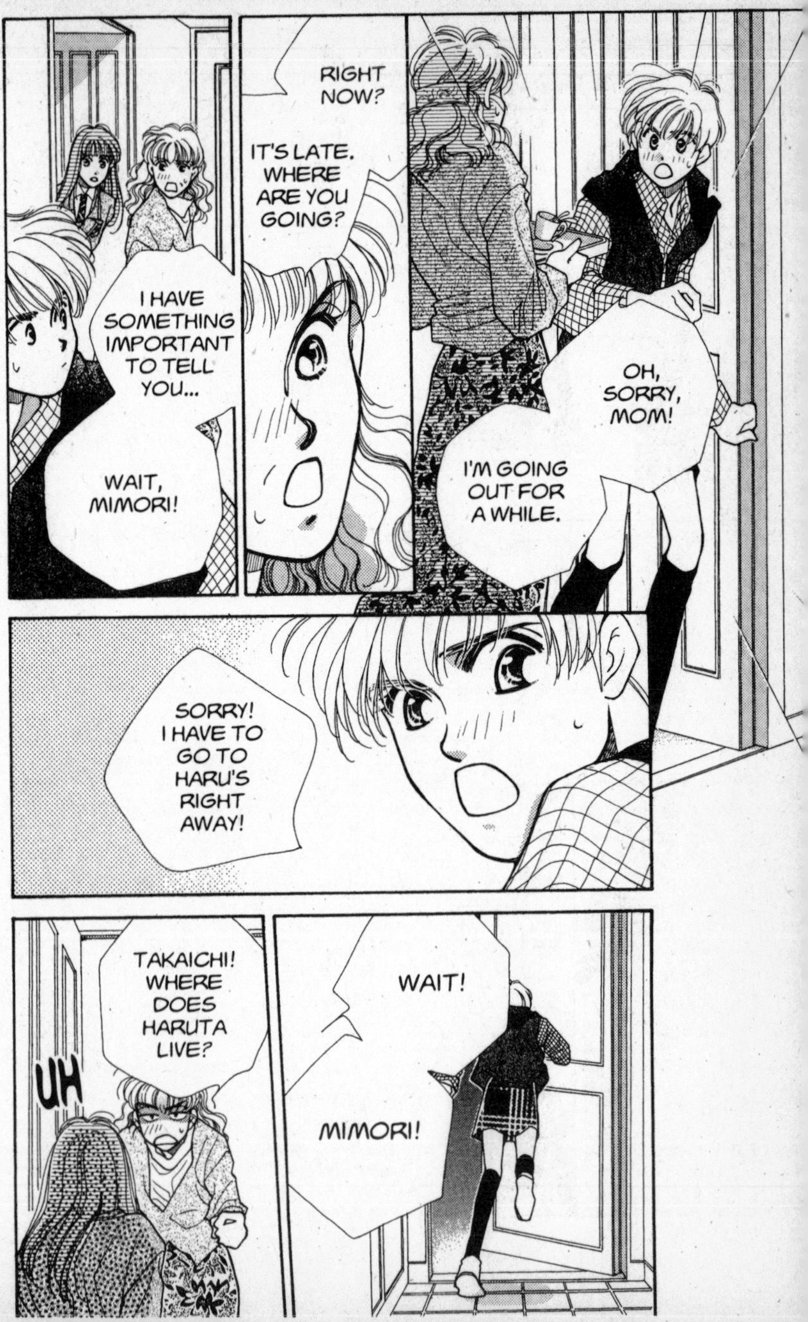
OH, SORRY, MOM!
I'M GOING OUT FOR A WHILE.
RIGHT NOW?
IT'S LATE. WHERE ARE YOU GOING?
I HAVE SOMETHING IMPORTANT TO TELL YOU...
WAIT, MIMORI!
SORRY! I HAVE TO GO TO HARU'S RIGHT AWAY!
WAIT!
MIMORI!
TAKAICHI! WHERE DOES HARUTA LIVE?
UH

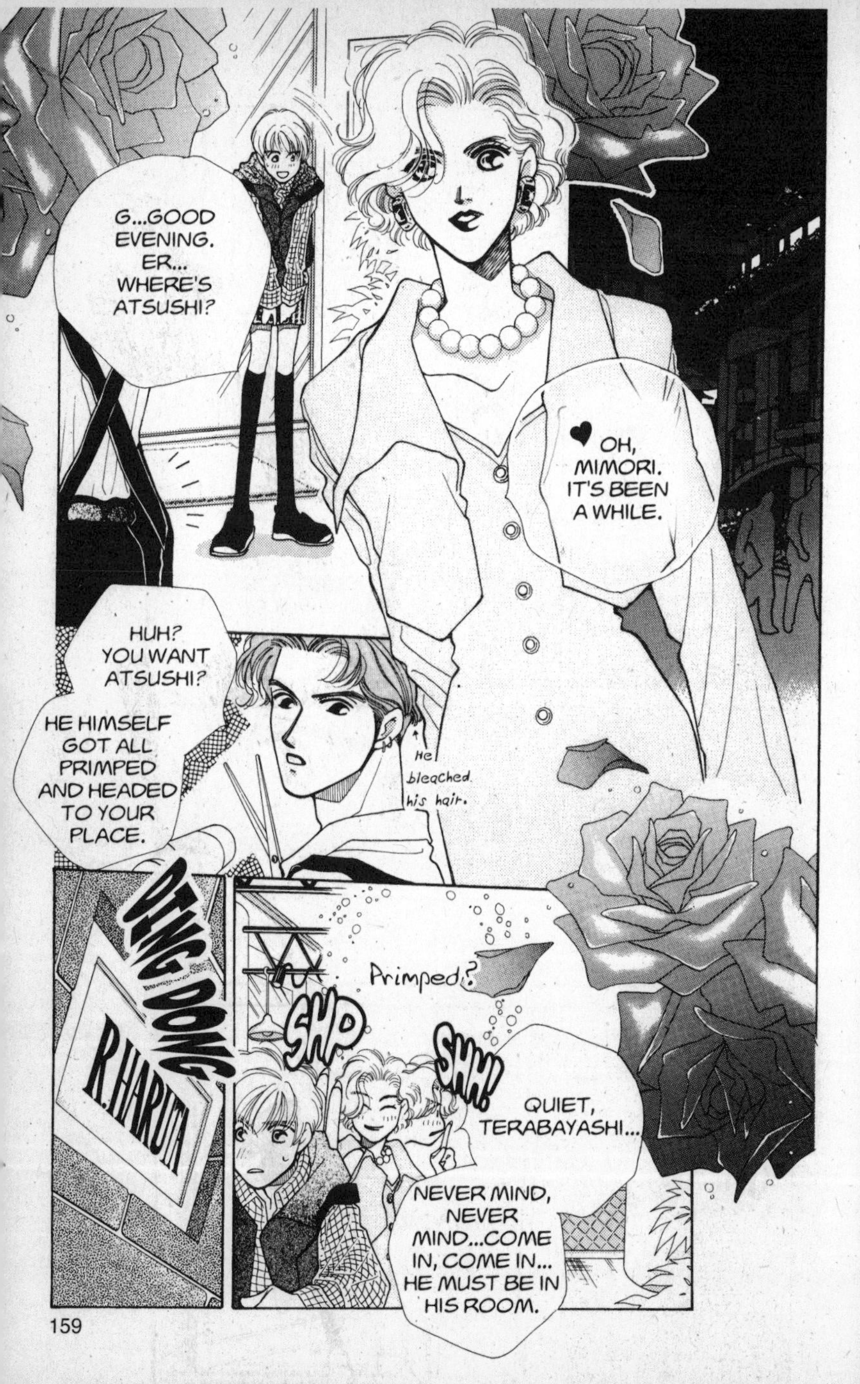
G...GOOD EVENING. ER... WHERE'S ATSUSHI?
OH, MIMORI. IT'S BEEN A WHILE.
HUH? YOU WANT ATSUSHI?
HE HIMSELF GOT ALL PRIMPED AND HEADED TO YOUR PLACE.
He bleached his hair.
Primped?
SHP
SHH!
QUIET, TERABAYASHI...
NEVER MIND, NEVER MIND...COME IN, COME IN... HE MUST BE IN HIS ROOM.
DING DONG
R.HARUTA

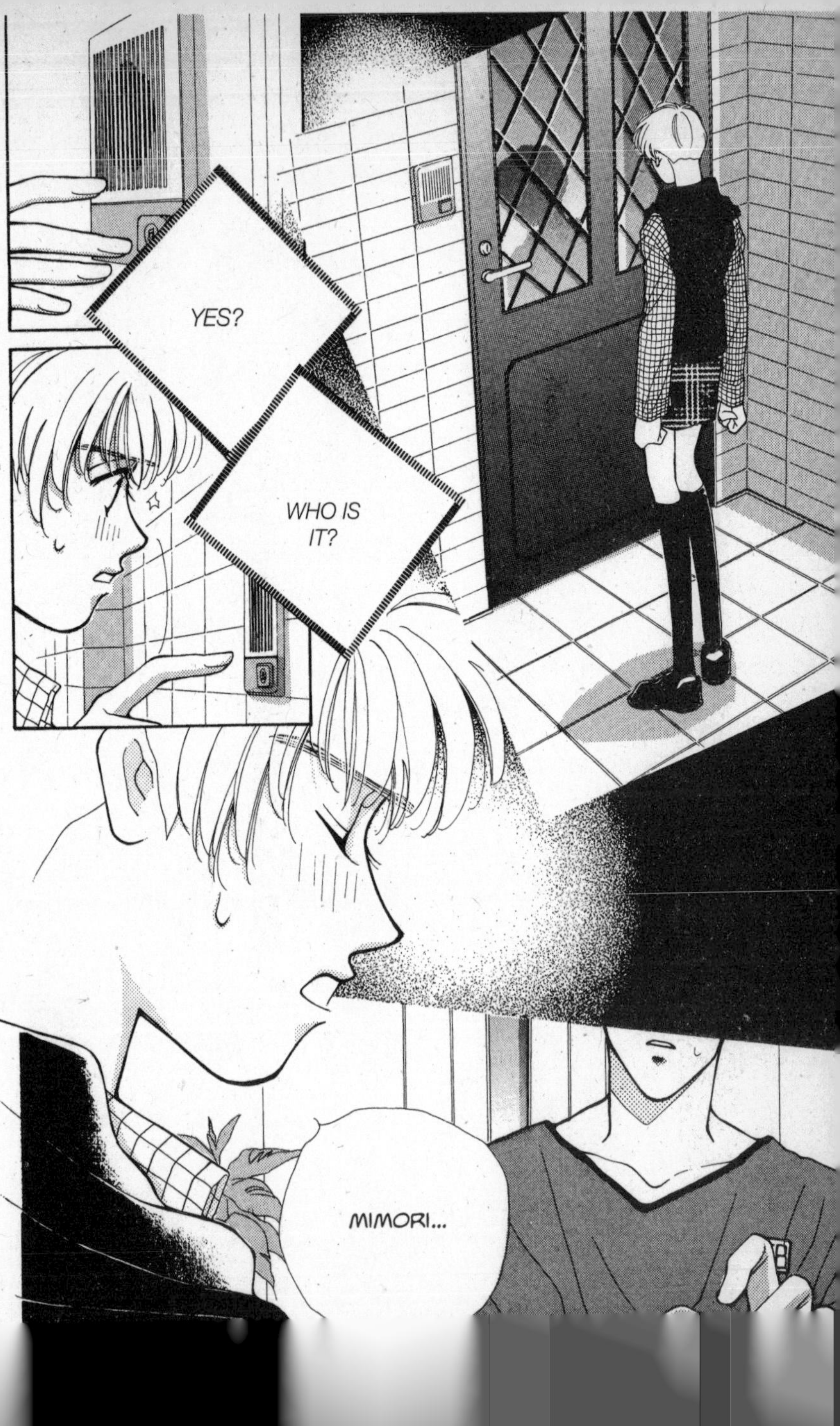
YES?
WHO IS IT?
MIMORI...

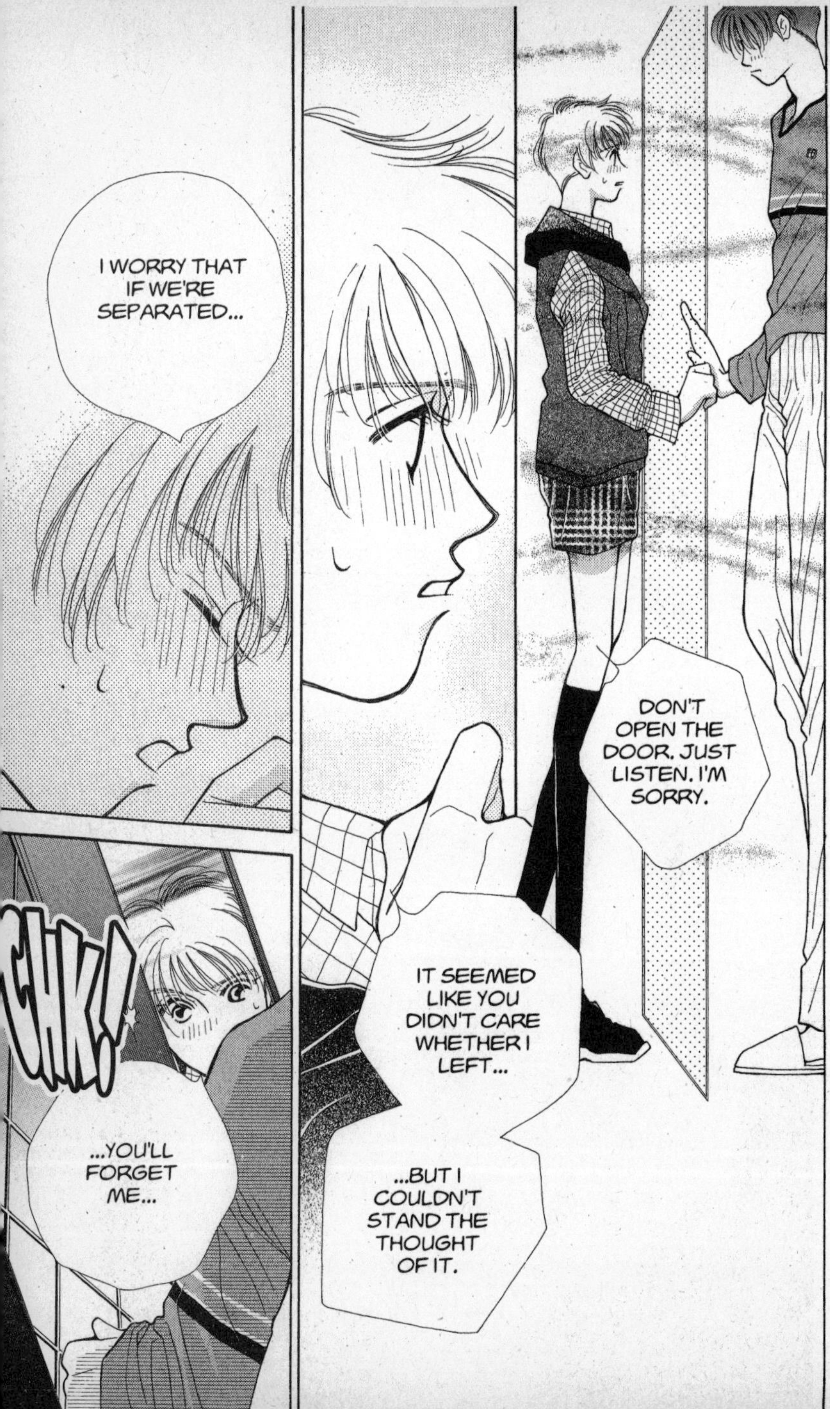
DON'T OPEN THE DOOR. JUST LISTEN. I'M SORRY.
IT SEEMED LIKE YOU DIDN'T CARE WHETHER I LEFT...
...BUT I COULDN'T STAND THE THOUGHT OF IT.
I WORRY THAT IF WE'RE SEPARATED...
CHK!
...YOU'LL FORGET ME...

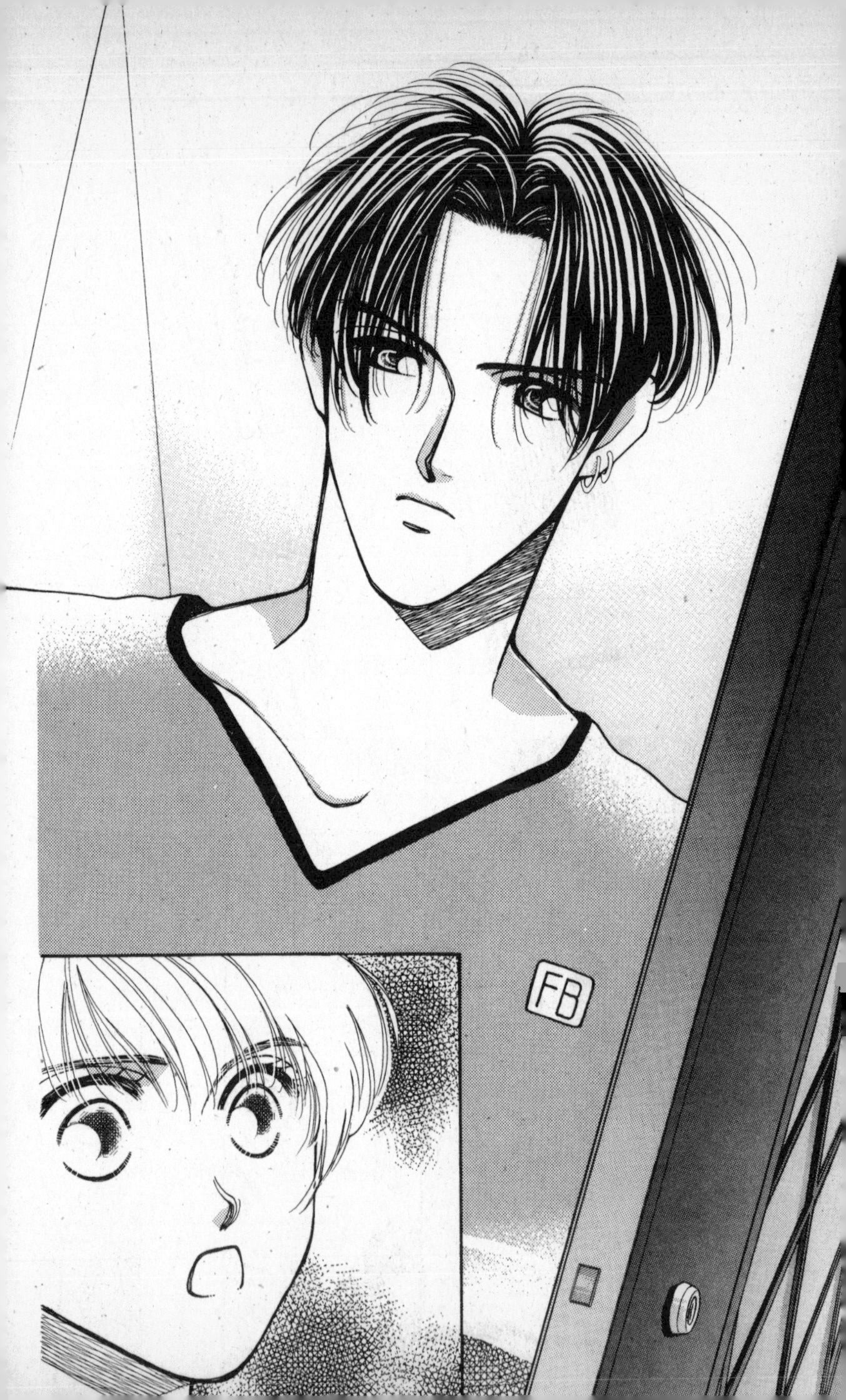
FB

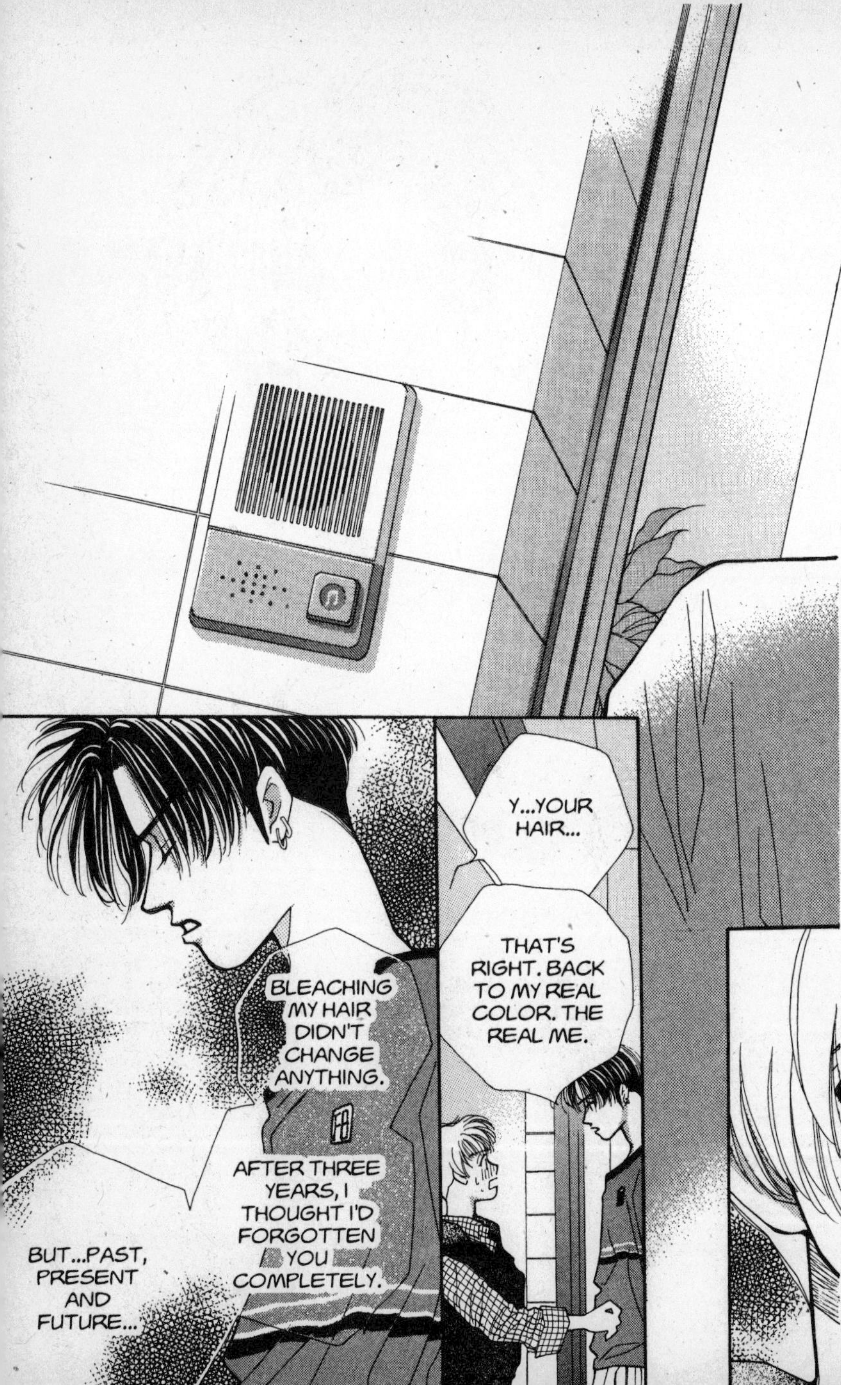
Y...YOUR HAIR...
THAT'S RIGHT. BACK TO MY REAL COLOR. THE REAL ME.
BLEACHING MY HAIR DIDN'T CHANGE ANYTHING.
AFTER THREE YEARS, I THOUGHT I'D FORGOTTEN YOU COMPLETELY.
BUT...PAST, PRESENT AND FUTURE...

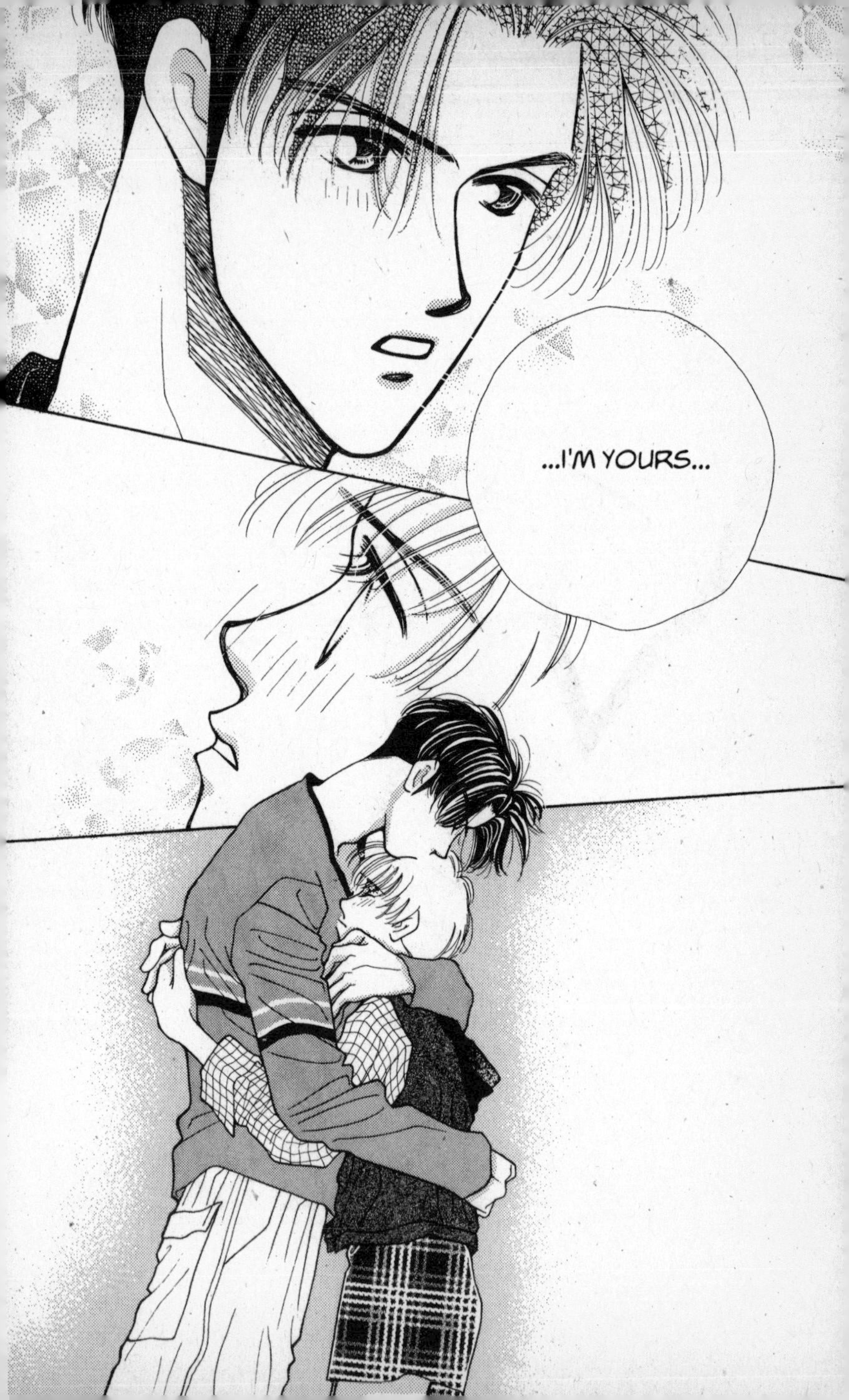
...I'M YOURS...

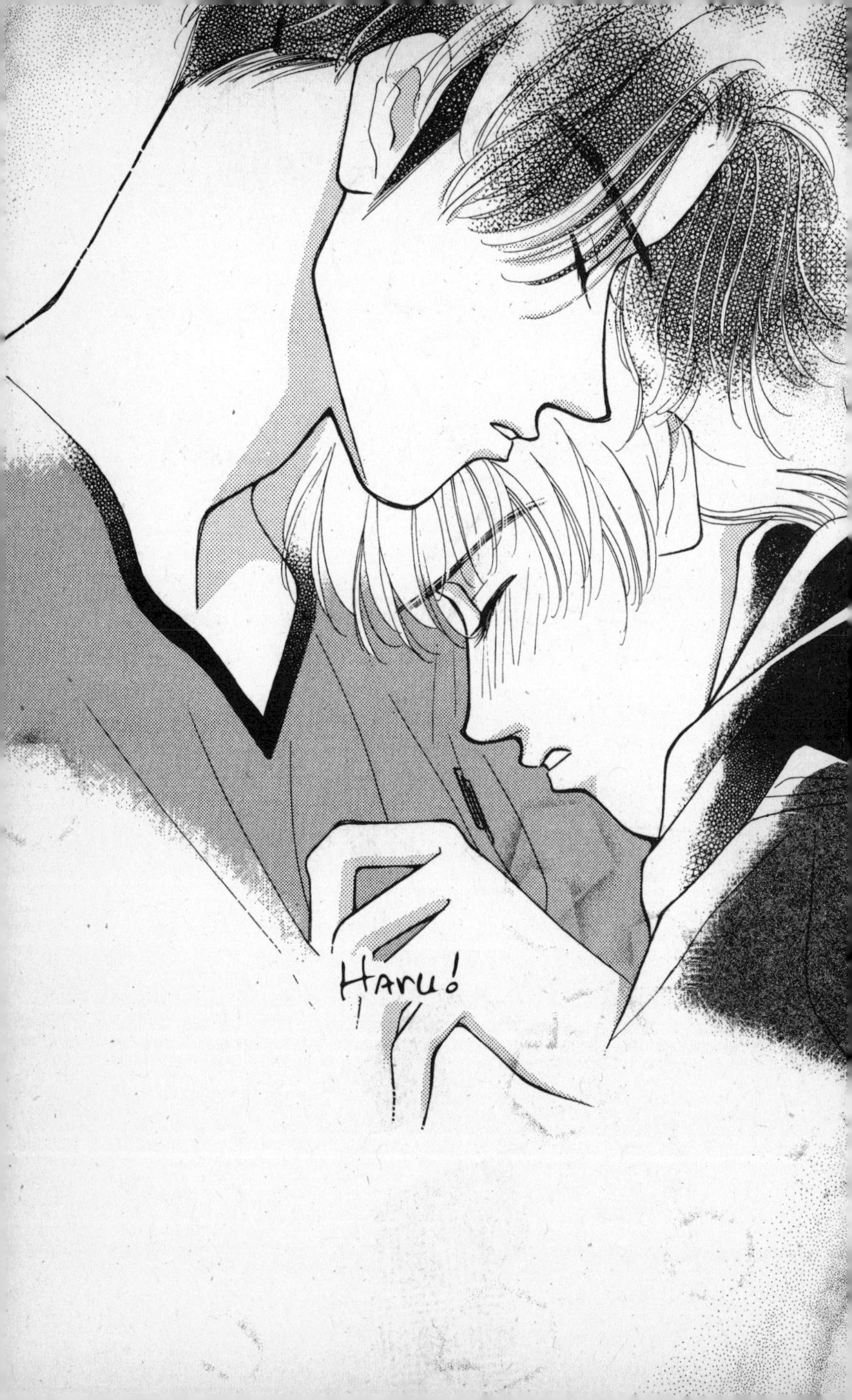
Haru!

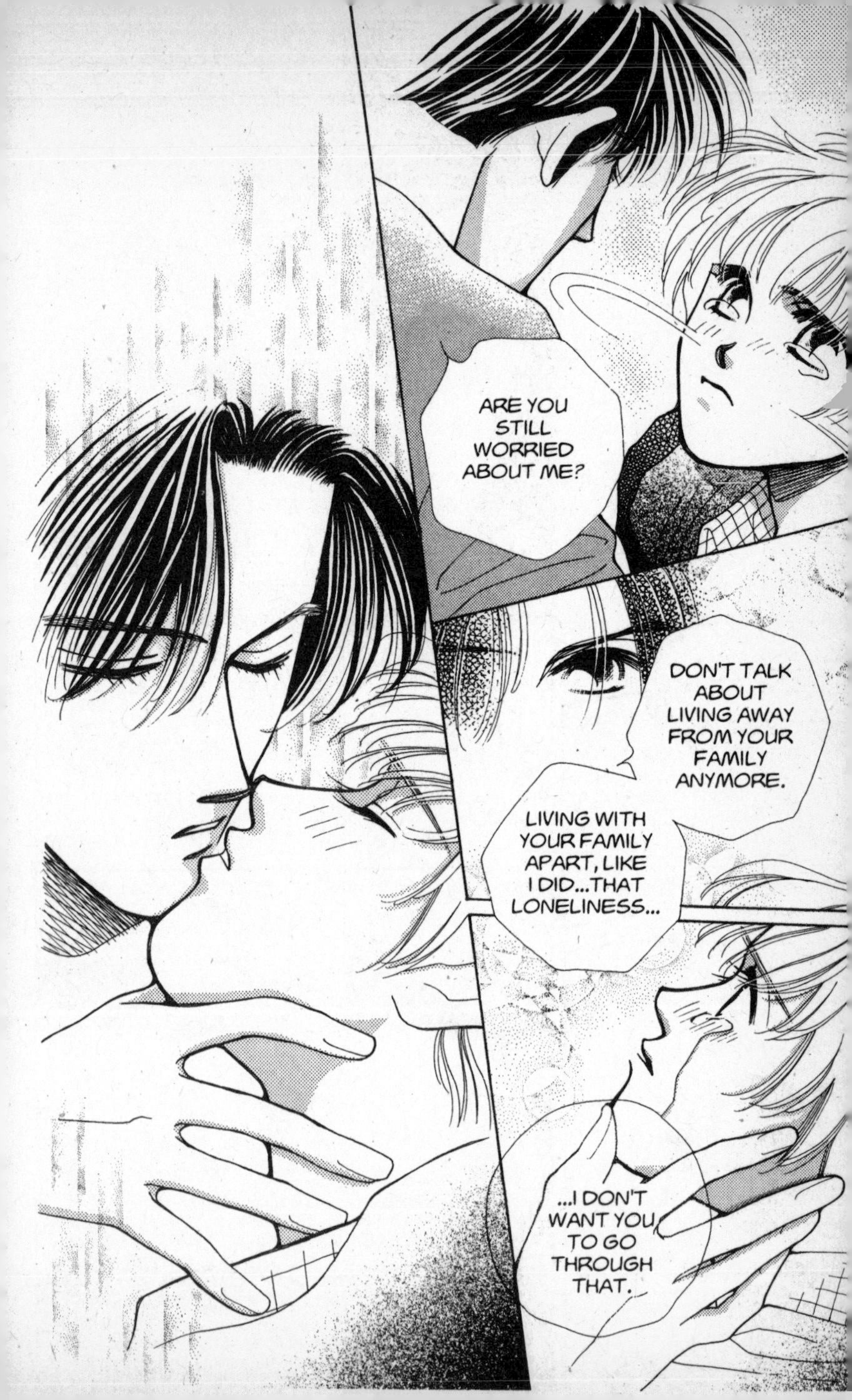
ARE YOU STILL WORRIED ABOUT ME?
DON'T TALK ABOUT LIVING AWAY FROM YOUR FAMILY ANYMORE.
LIVING WITH YOUR FAMILY APART, LIKE I DID...THAT LONELINESS...
...I DON'T WANT YOU TO GO THROUGH THAT.

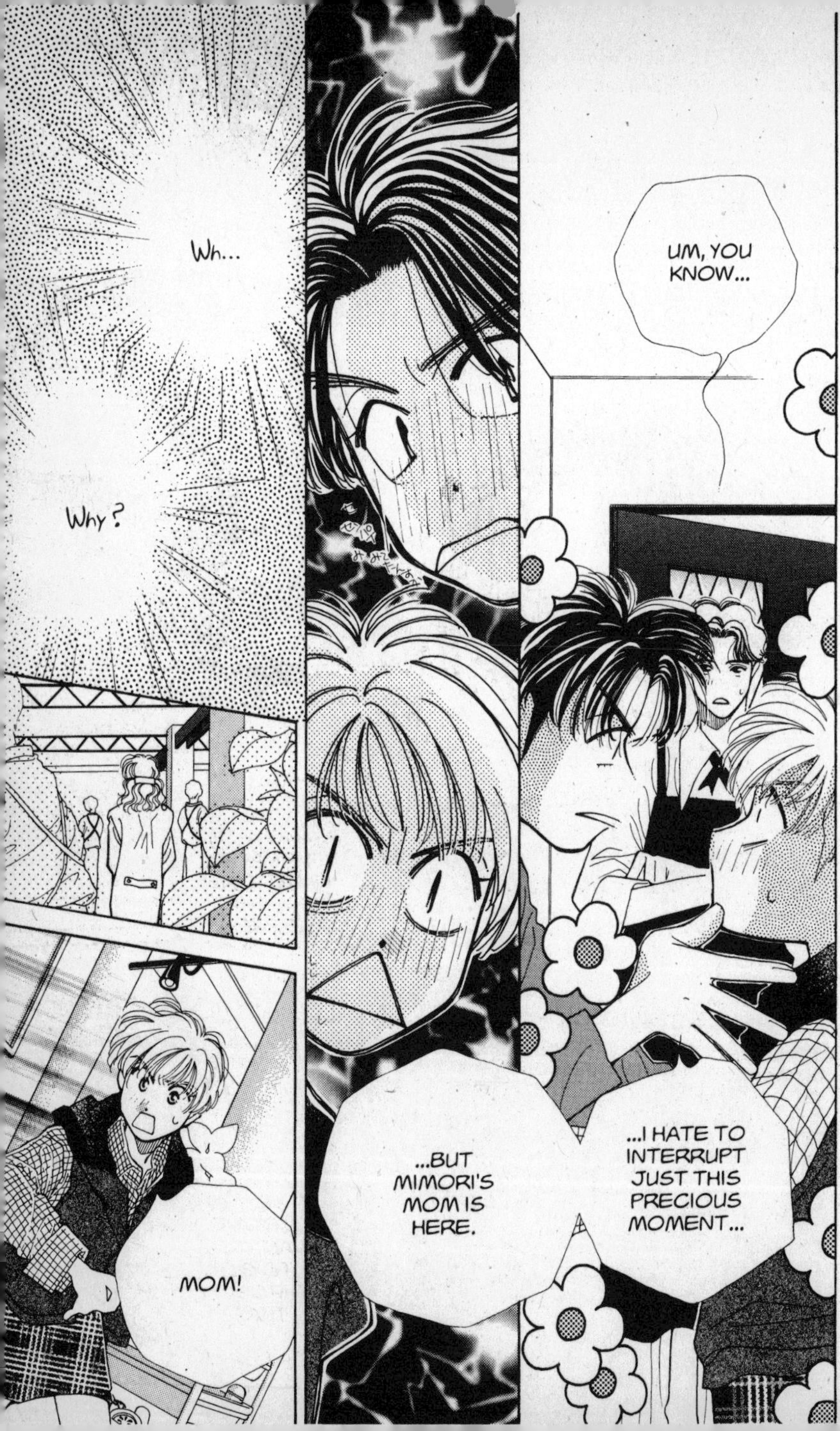
UM, YOU KNOW...
...I HATE TO INTERRUPT JUST THIS PRECIOUS MOMENT...
...BUT MIMORI'S MOM IS HERE.
Wh...
Why?
MOM!

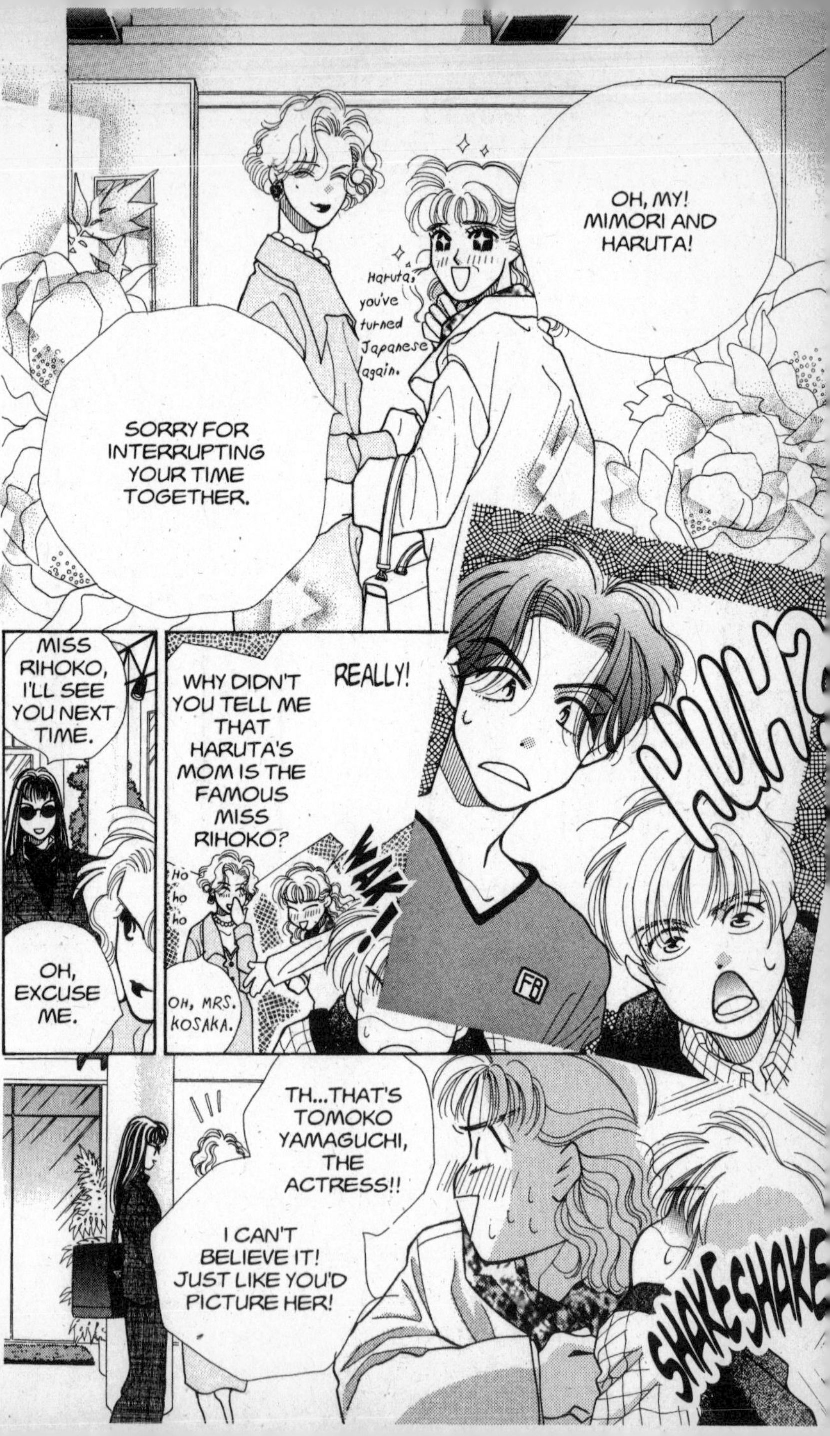
OH, MY! MIMORI AND HARUTA!
Haruta, you've turned Japanese again.
SORRY FOR INTERRUPTING YOUR TIME TOGETHER.
HUH?
REALLY!
WHY DIDN'T YOU TELL ME THAT HARUTA'S MOM IS THE FAMOUS MISS RIHOKO?
WAK!
Ho ho ho
OH, MRS. KOSAKA.
MISS RIHOKO, I'LL SEE YOU NEXT TIME.
OH, EXCUSE ME.
SHAKE SHAKE
TH...THAT'S TOMOKO YAMAGUCHI, THE ACTRESS!!
I CAN'T BELIEVE IT! JUST LIKE YOU'D PICTURE HER!

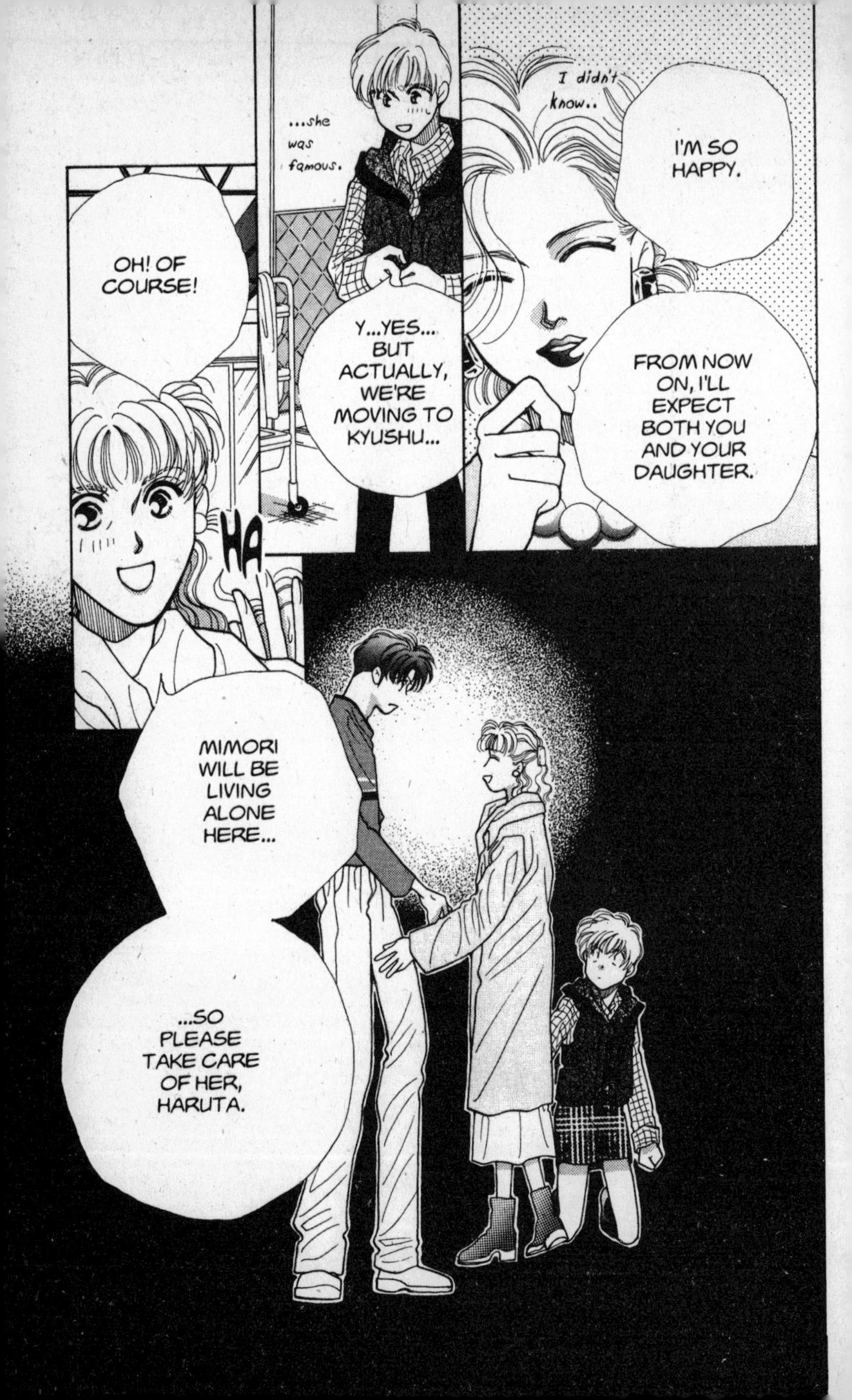
I'M SO HAPPY.
I didn't know..
FROM NOW ON, I'LL EXPECT BOTH YOU AND YOUR DAUGHTER.
...she was famous.
Y...YES... BUT ACTUALLY, WE'RE MOVING TO KYUSHU...
OH! OF COURSE!
HA
MIMORI WILL BE LIVING ALONE HERE...
...SO PLEASE TAKE CARE OF HER, HARUTA.

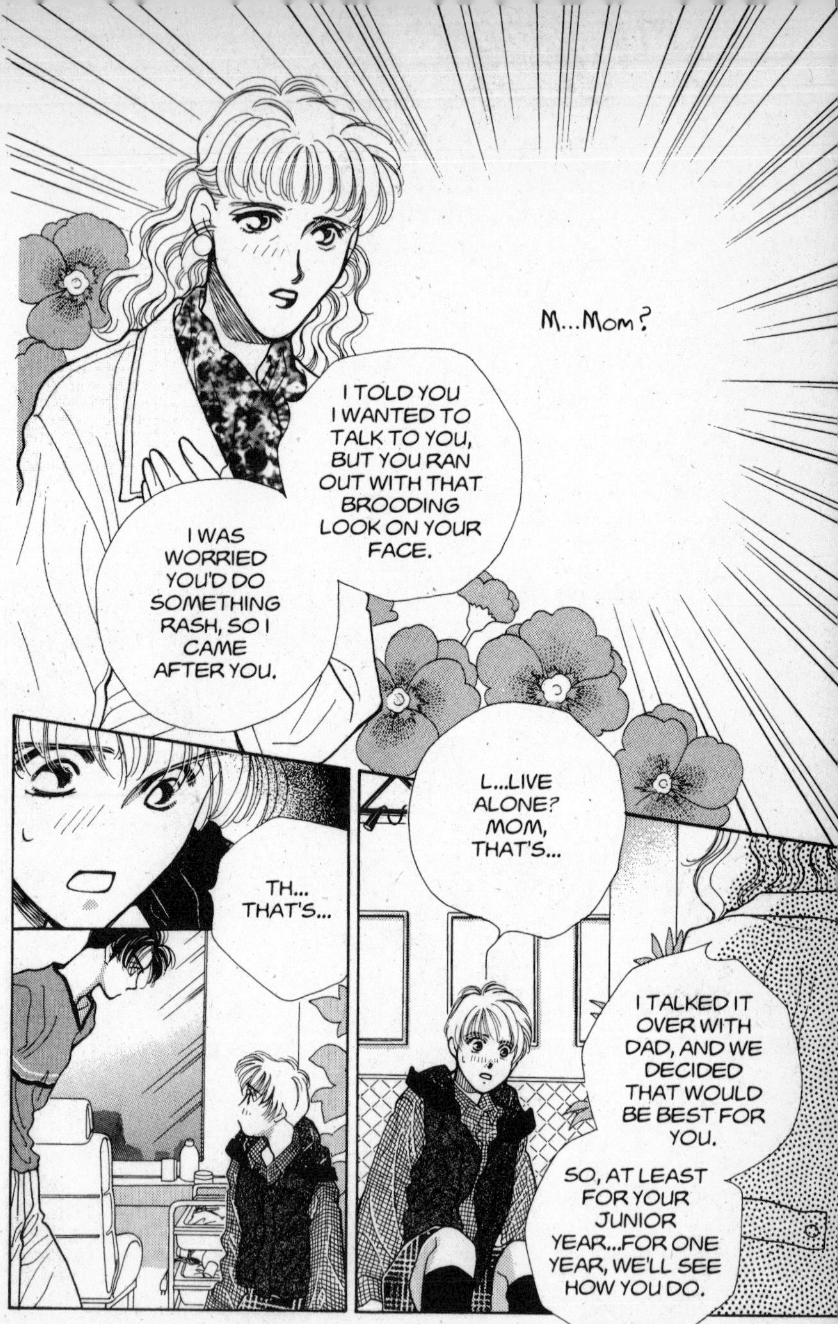
M...Mom?
I TOLD YOU I WANTED TO TALK TO YOU, BUT YOU RAN OUT WITH THAT BROODING LOOK ON YOUR FACE.
I WAS WORRIED YOU'D DO SOMETHING RASH, SO I CAME AFTER YOU.
L...LIVE ALONE? MOM, THAT'S...
I TALKED IT OVER WITH DAD, AND WE DECIDED THAT WOULD BE BEST FOR YOU.
SO, AT LEAST FOR YOUR JUNIOR YEAR...FOR ONE YEAR, WE'LL SEE HOW YOU DO.
TH... THAT'S...

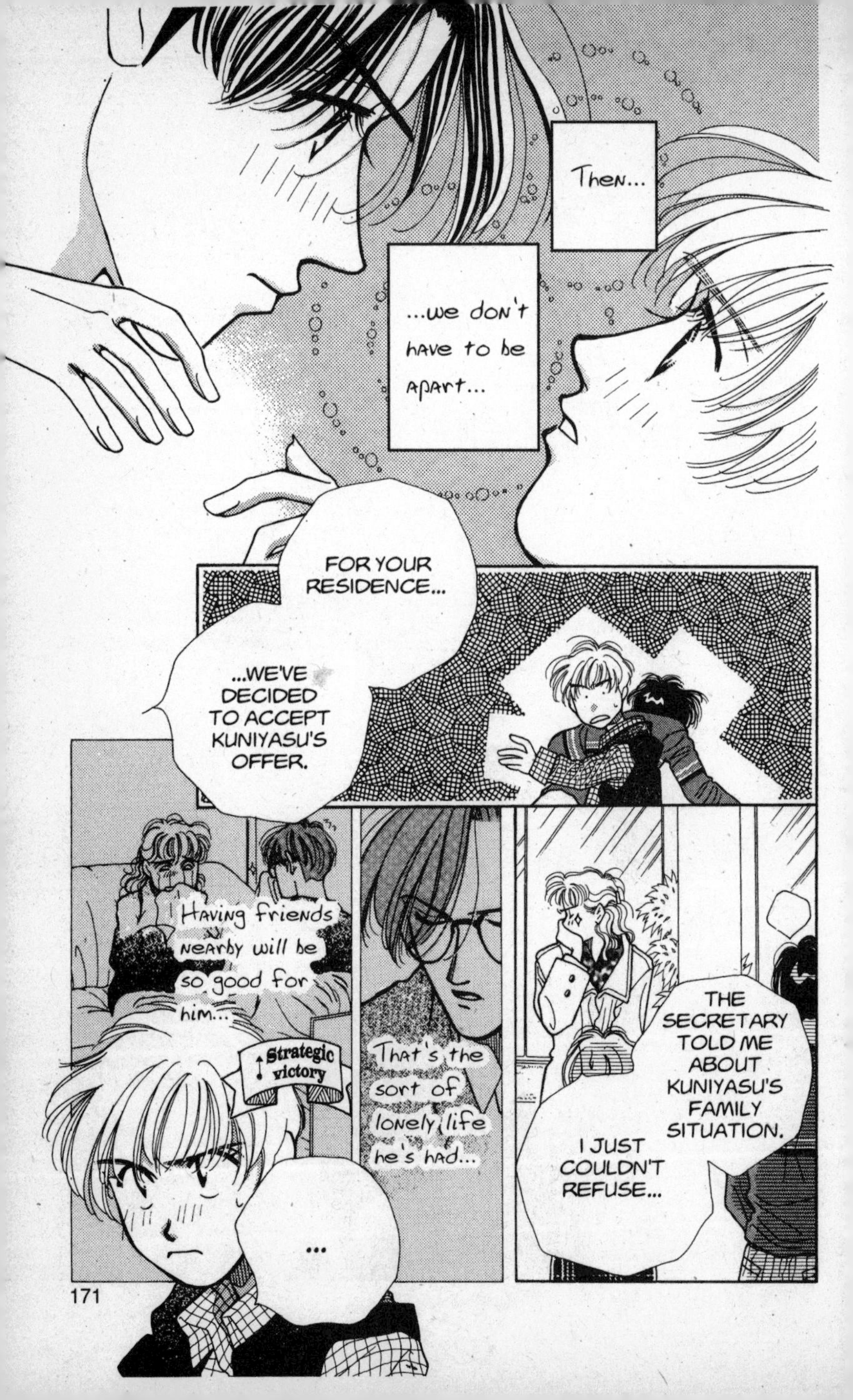
Then...
...we don't have to be apart...
FOR YOUR RESIDENCE...
...WE'VE DECIDED TO ACCEPT KUNIYASU'S OFFER.
THE SECRETARY TOLD ME ABOUT KUNIYASU'S FAMILY SITUATION.
I JUST COULDN'T REFUSE...
That's the sort of lonely life he's had...
Having friends nearby will be so good for him...
Strategic victory
...

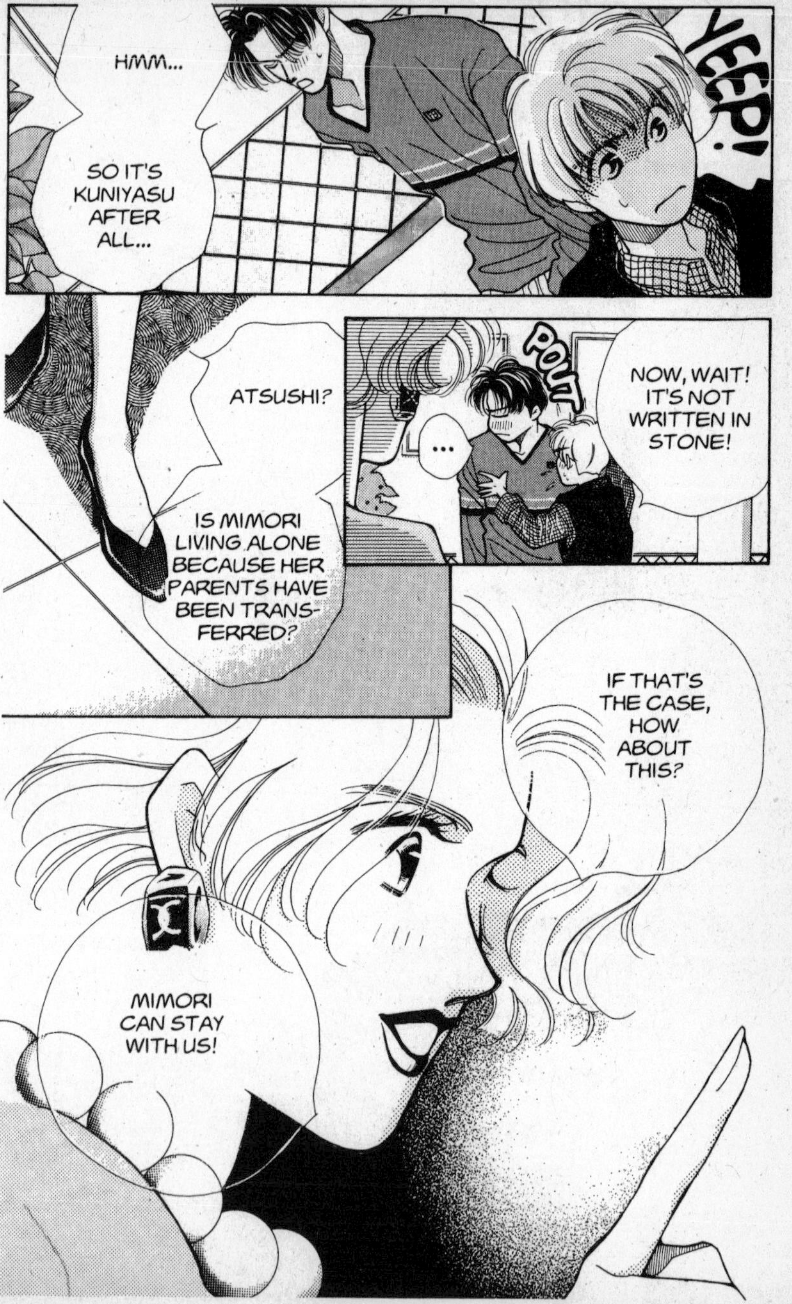

YEEP!
HMM...
SO IT'S KUNIYASU AFTER ALL...
NOW, WAIT! IT'S NOT WRITTEN IN STONE!
POUT
...
ATSUSHI?
IS MIMORI LIVING ALONE BECAUSE HER PARENTS HAVE BEEN TRANS-FERRED?
IF THAT'S THE CASE, HOW ABOUT THIS?
MIMORI CAN STAY WITH US!

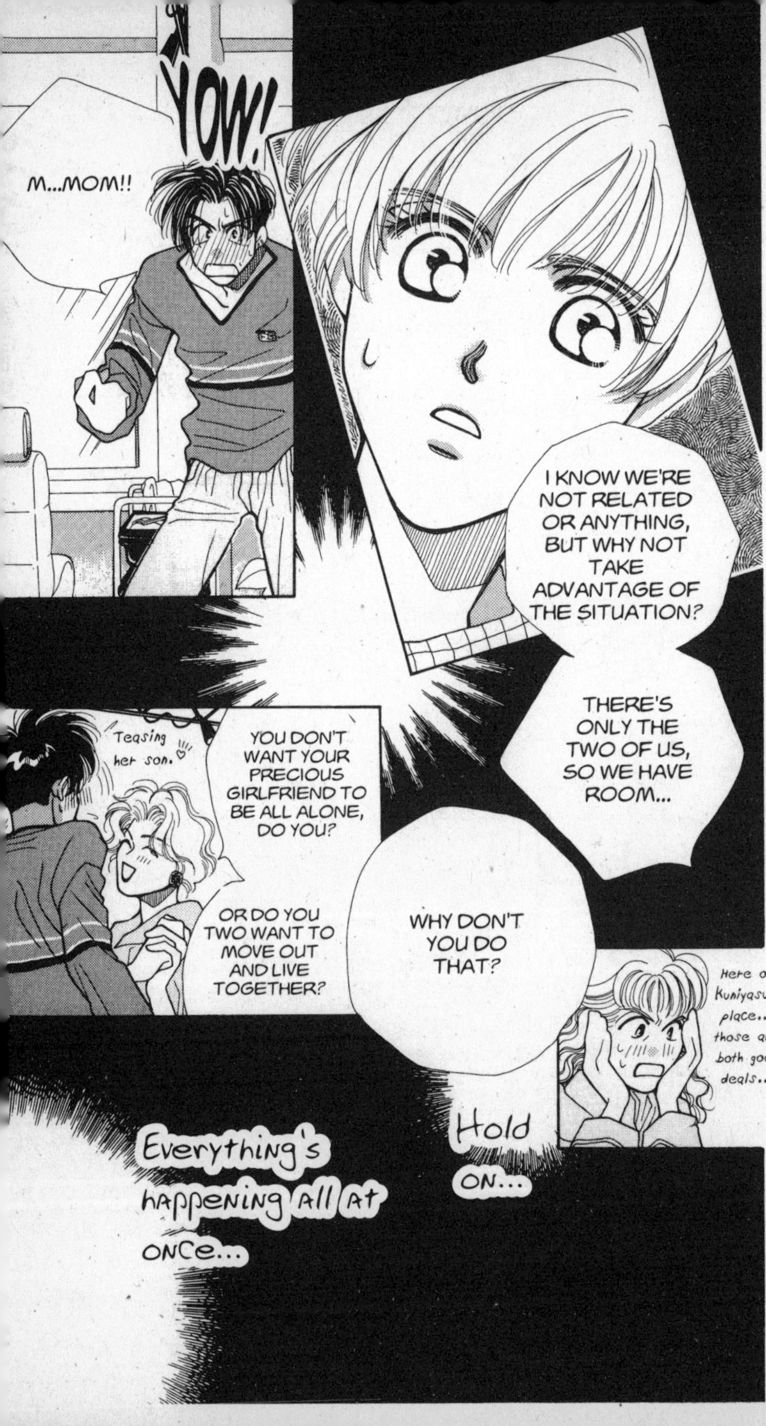
I KNOW WE'RE NOT RELATED OR ANYTHING, BUT WHY NOT TAKE ADVANTAGE OF THE SITUATION?
THERE'S ONLY THE TWO OF US, SO WE HAVE ROOM...
YOW!
M...MOM!!
YOU DON'T WANT YOUR PRECIOUS GIRLFRIEND TO BE ALL ALONE, DO YOU?
Teasing her son.
OR DO YOU TWO WANT TO MOVE OUT AND LIVE TOGETHER?
WHY DON'T YOU DO THAT?
Here or Kuniyasu's place... those are both good deals...
Hold on...
Everything's happening all at once...

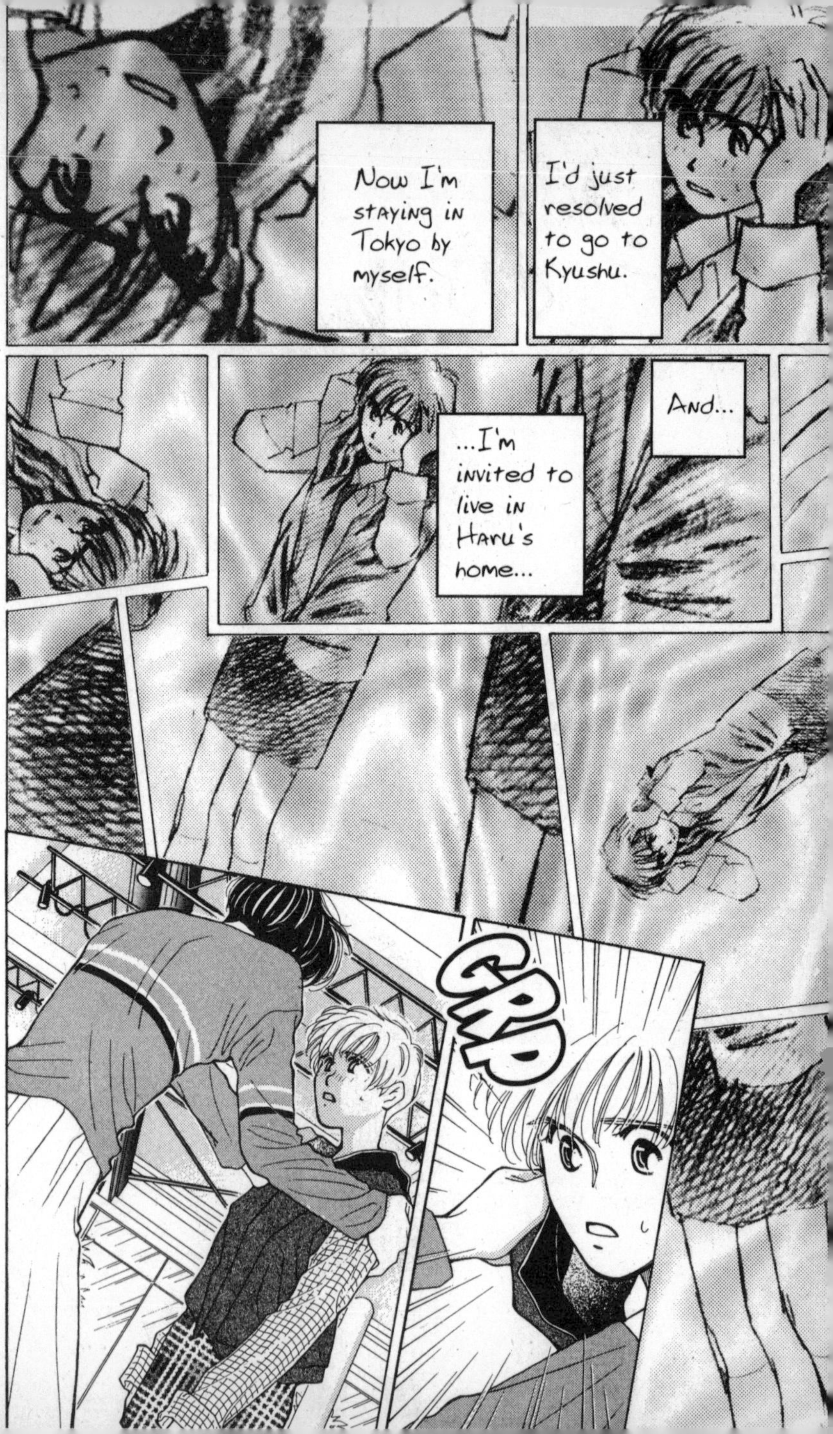
I'd just resolved to go to Kyushu.
Now I'm staying in Tokyo by myself.
And...
...I'm invited to live in Haru's home...
GRP

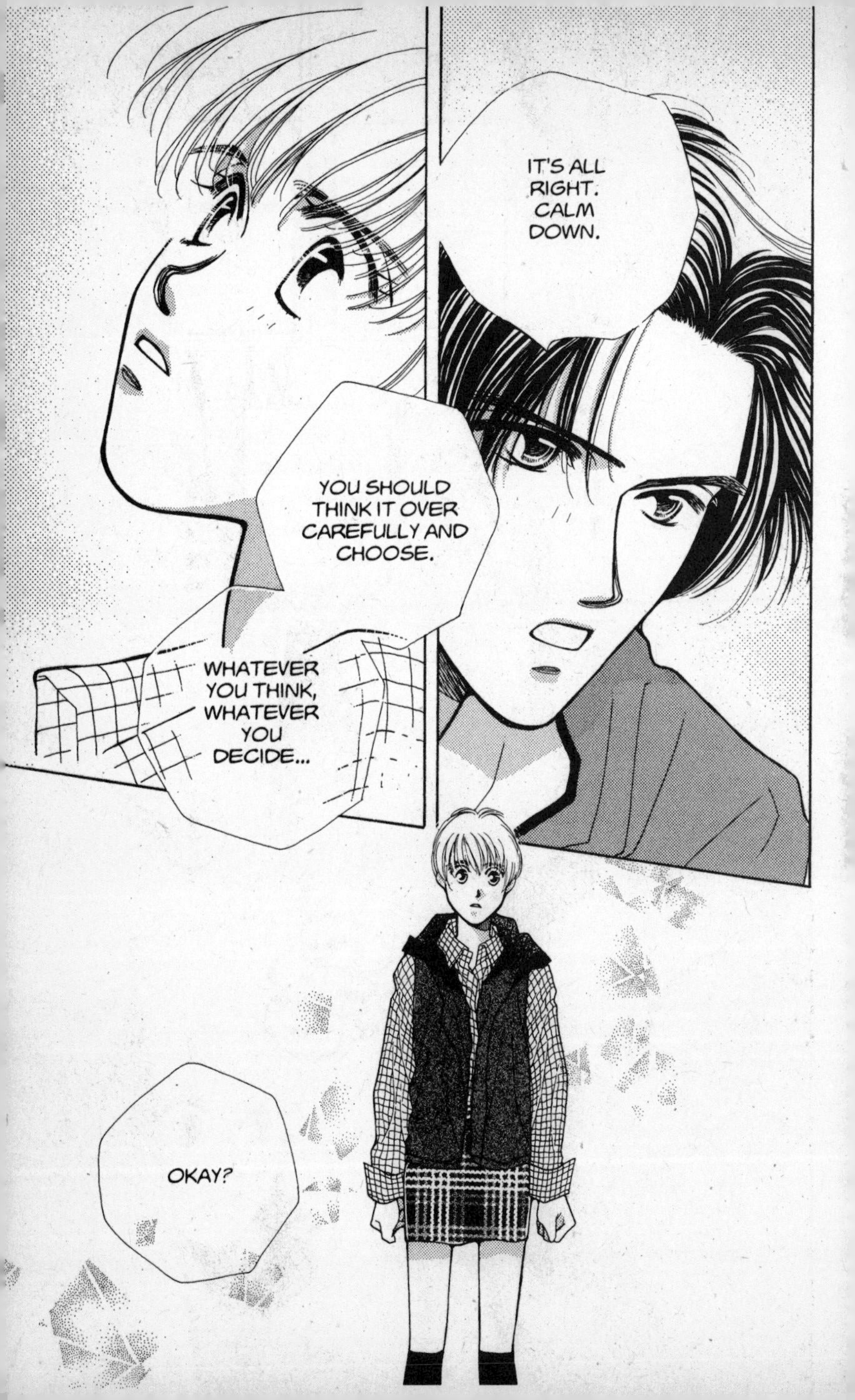
IT'S ALL RIGHT. CALM DOWN.
YOU SHOULD THINK IT OVER CAREFULLY AND CHOOSE.
WHATEVER YOU THINK, WHATEVER YOU DECIDE...
OKAY?

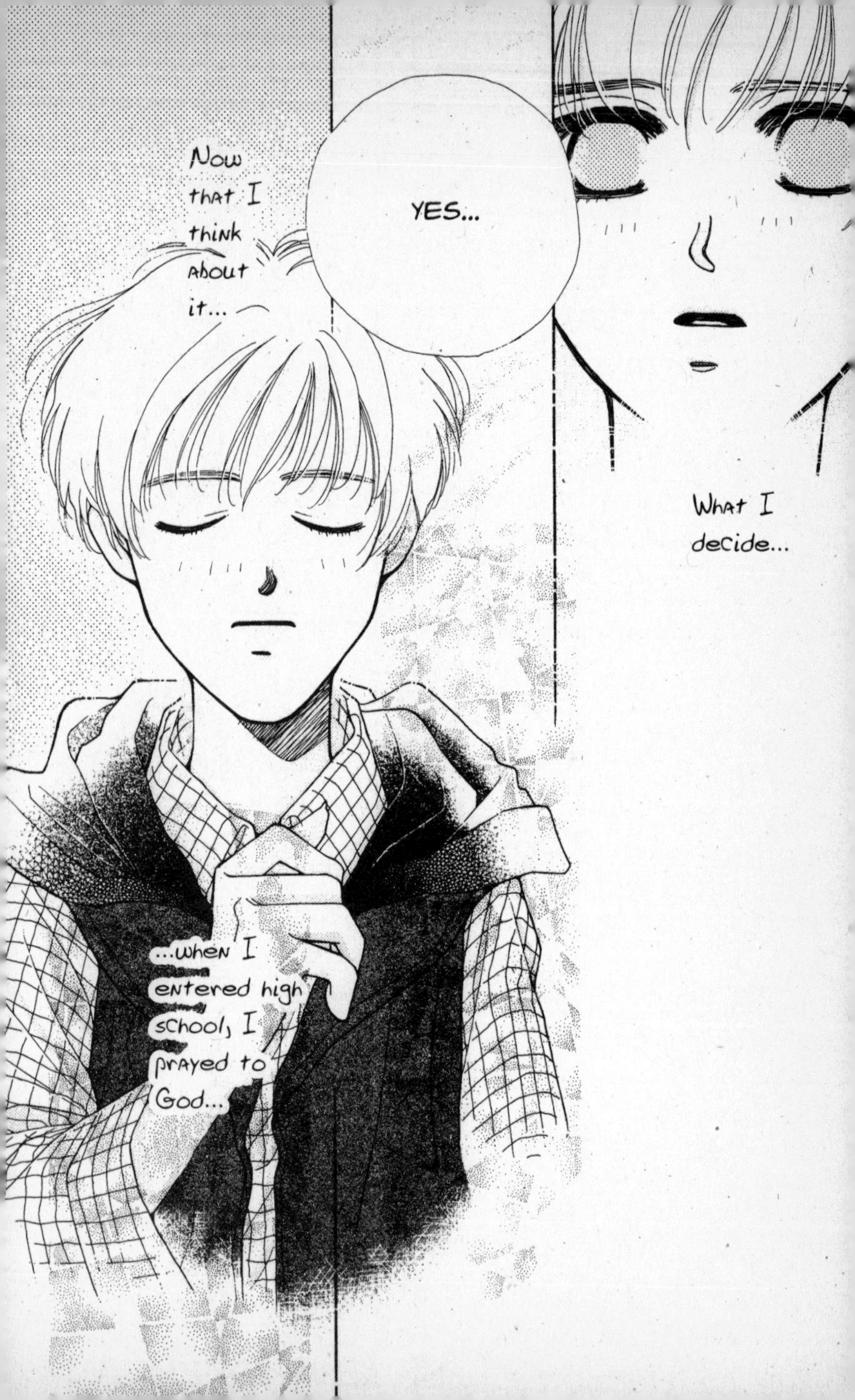
What I decide...
YES...
Now that I think about it...
...when I entered high school, I prayed to God...

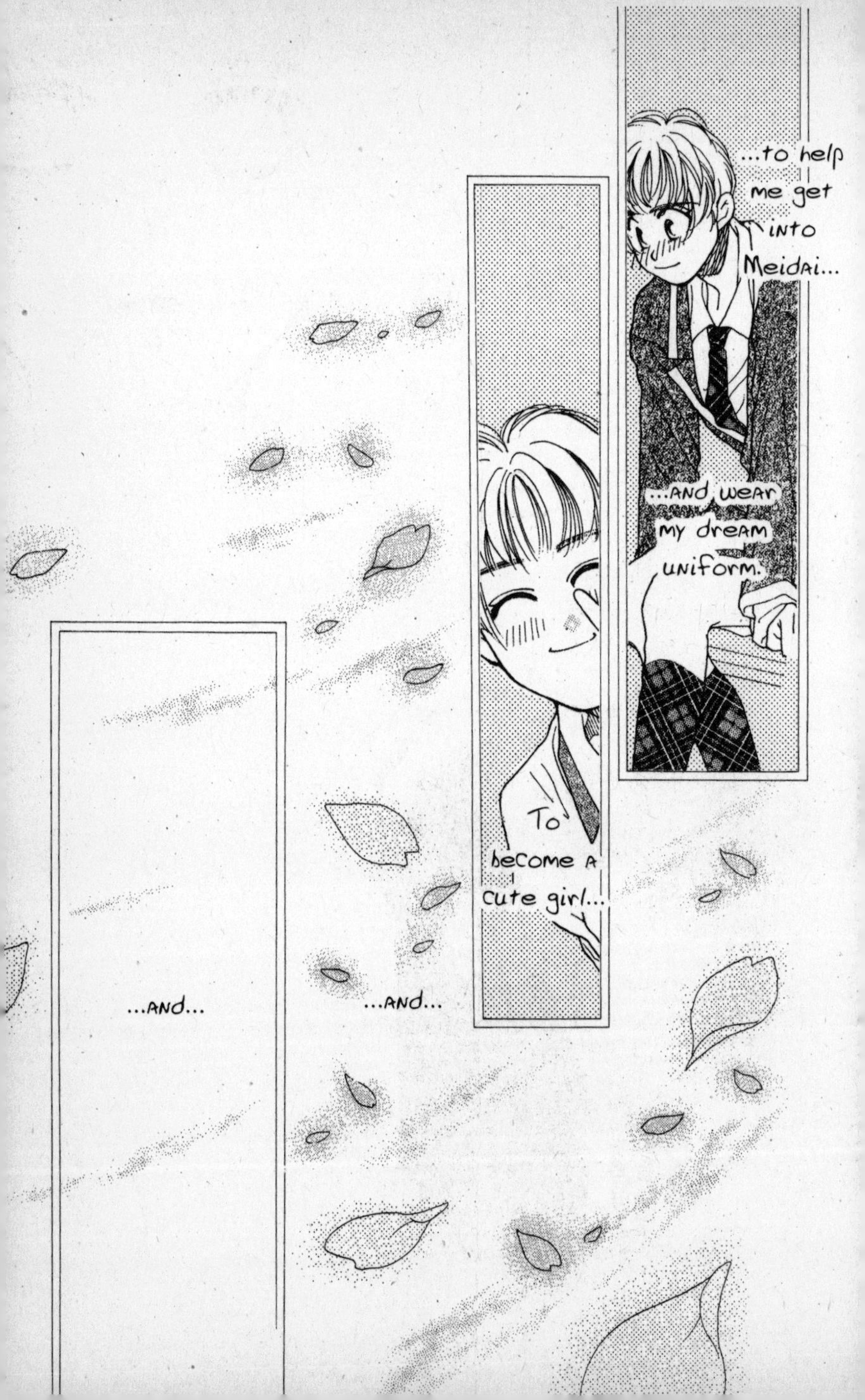
...to help me get into Meidai...
...and wear my dream uniform.
To become a cute girl...
...and...
...and...

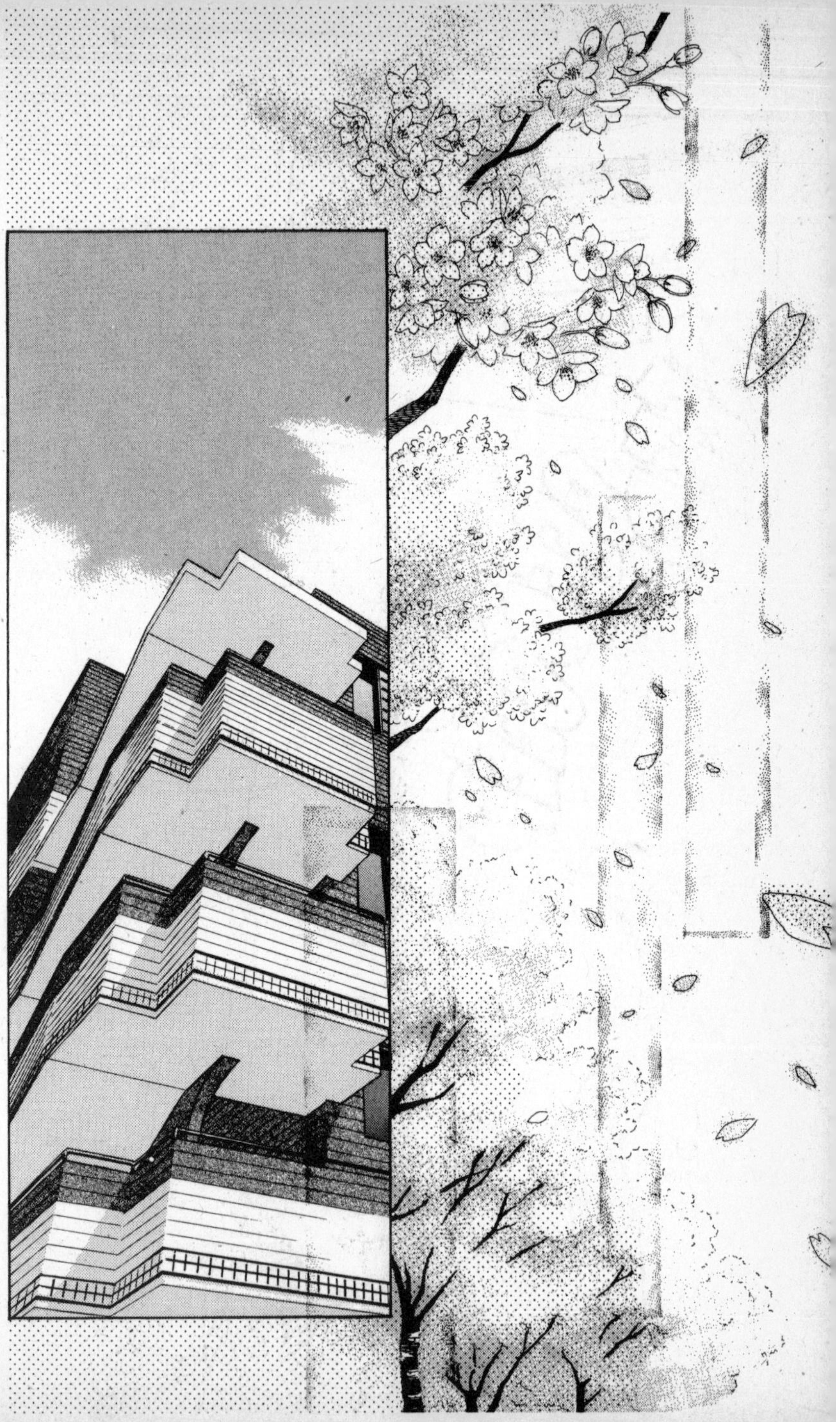

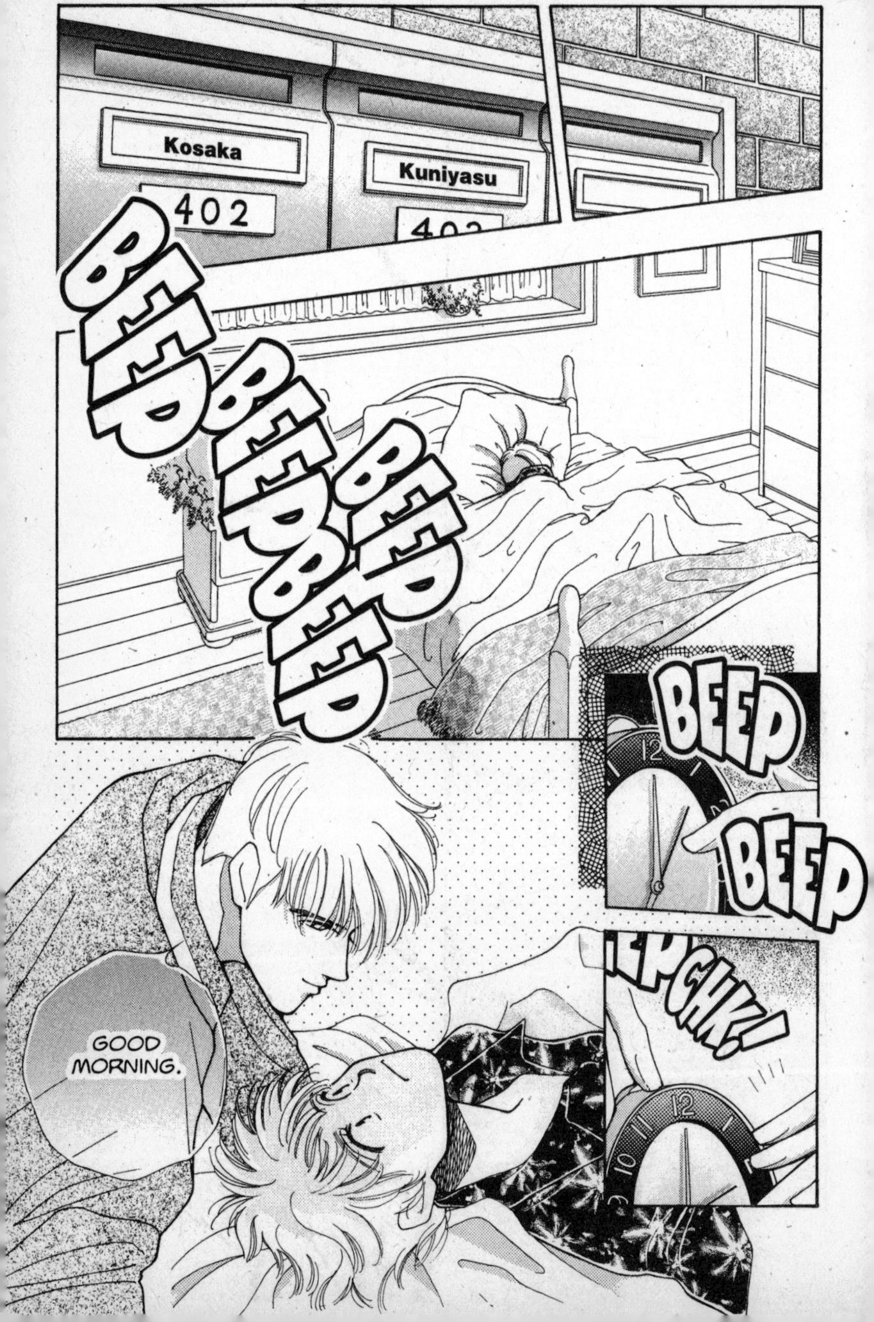
Kosaka
402
Kuniyasu
BEEP
BEEP
BEEP
BEEP
BEEP
CHK!
GOOD MORNING.

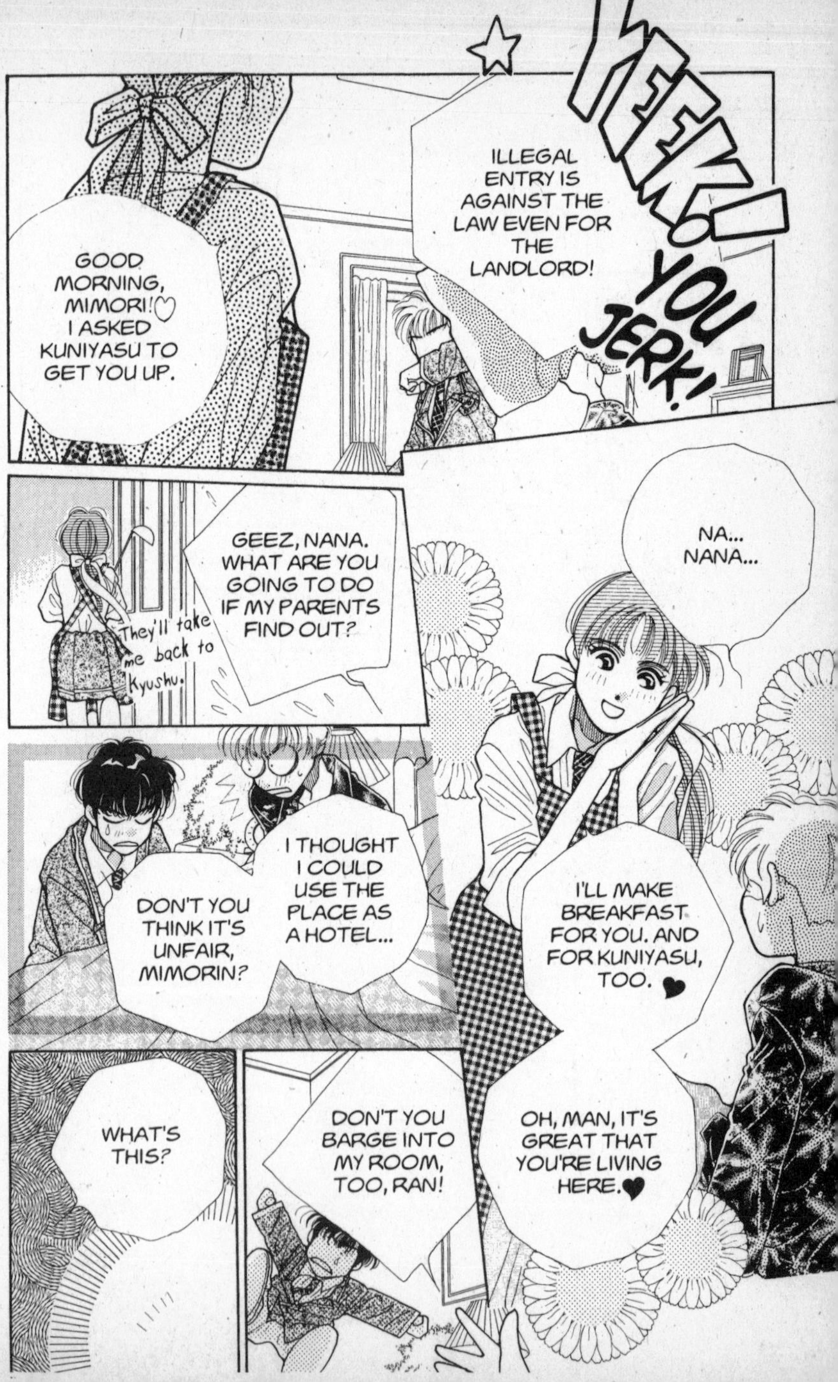
YEEK!
ILLEGAL ENTRY IS AGAINST THE LAW EVEN FOR THE LANDLORD!
YOU JERK!
GOOD MORNING, MIMORI! ♡ I ASKED KUNIYASU TO GET YOU UP.
NA... NANA...
I'LL MAKE BREAKFAST FOR YOU. AND FOR KUNIYASU, TOO. ♥
OH, MAN, IT'S GREAT THAT YOU'RE LIVING HERE. ♥
GEEZ, NANA. WHAT ARE YOU GOING TO DO IF MY PARENTS FIND OUT?
They'll take me back to Kyushu.
I THOUGHT I COULD USE THE PLACE AS A HOTEL...
DON'T YOU THINK IT'S UNFAIR, MIMORIN?
DON'T YOU BARGE INTO MY ROOM, TOO, RAN!
WHAT'S THIS?

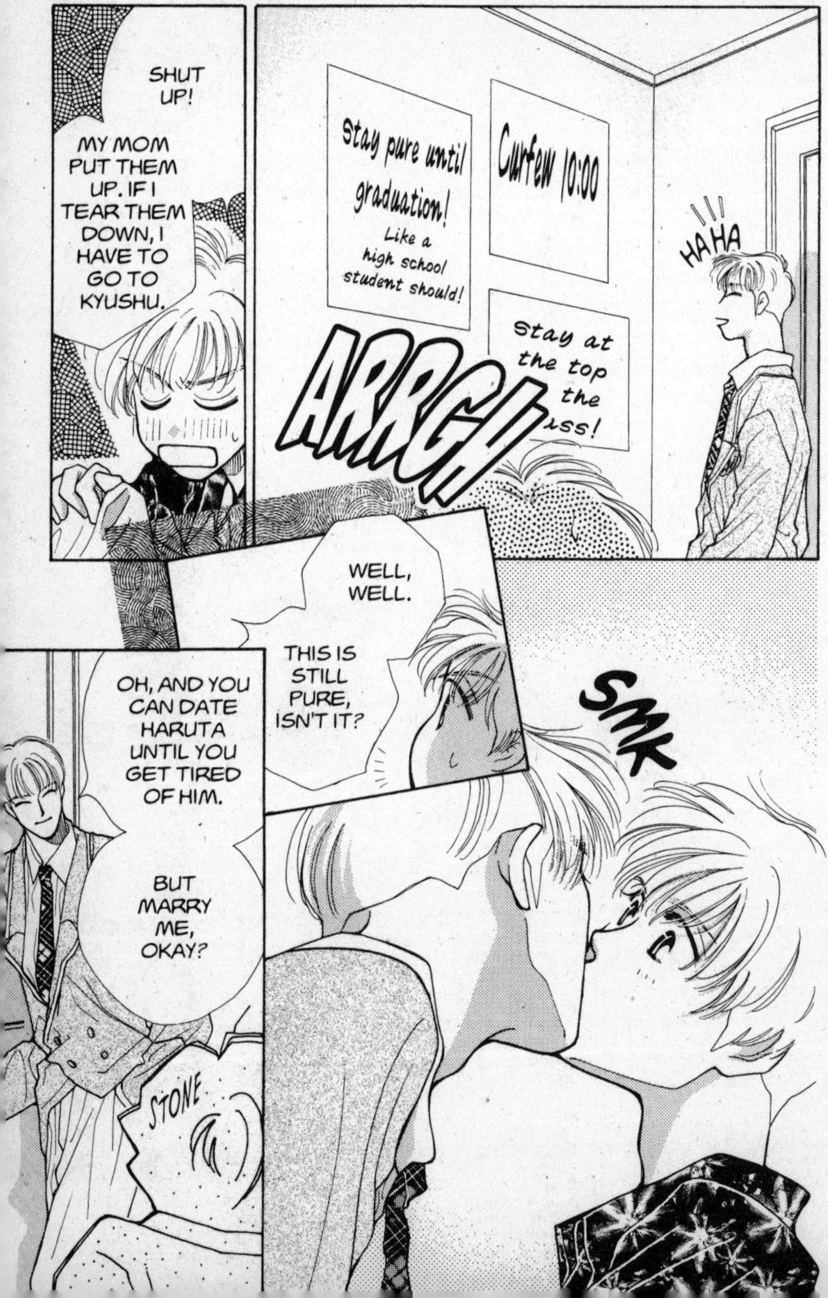
Stay pure until graduation!
Like a high school student should!
Curfew 10:00
Stay at the top the
ss!
HAHA
ARRGH
SHUT UP!
MY MOM PUT THEM UP. IF I TEAR THEM DOWN, I HAVE TO GO TO KYUSHU.
WELL, WELL.
THIS IS STILL PURE, ISN'T IT?
SMK
OH, AND YOU CAN DATE HARUTA UNTIL YOU GET TIRED OF HIM.
BUT MARRY ME, OKAY?
STONE

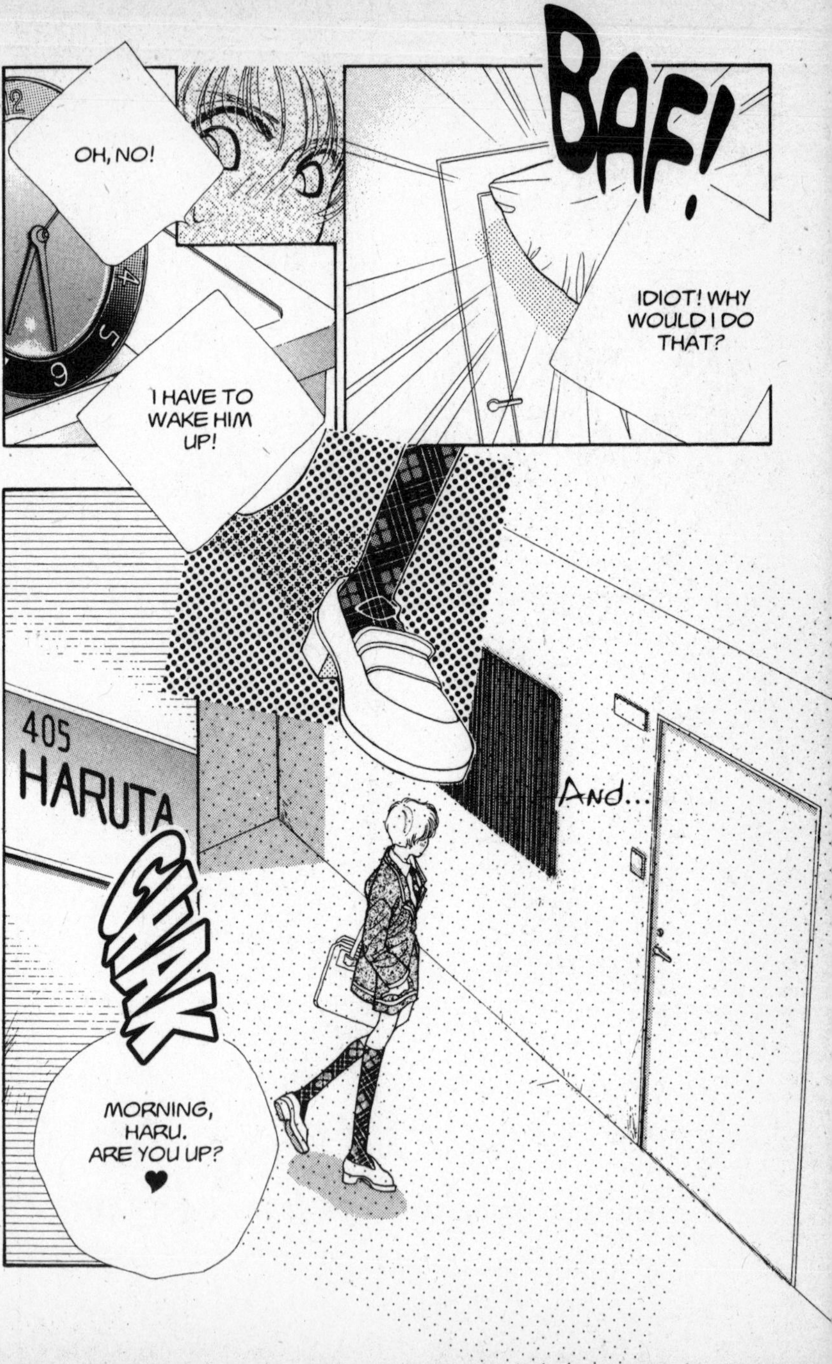
BAF!
IDIOT! WHY WOULD I DO THAT?
OH, NO!
I HAVE TO WAKE HIM UP!
405
HARUTA
And...
CHAK
MORNING, HARU. ARE YOU UP? ♥

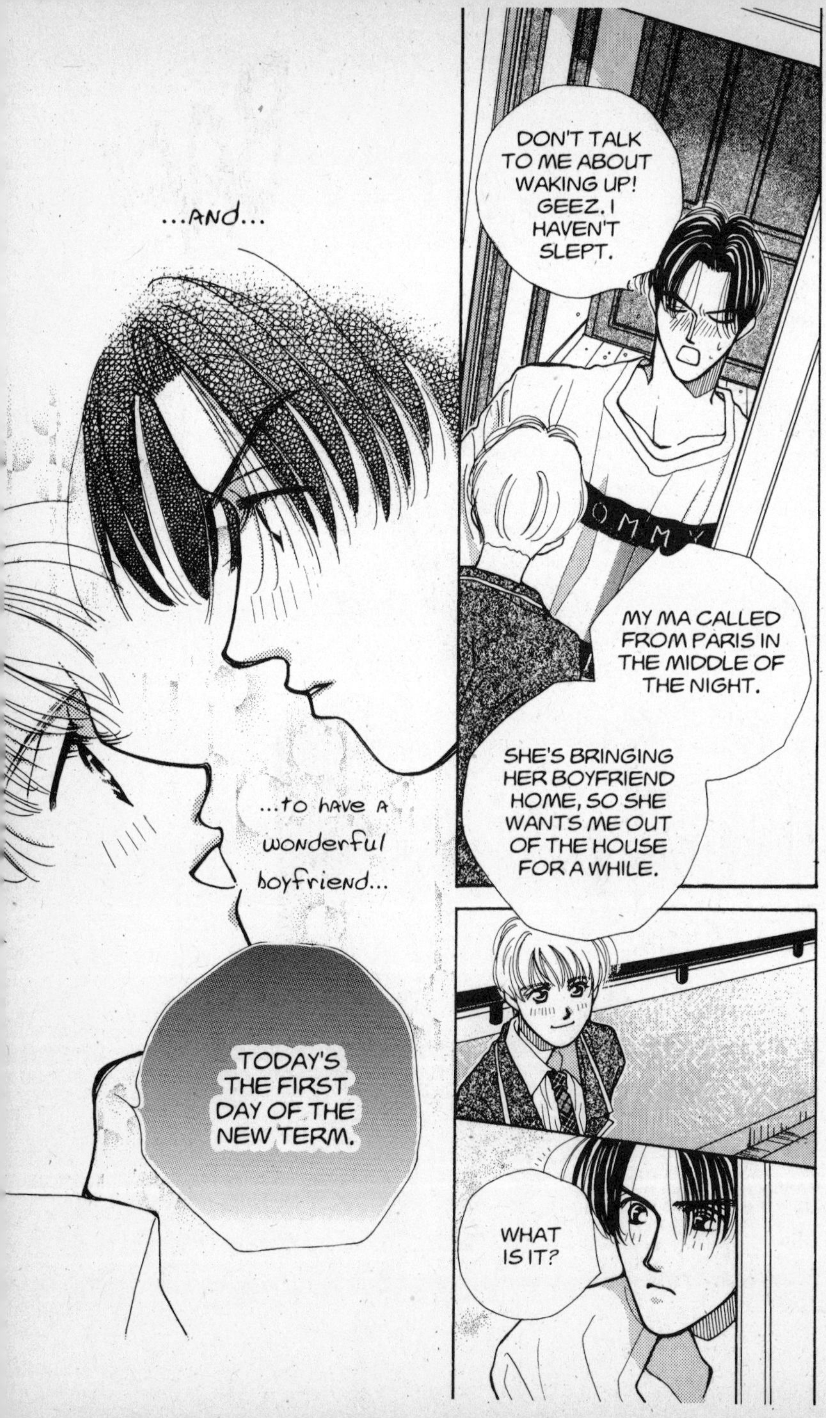
DON'T TALK TO ME ABOUT WAKING UP! GEEZ. I HAVEN'T SLEPT.
MY MA CALLED FROM PARIS IN THE MIDDLE OF THE NIGHT.
SHE'S BRINGING HER BOYFRIEND HOME, SO SHE WANTS ME OUT OF THE HOUSE FOR A WHILE.
WHAT IS IT?
...AND...
...to have a wonderful boyfriend...
TODAY'S THE FIRST DAY OF THE NEW TERM.

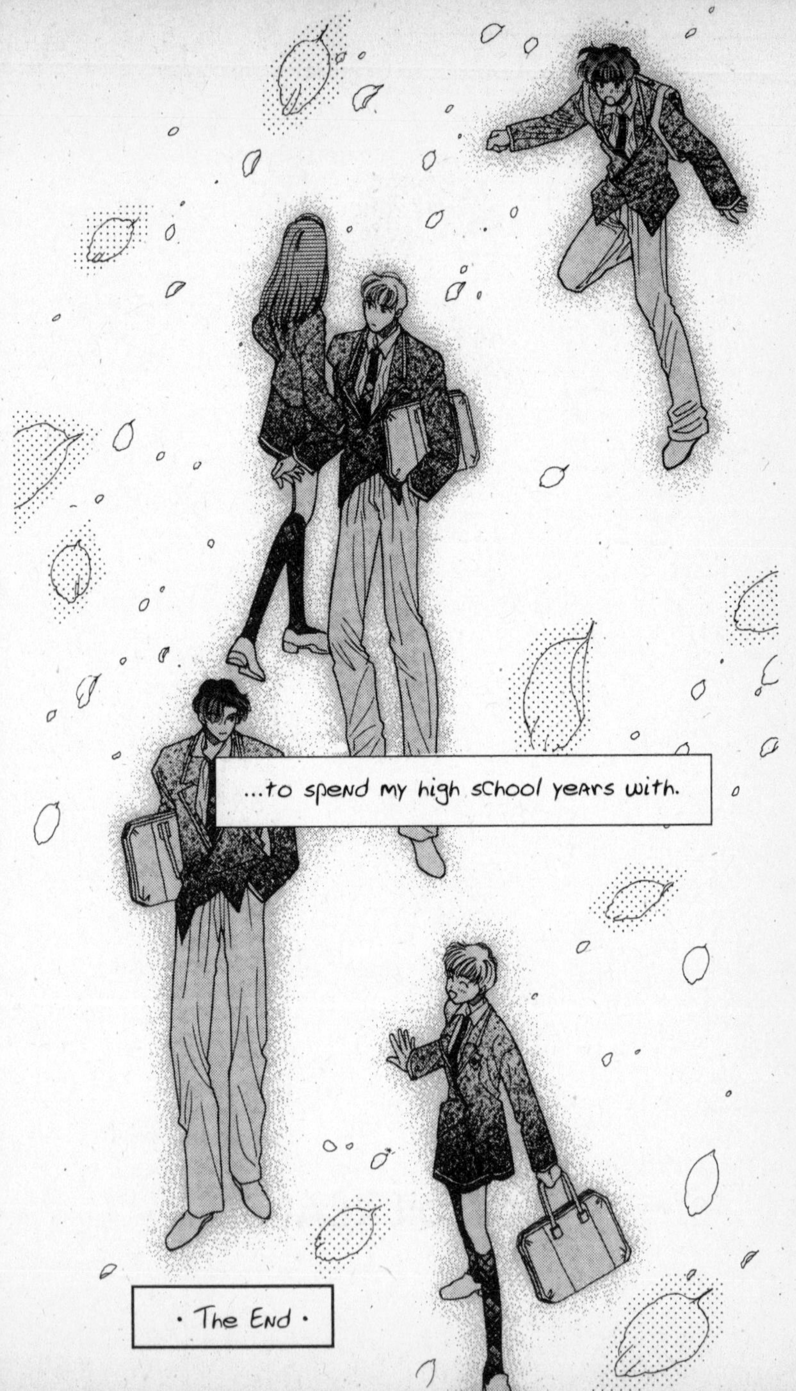
...to spend my high school years with.
• The End •

• **THANK YOU FOR READING!** •

CHARACTER RANKING

Here are the results of the character rankings I solicited at the end of Volume 4. Ta-da! Thank you for all your votes, but Japanese can be a misleading language! I asked you to tell me what kind of characters you longed for, but many people seemed to misinterpret my request. I wanted to know which characters you long for, not things you long to do to the characters! ☺ Sorry. Seriously, ☺ I've announced the top four; here are the rest!

Thanks go to R.H. and E.I. for their help in compiling the votes.

No. 5 Takashi Kurosaki 65 points

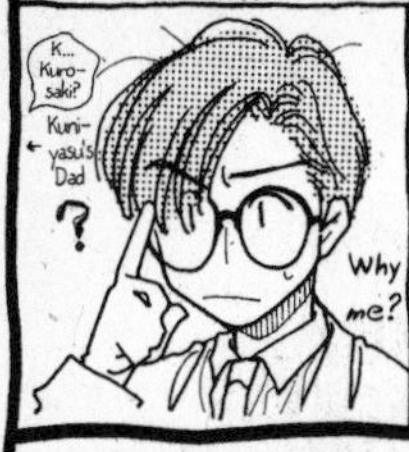
K... Kuro-saki?
Kuni-yasu's Dad
?
Why me?

He didn't appear much, but he ranked higher than Nana! :)
He wears a ring!! He has a wife and child!
Those of you who have impure thoughts, don't!! :)

No. 6 Ryotaro Terabayashi 61 points

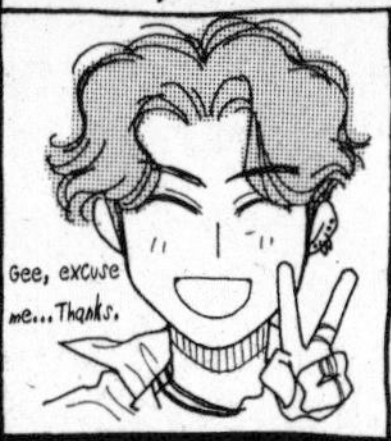
Gee, excuse me...Thanks.

This character also didn't appear much. There's a real-life model for him, you know. :) It's an inside story. :) I wonder if someone has the video... sob sob

No. 7 Nana Takaichi 60 points

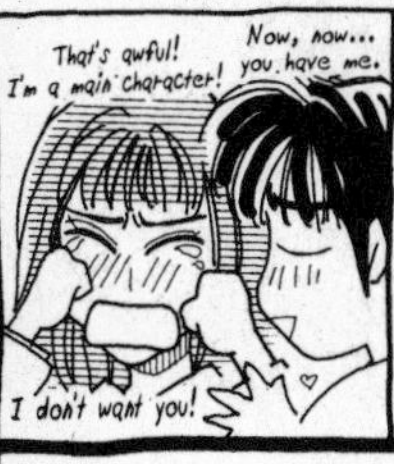
That's awful! I'm a main character!
Now, now... you have me.
I don't want you!

I didn't know she was so hated. But there are those who liked her...

I think it's because of you!!

No. 8 Kazuo Kosaka 28 points

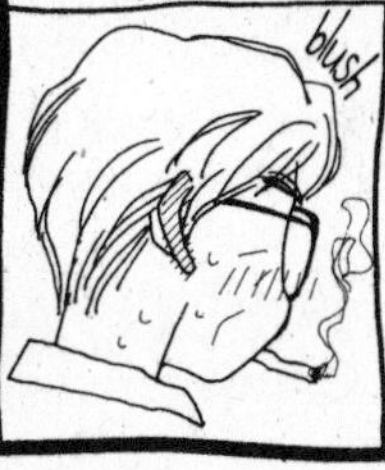
blush

It seems he got votes because he was so understanding. On the other hand, nobody liked Mimori's mom. :)

No. 9 Rihoko Haruta 12 points No. 10 Izumi Kosaka 9 points
No. 11 Mover from the moving company No. 12 Miwa Kosaka 3 points
No. 13 Takuya Inagaki (supervisor at the fast-food place) 2 points
The votes at the end were to get a laugh, I think. :)
Also, Miss Ayanokoji and the elementary-school Haruta got 1 point each...
and Kawashima got 3 points...
Sorry!!

That's it. We were all surprised that the top four came out so far ahead of the others, and that Nana scored so low. Um...it's my fault. I'm sorry. The battle between Kuniyasu and Haruta was close. On 3/27/1996, the time of this writing, they were 5 points apart. Those of us tallying the votes enjoyed this. As promised, we will choose 3 voters at random to receive a present, which will be paid for out of my pocket. It should arrive about the time this book is on the stands. The winners will know when they receive their presents. I'm not lying! The color postcards I promised before were sent to 200 lucky people whose names were drawn! I also sent New Year's cards to 50 people drawn from the entries!

Sorry there were so few. I apologize to everyone who didn't get a card. But please keep on writing, okay? I'll try to answer as many letters as possible with my new postcard printing software.
Sob sob...I'm so sorry.

And so...To all of you who read until the end, you kindly people who didn't even consider taking the books to a used bookstore, and all you others, (tears) really, thank you for reading through to this volume. You probably have your own ideas about the series, but for me, the characters continue to live their lives as usual in their world. Sorry, but I didn't want it to end, so I finished the story in an open way. I don't know what will happen next. They're still in their sophomore year in high school. I don't know (um...this is kind of embarrassing) which of the two boys Mimori will choose. (smile) This will make you hate me, but I ended it ambiguously by choice. It's okay for you readers to do whatever you like with the story!

I've written this in other places, but I'm going to do it again. Thank you for your letters. I got many of your responses while I was writing the series, and that made me very happy. This place, that scene, that dialog was good, and things like that. When it came to things that I really wanted to write, it touched me very deeply.

I'm not good at trying to entertain readers, or arranging the story to leave you speechless, or surprising you. I feel like that kind of thing is looking down on the readers. Maybe professionals should be like that, but I'm just writing things that I enjoy, and if you happen to like it, LUCKY! That's how I like to do things. That's my aspiration. Even with the characters. If I didn't enjoy it anymore, I wouldn't be able to continue, I don't think.

So, I'm ending **Tokyo Boys and Girls** while you're still saying, "I want to read the next episode,"and, "continue on with the story."

...even though it might be just flattery.

Truly, thank you very much. I hope we meet again.

M. KOHSAKA
Um...since Haru dyed his hair black, he's become popular. It makes me nervous. Anyway...onward to losing my virginity! ♥
Her apartment is #403.

A. HARUTA
Kuniyasu irritates me. I can't stand his hairdo. I wish he'd do something about it. Also...well...I want to hurry up and do it...
Not smoking!
(There's no #404)

N. TAKASHI
Sigh. Kuniyasu really doesn't like me...maybe I should look for a new guy.

R. SHINGO
I'm going to continue working part-time jobs so I can go on a trip with Nana this summer!! An overnighter, of course!

K. KUNIYASU
Huh? What's that? Kosaka's still a virgin? Really? Is that so? Hmm... I see. Delighted.
well, see you...

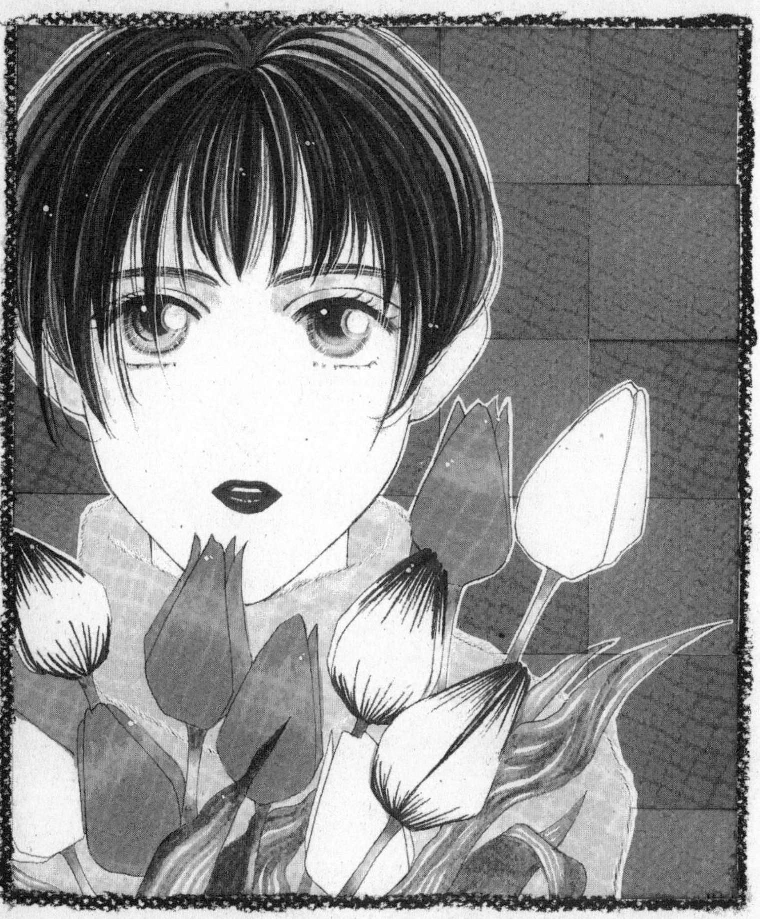

• SPECIAL THANX"

STAFF: N. KAIHO, R. HAYATSU, E. ITOH, M. KOREEDA

HELP: A. SAKAKURA, Y. IWAI, S. MARUYAMA, A. NAGAKUBO,

Y. TOSHIOKA, A. WADA, K. HARA, Y. IMAIZUMI,

H. KASAI, M. SEKIUCHI, M. TAKEUCHI"

T. SHIMAZAKI special thanx!!

Miki Aihara was born in the Shizuoka prefecture of Japan and currently lives in Tokyo. She made her debut in 1991 with *Lip Conscious!*, published in *Bessatsu Shôjo* Comic. Her immensely popular manga *Hot Gimmick* is published in English by VIZ Media. Aihara moves houses frequently, and loves to go to movies and shop for clothes. One of her hobbies is keeping tropical fish.

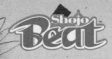

TOKYO BOYS & GIRLS VOLUME 5
The Shojo Beat Manga Edition

STORY AND ART BY
MIKI AIHARA

English Adaptation/Shaenon Garrity
Translation/JN Productions
Touch-up Art & Lettering/Bill Schuch
Design/Courtney Utt
Editor/Urian Brown

Managing Editor/Megan Bates
Director of Production/Noboru Watanabe
Vice President of Publishing/Alvin Lu
Vice President & Editor in Chief/Yumi Hoashi
Sr. Director of Acquisitions/Rika Inouye
Vice President of Sales & Marketing/Liza Coppola
Publisher/Hyoe Narita

Printed in the U.S.A.

Published by VIZ Media, LLC
P.O. Box 77010
San Francisco, CA 94107

Shojo Beat Manga Edition
10 9 8 7 6 5 4 3 2 1
First printing, July 2006

PARENTAL ADVISORY
TOKYO BOYS & GIRLS is rated T+ for Older Teen and is recommeded for ages 16 & up. This volume contains strong language and sexual themes.

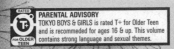

store.viz.com

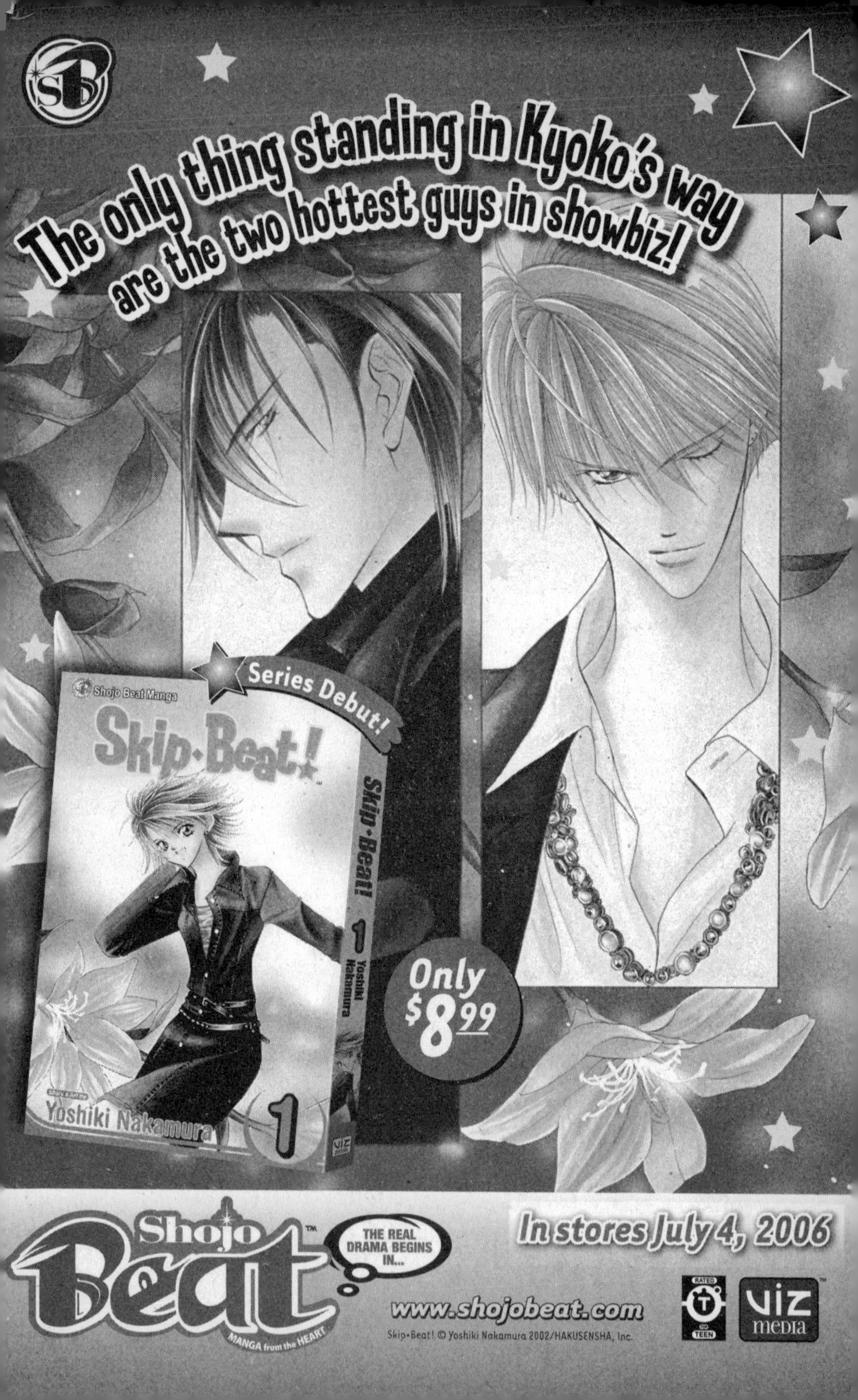

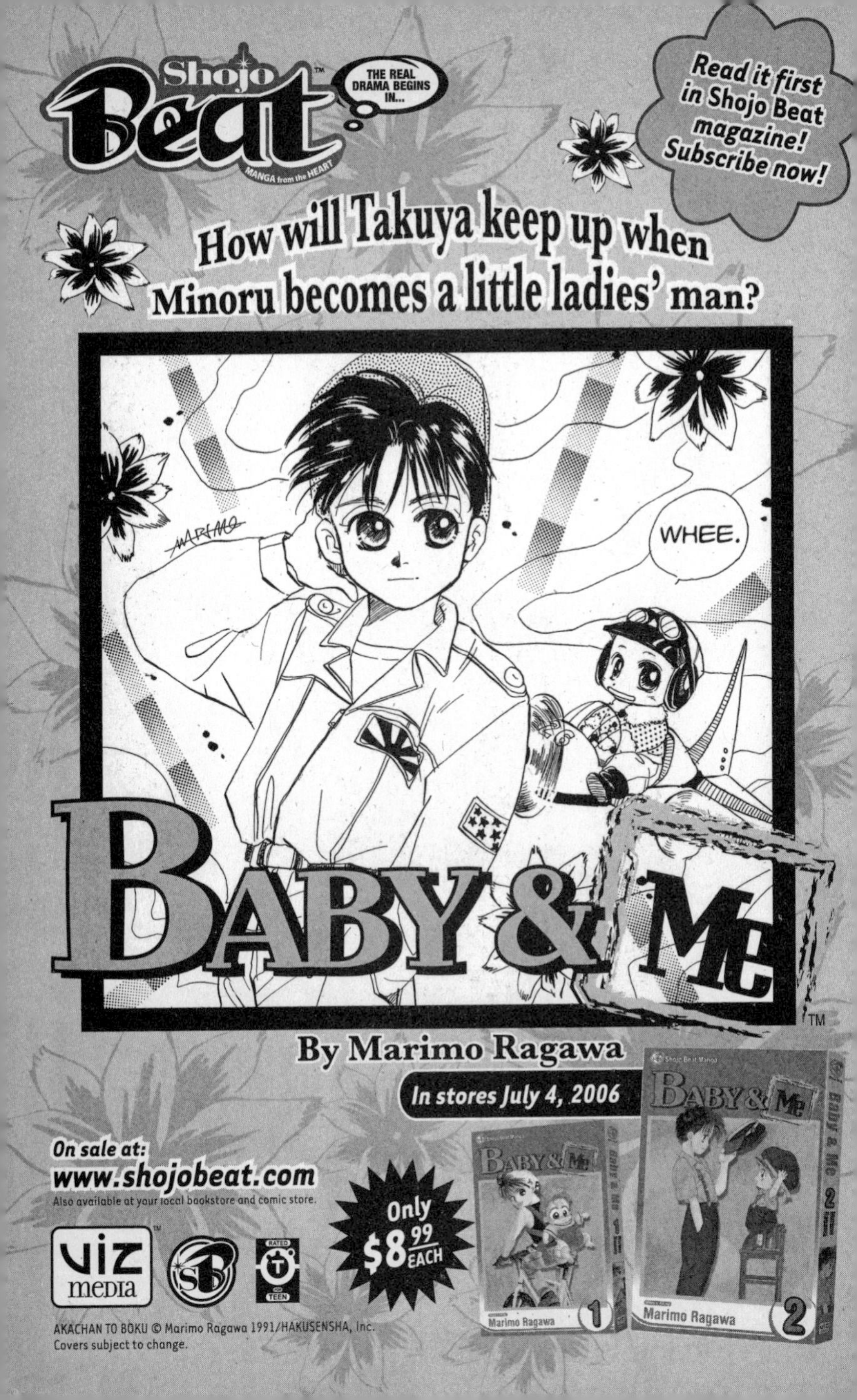
Shojo Beat
MANGA from the HEART
THE REAL DRAMA BEGINS IN...
Read it first in Shojo Beat magazine! Subscribe now!
How will Takuya keep up when Minoru becomes a little ladies' man?
MARIMO
WHEE.
BABY & ME
By Marimo Ragawa
In stores July 4, 2006
Shojo Beat Manga
BABY & ME
Marimo Ragawa
1
2
Only $8.99 EACH
On sale at:
www.shojobeat.com
Also available at your local bookstore and comic store.
VIZ media
RATED T TEEN
AKACHAN TO BOKU © Marimo Ragawa 1991/HAKUSENSHA, Inc.
Covers subject to change.